Privatizing Education

Privatizing Education

Can the Marketplace Deliver Choice, Efficiency, Equity, and Social Cohesion?

edited by

Henry M. Levin

National Center for the Study of
Privatization in Education
Teacher College, Columbia University

Member of the Perseus Books Group

Copyright © 2001 by Westview Press, A Member of the Perseus Books Group

Westview Press books are available at special discounts for bulk puchases in the United States by corporations, institutions, and other organizations. For more information, please contact the Special Markets Department at The Perseus Books Group, 11 Cambridge Center, Cambridge MA 02142, or call (617) 252-5298

Published in 2001 in the United States of America by Westview Press, 5500 Central Avenue, Boulder, Colorado 80301-2877, and in the United Kingdom by Westview Press, 12 Hid's Copse Road, Cumnor Hill, Oxford OX2 9JJ

Find us on the World Wide Web at www.westviewpress.com

Library of Congress Cataloging-in-Publication Data
   Privatizing education : can the marketplace deliver choice, efficiency,
   equity, and social cohesion? / edited by Henry M. Levin.
      p. cm.
   Includes bibliographical references and index.
   ISBN 0-8133-6640-2
    1. Privatization in education—United States.   I. Levin, Henry M.
LB2806.36 .P49 2001
379—dc21   00-054656

10   9   8   7   6   5   4   3

Contents

Preschools and Higher Education

International Dimensions

Charter Schools

Perspectives of Stakeholders

Evaluation Designs

Illustrations

Acknowledgments

This book had its origins in the paucity of nonpartisan sources of information on a major policy issue: privatization of public education. Although the last decade of the twentieth century saw a burgeoning privatization movement that included educational vouchers, tuition tax credits, and educational management organizations, there was little balance. Rather, most sources focused on only one side of the issues and ignored or denigrated the other side. Productive discourse in a democracy depends upon the presentation of contending views on controversial subjects, and educational privatization is one of the most contentious topics of our times. The broaching of this idea to Arthur Levine, president of Teachers College, Columbia University, was met with overwhelming encouragement to proceed. Levine's view that the purpose of a university is to take risks and establish studies even in the most sensitive areas is a breath of fresh air in these times of political correctness. I owe a great deal to him in launching the National Center for the Study of Privatization in Education (NCSPE), not only because of his academic support but also because of his assistance in acquiring funding.

The first major event in launching the NCSPE was to sponsor a two-day conference at Teachers College on April 9–10, 1999. The theme of the conference was "Setting the Agenda" for the NCSPE. Toward that end some fifteen papers were sought from noted experts in a variety of fields. Revised versions of thirteen of those papers constitute the contents of this volume. It is hoped that they come together as a unified whole in addressing the overall mission of the NCSPE. I wish to thank these authors for their thoughtfulness and cooperation in constituting both the conference and this book.

During the 1998–1999 academic year I was in my thirty-first year at Stanford University with a plan to take early retirement at the end of the year. However, with almost 3,000 miles between Stanford and Teachers College, I needed considerable help in arranging the logistics of the conference. Dana Taylor served in this role most capably, resulting in a conference that flowed smoothly and without hitches. I owe her a great debt for taking much of this burden off my shoulders. My luck continued with the production and editing of the manuscript. My colleague, Zuki Karpinska, took major responsibility for assembling the chapters and putting them in the form required by the publisher. I have the greatest admiration for her ingenuity and enterprise in working with so many separate authors in a productive way, and I am extremely grateful for her assistance. I also wish to thank my colleagues Patrick McEwan, Janelle Scott, and Parag Joshi for their general support and encouragement, and Maggie Barber for her editing of the final manuscript.

The conference on which this book is based was supported by generous funding from the Achelis and Bodman Foundations and the Ford Foundation. Production of this volume also benefited from these entities and the Pew Trusts. I wish to acknowledge my appreciation to all of these funding sources.

Finally, I wish to thank my wife, Pilar Soler, and my youngest daughter, Bianca Levin-Soler, for their support and tolerance in putting up with such a mercurial and enigmatic husband and father who has been preoccupied with launching this publication.

Henry M. Levin

Introduction

1

Studying Privatization
in Education

HENRY M. LEVIN

Introduction

At the start of the twenty-first century we are witnessing forces pushing for dramatic changes in our public and private institutions. Among these forces is the rise of the Internet, which promotes access to prodigious quantities of information and new ways of communication. At the same time, the workplace has changed as a consequence of both these influences and of global competition, placing a greater premium than ever on formal schooling and lifelong learning. These developments demonstrate an increasing emphasis on decentralization of decisionmaking and a much greater reliance on the marketplace. The educational system is hardly immune from these forces. Private providers have become competitors with government institutions at all educational and training levels, and educational policy is moving increasingly toward decentralized solutions and the marketplace.

In particular, privatization of education—in whatever form—has become a prevalent dimension of educational debate and operations. For-profit and nonprofit educational management organizations (EMOs) have proliferated and expanded efforts to operate schools through contracts with local school districts and charter schools. A more radical development—publicly funded educational vouchers for use in private schools—is on the ascendant and has already been adopted in Cleveland, Milwaukee, and Florida. Educational vouchers provide a certificate that parents can use to pay all or a portion of tuition at any school that meets state guidelines for eligibility, and there are increasing numbers of voucher and scholarship programs through private organizations. Charter schools—public schools that are largely exempt from state and local regulations—have been initiated in most states. They embrace many features of privatization in augmenting school choice in local communities. Further, many are operated by private firms or EMOs under contracts funded with public dollars. Such contracting is taking place with increasing frequency among conventional public schools. In addition to these mechanisms, tuition tax credits and tax deductions provide tax benefits to parents who pay tuition at private schools and, in some cases, other educational expenses.

The prospect of markets in education and private sponsorship of public school entities inspire strong emotions and debate. People tend to view these developments through the prisms of their own ideologies, and there is little constructive discourse by adherents and detractors. A cursory review of websites on educational privatization demonstrates how there is little balanced perspective assessing the potential benefits and costs. Rather, each side tends to elaborate and, often, to overstate its position and exaggerate the strength of the evidence supporting its stance. Thus, there are great obstacles to obtaining a nonpartisan and fully informed view, and even though most onlookers have an opinion on the subject, they lack even rudimentary information.[1] Recognition of the seriousness of this gap was the stimulus that led to the establishment of the National Center for the Study of Educational Privatization (NCSPE) at Teachers College, Columbia University. The priority of the NCSPE is not to support one side or the other but to study the privatization phenomenon and to communicate helpful analytical frameworks and pertinent evidence.

This volume is the outcome of a conference that was convened in April 1999 to set the agenda for the NCSPE. We invited contributions that would address all levels of education and many different aspects of educational privatization. The chapters in this volume are the product of that conference. Before reviewing them and the directions that they suggest, it is useful to provide a brief picture of privatization in education.

What Is Privatization in Education?

Private schools preceded public schools historically in the United States and in other countries, so the phenomenon of schools operated by private authorities is hardly new. Privatization of education can take many forms. The most common interpretation is the establishment of schools operated by nongovernment authorities, whether for-profit or not-for-profit. But public schools often contract with private providers for services like transportation, food services, textbooks, maintenance, instructional programs, and professional development. The new twist in recent years is that private contracts are entered with EMOs to operate the entire school, including the "core" educational mission. EMOs hire and supervise teachers and school staffs, set the curriculum, determine school organization and decisionmaking, and assess student progress. Such contracts are increasing among charter schools as well as conventional public schools operated by school districts.

The intermingling of public and private dimensions of education has a long history. Consider what Adam Smith said about education in his major 1776 classic, *The Wealth of Nations.* Smith divides the public purposes of education into two parts: that which can be acquired through daily experience "without any attention of government," and that for which "some attention of government is necessary" (Smith, 1937, p. 734). Thus, even when public educational goals are evident, they will be met by some combination of nongovernmental and government-sponsored experiences. In the financing of education, Smith also notes a dichotomy between public and private educational finance. He suggests that the most fundamental parts of education can be satisfied through "establishing in every parish or district a little school, where children may be taught for a reward so moderate, that even a common labourer may afford it; the master being partly, but not wholly paid by the public; because, if he was wholly, or even principally paid by it, he would soon learn to neglect his business" (Smith, 1937, p. 737). At about the same time, Thomas Paine recommended a voucher-type system for the American colonies in which education would be provided on the basis of government funding with freedom of choice and local ministers monitoring schools to ascertain if they were doing their jobs (West, 1967).

These early views show the complexity of the subject and the various forms of shifts toward privatization. Precisely what is meant by "privatization" will vary according to the perspective that one uses to judge the phenomenon. For example, shifts toward greater privatization can be found in the financing of education; sponsorship of schools; operation of schools; composition of educational benefits; and the emergence of for-profit schools.

Financing of Education.   As Smith noted, education can be funded from either public or private sources or a combination of the two. It is clear that an overwhelming share of funding for education in the United States is derived from public sources.[2] Families add to these resources by raising financial support for public schools, sending children to private schools, and providing educational experiences for children outside of the regular school day or school year. It is common for parent-teacher organizations and local public school foundations to solicit private contributions for support of their public schools.

Milton Friedman's (1962) original voucher plan called for a modest, publicly funded voucher for each child with unlimited opportunity for families to supplement the public voucher with their own funds. Thus, although the bulk of school funding at the kindergarten through twelfth grade levels is derived from public sources at present, there is a call under some plans for greater private contributions. At the same time, a shift in policy toward public educational vouchers and tuition tax credits would expand public funding for children in private schools. This might induce greater participation in private schooling (another form of privatization), but at public expense. West (1991) has argued that all education should be financed privately, since it is families who receive the benefits rather than society. Although this libertarian view is not a common one, it is an important voice in the debate over how to finance education and choices between educational vouchers and tuition tax credits.[3] It is clear that the mix of public versus private funding is a major issue.

Sponsorship of Schools.   A traditional breakdown between public and private schooling is sponsorship. About 53 million U.S. students at the elementary and secondary levels are in government-sponsored schools at state and local levels; about 6 million are in schools that are sponsored by nongovernmental or private entities. Usually we refer to government-sponsored schools as *public* schools and nongovernmental schools as *private* schools. However, as I have noted elsewhere (Levin, 1987), public schools may produce considerable private benefits and independent schools may produce extensive public benefits. In 1997 there were about 88,000 public schools and about 28,000 private schools.

Educational vouchers and tuition tax credits would certainly expand participation in private schools by reducing the costs to families. Vouchers would cover all or part of the tuition, and tax credits would diminish the tax burden of the family (James and Levin, 1983). The expected result would be to increase the numbers of students placed in private schools—a direct increase in privatization. Empirical estimates of such shifts suggest they would be relatively modest (Lankford and Wyckoff, 1992).

Operation of Schools.   But *sponsorship* of schools is not necessarily tantamount to school *operation*. A third way of viewing a shift in privatization is to draw a distinction between public and private operation of schools. Most public schools are managed by public authorities such as school boards and publicly employed managers established under state law for such purposes. Virtually all private schools are operated by private entities, usually the ones that sponsor the school. But public schools can be operated by private entities in many different ways, the most common being contracting (Hill, Pierce, and Guthrie, 1997). Government agencies such as school districts can contract with EMOs to run their schools. Under such arrangements the public school authorities agree to provide funding for the delivery of particular services under a specific set of guidelines. EMOs are given the authority to staff and manage the school, set curriculum and instructional strategies, sponsor professional development, establish school policies, and, in some cases, determine pay scales and working conditions as well as performance incentives.

With the advent of charter schools, this arrangement has become more common. In some states, like Michigan, a substantial number of charter schools—and the majority of new charter schools—are operated by EMOs (Miron, 2000). Some school districts have also engaged EMOs to run specific public schools that are not charter schools, often to compete with local charter schools. The complexity of the public-private relationship can be seen in these examples. Although the schools remain public and receive public funding, there is a movement toward privatization of school operations.

Composition of Benefits. K–12 education is characterized by two types of benefits: public and private. Public benefits accrue to society beyond students' and their families' direct participation in the educational system. Even families without children in school benefit from a more productive, civil, and democratic society. Schools represent the one institution that all students must participate in and are designed to confer a common language, heritage, values, knowledge of institutions, and modes of legitimate behavior to the young. Presumably this creates a better society for all, conferring public benefits (Wolfe, 1995) or what Milton Friedman (1962) calls "neighborhood" benefits. But in addition, participation in schooling tends to improve the income, employment prospects, status, knowledge, and other desired results for the individuals who receive the education. Economists and sociologists have devoted themselves to measuring these results as well as their social implications. For example, economists have attempted to calculate increased productivity and income at both the individual and social levels and have estimated both private and social rates of return on investment (Carnoy, 1995).

An educational system can focus on producing more social benefits by increasing the number of common experiences among schools to achieve greater social cohesion and democratic functioning across society. Or the system can increase the amount and scope of choice of parents to expand the responsiveness of schools to the specific wishes of their students and families. In the former case, the goal of a greater common experience is to produce social benefits; in the latter case, the goal of meaningful choice is designed to address private benefits. Of course, some aspects of schooling such as an increase in employability of graduates may increase both private and social benefits in the sense that greater or more remunerative employment for individuals will provide society greater tax revenues and lessen its dependence on public services.

If the educational system increases school choice and decreases the common educational experiences among schools, there is a shift toward privatization of benefits, even within public school systems. Most current educational reforms tend to move schools toward a market model, with greater choices within and among districts and among charter and magnet schools. There is also a tendency to increase differentiation among schools (according to themes like science, the arts, technology, and character) in order to make choice meaningful. Choice approaches provide incentives to schools to pursue market niches that are sensitive to the "private" preferences of families rather than to emphasize the common educational experience that serves as the basis for most public benefits. Thus, increasing privatization can also mean a greater focus on the private benefits of schooling than on the social or public benefits.

For-profit Providers.   The apparent shift toward privatization in education is further compounded by the visible entry of for-profit providers. Traditionally, for-profit schools in the K–12 sector have been rare, often concentrating on market niches, such as a special education service that is typically covered by public funding, or the education of underperforming students at private expense. But today there are increasing numbers of more conventional, for-profit schools or for-profit firms that are contracting as EMOs to operate schools in the public sector. For example, among Michigan's 165 charter schools in the 1999–2000 academic year—about 10 percent of the national total—three-quarters were contracting out all or part of their services to for-profit EMOs (Miron, 2000). To some observers, the entry of for-profit providers in education is a much more important manifestation of the expansion of privatization than any other criterion.[4]

Evaluating the Privatization Phenomenon

Much of the effort of the NCSPE is devoted to evaluating the different forms of privatization and comparing them and their consequences to the current system. In order to understand the arguments for and against educational vouchers and educational privatization, it is important to identify the criteria that have emerged in the public debate. Each of these criteria is highly important to particular policymakers and stakeholders: (1) freedom to choose; (2) efficiency; (3) equity; and (4) social cohesion.[5]

1. *Freedom to choose*—For many advocates of educational privatization, the freedom to choose the kind of school that emulates their values, educational philosophies, religious teachings, and political outlooks is the most important issue in school reform. This criterion places a heavy emphasis on the private benefits of education and the liberty to ensure that schools are chosen that are consistent with the child-rearing practices of families.

2. *Efficiency*—Perhaps the most common claim as to privatization is that it will improve efficiency by producing better results given the resources. Numerous studies have attempted to measure differences in student achievement between public and private schools generally and between students using vouchers in private schools and public students (e.g., in voucher demonstrations as summarized by McEwan, 2000).

3. *Equity*—A major claim among opponents of privatization is that it will create greater inequity in educational resources, opportunities, and results according to gender, social class, race, language origins, and geography. Voucher and privatization advocates argue to the contrary that the ability to choose schools will open possibilities to students locked into inferior neighborhood schools and that the competitive marketplace will have great incentive to meet the needs of all students more fully.

4. *Social cohesion*—As set out above, a major public purpose of schooling is to provide a common educational experience with respect to curriculum, values, goals, language, and political socialization so that students from many different backgrounds will accept and support a common set of social, political, and economic institutions. The challenge is whether a marketplace of schools competing primarily on the basis of meeting the private goals of parents and students will coalesce around a common set of social, political, and economic principles in the absence of extensive regulations or powerful social incentives.

It is important to note that there is no single privatization, voucher, or charter school plan, even though collectively these reforms are often lumped together in the debate. Different plans emphasize different mixes of priorities among the four criteria identified above. Within limits, the plans are highly malleable and can be designed to meet specific objectives. Plans can be constructed with particular features to address each of the four policy criteria by using three policy instruments: (1) finance; (2) regulation; and (3) support services. As an example, we can apply these policy instruments to the construction of voucher plans.

1. *Finance* refers to the overall value of the educational voucher, how it is allo-

cated, and whether families can add to it. A large voucher means there will be more options arising in the marketplace with greater freedom of choice and competition. If a voucher is differentiated by educational need (e.g., larger vouchers for the handicapped or the poor), then issues of equity will be addressed. Schools will be able to obtain additional resources for such students, will have greater incentives to attract such students, and will be able to provide richer programs to address their needs. If families can add on to vouchers from their private resources, as Friedman (1962) proposed, then higher-income families will be advantaged in the educational marketplace, as they will be able to send their children to more expensive and restrictive schools (with potential increases in inequities relative to the current system).

2. *Regulation* describes the requirements for participating in the voucher system as well as any other rules that must be adhered to by schools and families in using vouchers. Presumably, only schools that meet certain standards will be eligible to redeem vouchers. Therefore, eligibility rules will have a heavy influence on freedom of choice. Some voucher plans have emphasized a common curriculum and uniform testing as a condition of school participation to ensure that students are meeting goals of social cohesion and that schools can be compared for their productive efficiency. Admissions requirements have also been a matter of scrutiny; schools with more applicants than available spaces will be required to choose some students by lottery to assure fairness in selection procedures. Eligibility for vouchers might also be restricted to certain populations in the name of equity. For example, public and private voucher plans in the United States have been generally limited to children from poor families in order to give them choices outside of their neighborhoods. Florida legislation limits vouchers to children in public schools that had "failed" according to state criteria.

3. *Support services* comprise those types of publicly provided services to increase the effectiveness of the market in providing freedom of choice, productive efficiency, and equity. Competitive markets assume that consumers will have access to a wide variety of choices as well as useful information for selecting among them. In the United States the availability of public transportation is limited, necessitating a system of transportation from neighborhoods to schools of choice. In the absence of that, school choices and competition for students will be limited, reducing the competitive efficiency of schools and creating inequities for those who cannot afford private transportation. Information needs to be made widely available to families so they can make informed choices in selecting schools for their children. Accurate information on school programs and effectiveness, as well as other important aspects of school philosophy and practice, would be collected and disseminated to assist parents in their decisionmaking.

Different voucher proposals (and state guidelines for charter schools) have incorporated different designs that utilize these three policy instruments to achieve specific goals. For example, Friedman's original proposal focused primarily on freedom of choice and productive efficiency, establishing a flat voucher at a modest level; parents would be able to add to the voucher. No provisions were made for transportation or information (somewhat inhibiting the goal of choice), and regulation was minimal. Of course, the lack of information and transportation would likely reduce opportunities, especially for families with modest resources—a challenge for equity. But these omissions would reduce costs and government intrusion, presumably raising productive efficiency. Social cohesion was addressed with the suggestion of a minimal curriculum provision that is not described further.

In contrast, a plan by Christopher Jencks prepared for the U.S. Office of Economic Opportunity (Center for the Study of Public Policy, 1970) placed much greater emphasis on equity, social cohesion, and freedom of choice.[6] It provided larger vouchers to the poor, regulated admissions, standardized tests for common areas of curriculum, and provided both transportation and information. But the high potential costs of transportation, information, and regulation suggest a sacrifice of overall productive efficiency. This proposal put great emphasis on increasing choice, particularly for families who lack resources, but extensive regulations would also inhibit freedom of choice more generally by imposing admissions, curriculum, and testing requirements on schools.

In contrast to these general voucher plans, the privately financed voucher plans and publicly financed arrangements in Milwaukee and Cleveland are restricted to students from lower-income families, with an obvious emphasis on increasing opportunities for these children alone. However, these are viewed as pilot programs by many advocates and as a prelude to a larger voucher system. Voucher plans for the poor vary considerably with respect to value of the voucher, regulation, and support services, with the two public plans encompassing substantial regulation while providing transportation and some information. In most of the private voucher endeavors, the voucher has been set at a low value, requiring parents to make up the remainder of the funds as a gesture of sacrifice and shared responsibility.

It is clear that the way a privatization plan is designed will have profound implications. Different stakeholders have different expectations and preferences.[7] Those who have strong preferences for freedom of choice may resist any regulation that limits parental augmentation of vouchers or that sets curriculum and admissions guidelines, even if they expand equity and social cohesion. Because of the potential conflicts among the criteria, there is no single design that will meet the goals and priorities of all stakeholders. Virtually any design that incorporates all four criteria will have to be based on compromises and trade-offs.

Setting the Agenda

Individually, each part and chapter in this volume represents a contribution toward setting an agenda for the study, analysis, and dissemination of the knowledge base on educational privatization. Collectively, the authors have attempted to capture a variety of dimensions and issues, national and international, that represent what is known and projected about educational privatization. In the best sense of the term, each of the chapters provides a "status report" of its area of coverage and suggestions that might be undertaken by the NCSPE and other entities.

Chapter 2, "Educational Vouchers and the Media," by noted journalists Lee Mitgang and Christopher Connell, analyzes the role of the media in presenting complex issues like educational vouchers to a mass audience. They argue that the role of the media has increased in importance and that there are questions as to how well and how fairly the media are covering the subject. The central tension is underlined by the fact that the topic is highly controversial and inextricably tied to ideology. In addition, much of the empirical research is derived from statistical models and experiments (cf. Chapter 13 by David Myers and Chapter 14 by Fred Doolittle and Wendy Conners) that will appear to be arcane and even inscrutable in their technical detail to most citizens and policymakers. After reviewing the existing treatment of the voucher issue by the media, Mitgang and Connell conclude that reporters need greater familiarity with the intricacies of educational research as well as fair-minded resources to draw upon rather than those that are highly committed to one side or the other. Both of these conclusions are certainly sound recommendations for the NCSPE.

Implementation Issues

The two chapters in Part 2 address the challenges of legal systems and information. Every major change in the delivery of educational services must be evaluated in its legal context, which includes not only federal laws and their interpretation but also state laws that can differ considerably. In Chapter 3, "The Legal Status of Privatization and Vouchers in Education," Frank Kemerer examines the implications of educational privatization at federal and state levels. He notes that although much of the public discussion is about the application of the U.S. Constitution to educational vouchers and other forms of privatization, states may actually play a larger role. The federal constitution as well as recent U.S. Supreme Court decisions give states great authority in regulating almost all aspects of private schools, including teacher qualifications, curriculum, testing requirements, and compulsory ages of attendance. Within this context, Kemerer undertakes a systematic effort to review the legal framework for private schools across the states on such matters as admissions, collective bargaining, and the constitutionality, under federal and state laws, of vouchers, educational tax deductions, and tuition tax credits. He also sets a research agenda that will be responsive to the different stakeholders. Topics include making inventories of the legal frameworks, studies of the impact of privatization and choice on racial and ethnic segregation, state accountability measures, unions and collective bargaining, and monitoring disputes.

Any market system or system of educational choice assumes that such choices will be informed. But education is a complex phenomenon that defies simple description, and a major issue is how to provide useful information that is accessible, understandable, and relatively inexpensive. In Chapter 4, "Information and Choice in Educational Privatization," Mark Schneider studies this issue and attempts to integrate the decisionmaking process of families with their information requirements as well as elements of design and construction of an effective information system. Schneider draws heavily on his own studies, particularly the lessons learned from his important project aimed at designing and implementing a school information system in Washington, D.C. A particular concern is that an information system for schools be accessible to all potential choosers in a form that is amenable to their capabilities and needs. Although he explores the use of new technologies for dissemination, such as specially designed websites with search engines and information on schooling options, he is also concerned that this approach might have the effect of separating those who are knowledgeable about such technologies from those who are not. Thus, he emphasizes the need to be vigilant for differences in access to information that might increase stratification and segregation in schools.

Preschools and Higher Education

Part 3 also contains two chapters. Much can be learned from the market of preschools for two reasons. First, it has traditionally been private in responsibility and operations. Second, it is moving more and more toward the public sector, in many respects the opposite of the current shifts in K–12 education. In Chapter 5, "Preschools and Privatization," Ellen Magenheim examines a range of issues on both the supply and demand sides of the market. She places particular emphasis on what is "quality" in early childhood programs, a matter that is controversial and has implications for costs, finance, and information. She provides an especially strong review regarding the stakeholders and their interests. Magenheim concludes with a range of issues and three potential research projects that might address them in setting an agenda for future research.

At the other end of the spectrum, Arthur Levine addresses higher education in Chapter 6, "Privatization in Higher Education." This is an especially important topic because advances in information technology and distance learning have stimulated many alternatives to traditional higher education. No longer is institutional location a major constraint on the ability to attract and educate clients. Levine suggests that pressures for transforming content and delivery of higher education are rising because of changes in student demography and interests, emerging modifications of careers, and the high level of responsiveness and competitiveness of many of the private institutions and websites that are entering the marketplace. Levine also argues that the new alternatives are a response to rising costs of traditional education and changing attitudes about what constitutes higher education. In this chapter he provides many examples of new providers as well as older, established firms taking on education and training as "new product lines." He asserts that the speed with which this is taking place requires some urgency in developing a research agenda and provides some questions that need to be explored.

International Dimensions

Just as the K–12 sector can learn from preschool and higher education markets, there are lessons for building a study agenda from the international experience. The section on international dimensions attempts to acknowledge some of these lessons and their consequences. In Chapter 7, "Privatization Through Vouchers in Developing Countries: The Cases of Chile and Colombia," Martin Carnoy and Patrick McEwan evaluate what has been learned from experience in two nations. The Chilean case is most auspicious because of the fact that Chile has had a nationwide voucher system for almost two decades. Carnoy and McEwan report on their extensive studies of Chile's vouchers on the distribution and sponsorship of schools, student characteristics in public and private schools, the apparent impact of vouchers on student achievement, and the impact of competition on school performance. They also survey the experience with targeted vouchers for low-income secondary school students in Colombia. Their main lessons seem to be cautionary in warning against simplistic generalizations that ignore the context and specific design specifications of voucher plans. Details count for a great deal in determining results.

Whereas Carnoy and McEwan survey privatization in two industrializing countries, Geoffrey Walford in Chapter 8 ("Privatization in Industrialized Countries") surveys industrialized nations, especially England and Wales and the Netherlands. He describes in detail the development of privatization mechanisms in the two settings and their dynamics over time. He also tries to point out the consequences of the changes in arrangements that have taken place. The detailed attention to the history and setting of the efforts at privatization are particularly valuable, given the importance of context and details on educational impacts. For example, Walford points out that privatization in the Netherlands is extensive in theory but highly constrained in practice by extensive government regulation. He points to the need for separate studies on individual countries as well as comparative studies that might unearth what has been learned. He also recommends that such case studies lead to more intensive research on those countries that have the most to teach us.

Charter Schools

Chapters 9 and 10 are devoted to a uniquely U.S. movement: charter schools. This movement combines deregulation, school choice, and considerable privatization to the degree that private EMOs have contracted with charter school sponsors to manage many of the schools. In Chapter 9, "Assessing the Growth and Potential of Charter Schools," Pearl Rock Kane and Christopher Lauricella survey the charter school movement, which has grown rapidly. In addition to descriptive statistics on charter schools and breakdowns by states, they also explore specific dimensions. They caution us that charter school regulations vary considerably from state to state and that generalization is thus a hazardous undertaking. They pursue such topics as accountability, innovation, choice, autonomy, governance practices, parental involvement, and a host of others. Kane and Lauricella also provide an ambitious research agenda on charter schools. In this case, the explosion of charter schools has outpaced vastly an understanding of their consequences.

Available surveys do depict the overall landscape of charter schools, but they must be supplemented by detailed information on charter school life, best undertaken with intensive case study. In Chapter 10, "Privatization and Charter School Reform: Economic, Political and Social Dimensions," Amy Stuart Wells and Janelle Scott report some of the findings from UCLA's study of charter schools. Of particular interest is how different facets of privatization are found in different charter schools, as well as their consequences. Their team undertook an intensive study of seventeen charter schools in ten districts distributed across California. Although their overall study was more extensive, they distilled an analysis of dimensions on privatization including the source of finances, use of EMOs, extent of public-private partnerships, control of enrollments, racial segregation, and community involvement. They find that one impact of charter school policies is the expansion of financial and other inequalities among these schools. Wells and Scott conclude their chapter with an extensive research agenda on the little-studied topic of charter schools.

Perspectives of Stakeholders

Clearly, the impact of privatization will depend very heavily on its implications for the major stakeholders. Two stakeholders that are likely to be deeply affected by change are poor families and teachers. The two chapters in Part 6 attempt to develop the consequences for each of these two constituencies. In Chapter 11, "Vouchers, Privatization, and the Poor," Gary Natriello explores the potential impact of a shift from a public bureaucratic model of education to one based on vouchers and the private provision of education. He sets out eight major stakeholder groups and examines how their interests might affect students from poor families. He argues that the interests and strategies of the stakeholders will mold the shape of privatization policies, and each of the stakeholders needs to be studied to ascertain its interests, possibilities for coalition, and potential strategies. He focuses his analysis on the potential effects of privatization and vouchers on the poor. He also provides an extensive list of studies that can be done on the stakeholders to refine this analysis.

Teachers are one of the most important stakeholders; their conditions of employment and teaching practices are directly affected by the organization of schools and the way that they are financed. In Chapter 12, "Teachers and Privatization," Caroline Hodges Persell considers issues privatization raises for teachers and teaching. Although she also briefly reviews the other stakeholders, her focus is teachers. Persell draws upon a large body of theoretical and empirical literature to better understand the complex issues surrounding teachers and privatization. This includes privatization experiences in other areas, such as deregulation of airlines and privatization of health services, to evaluate the lessons learned. Finally, she sets out a research agenda to examine teacher recruitment, retention, and qualifications; potential value conflicts for teachers; and the stability and effects of different institutional forms on teacher behavior.

Evaluation Designs

Because there has been relatively little privatization of education in the past, most assertions about the consequences of privatization lack evidence. In large measure this has produced advocates and detractors, each making claims about the impact of privatization that cannot be buttressed by available data. The one exception has been the recent attempt to carry out experimental and statistical research that compares student achievement in public and private schools, as well as students receiving and not receiving vouchers. These studies have been both experimental and nonexperimental. The two chapters in Part 7 therefore represent highly systematic attempts to set out guidelines for designing, implementing, and interpreting such studies. In Chapter 13, "Criteria for Evaluating School Voucher Studies," David E. Myers attempts to place such studies within a policy framework. He addresses specifically the issues of measurement of the appropriate constructs, validity of results and their use, and the generalization of results to a broader policy context. Myers draws heavily on his experience in codesigning and implementing a notable voucher experiment in New York City. Accordingly, he raises important issues that emerged in that pioneering study.

In contrast, Chapter 14 ("Designing Education Voucher Experiments: Recommendations for Researchers, Funders, and Users") provides a somewhat different context for considering educational voucher experiments. Fred Doolittle and Wendy Connors draw upon the wealth of experience gained by the Manpower Demonstration Research Corporation in their three decades of designing and running social experiments. The authors set out a step-by-step approach by raising the questions that are pertinent to conducting experiments. They also attempt to paint a comprehensive picture of the issues that arise and their possible solutions, almost a brief handbook on the subject that should be valuable to anyone who attempts to design, implement, or interpret such studies. In many respects, the entire chapter sets an agenda for conducting experimental research on educational vouchers and privatization. Presumably, the dearth of evidence suggests that a major role of the NCSPE should be to promote, carry out, and summarize studies on the impacts of different forms of privatization according to the four criteria set out above: freedom of choice, productive efficiency, equity, and social cohesion. Chapters 13 and 14 provide a framework for undertaking at least part of that task.

Surveying the Horizon

Taken as a whole, the chapters in this volume embrace many different issues that need to be pursued if we as a nation are to understand educational privatization and its consequences. Together they produce an agenda that will be valuable not only to the NCSPE but also to any other organizations that wish to investigate educational privatization.[8] It is with these important goals in mind that we present our research.

Notes

1. Public Agenda (1999). *On Thin Ice: How Advocates and Opponents Could Misread the Public's Views on Vouchers and Charter Schools.* New York: Public Agenda.

2. Of course, we should not lose sight of the fact that parents, nonparents, and businesses pay taxes to support public schools, so ultimately all of the funds are derived through the private sector.

3. In general, libertarians prefer tuition tax credits because they are a finance mechanism that is independent of schooling so that they are less likely to be entangled with regulation of schools than are educational vouchers. In contrast, cultural conservatives such as William Bennett are more open to educational vouchers because they prefer a specific curriculum for all schools or the mastery of a specific canon of knowledge.

4. Paradoxically, there is little evidence that any of these firms have reached profitability at the present time. Indeed, one of the earliest of the for-profit firms, Tesseract (formerly EAI) lost about $11 million on $37 million in revenues in 1999 and has filed for bankruptcy. Edison Schools lost about $27 million on revenues of about $217 million, although it continues to expand rapidly. See "For-Profit Schools" in *Business Week* (2000).

5. This section draws heavily on H.M. Levin (1999).

6. Also see J.E. Coons and S. Sugarman (1978) and J.E. Chubb and Moe (1990) for different versions of voucher plans.

7. My own insights and understanding on these issues have been enhanced by a prescient doctoral dissertation carried out by one of my students some two decades ago (Catterall, 1982).

8. A rich new source of information on what is known and not known and what needs to be learned about educational vouchers is *School Vouchers* (2000). This agenda was constructed by a group representing all sides of the issue that was convened by Jack Jennings of the Center on Education Policy.

References

Carnoy, M. (1995). Rates of return to education. In M. Carnoy, *International encyclopedia of economics of education* (2d ed.), pp. 364–369. New York: Elsevier Science.

Catterall, J. (1982). *The politics of education vouchers.* Unpublished doctoral dissertation, Stanford University, School of Education, Stanford University.

Center for the Study of Public Policy. (1970). *Education vouchers: A report on financing elementary education by grants to parents.* Cambridge: Center for the Study of Public Policy.

Center on Education Policy. (2000). *School Vouchers.* Washington, D.C.: Center on Education Policy.

Chubb, J.E., and Moe, T.M. (1990). *Politics, markets, and America's schools.* Washington, D.C.: Brookings Institution.

Coons, J.E., and Sugarman, S. (1978). *Education by choice.* Berkeley: University of California Press.

For-profit schools. (2000, February 7). *Business Week,* pp. 65–78.

Friedman, M. (1962). The role of government in education. In M. Friedman (ed.), *Capitalism and freedom.* Chicago: University of Chicago Press, chap. 6.

Hill, P., Pierce, L., and Guthrie, J. (1997). *Reinventing public education: How contracting can transform American schools.* Chicago: University of Chicago Press.

James, T., and Levin, H.M. (1983). *Public dollars for private schools: The case of tuition tax credits.* Philadelphia: Temple University Press.

Lankford, H., and Wyckoff, J. (1992). Primary and secondary school choice among public and religious alternatives. *Economics of Education Review* 11(4), 317–338.

Levin, H.M. (1987). Education as a public and private good. *Journal of Policy Analysis and Management* 6, pp. 628–641.

Levin, H.M. (1999). The public-private nexus in education. *American Behavioral Scientist* 1(43), 124–137.

McEwan, P.J. (2000). *Comparing the effectiveness of public and private schools: Review of evidence and interpretations.* Occasional Paper No. 3. New York: National Center for the Study of Privatization in Education, Teachers College, Columbia University. Available at [www.tc.columbia.edu/ncspe].

Miron, G. (2000, April). *What's public about Michigan's charter schools: Lessons in school reform from statewide evaluations of charter schools.* Paper presented at the annual meeting of the American Educational Research Association, New Orleans.

Public Agenda. (1999). *On thin ice: How advocates and opponents could misread the public's views on vouchers and charter schools.* New York: Public Agenda.

Smith, A. (1937). *Wealth of nations* (Modern Library ed.). New York: Random House.

U.S. Department of Education, National Center for Education Statistics. (1999). *Digest of Education Statistics, 1998* (NCES 1999–036). Washington, D.C.: U.S. Department of Education, Office of Educational Research.

West, E.G. (1967). Tom Paine's voucher scheme for public education. *Southern Economic Journal* 33, pp. 378–382.

_____. (1991). Public schools and excess burdens. *Economics of Education Review* 10, 159–170.

Wolfe, B.L. (1995). External benefits of education. In M. Carnoy (ed.), *International encyclopedia of economics of education*, (2d ed.). New York: Elsevier Science, pp. 159–163.

2

Educational Vouchers
and the Media

LEE D. MITGANG AND CHRISTOPHER V. CONNELL

As education stories go, the school voucher debate features all the expected complications, excess emotionalism, and partisanship of such other long-running, unresolved feuds as bilingual education or phonics–versus–whole language. But in key respects, the voucher argument stands apart. Since 1955, when economist Milton Friedman first proposed replacing the traditional system of public schooling with a voucher system, the debate has escalated to a level of complexity and contentiousness that poses special challenges for any print or broadcast journalist seeking to cover the issue accurately, fairly, and perceptively.

John Witte (1999), director of the Robert M. LaFollette School of Public Affairs at the University of Wisconsin–Madison, whose research on the nearly decade-old Milwaukee private school choice experiment has placed him in the eye of the storm, brands the media's handling of the story as "choice theater." In his forthcoming book, *The Market Approach to Education: An Analysis of America's First Voucher Experiment*, Witte argues that the growth in the media's fascination with the voucher story can be explained not simply by the idea's potential merits but by its high drama and "man-bites-dog" qualities that reporters crave and that more workaday education stories generally lack. Choice, Witte (1999) writes,

provides a truly radical departure from education as usual. For those concerned with the course and quality of education now or in the future, it challenges the basic framework of the policy regime. It also focuses attention on parents as critical actors in a system where they are often neglected or relegated to quite subservient support roles. And finally, if packaged properly, it invokes deep value structures revolving around the twin poles of freedom of choice and the unjust denial of equal opportunity. . . . As national actors became involved, this further expanded media coverage in a synergistic upward spiral.[1]

The public consequences of the media's handling of the voucher story have multiplied during the 1990s as publicly and especially privately funded voucher plans spread. From 1990 to 1995, Milwaukee was the nation's single laboratory for publicly funded vouchers. Even there, however, the voucher experiment was so limited and specialized that it was easy for many journalists beyond the city limits to regard it as interesting but idiosyncratic, with only debatable applicability to other cities. Between 1990 and 1993, the voucher cause also suffered a series of setbacks as statewide voucher ballot initiatives in California, Colorado, and Oregon were defeated soundly. Since then, however, the popularity of vouchers—as measured by opinion polls—has increased steadily.[2] And their constitutionality, although far from settled, has survived some important court tests. The apparent growth in the appeal of vouchers is especially striking among minority groups frustrated with the pace of improvement in neighborhood public schools. In 1996, Cleveland became the second city to permit vouchers and the first to allow their use for parochial schools (three years later, on the eve of the new school year, a federal court halted the issuance of vouchers to new students temporarily on grounds that it violated the constitutional separation of church and state). By 1998, provoucher corporations and foundations had committed some $250 million to establish privately financed voucher programs in forty-one cities, serving more than 13,000 children.[3] Privately funded voucher programs, in particular, have garnered extensive and respectful media coverage, even from newspapers that take a dim editorial view of public vouchers.[4] When, for example, Harvard's Paul E. Peterson reported in October 1998 that standardized test scores of 1,300 pupils participating in a privately financed voucher program in New York City improved slightly more than those of students who remained in public elementary schools, the findings received prominent play in *The New York Times, The New York Daily News, The New York Post, El Diario, The Washington Post, The Wall Street Journal, Education Week*, and *The Detroit News*.

In short, the voucher idea has risen in the media's eyes from the backwaters of school reform to the front pages. Although the number of students and schools involved remains miniscule in the universe of 53 million U.S. schoolchildren, the concept has attracted widespread interest in the 1990s for a variety of reasons:

- The public's fascination with market solutions during an economic boom;
- Dissatisfaction with government in general and public schools in particular;
- Strong advocacy by Republican governors and lawmakers of vouchers, tuition tax credits, charter schools, and other efforts to inject competition into K-12 education;
- Privatization of other municipal services in major cities;
- The move by the U.S. Supreme Court in *Agostini v. Felton* (1997) to undo its cumbersome edict in *Aguilar v. Felton* (1985) that forced Title I remedial classes at parochial schools into offsite trailers.

Former President George H. W. Bush sought to advance the cause of vouchers with a so-called GI Bill for Children. Congressional Republicans have made repeated, unsuccessful attempts since 1995 to promote vouchers as a cure for ailing public schools in the District of Columbia and elsewhere but were thwarted by President Bill Clinton's vetoes. Private benefactors—"voucher Medicis," as a *Wall Street Journal* editorial writer dubbed them—have stepped in where government has been hesitant to go.[5]

The jury is still out on the educational merits of vouchers. Reporters and policymakers need to keep in mind that the voucher movement is in its infancy, and any research, and any researcher, claiming to present "definitive" findings for or against the idea ought to be regarded with suspicion. Still, the ascent of vouchers to media prominence and political respectability has obliged reporters, editors, and editorial writers in many more cities and states to seek a deeper understanding of vouchers as a reform strategy.

Joe Williams, a veteran education reporter and resident voucher expert for the *Milwaukee Journal-Sentinel*, said he routinely fields calls from reporters from Texas, Arizona, New Jersey, New York, and other states where the idea of publicly funded vouchers has emerged as a possibility. "Vouchers are a tough subject, an emotional subject, and it's very hard for a general interest newspaper to wrap its arms around it," he told us.[6]

The Stakes and the Stakeholders

Journalists dealing with voucher stories have found themselves both ardently courted and acidly scrutinized by a cottage industry of organizations and individuals whose positions for or against the idea may be either overt or subtle. The groups that have established themselves as standard news sources include teachers' unions and others in the education "establishment";[7] national and local parent groups; religious organizations such as the National Catholic Education Association; liberal groups and First Amendment advocates such as People for the American Way, the NAACP, and Americans United for Separation of Church and State; conservative foundations and think-tanks including the Heritage Foundation, the Center for Education Reform, the Hudson Institute, the Institute for Justice, and the Lynde and Harry Bradley Foundation; organizations such as CEO America that champion and finance privately funded voucher plans; and nonpartisan educational research groups such as the Carnegie Foundation for the Advancement of Teaching.

Finally, the two major national political parties have staked out largely opposite positions on educational vouchers. The Republican Party has made vouchers a centerpiece of its education platform; Democrats, with only a few exceptions, have limited their support of school choice to public schools and the charter school movement.

Along with these national and local organizations, reporters on deadline or preparing in-depth articles habitually consult a list of established individual sources with widely varying degrees of expertise and objectivity on this issue. The most frequently quoted include: Chester E. "Checker" Finn Jr., a former education official in the Reagan administration who now heads the Thomas B. Fordham Foundation; Howard Fuller, former school superintendent of Milwaukee's public schools and currently with Marquette University's School of Education; Clint Bolick of the Institute for Justice, a conservative legal organization that has argued a number of voucher court cases; Frank Kemerer, a researcher at the University of North Texas; Henry Levin of Teachers College, Columbia University; Terry Moe of the Hoover Institute, coauthor of the 1990 Brookings Institution's influential *Politics, Markets, and America's Schools*; Alex Molnar of the University of Wisconsin–Milwaukee; Derek Neal of the University of Chicago; Paul Peterson of Harvard University; and John Witte of the University of Wisconsin.[8]

There is, then, no shortage of sources eager to talk with, and influence, reporters writing or preparing broadcast pieces on vouchers. What *is* in short supply, according to journalists we spoke with, are genuinely "honest brokers"—dispassionate individuals and organizations with no motive other than helping the press and the public get unvarnished facts about how vouchers work in practice, not theory, and about their soundness as an educational strategy.

Lynn Olson, senior editor of *Education Week,* echoed the comments of many of the journalists we contacted: "One of the hardest things about covering the voucher story is that there aren't any neutral people. There's a feeling that everyone has a vested interest."[9]

Much of the national print and broadcast reporting has painted the Milwaukee and Cleveland voucher experiments as human-interest stories—the "choice theater" alluded to by professor Witte: poor, determined mother struggles to save child from failing inner-city school. Or: African American/Democrat/urban lawmaker forms unlikely alliance with upstate white Republicans to battle intransigent education bureaucrats. From there, the articles typically segue into he said–she said, "balanced" accounts of the pros and cons of vouchers. The frequent result: Readers and viewers are left to sort out for themselves the validity of conflicting arguments by the partisans. Only infrequently does the reporting break out of the confines established by the arguments of advocates and foes.

Kim K. Metcalf, director of the Indiana Center for Evaluation at Indiana University, who was hired by the state of Ohio to conduct research on the Cleveland voucher experiment, found himself, like Witte before him in Milwaukee, in conflict with the more optimistic findings of Peterson of Harvard. Metcalf said that most reporters seemed at a loss over what to make of the conflicting research claims: "Unfortunately," said Metcalf, "most reporters knew only that two researchers were claiming different results from the same data, one from Harvard and one from Indiana. The result, I'm afraid, was that they came away assuming that no one could be believed and that everyone investigating the issue was doing so subjectively."[10] Metcalf has accused his rivals of distorting data from his early research for their own ends.[11] Peterson himself, in a recent article, acknowledged shortcomings in the competing studies about Cleveland: "In the end, firm conclusions cannot be drawn from the studies of the scholarship program in Cleveland. In neither our research nor that of the Indiana evaluation team was it possible to compare similar groups of students by means of [a randomized field trial]."[12]

Some advocates feel the media have paid too much attention to the disputes between the academic scorekeepers and not enough to what is actually transpiring in the communities and classrooms. "The coverage tends not to be as substantive as it ought to be," said Elliot Mincberg, general counsel for the antivoucher People for The American Way. "The typical voucher story will be: 'Here's John Jones or Jill Smith and they have a child in a terrible public school, and they've been scrimping and saving, and now with vouchers they will get to send him to a private school.' It's the bright, shiny kid syndrome. You don't see stories about the many, many kids who drop out of voucher schools or are pushed out of voucher schools in Milwaukee."[13]

Lacking the time to camp out inside schools or classrooms, reporters typically seek proxies for clues to the effectiveness of vouchers. They might look, for example, at how many parents sign up for the vouchers and whether enrollment is up or down in both the private and public sectors. They may examine attendance or dropout rates, even though those are often murky and open to multiple interpretations. Most often, they turn to standardized tests as the most telling barometer for performance—but those statistics are also among the most hotly disputed by researchers and voucher partisans. "It's hard for us to quantify. How do you really measure whether [vouchers] are a success?" said a Cleveland editor who asked not to be identified. "How are reporters to place a new school's test scores in appropriate perspective?" the editor asked. Did more parents sign their children up for neighborhood public schools because they were unswayed by vouchers, or because Cleveland restored full-day kindergarten?

The statistical duels among researchers have left even the most veteran reporters leery. When a new study lands on his desk, "I almost dread it," said Williams of *The Milwaukee Journal-Sentinel*. "We end up calling the same suspects and it becomes an argument over methodology." "We find it very confusing ourselves," said Scott Stevens, an education writer at the *Cleveland Plain Dealer*. "It's very difficult to put across to the public. You feel like you're trying to wade through a bunch of mumbo jumbo. You just end up shaking your head."[14] "There's no one straight on this one," agreed June Kronholz, a *Wall Street Journal* education correspondent who has covered the voucher story in Arizona, the Edgewood school district in San Antonio, Texas, and elsewhere. "Everybody's got a point of view."[15]

The Media's Challenges

In common with many educational policy issues, the press is the main gatekeeper of information as well as a shaper of the public's perceptions of the wisdom, popularity, and practicality of differing reform strategies. The media are the portals through which highly technical research—often with conflicting claims and arcane language—must pass to reach the voting public. It falls to journalists to translate research into language the lay public can grasp while doing justice to its intricacies. And it is left to the media to cut through the hyperbole on both sides: the often-inflated, premature claims of voucher proponents who portray the strategy as an elixir of school renewal, and the claims of opponents who insist vouchers would spell the end of public education and undermine the First Amendment.

Beyond their obligation to present clear, balanced accounts of voucher developments, the reporters we spoke with were keenly aware that vouchers are, as the *Plain-Dealer's* Stevens put it, "uncharted territory." They felt an added obligation to help readers understand the larger goals and stakes in this debate.

Richard Colvin, education writer of *The Los Angeles Times*, observed: "It's important to recognize what vouchers achieve for individual kids. We as middle-class reporters tend to think only about the systemic goals of vouchers, but we also have to think about the effects on individual lives. What do we say to lower-income parents where the schools are terrible? We have to realize that this is not just a bunch of right-wing nuts out to destroy public education. You can't ignore the political dimension."[16] "Our whole society is involved in a debate about market solutions," says Bella Rosenberg, special assistant to the president of the American Federation of Teachers (AFT). "There's a real contest of values going on. . . . The media in a democracy play a very important role in this debate."[17] "Interestingly," Metcalf of the Indiana Center for Evaluation told us, "only one reporter ever asked me, 'Based on the findings, what would [I] do with my own children?'"

In meeting the multiple challenges of brokering among conflicting claims and finding the larger meanings of the voucher debate, however, reporters with limited time and expertise, and with few dispassionate sources to turn to, have done what they regard as the next best thing: consider the source. Put another way, reporters at key moments in the history of the choice debate have placed great, and sometimes undue, weight on the pedigree of the authors or sponsoring organizations of voucher research. In practice, that has led to a widespread presumption in the media that voucher research conducted by Ivy League scholars and by prestigious foundations and think-tanks is, by definition, accurate, fair, and worthy of prominent coverage. In contrast, comments and research emanating from organizations and individuals considered partisan or self-interested, such as the teachers' unions, are often presumed to be automatically flawed or biased and tend to get far less press coverage or none at all.

A recent case in point was the press's handling of Peterson's research on the Cleveland voucher program. With no mention of Peterson's record as a provoucher partisan, *The New York Times* ran an uncritical 900-word story on his Cleveland research on September 18, 1997, that began: "In the first independent evaluation of Cleveland's groundbreaking school voucher program, a *Harvard University study* [emphasis ours] has found that the program was very popular with parents and raised the scores of those students tested at the end of the first year."[18] The journalist, not the university, confers the Harvard imprimatur here. A year earlier, Republican presidential hopeful Lamar Alexander, a former U.S. secretary of education and state governor, used similar shorthand to add credence to what he repeatedly referred to as "the Harvard study" during an August 22, 1996, appearance on the *NewsHour with Jim Lehrer*.[19]

Two months before the *Times* article appeared, the American Federation of Teachers, an unabashed foe of vouchers, had issued a report that called the Cleveland program "a cruel hoax" and went on to blast the methodology of the Peterson study. The AFT's report received no coverage in the *Times*. But a subsequent analysis of the two Cleveland studies by *Education Week's* Debra Viadero quoted several education experts as saying that both reports had methodological flaws, and each reflected the respective biases of its originators.

This uneven pattern of voucher news coverage was at work several years earlier at another critical juncture: the release of the Brookings Institution's landmark 1990 report, *Politics, Markets, and America's Schools,* by then Brookings senior fellow John E. Chubb and Stanford University political scientist Terry Moe. The report hit the education world and the media like a thunderclap. Here were two scholars from an establishment think-tank making the radical case, buttressed by social-scientific data and analysis, for a free-market model of education funding and governance. Chubb and Moe were embraced by the editorial pages of *The Wall Street Journal* and received wide coverage from newspapers, broadcasters, and news agencies around the country. Their report became the anthem of the prochoice community for the next three years and was demonized by Albert Shanker and others in the education community as an ideological assault on public education cloaked in scholarly garb. As Shanker put it in his weekly paid "Where We Stand" column on October 11, 1992:

> The curious fact is that almost no one who cites Chubb and Moe has read their book, although they have all read favorable things about it in newspaper editorials and op-ed pages. The few nontechnical people who have read it confess they could not follow the statistical analysis that makes up more than half the book and that is supposed to support the conclusions.[20]

While the Brookings study became a staple of the press's voucher coverage, the media largely ignored subsequent critiques of Chubb and Moe's findings and methods.[21]

The point here is not to pass judgment on the merits of any particular research effort or the ripostes that followed. We *are* suggesting that reporters, often lacking the expertise to adjudicate the contradictions themselves, make judgments on whether or not to give voucher research credence based on the scholarly bona fides of the authors. And at several critical junctures in the voucher debate, those judgments may have unwittingly caused the press to add to the vitriol of the voucher debate rather than to relieve it.

Such complexities and contradictions are not unique to vouchers, of course. But unlike almost any other education topic, reporters covering vouchers face the added challenge of reporting accurately and evenhandedly on a school reform strategy with not only disputed educational merits but also equally controversial and mercurial legal, political, economic, racial, and social dimensions. Several education reporters told us that the scrutiny their voucher stories routinely receive from both sides of the voucher divide is unlike anything else they cover. That is certainly the case for reporters in Milwaukee and Cleveland.

Williams of the *Milwaukee Journal-Sentinel* said that local radio talk-show hosts from both the left and right regularly dissect his coverage:

> It puts added pressure on us," he said. "It's almost like they count the number of paragraphs in our stories to make sure each side gets their share of space. But we also put a lot of pressure on ourselves. I've spoken with reporters at the *Cleveland Plain Dealer*, and we all feel that this is an important social experiment going on in our cities, and we have a responsibility to look at it from all sides and aspects.[22]

In describing the role of the media in the voucher debate and the challenges that news organizations set for themselves in covering this story, it should be emphasized that no journalist regards himself or herself as a dupe for voucher foes or partisans, or as a mere conveyor of facts gathered by others. The media have been an important contributor to the debate in their own right. At its best, news coverage and analysis can reflect the experience, expertise, and perspective gained from long service on the education beat. Viadero of *Education Week*, for example, has established herself as a respected in-house analyst of education research, capable of spotting the strengths and flaws of research on voucher programs.

Education correspondents from *The Los Angeles Times, Education Week, The Wall Street Journal,* and other news organizations have made pilgrimages to voucher hotbeds such as Milwaukee, Cleveland, San Antonio, and Arizona to visit schools, sit in classrooms, talk with community leaders, and offer fresh analytical insights based on firsthand observation. Colvin of *The Los Angeles Times*, who has covered vouchers since California's unsuccessful ballot initiative in 1993, has visited Milwaukee and weighed the merits of conflicting research on the schools there.

Some newspapers and columnists have gone farther, however, choosing to use their clout to play a direct and, at times, even partisan role in shaping the national voucher debate. *The Wall Street Journal* is the outstanding example of a nationally respected newspaper that has used its editorial and op-ed columns since the 1980s to crusade for vouchers. The *Journal's* editorial pages had much to do with bringing to national prominence Milwaukee's Annette "Polly" Williams, the

African American politician who helped found that city's voucher plan. On August 14, 1996, the *Journal's* op-ed page became the first public forum to carry the startling research of Peterson and his colleagues, which, in contrast to Witte's previous research, argued that Milwaukee's voucher program was producing measurable improvements in student achievement. (On this story, as with many others, the *Journal's* ardent editorial advocacy contrasts sharply with the meticulously straightforward and insightful coverage of voucher developments on its news pages.)

Two of the nation's most prominent African American columnists, Brent Staples of *The New York Times*, and William Raspberry of *The Washington Post*, have written articles making the case for experimenting with vouchers in minority communities where public schools are failing. Staples told us that his responsibility as a journalist is to "penetrate to the social point of the story, which is that conditions in city schools are unacceptable and that vouchers must be tried." He accused others in the media of "moral cowardice" for avoiding taking a definite stand on vouchers and falling back instead on he said–she said reporting in the face of apparent contradictions. At any rate, Staples's and Raspberry's columns in the liberal editorial pages of the nation's two most powerful dailies, added to the voices of such prominent provoucher African American politicians as Milwaukee's Polly Williams and former New York Congressman Floyd Flake, have opened fascinating new avenues for press coverage of the voucher debate.[23]

How well, then, are the media meeting the challenges of covering the voucher story? We posed that question to a number of researchers and advocates on the receiving end of press coverage. Several praised the coverage of vouchers by education beat reporters and by National Public Radio, but they were more critical of the rest of the press, particularly television.

Cecilia Rouse, an economics professor at Princeton University who waded into the voucher debate in 1997 with an econometric study of Milwaukee's choice program that found better math scores among participants, said she felt the half-dozen or so education writers who contacted her did a reasonably good job in their coverage: "Reporters treated me very well, and they honestly wanted to understand [my research]. About half of them did."[24]

Witte of the University of Wisconsin said that many out-of-town reporters he has dealt with seemed "lazy. They just wanted quick quotes and didn't want to actually read up about the [Milwaukee choice] program." Witte has higher regard for education writers, especially those in the Milwaukee area who he said had done quite well with the voucher story. "They knew the historical background and they knew how to look for the complications." But he added: "The visual media have portrayed [the Milwaukee choice program] as a glamorous experiment, with the African-American Polly Williams teaming up with our Republican Governor Tommy Thompson to rescue the children of Milwaukee from their public schools."[25]

People for the American Way's Mincberg told us that local reporters in cities with voucher experiments do a better job of digging than the national press. "In Cleveland there's been an enormous amount of local coverage of the nitty-gritty of vouchers—not just the educational controversy, but serious financial audits as well," said Mincberg. "The *Plain Dealer* and the *Columbus Dispatch* both reported that more than $1 million was spent on taxi cabs" ferrying voucher children to private schools. "Similarly in Milwaukee in the early years there were serious stories about fly-by-night voucher schools and schools educating phantom voucher students. That got into the Milwaukee press, but not much more. You heard very little about it outside Milwaukee," he said.[26]

Howard Fuller, former Milwaukee school superintendent and now a professor at Marquette University's School of Education, had this to say: "I've had a very mixed experience dealing [with the media.] The vast majority of reporters really know very little about it and don't understand the research . . . Many obviously bring a philosophical predisposition against them."[27] Checker Finn told us that "the problem for the media in general is the lack of sophistication." He continued: "One of two things happen. Either they take the researcher's view, or they fall back on their own interests, prejudices and usual sources of opinion. Not many people are able to look at response coefficients and figure out which are meaningful."[28] Finally, Peterson, arguably on the receiving end recently of more press coverage in the choice debate than any other researcher, told us that he found media accounts of his work generally accurate: "I think the media have done a pretty good job."[29]

Such comments by leading players in the voucher saga suggest that the media, especially local reporters and education specialists, have done reasonably well in presenting the public with the facts of the voucher story as it has evolved. But most reporters need help in sorting out its broad implications and technical complications. It should also be noted that because of its legal and political dimensions court reporters, state-house correspondents, and general assignment reporters as well as education writers routinely write about vouchers. Newspapers and networks that almost never ask a general-assignment reporter to cover a complicated military story, or assign a nonspecialist to the medical beat, think nothing of letting all hands have a go at complex education stories.

What Can Be Done?

From our review of the media's performance in covering the voucher story, two priorities were clear. First, most reporters need, and would welcome, a better grasp of the intricacies of education research. Second, they need ready access to a corps of reliable, fair-minded experts to help put voucher developments in perspective.

What services, studies, and activities might the new National Center for the Study of Privatization in Education (NCSPE) undertake to address those challenges? We suggest the following possibilities:

> First and foremost, the NCSPE should establish itself as an honest broker of voucher research and information for reporters on deadline.

Whatever the new center chooses to do, it should recognize from the start that it will have to demonstrate its expertise and, even more, its *neutrality*, to all parties in the debate—especially to a press corps grown justifiably suspicious of the motives of all news sources in the voucher saga. Reporters reflexively asked us, for example, who would be funding the NCSPE, who the staff was, who would be on the board of directors. In the long run, the answers to those questions may determine whether the center's efforts at being an honest broker in the voucher debate will succeed. "There is a tremendous need for someone to help sort out the mass of confusing information that accompanies discussion of vouchers and school choice more generally," says Metcalf.

Becoming a consumers' union of sorts for voucher developments and research, then, would require confronting several harsh challenges. To serve the media effectively and fit into the realities of deadlines, the NCSPE would ideally need access to voucher research at the same time it is released to the media—and *before* it makes headlines. Such prepublication access would require, by definition, that the NCSPE establish and maintain a reputation for neutrality and expertise with the press, the research community, and partisans on both sides of the debate. Inevitably, there will also be times when the NCSPE would be called for comment without having a chance to see the full research report. In either case, the timeliness of response is crucial to getting into a reporter's all-important first story, whether on the nightly news or in the morning edition of the newspaper. Most reporters are (or fancy they are) adept at summarizing the material they are presented with. The challenge is knowing how to help reporters on deadline distill the essence of research and place it in larger context.

> Second, the NCSPE should provide one-stop shopping for a rich compendium of voucher information, background and commentary.

Specifically, we found great receptivity to the idea of a voucher website. Such a site operated and maintained by the NCSPE might include:

- A voucher bibliography, consisting of books and scholarly articles on vouchers, with information and links on how to obtain them. Excerpts or summaries of hard-to-get or out-of-print texts or articles with special merit might be maintained online.
- A list of nonpartisan experts willing to assist reporters in analyzing the merits of research, news developments, and opinion polls on vouchers.
- Links to other Internet sites for organizations and individuals with an interest or expertise on vouchers.
- A historical summary of trends in opinion polls about vouchers, including the sponsoring organizations, the findings, and the exact wording of the poll questions.

The information in the website could also be conveyed to the media with periodic newsletters, which would serve the added function of calling attention to the center's other work and research.

Third, the NCSPE should stand ready to assist reporters in understanding the basics of educational research.

We found strong demand among reporters for such knowledge, not just for the voucher story but for any news development requiring an ability to evaluate the quality, methods, and conflicting claims of educational research. Online tutorials are one possibility. Working with the Hechinger Institute on Education and the Media at Teachers College, Columbia University, and the Education Writers Association in Washington, D.C., the NCSPE might consider offering weekend-long annual workshops on the basics of deciphering and evaluating research.

Fourth, consider conducting an independent study of how effectively the press is covering vouchers, and what further services the NCSPE might provide to increase that effectiveness.

Specifically, the NCSPE might conduct a national survey of education writers and editorialists to discover, for example, how many have actually visited districts with vouchers; how many have background or knowledge of educational research analysis; what sources they contact for guidance, background, or comment when doing voucher stories; and invite comments and suggestions about how a center like this might be helpful.

The questionnaire, or an accompanying cover letter, would also serve as an added vehicle for introducing the new center to the media.

On a deeper level, the NCSPE should not merely be about helping social scientists become more adept at the sound-bite game. To preserve the integrity and value of research, the NCSPE should encourage reporters and editors to slow down a bit, to take a more deliberate, knowledgeable approach to research, including polls. As one earlier study of media behavior put it, reporters confronting research should be as concerned with its scientific value as its entertainment value.[30]

Finally, the NCSPE should acquaint the media with research on the experiences with vouchers in other nations.

Through a website, newsletters, workshops, or other means, the NCSPE should place special priority on acquainting the media with the international dimensions of the voucher saga. Considerable research and commentary has been done on voucher systems in England, Scotland, Australia, and elsewhere by, for example, Frank Echols and J. Douglas Wilms of the University of British Columbia, Peter Cookson of Teachers College, Columbia University, and Kathryn Stearns in a 1996 Carnegie Foundation report, *School Reform: Lessons from England*. Given the scarcity of conclusive data from the U.S. experience, the NCSPE can help reporters gain powerful new perspectives on the possibilities and pitfalls of vouchers by directing them to the experiences of other nations.

Notes

1. Witte, J. (1999). *The Market Approach to Education: An Analysis of America's First Voucher Experiment*, p. 172.

2. In 1993, when the annual Phi Delta Kappa/Gallup Poll ("Public's Attitudes Toward the Public Schools") first asked adults about allowing students and parents to choose a private school to attend at public expense, 24 percent were in favor and 74 percent opposed. In the 1998 thirtieth annual poll, 44 percent were in favor and 50 percent opposed. Source: *Phi Delta Kappa International*, August 1998.

3. *Children First* (Winter 1999), published by the Children's Educational Opportunity Foundation of America, which funds private voucher programs; see pp. 22–23.

4. Chester E. Finn Jr., president of the Thomas B. Fordham Foundation, offers as an example the coverage by the *Dayton (Ohio) Daily News* of private vouchers in that city; the newspaper has editorialized against the publicly funded vouchers in Cleveland.

5. Shales, A. (1998, October 30). "Voucher Program Passes a Test." *Wall Street Journal*.

6. Telephone interview with Joe Williams, February 10, 1999.

7. The late Albert Shanker, president of the American Federation of Teachers, devoted more than forty of his weekly "Where We Stand" ad columns in *The New York Times* to attacks on vouchers.

8. Most of the news sources listed here appear in the Education Writers Association's

June 1998 backgrounder on vouchers provided to member reporters to help them balance their coverage.

9. Telephone interview with Lynn Olson and Mark Walsh of *Education Week*, February 5, 1999.

10. Written reply from professor Metcalf to questions about media coverage of vouchers, February 22, 1999.

11. Metcalf, K.K. (1998, September 23). "Advocacy in the Guise of Science." *Education Week*.

12. Peterson, P.E. (1999). "Vouchers and Test Scores: What the Numbers Show." *Policy Review*, January and February 199, Number 93. Peterson contends his newer research on privately funded school choice in New York City meets the standards of a randomized field trial.

13. Telephone interview with Elliot Mincberg, February 22, 1999.

14. Telephone interview with Scott Stevens, February 9, 1999.

15. Telephone interview with June Kronholz, February 4, 1999.

16. Telephone interview with Richard Colvin, February 10, 1999.

17. Telephone interview with Bella Rosenberg, February 24, 1999.

18. Lewin, T. (1997, September 18). "School Voucher Study Finds Satisfaction." *The New York Times*, p. 16.

19. Cited in "Research, Politics, and the School Choice Agenda," by Alex Molnar et al., in *Phi Delta Kappan*, November 1996.

20. Albert Shanker, "Chubb and Moe Revisited: Science or Ideology?" printed in *The New York Times* as a paid column, "Where We Stand," October 11, 1992.

21. One such critique, by professors Valerie Lee of the University of Michigan and Anthony S. Bryk of the University of Chicago, was largely ignored by news organizations when presented at an October 1, 1992, conference on school choice sponsored by the Economic Policy Institute in Washington, D.C. Their paper, "Science or Policy Argument? A Review of the Quantitative Evidence in Chubb and Moe's *Politics, Markets and America's Schools*," later appeared in Lee, V., and Bryk, A. (1993), "Science or Policy Argument? A Review of the Quantitative Evidence in Chubb and Moe's *Politics, Markets, and America's Schools*," in E. Rasell and R. Rothstein (eds.), *School Choice: Examining the Evidence* (Washington, D.C.: Economic Policy Institute). Lee and Bryk, noted for their previous research on the virtues of private and parochial schooling, concluded: "On an important matter of public policy . . . *Politics, Markets and America's Schools* comes up short as a piece of disciplined policy research."

22. Telephone interview with Joe Williams, February 10, 1999.

23. Staples made a particularly impassioned argument for vouchers in a lengthy article, "Schoolyard Brawl," in the January 4, 1998, edition of *The New York Times*. While virtually accusing teachers' unions and other voucher foes of outright racism for denying educational opportunities to minority children in the face of massive inner-city public school failure, he also conceded that "in terms of what ails us nationally" voucher programs and charters schools "are no more than pop guns deployed against a battle ship."

24. Telephone interview with Cecilia Rouse, February 5, 1999.

25. Telephone interview with John F. Witte, February 9, 1999.

26. Telephone interview with Elliot Mincberg, February 22, 1999.

27. Telephone interview with Howard Fuller, February 5, 1999.

28. Telephone interview with Chester E. Finn Jr., February 5, 1999.

29. Telephone interview with Paul Peterson, February 8, 1999.

30. Weiss, C., and Singer, E. (1988), *Reporting of Social Science in the National Media* (Russell Sage Foundation), p. 253. Their analysis also reached conclusions similar to ours about how journalists frequently compensate for their lack of sophistication about judging the scientific validity of research: "What we see . . . is that reporters and editors paid only passing attention to research quality. They looked to the positions, institutional affiliations, and reputations of social scientists as a way to judge the competence of their research" (p. 52).

References

Children's Educational Opportunity Foundation of America. (1999, Winter). *Children first.* Bentonville, Ariz.: Children's Educational Opportunity Foundation of America.

Chubb, J., and Moe, T. (1990). *Politics, markets, and America's schools.* Washington, D.C.: Brookings Institution.

Echols, F., Wilms, J., Cookson, P., and Stearns, K. (1996). *School reform: Lessons from England.* Princeton: Carnegie Foundation for the Advancement of Teaching.

Lee, V., and Bryk, A. (1993). Science or policy argument? A review of the quantitative evidence in Chubb and Moe's *Politics, markets, and America's schools.* In E. Rasell and R. Rothstein (eds.), *School choice: Examining the evidence.* Washington, D.C.: Economic Policy Institute.

Lewin, T. (1997, September 18). School voucher study finds satisfaction. *New York Times*, p. A16.

Metcalf, K. (1998, September 23). Advocacy in the guise of science. *Education Week.*

Molnar, A., Farrell, W., Johnson, J., and Sapp, M. (1996). Research, politics, and the school choice agenda. *Phi Delta Kappan* 78(3).

Peterson, P. (1999) Vouchers and test scores: What the numbers show. *Policy Review* 93.

Rose, L.C., and Gallup, A.M. (1998). The Thirtieth Annual Phi Delta Kappa/Gallup Poll of the public's attitudes toward the public schools. *Phi Delta Kappan* 80(1).

Shales, A. (1998, October 30). Voucher program passes a test. *Wall Street Journal.*

Shanker, A. (1992, October 11). Chubb and Moe revisited: Science or ideology? In the American Federation of Teachers "Where We Stand" advertising series in *New York Times*, sec. 4, p. 7.

Staples, B. (1998, January 4). Schoolyard brawl. *New York Times*, p. A35.

Weiss, C., and Singer, E. (1988). *Reporting of social science in the national media.* New York: Russell Sage Foundation.

Witte, J. (1999). *The market approach to education: An analysis of America's first voucher experiment.* Princeton: Princeton University Press.

Implementation Issues

3

The Legal Status of Privatization and Vouchers in Education

FRANK R. KEMERER

Privatization of schooling generates a host of complex legal issues that are usually overlooked in the literature. What barriers might federal and state constitutional law pose for privatization efforts? Is the autonomy of private organizations compromised by participating in these programs? Do students and teachers retain the same federal rights in public schools operated by private entities that they have in traditional public schools? How does privatization affect the role of teachers' unions and collective bargaining? It is important to explore these matters because they ultimately will affect the form that privatization takes and, consequently, its outcome.

For purposes of this chapter, I divide privatization into two categories: The first focuses on letting private organizations operate public schools either by contracting with school districts (known as "contracting-out") or through the charter school process; the second focuses on providing parents with publicly funded vouchers and tax benefits so that they can enroll their children in private schools. The first category is substantially different from the second in that the schools theoretically remain public. Under the second, it is assumed that private schools remain private. As we will see, these assumptions may not always be true.

We begin by discussing emerging legal issues related to letting private organizations operate public schools. We next examine emerging legal issues involving voucher and tax benefit plans. Following the legal review, we then consider stakeholder interests and the types of research studies that should be undertaken to address them.

Privatization Within the Public Sector

Privatization is not new to public schooling. School districts routinely contract with private organizations to provide such services as bus transportation, meals, maintenance, and special education for severely disabled children. For a time in the 1970s, "performance contracting" with private companies for segments of the instructional program, particularly remedial education, was popular, though it proved largely unsuccessful.[1] In a few sparsely populated states like Maine and Vermont, small township school districts for years have financed the attendance of their high school students in out-of-district public or in private schools in lieu of building a high school. More recently the concept of contracting-out has encompassed operating an entire public school.[2] There are a number of legal concerns directly related to the latter. In this section, we will focus briefly on four: restrictive constitutional provisions; the status of the schools operated by private entities; selective admissions; and the role of unions and collective bargaining.

Restrictive Constitutional Provisions

In formulating school reform initiatives that accommodate private organizations, state legislatures cannot ignore the strictures of their own state constitutions. Although there are only a few court decisions to study so far, they are informative as to what the legal concerns are. For example, Michigan has a state constitutional provision requiring the legislature to establish a public school system and prohibiting it from funding private schools.[3] A number of states have similar provisions.[4] The Michigan charter school statute allows persons and entities, including private organizations, to operate public school academies on a nonprofit basis.[5] Religious organizations are excluded, given the state constitution's antiestablishment-of-religion provision. The Michigan statute specifies that those granted charters are subject to state and federal law applicable to public school districts. In other words, the schools themselves are to be operated as public institutions. A lawsuit greeted passage of the charter legislation. Plaintiffs contended that the scheme violated the state constitution because the public school academies are not controlled by the state and because the charter school boards of directors are not publicly elected.

In 1997, the Michigan Supreme Court rejected the contentions and became the first state supreme court to uphold a charter school law, overruling two lower court decisions.[6] As a case of first impression, it may influence the decisions of courts in other states that allow private organizations to operate charter schools. At issue, as the court saw it, was whether the charter schools, known in Michigan as "public school academies," are sufficiently under the control of the state to be considered public schools. The court found it sufficient that a public body retains oversight through the charter-granting and -monitoring process. Moreover, the justices noted that the legislature, after the lower court rulings, amended the charter school law to require that all academy teachers be state certified and to clarify that the academies are subject to the rulemaking authority of the State Board of Education, thereby significantly limiting the autonomy of the charter schools.

Note how legislative concern about complying with the state constitution produced these two measures. Whether either can be justified in terms of improving academy effectiveness is irrelevant. The amendments exist to satisfy constitutional requirements. As dissenting Justice Patricia Boyle noted, "Freedom from regulation is precisely that element of the charter school concept that brings it into potential conflict with the constitution."[7]

The legal argument made in the Michigan case often is characterized as an unconstitutional delegation of governmental authority. Unconstitutional-delegation law is a judicial construction of state constitutional provisions vesting government entities with the establishment and control of public schools. The doctrine restricts the ability of a legislature to turn its responsibilities over to private entities altogether or without sufficient accountability measures.[8] Massachusetts has a constitutional provision prohibiting the use of public money for a school that "is not publicly owned and under the exclusive control, order and supervision of public officers or public agents authorized by the commonwealth or federal authority or both."[9] The Supreme Judicial Court of Massachusetts, the state's highest court, ruled in 1996 that the takeover of the Chelsea public school system by Boston University did not violate this provision. The court observed that "there is nothing in the concept of a public agent that precludes a private university from performing as an agent of the public."[10] Because the Chelsea School Committee exercises extensive supervisory control over the university's performance pursuant to the contract, the university acts as the agent of the school committee in educating the youth of the city. Consequently, there is no impermissible aid to a private entity and no unconstitutional delegation of the school committee's powers.

The situation is similar with regard to the Massachusetts charter school law. The statute allows the State Board of Education to grant a charter to a board of trustees to create what is called a "commonwealth charter school."[11] The trustees are public agents under the law, and the charter school is deemed a public school. However, there is no statutory restriction on allowing the board of trustees to contract with a private entity to run the school. Thus, the for-profit Edison Project is under contract to operate the Seven Hills Charter School in Worcester and the Boston Renaissance Public Charter School, one of the largest charter schools in the nation with over 1,200 students. There has been no reported litigation involving the practice.

There was, however, a challenge to the decision of a Pennsylvania school district to contract out one of its elementary schools to a private for-profit corporation. In a 4-2 decision in 1995, the Pennsylvania Supreme Court became the first supreme court to uphold the practice.[12] The Wilkinsburg school district, just outside Pittsburgh, concluded that the abysmal performance of students at its Turner Elementary School justified drastic reform. It contracted with Alternative Public Schools, Inc., to operate the school. The Wilkinsburg teachers' union bitterly opposed the move, eventually suing the district for violating state law. Although the school code at the time allowed contracting-out for various support services, there was no mention of contracting-out the entire educational program. The Pennsylvania Supreme Court agreed with the school district that the school code served as no bar to the district's contracting-out as a way of assuring that the district meets it obligation under the state constitution to provide "a thorough and efficient system of public education."[13] The majority noted that even if the code could be construed to prohibit contracting-out, such a restriction might be unconstitutional as restricting the district's ability to operate an efficient system of schooling.[14] What is important, the majority maintained, is the welfare of the student. In 1997, a Pennsylvania trial court ruled that the new state charter school law prohibits a private for-profit company from taking control of a public school and terminated the contract.[15] It will be interesting to see if the prohibition on privatization in the new charter school law will give the Pennsylvania high court another opportunity to confront the issue.

What can be learned from the Wilkinsburg episode? First, the Pennsylvania Supreme Court decision may constitute a groundbreaking precedent because many state constitutions have the same "thorough and efficient" terminology or variations thereof (e.g., "uniform," "efficient," and "general and uniform").[16] If so, a state law prohibiting private organizations from operating public schools under contract with a district or through a charter school law would be unconstitutional. Second, a carefully drafted privatization statute that spells out the conditions of contracting-out, the status of the school operated by the entity, the rights of students and teachers in the school, and the role of the teachers' union will go a long way toward mitigating conflict and forestalling litigation.

All but four state constitutions have provisions prohibiting states from aiding religious establishments. These antiestablishment provisions—together with provisions requiring that schools operating on a contract basis with private entities remain public schools—prevent contracting-out with religious establishments. But can a religious group obtain a charter to operate a school? In states where private organizations are not precluded from obtaining a charter, the answer appears to be yes—so long as the charter school is operated as a public school. For example, Arizona's very permissive charter school law allowing both nonprofit and for-profit private entities to receive charters stipulates that charter schools are public schools and must be nonsectarian in their operations.[17] Religious organizations increasingly view the charter school process as an opportunity for privatization in their favor.[18] There can be little doubt that litigation will increase on this issue.

In sum, it is too early to determine the extent to which state constitutions may limit the ability of legislatures and school districts to delegate the operation of public schools to private organizations. However, the Pennsylvania Supreme Court decision is noteworthy for the breadth of authority it suggests school districts have to do so.

When Is Private Public?

Based on the foregoing discussion, the prevailing view is that public schools operated by private organizations continue to be public. This is important because a body of law, much of it constitutional, has been built up around the operation of public schools. Under the terms of the Fourteenth Amendment to the U.S. Constitution, the state and its political subdivisions must accord persons their federal constitutional rights. This is known as the "state-action doctrine." As political subdivisions of the state, public schools must recognize all the protections of the U.S. Constitution that federal courts have applied to public school students and teachers. Subject to some limitations, these protections include the freedoms of speech, religion, and association; the right to be free from state-supported religious indoctrination; the right to be free from unreasonable searches and seizures; the right to due process before expulsion or job loss; and the right to equal protection of the laws. These hard-fought rights are not inconsequential in that they are beyond the power of government officials to circumscribe or ignore.[19]

By contrast, private schools function independently of the state. Since there is no state action, they are not required to extend constitutional rights to their constituents. As noted later in this chapter, the regulatory framework surrounding private schools is far less extensive than that for public schools. However, when a private organization is employed to operate a public school under contract with a school district or is given a charter to do so, the assumption is that the school the private organization operates is public and must accord constituents their constitutional rights. This is so because the authority of the private operators stems directly from a governmental agency or via a contract with a governmental agency and the operators are accountable to the governmental agency.

But suppose private entities are given considerable autonomy to operate public schools (i.e., they control hiring and firing, student discipline, etc.). Are the schools now state-licensed private institutions that are beyond the reach of the federal Constitution? It appears that the Wilkinsburg school board assumed so when it laid off twenty-four teachers at Turner Elementary School so that Alternative Public Schools, Inc., could hire its own staff. If viewed in this manner, the status of privatized schools is similar to that of private schools participating in a state voucher program (discussed below). Although there has been no litigation on the issue, it is certain to arise.[20]

Selective Admissions

Private organizations operating public schools cannot, of course, select the students they want to educate. However, troubling legal issues surface when the educational program is thematic. A school targeted to math and science students, for example, may have a largely upper-income Anglo student body. Conversely, a school catering to at-risk students may enroll mostly low-income minority students. Are these schools in violation of civil rights laws? One federal appellate court recently expressed concern about a provision of the Colorado Charter Schools Act defining at-risk students as those "who, because of physical, emotional, socioeconomic, or cultural factors, [are] less likely to succeed in a conventional educational environment." Although the court rejected a parent's discrimination challenge to the establishment of a charter school in Pueblo, Colorado, the judges noted, "We share the parent's concern with the practice of drawing classifications based on 'culture,' which might in some circumstances be used as a proxy for ethnicity, race, national origin or some other suspect classification."[21] It is important to note in this context that charter schools must comply with federal civil rights law to be eligible for federal charter school money.

Some state charter school laws try to mitigate the tendency of choice schools to be racially and ethnically isolated by requiring them to reflect the ethnic makeup of the school district within which they are located.[22] Several recent federal appellate court rulings indicate that the quest for ethnic diversity may not save these provisions from being declared unconstitutional as a violation of the Fourteenth Amendment's Equal Protection Clause.[23] A noted decision is the 1998 decision of the U.S. Court of Appeals for the First Circuit striking down the race-conscious admissions policy at the Boston Latin School, an academically competitive public choice school within the Boston public school system. Applying the strict-scrutiny test used by the U.S. Supreme Court to determine the constitutionality of race-based programs, the appellate court concluded in a 2-1 decision that the admissions policy "is, at bottom, a mechanism for racial balancing—and placing our imprimatur on racial balancing risks setting a precedent that is both dangerous to our democratic ideals and almost always constitutionally forbidden."[24] This is a serious matter, and in the last section of this chapter I address the need for carefully designed research studies pertaining to it.

A somewhat similar concern arises when choice schools, whether privatized or not, require parents to agree to contribute services to a school as a condition of student admissions. These arrangements raise questions whether state constitutional provisions providing for a free public education are being violated when low-income families cannot make the necessary commitment. To the extent such arrangements discriminate against minority families, they also may prove to be in violation of civil rights laws.

Much discussion appears in the school-choice literature over discrimination against children with disabilities in admissions and in the programming of choice schools, especially those operated by private entities.[25] The most prominent example concerns the Edison Project's Boston Renaissance School, which ran into trouble with the U.S. Department of Education's Office of Civil Rights in its treatment of children with disabilities through its inclusion policy.[26] So far, the case law has not developed in this area. However, the 1997 amendments to the federal Individuals with Disabilities Education Act (IDEA) require that if schools are chartered by a local education agency then the agency is responsible for providing special education programs and services to the child as though the child were in a traditional public school.[27] This relieves the charter school of a burden that could prove impossible to shoulder. If the charter school is chartered by the state, it has all the responsibilities of a local education agency to provide services to children with disabilities and receives a per-child federal allotment to do so, although the allotment may be insufficient.[28] The amendments also provide limited federal funding to underwrite the costs of special education at traditional private schools.[29] It is too early to know how the new amendments will affect the treatment of children with disabilities in privatization programs.

Collective Bargaining Rights

There are thirty-four states with collective bargaining laws, seven states that allow bargaining but have no enabling statutes, and nine that prohibit teacher–school board bargaining entirely. Privatization may have a profound effect on teachers' unions and collective bargaining in the forty-one states that permit bargaining, and that is why the two major teachers' unions oppose it. In this section I sketch some of the basic legal issues.[30]

Let's assume that a school district is considering privatizing one of its schools and plans to staff the school from its pool of teachers. Does the school district have to bargain with the teachers' union over the idea of privatization and how to go about it? Will the teachers at the privatized school remain in the district's teacher collective bargaining unit? If the teachers have a sizable role in the management of the school, will they be considered supervisors rather than employees and thus be ineligible to continue as union members? The answers to these questions will depend on the terms of applicable state laws, the decisions of state labor boards, and court rulings. It may be that irrespective of state law the collective bargaining agreement itself may prevent or condition contracting-out. Certainly, union leaders will do what they can through contract negotiation, as well as lobbying and litigation, to protect their members.

In Minnesota, for example, the state charter school law allows nonprofit organizations to operate charter schools and specifies that collective bargaining is permissible. However, the bargaining unit is to be separate from the sponsoring school district unless the employees of the school, its board of directors, the union, and the school district board agree otherwise.[31] When the Edison Project began operating a charter school in Duluth in 1997, the 1,100-member Duluth Federation of Teachers sought to include the charter school's teachers in the bargaining unit. The union argued that Edison, as a for-profit corporation, could not operate a charter school under the state charter law and that the teachers are employees of the Duluth school district. The Duluth school district noted that it had granted a charter to the Public School Academy, a nonprofit group, which in turn subcontracted with Edison. Under this arrangement, it argued, the teachers are employees of the academy and can under the charter school law opt to be part of the school district bargaining unit, bargain separately, or not bargain at all. The state mediation agency and a state district court agreed. The teachers remain nonunion. However, in a demonstration of its considerable political clout, the

Duluth union backed four successful anti-Edison candidates in the 1997 school board elections, giving the board a slim majority in favor of privatization.[32] Loss of political power is one of the key reasons why unions fear privatization and school choice in general.

Suppose that a school board contracts with a private corporation to operate one of its schools as a public school but allows the corporation to hire the teachers.[33] Under this scenario it may be that even though the school remains public, the teachers do not. However, it is likely that at the least the school district will have to bargain with the teachers' union over the effect of the decision on teachers. As noted earlier, the Wilkinsburg, Pennsylvania, school district furloughed twenty-four teachers when it contracted out its Turner Elementary School. The teachers' union successfully challenged that decision as a violation of the collective bargaining agreement. The district was forced to rehire the teachers and pay them over $250,000 in back pay and benefits.[34]

Letting privatized schools hire their own teachers could force teachers' unions into the domain of private labor law, where they have had little influence in the past and may not bargain at all. The same is true, of course, if a school operated by the private organization is or remains private. Labor relations in the private sector are conducted under the terms of the federal National Labor Relations Act (NLRA).[35] Since the NLRA does not extend bargaining to very small organizations,[36] does not extend bargaining rights to teachers at sectarian schools,[37] limits bargaining for teachers who function as managerial employees,[38] and often differs from state law in what is bargainable, the challenge to teachers' unions would be formidable. And they are sure to resist it. A case in point is litigation over a decision by the Farmington, Minnesota, school district to contract out its food services to a private for-profit corporation in 1995. The union sought to retain the food services workers in the union and requested a hearing before the Minnesota Bureau of Mediation Services. The private corporation was successful in removing the case to the National Labor Relations Board (NLRB). The NLRB determined that the private corporation, not the school district, was the employer of the workers and certified an election. The workers opted for no union, and the union sued in federal court, arguing that the NLRB has no jurisdiction because the workers were in reality employed by the district. The union pointed to the fact that the workers, although hired by the private corporation, have the same duties as those employed by the district; are subject to the regulations of the district while on duty; receive wages in accordance with the collective bargaining agreement between the district and the union; must be approved by the district to work on the premises; work the same number of days and hours as district employees; and so on. In short, the union argued that the NLRB had extended its jurisdiction to a political subdivision of the state, which is exempted from the coverage of the National Labor Relations Act. The court noted, however, that the NLRB had recently decided to extend jurisdiction to private employers, even if control of basic employment terms of their workers lies with statutorily exempt political subdivisions. Although troubled by this development, the court cited prior U.S. Supreme Court precedent in refusing to intervene.[39]

Vouchers, Tax Deductions, and Tax Credits

Voucher programs and similar measures to facilitate parental choice of private schools for children involve a somewhat different set of legal concerns. To date, only three publicly funded voucher programs have been enacted: Milwaukee, Cleveland, and the state of Florida. However, voucher bills have been introduced in a number of other states. Here we examine, first, whether constitutional law will even permit this form of privatization; and second, if so, whether the private schools become significantly public.

Constitutionality under Federal and State Law

In 1925, the U.S. Supreme Court ruled unanimously in *Pierce v. Society of Sisters* that parents have a right to choose a private school in lieu of a public school and that a state law to the contrary violates the property rights of private school operators under the Fourteenth Amendment.[40] *Pierce* often is cited in support of the right of parents to determine the education of their children. The Court noted that the concept of liberty "excludes any general power of the State to standardize its children by forcing them to accept instruction from public school teachers only. The child is not the mere creature of the State; those who nurture him and direct his destiny have the right, coupled with the high duty, to recognize and prepare him for additional obligations."[41] Of course, the Court did not say that the state as a matter of constitutional law must enfranchise parents with the means to exercise the right. Thus we have the contemporary quest for voucher and tax benefit plans to assist parents, especially those with limited incomes, in exercising their *Pierce* rights.

In 1973, the U.S. Supreme Court in *Committee for Public Education v. Nyquist* invalidated 6-3 a New York statute that encompassed a tuition grant program for low-income families and a tax deduction program that varied by income level for other families so that their children could attend private schools.[42] The Court ruled that both tuition aid programs violated the Establishment Clause of the First Amendment that prevents government from making laws "respecting an establishment of religion." Writing for the majority, Justice Lewis F. Powell noted that "if the grants are offered as an incentive to parents to send their children to sectarian schools by making unrestricted cash payments to them, the Establishment Clause is violated whether or not the actual dollars given eventually find their way into the sectarian institutions. Whether the grant is labeled a reimbursement, a reward, or a subsidy, its substantive impact is still the same."[43]

Although the Supreme Court majority in *Nyquist* found inconsequential the fact that the money first went to parents rather than directly to schools, the opinion included a telling footnote: "Because of the manner in which we have resolved the tuition grant issue, we need not decide whether the significantly religious character of the statute's beneficiaries might differentiate the present case from a case involving some form of public assistance (e.g., scholarships) made available *without regard to the sectarian-nonsectarian, or public-nonpublic nature of the institution benefited*."[44] In other words, if grants could be applicable either to public or to private school attendance, the constitutional outcome might be different. For this reason, the Court observed that its decision did not compel a conclusion that the GI Bill impermissibly advances religion. This commentary foreshadowed the Court's seminal ruling in *Mueller v. Allen* a decade later regarding the constitutionality of tuition tax deduction programs.

In *Mueller* the Supreme Court upheld 5-4 a Minnesota law that allows parents an income tax deduction for expenses incurred in providing tuition, textbooks, and transportation for children in public or private schools.[45] In a key passage, Justice Rehnquist observed in his majority opinion that "the historic purposes of the [Establishment] Clause simply do not encompass the sort of attenuated financial benefit, ultimately controlled by the private choice of individual parents, that eventually flows to parochial schools from the neutrally available tax benefit at issue in this case."[46] It did not trouble the majority that most of the benefits flow to parents of children in parochial schools.

Since *Mueller*, the Supreme Court has issued four decisions based on the *Mueller* precedent that suggest the Court is prepared to uphold a voucher system wherein the voucher goes to the parent and not to the school, the parent has a wide choice of public and private schools, and there is no favoritism extended to sectarian private schools.[47] In 1998, the justices had an opportunity to rule on vouchers when the decision of the Wisconsin Supreme Court upholding the Milwaukee voucher program came before them. The Milwaukee program was expanded in 1995 to encompass sectarian private schools. However, the Court opted not to take the case.[48] The action conveys no indication of how the justices feel about the matter. Although the Supreme Court to date has turned down opportunities to rule on the issue as noted below, most commentators believe that the time is nearing when the U.S. Supreme Court will accept a voucher case.

Deciding what the Court will do is only part of the calculus. There are fifty state constitutions and state supreme courts to consider as well. Assuming the Court adheres to the concept of federalism and allows the states to apply their own constitutions to contested voucher, tax deduction, and tax credit programs, the outcome becomes much more uncertain.[49] This is because state constitutions vary considerably in the degree to which they separate church and state. In addition, there are other restrictive provisions in many state constitutions. Moreover, it should not be overlooked that state supreme court judges in thirty-eight states, unlike federal judges, are elected and thus more attuned to political factors. A brief summary of state constitutional law in the context of school vouchers is presented here, based on the author's extensive analysis reported elsewhere.[50] The appendix contains a table placing each of the fifty states into one of three categories—restrictive, permissive, and uncertain—with regard to its likely orientation toward the constitutionality of state-funded school vouchers encompassing sectarian private schools.

The most restrictive state is Michigan, where the state constitution specifically prohibits a "payment, credit, tax benefit, exemption or deductions, tuition voucher, subsidy, grant or loan of public monies or property" directly or indirectly to support the attendance of students or employment of persons at nonpublic schools.[51] In a ruling on this section in 1971, the Michigan Supreme Court seemed to accept that this section bars voucher-like payments to parents whose children attend private school.[52] Another fifteen states have constitutional provisions restricting any form of aid directly or indirectly to sectarian private schools, constitutional provisions requiring public funds to be spent on public schools only, or state supreme court decisions interpreting the state constitution to this effect. For example, the Supreme Judicial Court of Massachusetts has issued unanimous advisory rulings on two occasions that the state constitution's restriction on spending public money for other than public education prohibits channeling money to students attending private schools in any form, including a tax deduction.[53] A voucher, tax deduction, or tax credit program faces an uphill battle in these states.

At the opposite extreme from Michigan are Wisconsin, Arizona, and Ohio. In 1998, the Wisconsin Supreme Court ruled that the expanded Milwaukee voucher program does not violate either the state or federal constitution by extending benefits to parents whose children attend sectarian private schools.[54] As already noted, the U.S. Supreme Court declined to take up this case on appeal. Early in 1999, the Arizona Supreme Court upheld a state statute allowing persons to claim a tax credit of up to $500 for donations they make to nonprofit groups funding scholarships for students to attend private religious and nonreligious schools.[55] The Arizona high court concluded that the plan violated neither the federal nor state constitution. The justices found the tax credit scheme indistinguishable from the Minnesota tax deduction plan upheld by the U.S. Supreme Court. Moreover, no public money would flow to private religious schools, a prohibition of the Arizona Constitution, because a tax credit is not "public money." Whatever benefit accrues to sectarian private schools, the court observed, is sufficiently attenuated to foreclose a breach of the state constitution. In 1999, the U.S. Supreme Court refused to hear the Arizona case.

In 1999, the Ohio Supreme Court found that the Cleveland school voucher program allowing families to send their children to religious and nonreligious private schools does not violate either state or federal constitutional prohibitions against state aid to religion.[56] However, the law's passage did violate a state constitutional provision prohibiting the enactment of bills addressing more than one subject. Within weeks of the ruling, the Ohio legislature reenacted the measure through a budget package geared specifically to education. Thereafter, opponents filed a lawsuit in federal court. The federal judge created a firestorm of opposition when, just before school was to open in the fall of 1999, he suspended the voucher program pending a ruling on its constitutionality. A few days later, the judge rescinded part of his order by allowing the program to continue for the 3,000 students already enrolled. Emergency motions were filed with the U.S. Court of Appeals for the Sixth Circuit asking that the entire order be rescinded so that 800 new voucher recipients could enroll. Before the appellate court could rule, the U.S. Supreme Court took the unusual action of granting the Ohio attorney general's request that the trial judge's preliminary injunction be set aside entirely.[57] What is particularly interesting about the Court's intervention is the lineup of justices in the 5-4 ruling. Those in the majority were Chief Justice William H. Rehnquist and Justices Sandra Day O'Connor, Antonin Scalia, Anthony M. Kennedy, and Clarence Thomas. The dissenters were Justices John Paul Stevens, David H. Souter, Ruth Bader Ginsburg, and Stephen G. Breyer. Although neither side issued an opinion, the inclination of the five in the majority to intervene at such a preliminary stage of litigation suggests a predisposition to hear a voucher case, if not rule favorably upon it. In December 1999, the federal district court declared the Cleveland voucher program unconstitutional, a decision later affirmed by the U.S. Court of Appeals for the Sixth Circuit.[58] Many commentators believe this case will wind up before the U.S. Supreme Court within the next two years.

In addition to Wisconsin, Arizona, and Ohio, there are eleven states where some combination of weak antiestablishment constitutional provisions, strong free exercise of religion provisions, the presence of a constitutional override provision on restricting appropriations for public education only, or supportive supreme court precedent suggests a permissive climate for state vouchers, tax deductions, and tax benefits (see the table in the appendix).

The remaining twenty states are listed as uncertain because of ambiguous constitutional terminology, the absence of authoritative case law, or pending litigation. In two of these—Maine and Vermont—the state supreme courts have addressed voucher-like programs called "tuitioning," whereby public school districts without high schools shoulder the costs of tuition paid by parents to send their children to private schools. In 1999, the Maine Supreme Judicial Court rejected a parental challenge to the exclusion of religious schools from the state's tuition reimbursement program.[59] If such schools were included, the court noted, unrestricted funds would flow directly into the coffers of religious schools, contrary to the thrust of the First Amendment prohibition against state aid to religion as interpreted by the U.S. Supreme Court. The Maine high court viewed the religion clauses of the state constitution as coextensive with those of the U.S. Constitution. A month later, the U.S. Court of Appeals for the First Circuit issued a similar ruling declaring the program unconstitutional under the federal constitution.[60] The U.S. Supreme Court refused to hear either case.

In June 1999, the Supreme Court of Vermont ruled that a school district's payment of student tuition to a Catholic high school violates the state constitution's Compelled Support Clause.[61] That clause provides that no person "ought to . . . or of right can be compelled to" support any place of worship. Noting the similarity between religious worship and religious education, the court found the absence of any restrictions on funding religious education a fatal flaw. The U.S. Supreme Court later refused to review the Vermont high court's ruling.

What is significant about the Maine and Vermont supreme court decisions is that both left the door open to the constitutionality of a voucher program that channels money to parents, not schools, and that limits the expenditure of public money to the secular components of private school curricula.[62] For this reason, both states are included in the uncertain category, despite the 1999 decisions.

It is clear from the foregoing discussion that the constitutional status of voucher and tax benefit programs will remain in a state of flux for the foreseeable future.

Private Schools and State Action: The Publicization of the Private School

A state can regulate private schools without violating the U.S. Constitution as long as the regulation is reasonable—a test that is difficult to fail. This point of law frequently is overlooked by private school proponents. In upholding the right of private schools to coexist with public schools, the U.S. Supreme Court noted in the 1925 *Pierce v. Society of Sisters* case that:

no question is raised concerning the power of the State reasonably to regulate all schools, to inspect, supervise and examine them, their teachers and pupils; to require that all children of proper age attend some school, that teachers shall be of good moral character and patriotic disposition, that certain studies plainly essential to good citizenship must be taught, and that nothing be taught which is manifestly inimical to the public welfare.[63]

States have relied on this passage for years to set standards for private schools encompassing such matters as compliance with health and safety regulations, length of the school year, and enrollment reporting. Less frequently, states have included state certification of teachers and curricular specifications. In 1996, the U.S. Court of Appeals for the Sixth Circuit upheld adding state student testing to the list.[64] Although there have been challenges to state regulations on the basis of unreasonableness and unconstitutional interference with First Amendment freedoms—especially religion—states generally prevail.[65] Private schools also are subject to selected federal civil rights laws (e.g., Title VII of the 1964 Civil Rights Act), although there often are exemptions for very small schools and for those that are religiously affiliated.[66] However, most private schools are not subject to a number of federal laws that require receipt of federal funding to be applicable (e.g., the IDEA and Title IX of the 1972 Education Amendments against sex discrimination). It is not yet known whether private schools participating in a publicly funded voucher program must comply with such laws, but it seems clear that neither the state nor school districts can provide support to schools that discriminate. In the case of the Milwaukee voucher program, the trial judge concluded that the private schools participating in the original program did not have to comply with IDEA.[67] Whether the state or the Milwaukee school district violates federal disability law by supporting such schools awaits a future court ruling.

Thus far, the flow of public dollars indirectly to private schools through the Milwaukee and Ohio voucher programs has not resulted in extensive new regulations on participating private schools, though some of the regulations, for example, the selection of Milwaukee voucher students on a random basis (except for siblings of pupils already enrolled) and exemption of students who are not of the school's faith from religious activities,[68] pose significant restraints on private school autonomy. One regulatory measure imposed by the Wisconsin State Superintendent of Public Instruction on the Milwaukee voucher program when it was new in 1991 does stand out, although it was later removed. The regulation required participating private schools, like public schools, to observe "all federal and state guarantees protecting the rights and liberties of individuals including freedom of religion, expression, association, unreasonable search and seizure, equal protection, and due process."[69] Regardless of its merit, this requirement alone fundamentally alters the relationship between a private school and its patrons and employees. Normally a matter of contract law, the relationship between a private school and both its students and teachers under this regulation becomes, to some extent, a matter of constitutional law. This is so because the regulation treats participating private schools as subdivisions of the state. As noted earlier, state action applies to public schools, but not to private schools. If applied to private schools participating in publicly funded voucher programs, the state-action concept and attendant legal responsibilities would threaten their independence by making them, in effect, public institutions.

There is nothing that precludes a state from enacting a statute or a state agency from adopting a regulation like the one described in Milwaukee. But suppose there is no such legislation or regulation. Could a parent or teacher successfully claim in federal court that a private school funded largely through vouchers or tax benefits must comply with constitutional safeguards? In a seminal ruling in 1982, the U.S. Supreme Court observed that the mere fact that "a private entity performs a function which serves the public does not make its acts state action."[70] The Court rejected the teachers' claims of violation of free speech and due process in connection with their termination at a private school that received nearly all its funding from the state for educating children with special learning needs. However, constitutional authority Robert O'Neil recently has written that the outcome might be different if *student* claims are at stake, if state regulation is comprehensive, and if private schools are substantially involved in performing the public function of educating students at public expense.[71]

Stakeholders and the Research Agenda

Based on the previous discussion, it is clear that there are a number of unanswered questions about how law affects educational privatization. Some of the answers await judicial decision. Others, however, require the attention of researchers. The remainder of this chapter discusses what research needs to be done and why.

Making an Inventory of the Legal Framework

State-level policymakers clearly are major stakeholders in the ongoing development of the legal framework for privatization. Careful drafting of privatization measures can help legislators avoid litigation or better defend against it once programs are in place. Still, the great variance among charter school laws suggests a rush to legislate before all the ramifications are understood.[72] The result is uncertainty over whether privatization is allowed and, if so, under what conditions. Uncertainty breeds litigation, some of which has been discussed previously.

Privatization through vouchers and tax benefits is on even shakier legal ground. Few studies have examined how state constitutional provisions in combination with evolving case law affect the design of programs that will withstand constitutional challenge.[73] Even with design features like these, there is no assurance that a court would uphold a voucher program encompassing sectarian private schools. Much will depend upon the wording of state constitutional provisions and upon the views of judges to the proper relationship between church and state.

The statutory and case law affecting privatization of education is growing rapidly. There is a pressing need to provide state policymakers with comprehensive up-to-date information so that they, in turn, can design legislation and implement regulations that are definitive and defensible. I would urge that more than simply inventorying legislation or grouping laws into broad categories (e.g., "weak" or "strong" charter laws) is necessary. What is needed is a continuing state-by-state study of constitutional, statutory, and interpretive case law in sufficient detail to be helpful to state-level policymakers.

Researching School Resegregation

Elsewhere, I have discussed the tendency of choice schools to be as racially and ethnically distinctive as traditional public schools.[74] A brief summary of that discussion is provided here. One-third of the public school student population and 22 percent of the private school student population are minority.[75] But the distribution is not uniform across school districts and schools. As Table 3.1 shows, more than three of every five American public schools are predominately Anglo, whereas nearly one in ten is predominately minority (data not available for private schools). In Minnesota and Wisconsin, public schools are even more predominately Anglo. By contrast, a higher percentage of charter schools than traditional public schools is predominately minority and a lower percentage is predominately Anglo in these states. In California the reverse is true. During the second year of charter school operation in Texas, nearly two-thirds of the charter schools served predominately minority students. Four schools enrolled more than three-quarters of all Anglo students in the charter school program. In Minnesota, half of the charter schools in 1996 were more than 80 percent Anglo, whereas nearly one-third were more than 80 percent minority. In Milwaukee, almost half of

TABLE 3.1   Racial/Ethnic Isolation in Public Schools and in Selected School
Choice Programs (numbers in percentages)

	Proportion of Minority Students in School		
	0 – 20% *(Mostly Anglos; few minorities)*	*>80 – 100%* *(Mostly minorities; few Anglos)*	*Total Percentage of Racially Distinctive Schools*
U.S. public schools[a]	61	9	70
Charter schools in ten-state study[b]	44	21	65
Public schools in California[b]	17	23	40
Charter schools in California[b]	37	17	54
Public schools in Texas[c]	22	27	49
Charter schools in Texas[c]	5	58	63
Public schools in Minnesota[d]	83	2	85
Charter schools in Minnesota[d]	50	31	81
Public schools in Wisconsin[e]	83	3	86
Milwaukee voucher program[e]	0	42	42

NOTE: In 1999, the Anglo concentration in charter schools remained the same but the
minority concentration declined to 23 percent among the larger number of operating
charter schools. Minnesota State Department of Education Data Center. Minnesota has
operated charter schools since 1991, the longest of any state.

the twelve nonsectarian private schools participating in the original voucher program were nearly all single-race, with another four serving a high concentration
of minority students. Adding the percentages of schools with high concentrations of Anglo students and with high concentrations of minority students in
each category of Table 3.1 reveals significant racial isolation in both traditional
public schools and choice schools. Extensive privatization is not likely to change
the situation and, indeed, may even make it worse.[76]

There are many reasons for racial and ethnic concentration, including location
of choice schools, curricular emphasis, availability of information for choosing
parents, and preference among both Anglo and minority parents for homogeneous environments. Still, what appears to be growing segregation of American
education by race/ethnicity and income is disturbing. Minority and low-income
families stand to lose in the long run if the political weakness that accompanies
isolation leads to discrimination in the provision of resources and thus con-

tributes to inferior education in either privatized schools or in traditional public schools. Society as a whole can be harmed if increased segregation in schooling results in lower achievement among minorities and the poor and decreased levels of tolerance for individual differences among all students.

Policymakers and educators are aware of the problem, and it is not unusual to see ethnic balance provisions in school choice legislation and contracting-out agreements. However, as noted earlier, these provisions appear unlikely to withstand legal challenge in federal court unless they can be justified as serving what is termed a "compelling state purpose" that is narrowly tailored to serve the state's goal—at least in the absence of strong supporting research findings. In several decisions, the U.S. Supreme Court has acknowledged that diversity is important in education.[77] Perhaps the best illustration is Chief Justice Warren Burger's observation in the 1971 Swann v. Charlotte-Mecklenburg Board of Education school desegregation ruling: "School authorities are traditionally charged with broad power to formulate and implement educational policy and might conclude, for example, that in order to prepare students to live in a pluralistic society each school should have a prescribed ratio of Negro to white students reflecting the proportion for the district as a whole." Doing this as an educational policy, he wrote, is within the broad discretionary powers of school authorities.[78] However, more recent decisions in public employment have cast doubt on the continuing validity of the assertion.[79] A related issue is that privatization could drain resources and motivated students away from traditional public schools to such a degree that students in the latter claim denial of equal educational opportunities under state law.[80] It is these same disparities that in the past triggered school finance litigation.[81]

In light of these concerns, there is need for research in the following areas:

1. How extensive is across- and within-school racial, ethnic, and income isolation in choice schools, both public and private? Why is it occurring? For example, if it can be shown that external factors such as lack of information, transportation, and school admissions policies are having a discriminatory effect, state school choice and privatization statutes may be vulnerable under state constitutional provisions guaranteeing a uniform and efficient system of education.
2. What are the educational and social harms of a school environment that is de facto segregated along racial, ethnic, and income lines?
3. Are the harms sufficiently significant that they overbalance the freedom of parents to self-segregate and the autonomy of privatized schools to select their students?

4. Are there remedies other than racial balance provisions that can pro-
    mote race and class integration—and be upheld by courts?

The scathing attack on the use of social-science research in the recent *Wessman
v. Gittens* racial balance case involving the Boston Latin School demonstrates the
need for studies to be very carefully designed and implemented if judges are to
take them seriously. In *Wessman*, the two-judge federal appellate court majority
denounced the quality of research presented by the school to justify its racial balance program. The school sought to show by testimony from its administrators
and a social-science expert witness that low teacher expectations account for the
weaker test scores of minority students on the admissions test. The court found
the administrators' testimony unconvincing and the findings of the expert witness flawed. The witness had not done a study of the Boston school system. Instead, he drew an analogy to his research on school climate in the Kansas City
school system. The court was not impressed: "When scientists (including social
scientists) testify in court, they must bring the same intellectual rigor to the task
that is required of them in other professional settings."[84] Since the findings of the
expert witness were not scientifically derived, "it follows inexorably that, with no
methodological support, he could not produce a meaningful analysis of causa-
tion and, accordingly, his conclusions cannot bear the weight of the School Committee's thesis." By contrast, the two judges in the majority in a 1999 Ninth Circuit appellate decision upholding a race-conscious admissions policy at UCLA's
research-oriented laboratory school were much more accepting of the expert testimony presented in that case.[85]

Assessing State Accountability Measures

As I have noted earlier here and elsewhere, a pressing concern is the relationship
between state regulation of privatization efforts and institutional autonomy.[86] In
a free market, private providers are supposed to vary in quality. When the profit
motive is introduced, there is concern that providers will be more interested in
money than in serving public needs. There may be needs that privatization will
not or cannot fill absent sufficient funding (e.g., the education of severely disabled children in the least restrictive environment).[87] Thus, markets require some
level of government regulation to hold providers to socially acceptable minimum
standards. Too little regulation fails to ensure adequate accountability for the expenditure of taxpayer money; too much regulation threatens to make private
schools quasipublic and thereby undermine the purpose of fostering alternatives
to the public educational system. Private school stakeholders will shy away from

programs that severely compromise their ability to operate independently of the state, and parents will shy away from privatization efforts that abuse public trust. There is a need for comprehensive assessment of state regulation of privatized schools to learn what regulatory measures are being employed; whether monitoring is actually occurring; whether the regulation serves a useful purpose; what the impact of regulation on institutional autonomy is; and whether deregulation of choice schools has affected the regulation of traditional public schools. It also will be important to monitor litigation filed by private religious schools and their patrons against regulations that they charge undermine their free exercise of religion under both federal and state constitutions.

Studying Unions and Collective Bargaining

A review of education and legal literature reveals a dearth of research on the relationship between privatization and collective bargaining. Yet unions have the political clout to affect significantly both the legal framework and the practice of privatization. A study should be undertaken of the involvement of the two major teachers' unions in shaping privatization programs through legislative lobbying and collective bargaining. What features should privatization measures have that will lessen the opposition of teachers' unions? How will privatization affect the role and influence of teachers' unions? Are state collective bargaining laws applicable to privatization? How hospitable will the National Labor Relations Act be to efforts to unionize teachers in privatized public schools that are not subject to state labor laws?

Monitoring Disputes

The relative freedom of privatized schools from much state and federal regulation raises questions regarding the right of constituents to challenge negative decisions. Students in public schools are entitled to due process before they can be disciplined, as are teachers threatened with termination. Will parents whose children are not admitted to privatized schools or are suspended or expelled assert constitutional rights? Similarly, will teachers who lose their positions do so? Monitoring litigation will reveal the judicial stance on whether the U.S. Constitution follows constituents into the privatized educational arena. Monitoring attrition of students and teachers from choice schools will shed light on the reasons for leaving and on whether there is a need for a formal grievance procedure for channeling and resolving conflicts. Clearly, the stakeholders in this aspect of privatization are the parents who entrust their children to privatized schools and teachers who choose to teach in them.

Conclusion

Given that so many of the legal issues surrounding privatization are unresolved and given the importance of the outcomes to legislators, parents, union leaders, private and public school officials, and society in general, the need for research is great. As we have seen, the emerging case law applying state constitutional provisions to privatization measures will play a major role in determining the legal framework within which privatization takes place. There is a need to monitor legal developments carefully and to alert policymakers to them to forestall poorly developed and implemented privatization programs that harm students and breed litigation. Beyond monitoring, there is a great need for carefully designed studies to determine how privatization affects racial and economic balance in American education and to identify which design features are most likely to promote equality of opportunity without undermining institutional autonomy and individual initiative inherent in the act of choosing. Teachers' unions and collective bargaining will play a major role in privatization, yet empirical research on their involvement is lacking. Finally, there is a need for research on whether the constitutional rights available to public school students and teachers exist in privatized schools and, if not, whether their absence has a detrimental effect on the educational environment and on the resolution of disputes.

[a]*Digest of Education Statistics 1997,* U.S. Department of Education, National Center for Education Statistics; data are for fall 1995.

[b]*A Study of Charter Schools: First Year Report* (1997). U.S. Department of Education, Office of Research and Improvement. These data show racial concentration of charter schools in ten states operating charter schools in 1995–1996. Data in the second-year and third-year reports (1998, 1999) were calculated differently but show little change, even though the number of states studied increased to twenty-four in 1997–1998. The 1997 report is used here for comparison purposes.

[c]*Texas Open-Enrollment Charter Schools: Second Year Evaluation* (1998). Texas Education Agency. Data show racial/ethnic concentration of student bodies of the nineteen open-enrollment charter schools during their second year of operation in 1997–1998.

[d]*Minnesota Charter Schools Evaluation* (1996). University of Minnesota Center for Applied Research and Educational Improvement. Data show ethnic concentration of student bodies of sixteen charter schools in ten different communities in 1996. Minnesota has operated charter schools since 1991, the longest of any state.

[e]*Fifth Year Report: Milwaukee Parental Choice Program* (1995). Data show racial concentration of student bodies of nonsectarian private schools participating in the voucher program during 1990–1994. Five of the twelve schools were more than 80 percent minority; four were substantially minority. Data are not available for three of the schools.

Appendix

TABLE 3.2   State Constitutional Orientation Toward Vouchers Encompassing Sectarian Private Schools[a]

State	Restrictive	Permissive	Uncertain
AK	X		
AL		X	
AR			X
AZ		X	
CA	X		
CO			X
CT			X
DE	X		
FL			X[b]
GA			X
HI	X		
IA			X
ID	X		
IL			X
IN			X
KS	X		
KY	X		
LA			X
MA	X		
MD		X	
ME			X
MI	X		
MN			X
MO	X		
MS		X	
MT			X
NC			X
ND	X		
NE		X	
NH			X
NJ		X	
NM			X
NV			X
NY		X	
OH		X	
OK	X		

TABLE 3.2   (*continued*)

State	Restrictive	Permissive	Uncertain
OR			X
PA		X	
RI		X	
SC		X	
SD	X		
TN			X
TX			X
UT		X	
VA	X		
VT			X
WA	X		
WI		X	
WV		X	
WY	X		

[a]For purposes of this table, it is assumed that a state voucher program would encompass private religious schools.
[b]Litigation pending.

Notes

1. See Carol Ascher et al. (1996). *Hard Lessons: Public Schools and Privatization.* New York: Twentieth Century Fund Press, pp. 23–42.

2. As of the beginning of 1999, there were about 100 public schools being managed by for-profit companies, up from sixty the year before. The expansion of charter school legislation to thirty-four states accounts for most of the growth. In twenty-one of these states, for-profit companies can run charters directly or through subcontracting with a public charter recipient. Anna Bray Duff, "Profiting from Public Schools," *Investor's Business Daily,* February 4, 1999. Private companies are increasingly eyeing the multi-billion dollar education sector as an investment opportunity. Edward Wyatt, "Investors See Room for Profit in the Demand for Education," *New York Times,* November 4, 1999. Not all efforts at privatization have been successful. The most prominent failures are the ill-fated arrangements negotiated in the early 1990s by the Hartford, Connecticut, school board and the Baltimore City School District with Education Alternatives, Inc. (EAI), a private for-profit company. The EAI experience has been well chronicled in the education literature. For an overview, see Patricia Cazares, "The Private Management of Public Schools: The Hartford, Connecticut, Experience," ERIC Document Reproduction Service No. ED 407738 (1997); and Sherri Doughty, "The Private Management of Public Schools: The Baltimore, Maryland, Experience," ERIC Document Reproduction Service No. ED 407739 (1997). *See* Carol Asher et al., *Hard Lessons,* for a detailed discussion. EAI had a more favorable experience in Miami-Dade County, Florida, where it served as a consultant over a five-year

span to implement its Tesseract curriculum in an elementary school. See Deborah L. Edwards, "The Private Management of Public Schools: The Dade County, Florida, Experience," ERIC Document Reproduction Service No 407740 (1997).

3. Mich. Const., art. 8, sec. 2.

4. Other state constitutional provisions limiting public funding to public schools only include Cal. Const., art. 9, sec. 8; Colo. Const., art. 5, sec. 34; Neb. Const., art. 7, sec. 11; N.M. Const., art. 4, sec. 31; and Wyo. Const., art. 3, sec. 36, and art. 7, secs. 4 and 7. Alabama and Pennsylvania's similar constitutional provisions can be overridden by a two-thirds vote of the legislature. Ala. Const., art. 4, sec. 73; Penn. Const., art. 3, sec. 30. Virginia's constitution allows funding for educational purposes at nonsectarian private schools. Va. Const., art. 8, sec. 10. Kentucky's constitution allows voters to decide the matter. Ky. Const., sec. 184. In other states such as Connecticut, Delaware, Rhode Island, and Texas, constitutional provisions restricting funding to public schools are limited to certain sources of funding, e.g., the public school fund, thus arguably allowing the use of other public monies for private school funding. For a full discussion including interpretive law and citations, see Frank Kemerer, "State Constitutions and School Vouchers," *Education Law Reporter* 120 (October 2, 1997).

5. Mich. Comp. Laws Ann. sec. 380.501 et seq. (West 1997).

6. *Council of Orgs. and Others for Educ. About Parochiaid, Inc. v. Governor*, 566 N.W.2d 208 (Mich. 1997).

7. *Council of Orgs.*, 566 N.W.2d at 224.

8. See Julie Vallarelli (1992). "Note: State Constitutional Restraints on the Privatization of Education," *Boston Law Review* 72, pp. 390–393. A good example of the restraint non-delegation law can impose on a state legislature is a 1976 Rhode Island Supreme Court decision striking down a statute requiring public school districts to bus children residing within their boundaries to private schools. The court found the statute an unconstitutional delegation of legislative authority to private entities because it did not limit the ability of a private school to pass on its transportation costs to public school districts. *Jennings v. Exeter-West Greenwich Regional School Districts Committee*, 352 A.2d 634 (R.I. 1976). In effect, the statute allowed private schools to determine not only which townships had to provide busing but also how far students were to be bused. For delegation to be valid, the court set forth two conditions. First, the public policy of the legislation has to be clearly specified. Second, there must be sufficient regulation to prevent private actors from exercising power in their own self-interest. Thereafter, the legislature corrected the problem by establishing the geographic parameters within which transportation services to private schools could be provided. Three years later, the court found the changes acceptable. *Jamestown School Committee v. Schmidt*, 405 A.2d 16 (R.I. 1979).

9. Mass. Const., art. 18. In two decisions, the Supreme Judicial Court of Massachusetts unanimously advised that channeling money to students to pay for private schooling would violate this provision. *Opinion of the Justices to the House of Representatives*, 259 N.E.2d 564 (Mass. 1970); *Opinion of the Justices to the Senate*, 514 N.E.2d 353 (Mass. 1987).

10. *Fifty-One Hispanic Residents of Chelsea v. School Committee of Chelsea*, 659 N.E.2d 277, 282 (Mass. 1996).

11. Mass. Gen. Laws Ann. Ch. 71, sec. 89(a) (West 1997).

12. *School District of Wilkinsburg v. Wilkinsburg Education Association*, 667 A.2d 5 (Penn. 1995). For a critical analysis of the decision, see Kimberly Colonna (1996), "Com-

ment: The Privatization of Public Schools: A Statutory and Constitutional Analysis of the Context of the *Wilkinsburg Education Association v. Wilkinsburg School District*," *Dickinson Law Review* 100.

13. Penn. Const., art 3, sec. 14.

14. "Here, it is conceivable that even if the Public School Code were to be interpreted to prohibit subcontracting of teachers, and that interpretation were to pass constitutional muster under most conditions, there may be other conditions, which the school district here insists there are, which would render this application of the Public School Code unconstitutional. We agree." *School District of Wilkinson*, 667 A.2d at 8.

15. The decision in *Wilkinsburg Education Association v. School District of Wilkinsburg* was handed down by the Court of Common Pleas, Allegheny County, Pennsylvania, August 6, 1997. The decision can be found in the *Pittsburgh Legal Journal* 146 (1998), beginning on p. 64. The relevant charter school provisions are Penn. Stat. 24 P.S. secs. 17-1715-A and 17-1717-A (1998). For an in-depth discussion of the three-year experience with contracting-out the Turner Elementary School, see Eleanor Chute, "A New Page Turns on Revisionist Tale; Outcomes Debated As School District Resumes Control," *Pittsburgh Post-Gazette*, June 29, 1998. For an earlier account, see Monica Haynes, "Studying a Revolution in Education," *Pittsburgh Post-Gazette*, March 19, 1995.

16. See generally Allen W. Hubsch, "Education and Self-Government: The Right to Education Under State Constitutional Law," *Journal of Law and Education* 18 (1989). In an appendix, Hubsch lists the primary constitutional provision of each state that pertains to the establishment of an educational system.

17. Ariz. Rev. Stat. secs. 15-181 and 15-183E.2 (1997). In a 1998 decision, the Court of Appeals of Arizona ruled that the State Board of Education's investigation into the creditworthiness and religious affiliation of a proposed charter school's board of directors was proper, given the necessity of assuring that charter schools and their operations are financially secure and nonsectarian. The school was denied a charter. The court broadly construed the investigatory powers of the state board and its authority under the state statute to determine criteria for granting charters.

18. See, e.g., Lynn Schnaiberg, "Buildings in Hand, Church Leaders Float Charter Ideas," *Education Week*, February 10, 1999. See also Anemona Hartocollis, "Religious Leaders Map Plans to Use New Law for Publicly Financed Charter Schools," *New York Times*, December 29, 1998, and Anemona Hartocollis, "A Charter School Legislator Says Religious Use Is Misuse," *New York Times*, December 30, 1998.

19. The author has a special interest in this area of the law. See, e.g., Frank R. Kemerer and Kenneth L. Deutsch, *Constitutional Rights and Student Life* (St. Paul, Minn.: West Publishing Company, 1979, and supp. 1984).

20. The issue is as yet little discussed in the education and legal literature. However, one recent law review article provides an interesting and thought-provoking analysis. See Justin Goldstein, "Exploring Unchartered Territory: An Analysis of Charter Schools and the Applicability of the U.S. Constitution," *Southern California Interdisciplinary Law Journal* 7 (Summer 1998).

21. *Villaneuva v. Carere*, 85 F.3d 481 (10th Cir. 1996), p. 488.

22. For example, the North Carolina statute states that "within one year after the charter school begins operation, the population of the school shall reasonably reflect the racial and ethnic composition of the general population residing within the local school administrative unit in which the school is located or the racial and ethnic composition of the special

population that the school seeks to serve residing within the local school administrative unit in which the school is located. The school shall be subject to any court-ordered desegregation plans in effect for the local school administrative unit." N.C. Gen. Stat., 115C-238.29F(g)(5) (1997). Despite the provision, half of the state's fifty-seven charter schools violated the ethnic diversity provision in 1999 by enrolling a disproportionate percentage of black students. The chairman of the State Charter School Advisory Committee recognized that closure is likely unless the law is changed. He added, "I suspect you'll see a change in the legislation before you see the state closing down successful schools." Tim Simmons, "Charter Schools Still Tilt Racially," *The (Charlotte) News and Observer,* January 3, 1999.

23. See *Tuttle v. Arlington County School Board,* 195 F.3d 698 (4th Cir. 1999), *cert. denied,* 120 S.Ct. 1552 (2000) (oversubscribed public school's use of race/ethnicity factor in admissions to achieve racial and ethnic diversity violates the Fourteenth Amendment Equal Protection Clause); *Eisenberg v. Montgomery County Public Schools,* 197 F.3d 123 (4th Cir.1999), *cert. denied,* 120 S.Ct. 1420 (2000) (denial of a white student's transfer to a magnet school in order to maintain racial diversity in district schools violates the Fourteenth Amendment Equal Protection Clause); *Wessman v. Gittens,* 160 F.3d 790 (1st Cir. 1998) (race-conscious admissions policy at academically competitive public school violates the Fourteenth Amendment Equal Protection Clause). But see *Hunter v. Regents of the University of California,* 190 F.3d 1061 (9th Cir. 1999), *cert. denied,* 121 S.Ct. 186 (2000) (university interest in operating a laboratory elementary school is sufficiently compelling to permit use of race-based admissions criteria), and *Brewer v. West Irondequoit Central School District,* 212 F.3d 738 (2nd Cir., May 11, 2000) (case remanded to trial court to determine whether school district's interest in reducing racial isolation is sufficiently compelling and narrowly tailored to justify prohibiting a white student from transferring out of a mostly minority urban school district). See also and compare the federal district court rulings in *Comfort v. Lynn School Committee,* 100 F. Supp. 2d 57 (D. Mass. 2000) (preliminary injunction will not issue where plaintiffs cannot show that racial balance program for elementary and middle schools is clearly unconstitutional), and *Equal Open Enrollment Association v. Board of Education of Akron City School District,* 937 F. Supp. 700 (N.D. Ohio 1996) (prevention of racial segregation is not sufficiently compelling to justify policy prohibiting white students from transferring out of urban school district).

24. *Wessman v. Gittens,* 160 F.3d 790 (1st Cir. 1998), p. 799.

25. See, e.g., Nancy J. Zollers and Arun K. Ramanathan, "For-Profit Charter Schools and Students with Disabilities: The Sordid Side of the Business of Schooling," *Phi Delta Kappan* (December 1998). For a thorough discussion, see Laura Rothstein, "School Choice and Children with Disabilities," in Stephen Sugarman and Frank Kemerer, eds., *School Choice and Social Controversy: Politics, Policy, and Law* (Washington, D.C.: Brookings Institution Press, 1999).

26. See Peggy Farber, "The Edison Project Scores—and Stumbles—in Boston," *Phi Delta Kappan* (March 1998); John Chubb, "Edison Scores and Scores Again in Boston," *Phi Delta Kappan* (November 1998); and Peggy Farber, "Edison's Score Remains Unchanged," *Phi Delta Kappan* (November 1998).

27. 20 U.S.C. sec. 1413(a)(5) (1997). See Joseph R. McKinney, "Charter Schools' Legal Responsibilities Toward Children with Disabilities," *Education Law Reporter* 126 (August 10, 1998). The Individuals with Disabilities Education Act is one of three federal disability laws that apply to public schools and schools operated by private entities as public schools. The second is section 504 of the 1973 Rehabilitation Act, which prevents discrimination

on the basis of disability in any federally assisted program. See 29 U.S.C. sec. 794 (1997). The third is Title II of the Americans with Disabilities Act, which applies to public schools and requires much the same as section 504. See 42 U.S.C. secs. 12181–12189 (1997).

28. The recent U.S. Supreme Court decision interpreting IDEA to require a school district to provide one-on-one nursing services to monitor a student's life-support equipment adds to the problem. *Cedar Rapids Community School District v. Garret F.*, 119 S.Ct. 992 (1999).

29. 20 U.S.C. sec. 1412(a)(10)(A) (1997).

30. Dispassionate discussion of the matter is rare. For an excellent, unbiased overview of the legal complexities involved, see William Buss, "Teachers, Teacher Unions, and School Choice," in Sugarman and Kemerer, *School Choice and Social Controversy*.

31. Minn. Stat. Ann. sec. 124D.10, subd. 21 (West 1998).

32. See Tom Wilkowske, "Minnesota Agency Likely to Intervene in Duluth School Dispute," *Duluth News-Tribune*, October 16, 1997, and Larry Oakes, "Duluth's Edison Experiment," *Minneapolis Star Tribune*, January 28, 1998.

33. How close a relationship the school has to the public sector may not affect its status as a private employer. The Supreme Judicial Court of Maine ruled that a private school serving a large number of public school students under contract with a public school district remained a private school and could not be considered a public employer under the state labor relations law for purposes of teacher unionization. *Lee Academy Education Association v. Academy*, 556 A.2d 216 (Maine 1989).

34. "The Turner Chronology," *Pittsburgh Post-Gazette*, June 29, 1998. In Minnesota, the state supreme court ruled in 1993 that even though the school district collective bargaining agreement with the food service union did not limit the managerial right of the district to contract out food services, the district was required under state labor law to bargain with the union over the *effect* of its decision. The school district could not unilaterally contract out food services work and discharge employees while the collective bargaining agreement was operative. The court upheld the arbitrator's award of reinstatement with full seniority and back pay for all food service workers. *Independent School District v. School Service Employees Union Local 284*, 503 N.W.2d 104 (Minn. 1993). The Hartford Principals and Supervisors Association challenged the school board's contracting-out agreement with Education Alternatives, Inc. (EAI), as a repudiation of the collective bargaining agreement and violation of the rights of union members under the Teacher Negotiation Act. However, the Superior Court of Connecticut sidestepped the issue, deciding the matter on the grounds that the termination of the contract with EAI mooted the case. *Supervisors Association v. Connecticut State Board of Labor Relations*, 1998 WL 13943 (Conn. Super., January 7, 1998).

35. 29 U.S.C. secs. 151–169 (1988).

36. The National Labor Relations Board, which enforces the National Labor Relations Act, applies discretionary monetary standards frequently based on the employer's annual revenues to determine when an employer falls within the terms of the act.

37. *NLRB v. Catholic Bishops of Chicago*, 440 U.S. 490 (1979).

38. *NLRB v. Yeshiva University*, 444 U.S. 672 (1982).

39. *International Union of Operating Engineers, Local 70 v. National Labor Relations Board*, 940 F. Supp. 1439 (D. Minn. 1996).

40. *Pierce v. Society of Sisters*, 268 U.S. 510 (1925).

41. *Id.* at 535.

42. *Committee for Public Education v. Nyquist*, 413 U.S. 756 (1973).

43. *Id.* at 786.

44. *Id.* at 782, n. 38 (emphasis added).

45. Currently, Minnesota families, regardless of income, can deduct from their state tax such expenses as private school tuition, fees, nonreligious textbooks, and instructional materials up to $1,625 for grades K-6, and up to $2,500 for grades 7–12. Minn. Stat. sec. 290.01 (1998). Minnesota also has a tax credit law that affords low-income families a credit toward the state tax for the same education-related expenses, excluding private school tuition. Minn. Stat. sec. 290.0674 (1998).

46. *Mueller v. Allen*, 463 U.S. 388 (1983), p. 400.

47. The four cases are *Witters v. Washington Department of Services*, 474 U.S. 481 (1986) (Establishment Clause does not prevent the provision of vocational rehabilitation services to aid a blind student to pursue studies at a Christian college to become a minister); *Zobrest v. Catalina Foothills School District*, 509 U.S. 1 (1993) (Establishment Clause does not bar a school district from providing a sign-language interpreter under the federal Individuals with Disabilities Education Act to a deaf student attending classes at a Catholic high school); *Rosenberger v. Rector and Visitors of the University of Virginia*, 515 U.S. 819 (1995) (providing student activity fees to third party printers of a student religious newspaper does not violate the Establishment Clause); and *Agostini v. Felton*, 117 S.Ct. 1997 (1997) (allowing public school teachers to deliver compensatory education on sectarian private school campuses is a neutral governmental program that provides benefits without regard to the sectarian-nonsectarian or public-nonpublic nature of the institution and thus does not violate the Establishment Clause). For an authoritative discussion of how the current U.S. Supreme Court will likely rule on a voucher system, see Jesse Choper, "Federal Constitutional Issues," in Sugarman and Kemerer, *School Choice and Social Controversy*. Choper concludes that the thinking of one justice—Sandra Day O'Connor—will determine how the current Court rules on the subject.

48. *Jackson v. Benson*, 578 N.W.2d 602 (Wis.), *cert. denied*, 119 S.Ct. 466 (1998).

49. Some commentators maintain that once the Supreme Court upholds a voucher program, it will preclude states from applying their more stringent antiestablishment provisions to the matter because doing so would violate both the Equal Protection Clause of the Fourteenth Amendment and the rights of parents to exercise their religious beliefs under the First Amendment. See, e.g., Joseph P. Viteritti, "Choosing Equality: Religious Freedom and Educational Opportunity Under Constitutional Federalism," *Yale Law and Policy Review* 15 (1996). However, to date, the Court has recognized that the Establishment Clause of the First Amendment does not trump more restrictive state constitutional provisions. Thus, although the Court ruled in *Witters v. Washington Department of Services for the Blind* that the Establishment Clause does not prevent the state from providing vocational rehabilitation services to aid a blind student at a Christian college, the justices noted that on remand the Washington State Supreme Court was free to consider the matter under the more stringent provisions of the state constitution. The latter did so and struck the program down as unconstitutional. *Witters*, 771 P.2d 1119 (Wash. 1989). This was an Establishment Clause case, however, and did not directly involve the free exercise of religion.

50. See Frank Kemerer, "State Constitutions and School Vouchers," *Education Law Reporter* 120 (October 2, 1997). See also Frank Kemerer, "The Constitutional Dimensions of School Vouchers," *Texas Forum on Civil Liberties and Civil Rights* 3 (1998).

51. Mich. Const., art. 8, sec. 2.

52. *In re Proposal C*, 185 N.W.2d 9, 26 (Mich. 1971).

53. *Opinion of the Justices to the House of Representatives*, 259 N.E.2d 564 (Mass. 1970); *Opinion of the Justices to the Senate*, 514 N.E.2d 353 (Mass. 1987). In the latter, the Massachusetts high court noted that the "language of our anti-aid amendment is 'much more specific' than the First Amendment to the U.S. Constitution." *Id.* at n. 4.

54. *Jackson v. Benson*, 578 N.W.2d 602 (Wisc.), *cert. denied*, 119 S.Ct. 466 (1998). In ruling on the state constitution issue, the Wisconsin high court concluded that its antiestablishment provision is coextensive with the Establishment Clause of the First Amendment. The high court drew on U.S. Supreme Court precedents, including *Mueller v. Allen* and its progeny, to uphold the Milwaukee program. Article 1, section 18 of the Wisconsin Constitution reads in part, "nor shall any person be compelled to attend, erect or support any place of worship, or to maintain any ministry, without consent; nor shall . . . preference be given by law to any religious establishments or modes of worship; nor shall any money be drawn from the treasury for the benefit of religious societies, or religious or theological seminaries." The trial court and the court of appeals had construed this section to be more restrictive than its federal counterpart and on that basis struck down the Milwaukee voucher program. Other state supreme courts have interpreted their state constitutional antiestablishment provisions to mean the same as the Establishment Clause as the First Amendment. Among them are Alabama, Maine, North Carolina, New Jersey, and Ohio. In a few states, the state supreme court has suggested, but not ruled, this to be the case. Thus, how the U.S. Supreme Court eventually rules on the voucher issue may have great influence on the law in these states.

55. *Kotterman v. Killian*, 972 P.2d 606 (Ariz.), *cert. denied*, 120 S.Ct. 283 (1999).

56. *Simmons-Harris v. Goff*, 711 N.E.2d 203 (Ohio, 1999).

57. *Zelman v. Simmons-Harris*, 120 S.Ct. 443 (mem.).

58. *Simmons-Harris v. Zelman*, 72 F. Supp.2d 834 (N.D. Ohio 1999), *aff'd,* 2000 WL 1816079 (6th Cir. December 11, 2000).

59. *Bagley v. Raymond School Department*, 728 A.2d 127 (Maine), *cert. denied*, 120 S.Ct. 364 (1999).

60. *Strout v. Albanese*, 178 F.3d 57 (1st Cir.), *cert. denied*, 120 S.Ct. 329 (1999).

61. *Chittenden Town School District v. Vermont Department of Education*, 738 A.2d 539 (Vt.), *cert. denied sub nom., Andrews v. Vermont Department of Education*, 120 S.Ct. 626 (1999). Unlike the Maine Supreme Judicial Court, the Supreme Court of Vermont based its decision exclusively on the state constitution. The court noted that whatever the U.S. Supreme Court might decide in the future about a voucher program would not affect its interpretation of the state constitution.

62. The Supreme Judicial Court of Maine observed in *Bagley* that "while it may be possible for the Legislature to craft a program that would allow parents greater flexibility in choosing private schools for their children, the current program could not easily be tailored to include religious schools without addressing significant problems of entanglement or the advancement of religion. It is up to the Legislature, not the courts, to determine whether and how to attempt to structure such a program." 728 A.2d at 146. The

Supreme Court of Vermont noted that "schools to which the tuition is paid by the district can use some or most of it to fund the costs of religious education, and presumably will. We express no opinion on how the State of Vermont can or should address this deficiency should it attempt to craft a complying tuition-payment scheme. We only decide that the current statutory system, with no restrictions on the purpose of use of the tuition funds, violates Article 3." *Chittenden*, 738 A.2d at 562.

63. *Pierce v. Society of Sisters*, 268 U.S. 510 (1925), p. 534.

64. *Ohio Association of Independent Schools v. Goff*, 92 F.3d 419 (6th Cir. 1996).

65. See the list of decisions in *New Life Baptist Church Academy v. East Longmeadow*, 885 F.2d 940, 950–951 (1st Cir. 1989). The most notable exception to general deference to the state is a 1976 Ohio Supreme Court ruling, *State v. Whisner*, 351 N.E.2d 750 (Ohio 1976) (state board's minimum regulations for private elementary schools were so intrusive as to violate parents' right to freedom of religion and their right to control their children's upbringing).

66. Title VII of the 1964 Civil Rights Act, which prevents discrimination on the basis of race, color, religion, sex, and national origin in public and private employment, applies to organizations with fifteen or more employees for each working day in each of twenty or more calendar weeks in the current or preceding year. 42 U.S.C.A. sec. 2000e (b) (West 1999). The act does not apply to a religious corporation, association, educational institution, or society with respect to the employment of individuals of a particular religion to perform work. 42 U.S.C.A. sec. 2000e-1 (a) (West 1999).

67. *Davis v. Grover*, No. 90 CV 2576 (Dane Cir. Ct., August 6, 1991), at p. 23. The holding was not taken up on appeal. Whether it is an anomaly remains to be seen.

68. Wis. Stat. Ann. 119.23 (3)(a) and (7)(a)4 (West 1999). The apparent antipathy of Wisconsin legislators toward state-level education bureaucracy resulted in the deletion of most accountability measures from the Milwaukee voucher legislation when it was expanded in 1995 to encompass religious private schools.

69. The requirement was eliminated in 1998 after the voucher program had been amended to include private religious schools. The action resulted from negotiations between the legislature's Joint Committee on Administrative Rules and the Wisconsin State Department of Public Instruction. It was agreed that in exchange for the department's removal of the student rights list from the departmental administrative rule, participating private school administrators and principals would be asked to sign and return a letter stating that Judge Susan Steingass had ruled in her 1990 trial court decision that the student rights list applied to private schools participating in the program. The letter to be signed also states that Judge Steingass had ruled that the Department of Public Instruction has an obligation to advise participating schools of these state and federal provisions. In short, the department was forced to drop the student rights requirement but not without acknowledging that they should apply.

70. *Rendell-Baker v. Kohn*, 457 U.S. 830 (1982), p. 842.

71. Robert O'Neil, "School Choice and State Action," in Sugarman and Kemerer, *School Choice and Social Controversy*.

72. See *A National Study of Charter Schools, Third Year Report*, U.S. Department of Education, 1999, pp. 12–15. See also Jennifer T. Wall, "The Establishment of Charter Schools: A Guide to Legal Issues for Legislators," *Brigham Young University Education and Law Journal* 1998 (1998) (noting the variability in charter school legislation and discussing issues that legislators should address).

73. The absence of studies prompted this author to assemble an inventory of state constitutional provisions and case law in all fifty states with the purpose of identifying those design features that give vouchers the best chance of passing constitutional muster in states where the legal environment appears supportive. See Frank R. Kemerer, "State Constitutions and School Vouchers," *Education Law Reporter* 120 (October 2, 1997). The conclusions from that research are as follows as set forth in Frank R. Kemerer, "The Constitutional Dimension of School Vouchers," *The Texas Forum on Civil Liberties and Civil Rights,* Vol. 3 (1998), pp. 178-179.

First, the voucher must flow to parents and not to institutions. Most states have a constitutional provision that prohibits direct expenditure of public money for sectarian purposes. The simplest way to accomplish this is to provide parents with certificates redeemable for educational services at approved schools and have the schools return the certificates to the state for payment. To avoid the problems experienced in litigation in Wisconsin and Ohio, the legislature should tailor the amount of the voucher to the cost of instruction. This avoids the appearance of giving sectarian private schools a windfall which then can be diverted for sectarian purposes.

Second, the legislature must give parents a wide choice of public and private schools. Expansion of the Milwaukee voucher program to include sectarian private schools but not public schools foundered on this point in litigation at the trial court level in 1997. Although the Wisconsin Supreme Court was not bothered by the exclusion, exclusion of public schools could be a stumbling block in other jurisdictions.

Third, the legislature must state clearly the public purpose of the state voucher program. This will help it survive a challenge under the public purpose provision that is common in state constitutions. The most convincing purpose is to enfranchise middle and low income families with the means to seek improved educational opportunities for their children so that the legislature clearly advances the state's interest in an educated citizenry. From an equity perspective, the present educational system accords the wealthy greater opportunities to control their children's education through choice of residence or payment of private school tuition. Legislatures effectively can demonstrate such a public purpose by varying the amount of the voucher with income level: The lower the income, the greater the voucher.

Fourth, legislators must include sufficient accountability measures to demonstrate that the voucher program will achieve the public purpose. These might include prohibiting discrimination in admissions, promoting toleration, requiring compliance with financial audits, and requiring students to participate in state-level testing programs.

74. See Frank Kemerer, "School Choice Accountability," in Sugarman and Kemerer, *School Choice and Social Controversy.*

75. Statistics, 1997. *Private School Universe Study, 1993–1994.* U.S. Department of Education, National Center for Education Statistics, 1996.

76. Arizona has a very permissive charter school law that accommodates private schools. Charter schools are not required to reflect the racial composition of the districts within which they are located. A recent study compares the racial and ethnic composition of individual Arizona charter schools with that of regular public schools in the same neighborhoods or attendance zones, rather than with all public schools in the state. It shows extensive racial clustering, with charter schools typically 20 percentage points higher in white enrollment than regular public schools serving the same area. Charters

with a majority of ethnic minority students tend to be either vocational-ed secondary schools or alternative schools for students expelled from traditional public schools. The researchers conclude that "the ethnic separation on the part of Arizona's charter schools, though de facto, is an insidious by-product of unregulated school choice." Casey D. Cobb and Gene V. Glass, "Ethnic Segregation in Arizona Charter Schools," *Education Policy Analysis Archives* (January 14, 1999) <epaa.asu.edu/epaa/v7n1/>.

77. See, e.g., *University of California Regents v. Bakke*, 438 U.S. 265 (1978).

78. *Swann v. Charlotte-Mecklinburg Board of Education*, 402 U.S. 1 (1971), p. 16.

79. See *Adarand Constructors, Inc. v. Pena*, 515 U.S. 200 (1995) (all racial classifications, including those that are benign, are to be subjected to detailed judicial scrutiny to ensure that individual equal protection rights are not abridged).

80. The U.S. Supreme Court ruled in *San Antonio Independent School District v. Rodriguez*, 411 U.S. 1 (1973), that claims of financial disparities among school districts do not constitute a denial of equal protection under the Fourteenth Amendment of the U.S. Constitution. However, such claims have been successful in state courts based on various provisions of state constitutions.

81. For a discussion, see "Note: The Limits of Choice: School Choice Reform and State Constitutional Guarantees of Educational Quality," *Harvard Law Review* 109 (1996). See also Kevin S. Huffman, "Charter Schools, Equal Protection Litigation, and the New School Reform Movement," *New York University Law Review* 73 (1998).

84. *Wessman v. Gittens*, 160 F.3d 790 (1st Cir. 1998), p. 805.

85. *Hunter v. Regents of the University of California*, 190 F.3d 1061 *cert.denied,* 121 S.Ct. 186 (2000)(9th Cir. 1999). The research presented in *Hunter* appears to be both more extensive and more targeted than that presented in the *Wessman* case. The two judges in the majority also were more willing to defer to the experts, noting that "courts should defer to researchers' decisions about what they need for their research" (p. 1066). The dissenting judge, however, was much more critical.

86. Frank Kemerer et al. "Vouchers and Private School Autonomy," *Journal of Law and Education* 21 (1992); Frank Kemerer, "School Choice Accountability," in Sugarman and Kemerer, *School Choice and Social Controversy*; Frank Kemerer, "Legal Issues Involving Educational Privatization and Accountability," Occasional Paper #6, National Center for the Study of Privatization in Education, 2000. Available: http://www.tc.columbia.edu/ncspe. See also the exchange between Kemerer and William Bentley Ball: Frank Kemerer, "The Publicization of the Private School," *Education Week*, January 8, 1992; William Bentley Ball, "False Assumptions on Voucher Programs and the Law," *Education Week*, February 12, 1992; Frank Kemerer, "Kemerer Responds to Ball on Vouchers, 'Publicization,'" *Education Week*, March 4, 1992. Ball argued most of the significant religion cases before the U.S. Supreme Court involving public school aid to, and regulation of, private schools.

87. A recent University of Michigan study showed that charter schools in that state tend to serve the least expensive students to educate. Thus, for example, charter school operators are more inclined to open elementary schools than secondary schools where the costs per student are greater. Tamar Lewin, "In Michigan, School Choice Weeds out Costlier Students," *New York Times*, October 26, 1999. Considering that charter schools are usually underfunded, this should not be surprising. When private for-profit organizations operate charter schools under contract with a public entity, the effort to economize is even more pronounced.

4

Information and Choice in Educational Privatization

MARK SCHNEIDER

There is at least one thing upon which most parents agree: A good education is critical to the quality of their child's future. This widely held belief is supported by a set of strong empirical studies linking education to a host of desirable outcomes. Unfortunately, there is disagreement about which aspects of education matter the most, a disagreement that to date research has not been able to resolve. Thus, even though we as a society want good schools and spend considerable amounts of money to achieve them, we aren't sure about what works best.

To this add the fact that debates about education are often colored by broader ideological disagreements. This creates a volatile combination that has produced conditions for political conflict, as well as the basis for the continuous waves of educational reform that have swept through the nation's schools.

Although school reform was a relatively constant phenomenon during the twentieth century, its form continually changed over the decades. In the past, educational reform movements often focused on curriculum and teaching methods. In contrast, many of today's reforms center on issues of governance (Chubb

The work reported in this chapter has been supported by the National Science Foundation and the Smith Richardson Foundation.

and Moe, 1990; Clune and Witte, 1990; Henig, 1994; Smith and Meier, 1995; Anhalt et al., 1995; Ravitch and Viteritti, 1996). A core belief underlying many new reform proposals is that education cannot be improved unless new actors are brought into the decisionmaking arena, changing the way in which educational policy decisions are made, shifting power toward parents, and exposing overly bureaucratized school systems to some form of market discipline. As these beliefs have crystallized, school choice has become one of the most widely implemented—and one of the most controversial—reform mechanisms designed to change the organization of schools and to enhance performance.

Although school reform comes in many forms, many if not most seek to create marketlike forces to which schools must respond—by becoming more flexible, more responsive to the needs of their students and parents, and improving the quality of education. But a central argument is that the behavior of parents must also change—and many reforms are designed to give parents incentives to become better shoppers and thereby unleash competitive forces among an expanded set of alternatives.

Unfortunately, scholars and policymakers actually know very little about how parent-consumers come to learn about the quality of the schools they would be choosing. Scholars know little about the information sources parents use, the quality of that information, and how parents use it to choose schools for their children. Scholars know even less about how to intervene in the flow of school information to increase parents' information levels. There is also the question of "feedback" between choice and parents' information levels. Many advocates have adopted a field-of-dreams approach: Build a system of choice and parents will come to use it—but the strength of the empirical foundations for this position has not yet been established.

In short, we assume that more information will lead to better parental choices and better schools, but the foundations for such assumptions are undeveloped. In this chapter, I explore some questions related to the role of information in school choice.[1] I first discuss how much information parents need to make choice work, contrasting "limited rationality" to "full information rationality." This essential distinction allows us to set realistic expectations for what parents should know and how many parents should know it.

It is also important to remember that in any market-oriented school choice reform, parents are not the only stakeholders. Although my main focus in this chapter is parents, I also discuss the roles of schools (the providers of education) and government (the funders) in managing information. Most everyone in the debate favors transparency of information, yet actions frequently belie this commitment—and often for obvious reasons.

Parents as Stakeholders: Choice at the Individual Level

Let us begin with H.A. Simon's (1986) observation that any realistic model of rational behavior must "describe a person who is limited in computational capacity, and who searches very selectively through large realms of possibilities in order to discover what alternatives of action are available, and what the consequences of each of these alternatives are" (p. 295).[2] One task is to specify the factors that affect the ability of parents to engage in this procedural or boundedly rational behavior and to identify whether school choice affects the incentives of parents to behave rationally. Moreover, traditional economic models assume full information, but a realistic model of choice must incorporate the idea that citizens can use shortcuts to get enough information to make appropriate choices. Although this is recognized in work on political behavior and citizen information about many public policies (see, e.g., Althaus, 1995; Iyengar, 1989; Sniderman, Brody, and Tetlock, 1991; Zaller, 1992; Popkin, 1991; Lupia, 1992, 1994; Lupia and McCubbins, 1998), it is often overlooked in work on parent information about the schools.

Without recognizing these limits, we may establish impossibly high standards by which to judge parents' information levels—and then criticize school choice because we find parents are relatively uniformed about the schools. I contend that we must consider how much information is actually required in order to make choice work.

Citizen Information Levels and Consumer Information Levels

Social scientists have repeatedly documented that citizens have scant information about public goods. But it is surprising to discover that levels of information about private goods are often quite similar to the limited information found about public goods and politics. In a survey of the relevant literature, F.R. Kardes (1994, p. 400) summarizes the major conclusions of the work on consumer behavior: "The typical consumer is exposed to a relatively small subset of available information about products and services, and the consumer attends to an even smaller subset of information to which he or she has been exposed. Not all information is encountered, and not all encountered information is attended to and processed."

In addition to the relatively low level of information consumers hold about products and services, many studies of information search find that "consumers have surprisingly little enthusiasm for the pursuit, even when buying expensive or socially risky goods" (Bloch, Sherrel, and Ridgway, 1986, p. 119). Research also shows that consumers typically spend little time gathering and analyzing information about the products and services they purchase (see, e.g., Fiske and Taylor, 1991; Cohen and Chakravarti, 1990; Tybout and Artz, 1994).

Consumer research has only relatively recently begun to document the degree to which consumers have information about their alternatives in private markets. However, at least since the pioneering work of Lazarsfeld et al. (1944), political scientists have shown that most citizens have extremely poor information about the choices they face in the political arena. The evidence is so consistent that L. Bartels (1996, p. 194) describes the current consensus about political information levels in no uncertain terms: "The political ignorance of the American voter is one of the best documented data of modern political science."

Since electoral politics are distant and removed from the daily world of most citizens, knowledge about candidates might be lower than knowledge about *policies* of government that may directly affect them. However, J. Zaller (1992) dismisses the suggestion that citizens are likely to learn more about matters that are important to them, arguing that the "tendency appears not to be very great or very widespread" (p. 18; see also Price and Zaller, 1993; Kuklinski et al., 1996; cf. Delli Carpini and Keeter, 1996).

Not surprisingly, these issues have emerged in the study of school choice. Although researchers in other fields have developed more realistic standards by which to judge information levels, many school researchers compare parents to some mythical, fully informed shopper and, not surprisingly, find them wanting. For example, a recent Twentieth Century Fund report argued that parents are not "natural 'consumers' of education" and that "few parents of any social class appear willing to acquire the information necessary to make active and informed educational choices" (Ascher et al., 1996, p. 40–41). It is an easy step from this position that parents are not well informed to the rejection of school choice—after all, how can uninformed parents make good choices about their children's schools?

I do not want to deny the fact that parents are often uninformed about many aspects of their children's schools that *we* think they should know about. In Table 4.1, I report some evidence on this point drawn from a survey that my colleagues and I undertook of parents in four local school districts.[3] Parents were asked to estimate the level of several dimensions in their child's school; official reports supplied the actual conditions. Table 4.1 reports "distance" scores that measure how close (in absolute value) a parent's estimate is to the actual performance of their child's school in each dimension.[4] For example, if a parent estimated that 60 percent of students in her child's school were reading at or above grade level and the actual performance level was 50 percent, the distance score equals 10 points.

TABLE 4.1   Means and Standard Deviations of Information Accuracy in Four
School Districts

District Location	Distance Score for Reading	Distance Score for Class Size	Distance Score for Hispanic Percent	Distance Score for Black Percent
New Jersey	14.8 (13.5)	6.3 (4.7)	6.7 (7.0)	8.2 (7.7)
New York	24.0 (16.6)	6.2 (6.4)	17.6 (14.6)	15.8 (14.2)
	N=1206	N=1264	N=1330	N=1324

Standard deviations in parentheses. source: Survey of parents.

Looking at these distance scores, two things are clear. First, parents do not have pinpoint accuracy about basic school-level factors. Second, parents in New York City are less accurate about their schools than suburban parents. For example, the average distance between the percentage of students reading at grade level estimated by parents and the actual performance is 24 points, and New York parents were off by an average of more than 15 points in their estimate of the size of the black student population and more than 17 points in the estimate of the size of the Hispanic student population of their child's school. In contrast, distance scores are much lower among suburban parents, especially for the racial makeup of the schools, which may partly reflect the racial balancing around which the schools in both Montclair and Morristown are organized.

If we look further into the data, we would find that in addition to these city-suburban differences, education and race also affect accuracy. Building on differences such as these and in contrast to Ascher et al.'s (1996) broad indictment of parental information search behavior, more commonly the argument about parent information levels focuses on potential race and class biases in the flow of information and the subsequent quality of parental decisions. For example, G. Bridge (1978) has even called the lack of information the Achilles' heel of voucher systems.

Indeed, data from the Alum Rock demonstration program showed that parents with less formal education and those who had lower expectations for their children's educational attainment were less aware of the voucher program. And J. Henig (1994), in a survey of parents in Montgomery County, Maryland, found that even among parents whose children attended schools with magnet programs

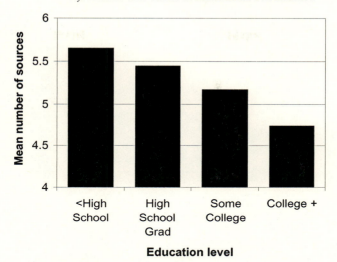

FIGURE 4.1   Total Number of Sources Parents Find
Useful, by Education
SOURCE: Parents survey.

many say they had never heard the terms "magnet school" or "magnet program." According to Henig (1994), this lack of even the most basic information was especially apparent among minorities, especially Hispanics.

Thus, many analysts who criticize choice argue that less educated parents will have difficulty making informed decisions about schools (see Bridge, 1978; Catterall, 1992; Wells and Crain, 1992), and that the differences in decisionmaking capabilities will directly lead to increased social stratification as well (Rose-Ackerman, 1992; Henig, 1994).

Stratification in the Search for Information

In our study, my colleagues and I found, not surprisingly, that education and race do indeed matter in the search for information about schools. The effects of these demographic characteristics are consistent, although not as large as the literature on political knowledge would have predicted. I believe that the most important effects may relate to patterns of networks.

Consider the following: We asked parents to judge the importance of a range of information sources in their search for information about schools. As seen in Figure 4.1, as education increases, parents rely on *fewer* sources of information.

At first glance, this may seem surprising. I had originally expected that parents

TABLE 4.2   Number of Educational Discussants Reported by Parents in New York and New Jersey

Number of Discussants	District 1	District 4	Morristown[a]	Montclair
0	38%	41%	20%	19%
1	18%	16%	12%	13%
2	20%	20%	21%	21%
3	24%	23%	48%	47%

[a]Percentages for Morristown do not total to 100 percent because of rounding error.
SOURCE: Parent survey.

with higher levels of education (and the higher income and cognitive skills attending education) would be casting their nets far and wide. But the reason for the inverse relationship stems from the *types* of sources parents use. Specifically, parents with higher levels of education rely on their friends (who are also more highly educated) to supply them with information about schools; they find other sources (especially formal sources of information in the media) less useful. In contrast, less-educated parents report using many more different sources of information. In short, highly educated parents find social networks particularly useful and do not need to search widely, whereas less-educated parents do not have such rich networks of information.

In this light, consider the data presented in Table 4.2. In New York City, the average number of educational discussants is 1.2 and the modal category is actually 0. In contrast, in New Jersey the mean is 1.95 and the modal category is 3. But perhaps more important, we found that parent networks about schools were so highly stratified by race and class that for low socioeconomic status and minority parents they were "networks to nowhere" (Schneider et al., 1997).

This pattern is particularly important because social contacts provide an efficient pathway to information about schools for more highly educated parents. In contrast, less-educated parents may rely more on media and other sources as they are forced to search more widely for information. Considering the overlap between race and education, it is not surprising that many of the patterns we found for parents with lower levels of education were also evident among parents who identify themselves as black, Hispanic, or Asian. I believe that these patterns are indicative of the ability of higher socioeconomic status parents to construct efficient networks of discussants about education, creating a way of getting useful information about the schools on the cheap.

I will return to some of the implications of this below.

The Benefits and Costs of Gathering Information
About Public Goods

Studies of information levels and how parents search for information are often structured in a benefit-cost framework. Using this framework, analysts argue that low citizen information levels are a result of simple benefit-cost calculations: Although accurate decisions about public goods may have beneficial consequences for individuals, the search for information is costly. All decisionmaking involves benefits (decision accuracy, e.g., choosing the "best" school for a child) as well as costs (cognitive effort; the costs of gathering and using information); thus individuals can be viewed as "cognitive misers" who seek to minimize costs while maximizing the rewards of accurate decisions (see, e.g., Simon, 1986; Fiske and Taylor, 1991; Sniderman, Brody, and Tetlock, 1991; Lodge and Stroh, 1993).

This view has led many social scientists to explore alternative models of the decisionmaking process. One approach explores the role of decision aids—shortcuts and heuristics—in helping citizens acquire the information they need to make informed choices.

Shortcuts to Decisions

The idea of shortcuts to decisions is not new to the study of politics and public policy. For example, S. Popkin's (1991) concept of the "reasoning voter" roots the question of information acquisition in a benefit-cost framework. Central to his argument is the concept of "low information rationality"—a method of economically combining learning and information from past experiences, daily life, the media, and political campaigns (Popkin, 1991, p. 7). Popkin (1991) views voters as investors and the vote as a reasoned investment in collective goods, made with costly and imperfect information under conditions of uncertainty (p. 10). The use of heuristics and the amount of information generated as a by-product of other aspects of life make citizen choices much more rational than the picture of ignorant citizens that is often drawn.

Similarly, J.H. Kuklinski and N.L. Hurley argue that there is growing evidence that the use of heuristics—specifically, taking cues from political elites—serves citizens well. Underlying this "new optimism" is the "idea that ordinary citizens can make good political judgments even when they lack general political acumen or information about the specific issue at hand by taking cues from political actors" (1994, p. 730). A. Lupia (1994) argued that:

As an alternative to the costly acquisition of encyclopedic information, voters may choose to employ information shortcuts. For example, voters can acquire information about the preferences or opinions of friends, coworkers, political parties or other groups, which they may then use to infer how a proposition will affect them. The appeal of these information shortcuts is that they generally require relatively little effort to acquire. (p. 63)

In their recent book, Lupia and M. McCubbins (1998) extend this argument. They make a distinction between "encyclopedic knowledge" and "ability knowledge." Whereas encyclopedic knowledge is essentially full or perfect information, ability knowledge is the outcome of selective attention and cognitive limits—individuals gather enough knowledge and employ efficient shortcuts to engage in actions and make choices that are sound. Lupia and McCubbins (1998) argue that "by forming simple and effective strategies about what information to use and how to use it, people can make the same decisions they otherwise would if they were expert" (p. 9). In this approach, people who lack detailed information not only use simple cues but also are systematic, selective, and strategic about the cues they do use (see Payne et al., 1993; Simon, 1957, on effort and accuracy in problem solving).[5]

In studying the flow of information about schools, we need to recognize that similar shortcuts may be available to parents. In other words, rather than look for encyclopedic knowledge, parents may have the ability to find information that they need to choose a good school for their children.

One such shortcut is visible cues to information. In this approach, we shift from the verbal information (on which political scientists have tended to concentrate in their study of "rational voters") to more basic visual cues about community conditions. Here the work of James Q. Wilson, George Kelling, and Wesley Skogan, who have argued that inner-city residents can use simple visual cues to judge the safety of urban neighborhoods, is critical.

Wilson and Kelling (1982) and C.M. Coles and Kelling (1996) develop the image of broken windows as an indicator of neighborhood decline. The process they describe is deceptively simple: If windows in a factory or a shop remain broken, a passerby walks away with the idea that no one cares about the neighborhood. More windows will then be broken, and the sense of disorder will intensify. In a self-propelling process, law-abiding individuals begin to avoid the area, thinking that the area is dangerous. This leaves the area open to criminals, and in fact the area becomes increasingly unsafe. Thus, in Kelling's view, even small disorders can lead to larger and larger disorders and ultimately to high crime rates.

W.G. Skogan (1990) has provided extensive survey data to support this link, showing a consistent relationship between citizen fears, experience with crime, and perception of neighborhood disorder in forty urban residential neighborhoods to documented conditions of graffiti, gang-related congregations, prostitution, drunkenness, and the like. In Skogan's (1990) work, people identified several forms of behavior as critical indicators of disorder. Among them were vandalism consisting of graffiti and damage to public spaces such as schools. Skogan (1990) confirmed that disorder and crime were intimately linked and, indeed, disorder was a more consistent indicator of neighborhood decay and crime than were other indicators such as poverty and racial composition. One fundamental lesson of this research is that individuals can use simple experiences to tell them about complex phenomena.

Although this body of work is mostly concerned with the relationship between observable conditions and crime, there are visual cues that parents can use to tell how well a school is working. My colleagues and I have shown that the observable physical condition of schools is correlated with performance (Schneider et al., 1999). Simply walking by a school and noting the presence of graffiti or the condition of the school building provides immediate cues to school performance. Similarly, a clean school free of graffiti is a safer school. In short, we argued that visual cues aid parents in selecting a school, allowing them to learn about the conditions about which they care. If a school building is in good working order and free of graffiti (especially interior graffiti), parents who care about academic performance can infer that these conditions mean better test scores. And parents who care about safety can infer that a school that is relatively free of graffiti is also a safer school. (On the availability of other heuristics for choosing schools see Bickers and Stein, 1998.)

One fundamental lesson learned from this line of research is that we must be careful not to overintellectualize our search for parent information levels: Although parents may not be able to report on reading scores or crime rates, they may have other ways of knowing that a school is good or not—and that ability knowledge can lead to appropriate choices.

Not Everyone Needs to Be Informed: The Concept of the "Marginal Consumer"

Increasing levels of parental information about schools is important; informed consumers should make better choices, and better-informed consumers should increase the efficiency of the market. However, many analysts have argued that in the current system of schooling parents are rationally ignorant and that the only way to increase the number of informed parents is to change the very nature of the schools themselves (i.e., increasing the benefit-cost ratio of parental knowledge by changing the nature of schools). These theories are driven by the idea that the incentives built into different institutional arrangements will affect individual decisionmaking processes, that individual parents will engage in more thoughtful and purposeful choice processes when school systems are designed to make their choices matter.

J. Chubb and T. Moe (1990) make this link the cornerstone of their argument for school choice: "In a system where virtually all the important choices are the responsibility of others, parents have little incentive to be informed or involved. In a market-based system, much of the responsibility would be shifted to parents (their choices would have consequences for their children's education), and their incentives to become informed and involved would be dramatically different" (p. 564). J.E. Coons and S.D. Sugarman (1978) make the same point but much more colorfully: "In a system with no options, ignorance might be bliss. In a system based on choice, ignorance is ruin" (p. 188).

Although this position has great intellectual appeal, I believe that Chubb and Moe, Coons and Sugarman, as well as other proponents of school choice err by implying that choice will lead to better schools by creating the conditions under which *all* parents will have incentives to become informed about schools and this large population of newly informed parents will generate competitive pressures on schools. I argue that this perspective overstates what we should *expect* from the average parent and I argue this perspective overstates what is *necessary* to generate competitive pressures and desirable outcomes.

Simply put, markets do not need all consumers to be informed; rather, competitive pressures can result even if a relatively small subset of consumers engage in informed, self-interested search. In this light, I argue that one of the major benefits of choice in inner-city school districts is that its creation allows parents, who my colleagues and I have termed "marginal consumers," to play an enhanced role in choosing and governing the schools.[6] As in any marketlike setting, marginal consumers pressure suppliers to increase efficiency and performance.

But efficiency isn't the only consideration for some scholars in the study of markets for public goods. Many scholars are concerned that if only some parents become informed, and if school choice gives them the opportunity to act on this information, then these more informed parents will make choices that ultimately harm the children of poorly informed parents. In short, informed parents might choose the best schools and leave the rest behind. I believe this argument ignores the possibility that competition can force other schools to improve. Thus, a critical question—with no satisfactory answer at present—is whether or not informed consumers do in fact increase the efficiency of educational outcomes for everyone or only for themselves.

The Role of Other Stakeholders
in the Provision of Information

The success of choice programs, and the quality of information parents have, will be affected by the extent to which education providers commit to disseminating quality information that parents can use. I see two barriers: First, many schools have no incentives to disseminate information widely and may, in fact, have incentives to misreport data; second, many school systems do not have the capacity (or are unwilling to redeploy existing resources) to support serious dissemination of quality information.

The Incentives for Schools to Report (or Misreport) Data

Many school officials at all levels feel besieged. Subject to constant criticism, their ability to isolate themselves behind a veil of professionalism and expertise has been eroding for decades. In addition, teaching is a difficult job, the rewards often few. Organizations under attack—and not just schools—might circle the wagons rather than seek more constructive responses. Moreover, as F. Hess (1999) has argued, although there are very strong incentives built into the governance of school systems for ambitious administrators to announce and launch new programs (and thereby create a name for themselves and win promotion), there are few incentives to put in place a monitoring system to assess the effects of these reforms, and there are no incentives whatsoever to broadcast failures. In short, although many school officials endorse the idea of transparency and of higher levels of parental information, their incentive systems may not reward or encourage behavior to make reliable information available.

But even if schools decide to make data available, there is no agreement as to what data should be reported. Moreover, there are no standard accounting rules that ensure uniformity across reports. Even a superficial scanning of school report cards demonstrates virtually no agreement about what should be reported and how it should be reported. In turn, schools have not only the incentive but also the opportunity to spin and even misreport data.

This has set up a bitter dispute between schools in different sectors, with each accusing the other of disseminating bad information or engaging in deceptive advertising and recruiting efforts. These charges are becoming more intense with the rapid spread of charter schools; they raise serious issues about the regulatory role of the state.

Consider this report from *The New York Times*, filed by Michael Winerip, who attended a "sales meeting" in Jersey City where Advantage Schools, Inc., a

Boston-based for-profit company, was pitching a new charter school for this heavily minority audience in one of the poorest school districts in New Jersey.

> This is the cutting edge of the school-choice movement, and it is stunning to behold because it is so radically different from what has come before in public education, and at the same time so much in sync with this era, when the free market is entrusted to deliver the best public-policy choices for us all. In the new education marketplace, public schools are expected to sell themselves aggressively, and the burden of figuring out what is real and what is hype falls not on regulators or district bureaucrats or boards of education but on parents. During the question period at that April meeting, Carlos Garcia asked what kind of guarantees went with all the company's promises. "What happens if my child does fall by the wayside?" Garcia asked. "I'm having that now, in another charter school."
>
> "You're asking what recourse you have if we don't do what we say," Madigan (the representative from Advantage Schools) responded. "I don't have a good answer for you. If this school doesn't do it, you tell other people and we don't keep in business."
>
> In short: Let the buyer beware.

Informed Parents and Bottom-Up Policing

Many advocates of school choice accept the principal of caveat emptor. As an example, consider Chubb and Moe (1990), who see vouchers as the means to free schools from the restrictive bureaucratic organization of public schooling. Specifically, they believe that vouchers have the capacity to create a publicly funded school system that is "almost entirely beyond the reach of public authority" (Chubb and Moe, 1990, p. 216). In their voucher plan, the entire school system would be driven by consumer choice, and the quality of schools would depend on the intelligence and diligence of parents. According to Chubb and Moe (1990), in a voucher system, "when it comes to performance, schools are held accountable from below, by parents and students who directly experience their services and are free to choose" (p. 217).

However—and this is critical—Chubb and Moe (1990) also note that "the state plays a crucial supporting role here in monitoring the full and honest disclosure of information by the schools—but it is only a supporting role" (p. 217). According to this argument, a bottom-up design of public schooling would force schools to be responsive to the needs and interests of students and parents rather than central administrators, but the state would ensure truth in advertising. What evidence do we have that school systems have the capacity to fulfill this role?

Many schools and school systems may not have the institutional capacity to produce and disseminate accurate information. For example, in my ongoing study in Washington, D.C., school officials claim that all their reporting systems are old and do not support one another, and my requests for even very basic data were refused. Of course, this refusal, although couched in terms of the inability of the school system to provide the information, was no doubt driven by suspicion that my research was going to hurt their schools and benefit charter schools. Nonetheless, the lack of capacity is evident: Almost all their recent effort to produce school report cards were delayed repeatedly by technical problems. As another example, they have no central listing of schools that have extended day programs, which is of increasing concern to a growing number of parents.[7]

In our work in New York, it took Paul Teske and me months to track down data on school performance over time; even after we located a school official who had most of the data, arranging for access required time-consuming negotiation. When New York City did release more recent information, its cross-sectional data were very difficult to use. We were even more stymied in our efforts to gather data on New Jersey districts over time (New Jersey's commitment to reporting school data seems to be a function of its budget situation). However, these experiences were downright positive compared to the hostility that I faced in my early meetings with school officials in Washington, D.C., who quite simply refused to cooperate in my search for information about schools and unabashedly expressed their desire that I "go away."

There are no easy fixes to these issues. In many school districts, a fundamental shift in the ethos of the organization may be necessary to have the schools commit to the dissemination of information and to the investment in computer systems and technical staff that may be necessary, even at a time when school districts are often under pressure to shed centralized staff.

The Role of Other Levels of Government and Business as Stakeholders

There are other stakeholders that can pressure schools and school systems to be more forthcoming in disseminating data. Although school boards and school systems are government entities, other agencies may be leverage points to increase the flow of information. After all, states have considerable statutory and constitutional authority over any local government entity, and they may be in a position to pressure local educational agencies to change behavior patterns. Moreover, as the standards movement takes hold, more uniform accounting rules may follow; with standardization, more uniform information might also flow.

The role of business deserves consideration. Increasingly, businesses are bearing the cost of school failures. Many firms decry the lack of qualified personnel for even entry-level jobs, and many businesses absorb high costs for training their workers—because the product of the schools have not mastered even the most basic skills. In turn, businesses are often a major constituency for school reforms. Moreover, large corporations that operate in many locations across the United States may also press for more transparency and uniformity.

Consider this excerpt from a paid-for column on the February 25, 1999, op-ed page of *The New York Times*, placed by Mobil:

> Because Mobil operates in so many diverse locales, we are all too familiar with the stubborn problems afflicting education in America: the lack of rigor and consistency in student and teacher standards, assessments and accountability. . .
>
> To improve academic performance, states need to move toward greater consistency in their standards and their tests.

To the extent that businesses believe in transparency in order to pressure schools into performing better, another potent player is added to the mix in favor of a more standardized approach to reporting school performance and more uniform dissemination of that information.

Increasing Information Levels

Let's assume we can establish reasonable standards for judging parents' information levels, and let's assume that political pressure mounts to disseminate information about the schools: How much do we know about how to increase parents' information levels? Analysts need to begin to think more carefully and creatively about outreach and information dissemination activities. This leads to a new set of research questions, about which little is really known:

- How does information get disseminated?
- How can we reduce the costs of acquiring such information?
- Who accesses the various sources of information and with what consequences?

Traditional Methods of Reducing Information Costs:
Networks, Formal Sources, and Intermediaries

Shopping for schools is a complex task: Schools are multidimensional, their quality difficult to measure. In addition, information about their performance is often hard to uncover. Facing such difficulties, parents must develop strategies to aid them in their search for information.

A large body of research has documented the use of shortcuts to decisionmaking involving complex choices. These studies often focus on the decisionmaker as an *individual* (see, e.g., Payne et al., 1993). However, decisions are usually not made by individuals acting in isolation. M. Granovetter (1985) identified the importance of social networks as modifiers of purely individual actions, arguing that the individual decisionmaker is not an atomistic actor deciding alone but rather is embedded in social networks.

One of the most important aspects of networks is that they reduce the costs of gathering information. Not surprisingly, networks have been found to be important in the search for information about schools: Word of mouth and talking to others are among the most common ways that parents learn about schools (Witte, 1991; Witte et al., 1992; Wilson, 1992, p. 22; Boyer, 1992, p. 33; and Glenn, McLaughlin, and Salganik, 1993, p. 59). But as noted above there are differences in the way these networks of information are constructed. Thus, there are fundamental questions about the quality of networks—the most traditional form of information dissemination—and these questions are more important for parents with less education or those who are from racial minority groups.

If we desire to increase parents' information levels, then we need to devise strategies to involve parents in larger and better networks. However, the quality of networks is largely determined by the social milieu in which an individual lives. Although my colleagues and I have presented evidence that school choice increases the number of other individuals parents talk with, the effect is overwhelmed by racially and class-defined residential patterns.

In addition to social networks parents often use intermediaries as sources of information, most of which are school-based institutions. Teachers, administrators, and other staff act as contact points in the dissemination of information. Schools also engage in outreach activities, for example, creating brochures, distributing newsletters, and so on. However, as I have just argued, school officials often have a vested interest in *not* providing accurate information and, indeed, they may not have the comparative information about alternate schools in the parents' choice set that can help them make appropriate choices. In addition, there are often large status gaps between professional educators and low-income parents, making it difficult for some parents to approach the professionals for information.

Community organization centers can play a role as intermediaries. But I believe the quality of the information they have is often incomplete, and their ability to accurately compare performance across schools is often lacking. The schools themselves often have little or no incentive to engage in this outreach and dissemination.

I accept Henig's (1994) argument that in any attempt to make school choice work the "most important steps could be those that relate to the collection and dissemination of more useful information about how the schools are performing" (p. 219). Following this, I believe that we need to learn more about the flow of information and look for points at which that flow can be improved. In particular, I believe that there are new techniques and changes in information technology that can transform the level of information. The most obvious technology change is the Internet, but even using the Internet to disseminate information can exacerbate inequalities and broaden the "digital divide."

In the rest of this chapter, then, I will discuss a project that I launched in Washington, D.C., in 1999. The motivation for the study was the rapid diffusion of choice in the nation's capital (mostly through the chartering of a large number of new schools). Supported by both the Smith Richardson Foundation and the National Science Foundation, I am working with several community-based organizations in Washington to construct a website with comparative information about charter and traditional public schools, to ensure that this site is accessible to a wide range of parents, and to ensure that the presentation of the data is user-friendly. This action component is coupled with a research component to measure the extent to which the site is used, by whom, and to what effect. (For a more complete discussion, see Schneider and Buckley, 2000.)

Constructing an Internet Site for Schools in the District of Columbia

The Internet has emerged as a revolutionary means to obtain information cheaply about a wide range of products. According to the U.S. Department of Commerce, businesses in virtually every sector of the U.S. economy are using the Internet to control purchasing costs, manage supplier relationships, streamline inventory, and, most important from our research perspective, reach new and existing customers more effectively (1998, p. 2). In turn, the use of the Internet is spreading at an incredibly rapid rate. For an idea of the magnitude of the change, consider the following: In 1993, fewer than 5 million Americans were connected to the Internet, by 1997 that number had grown to over 60 million, and by 2000 was 100 million (U.S. Department of Commerce, 2000). As many as 70 percent of all 12- to 19-year-olds go online in any week (Sweeny, 1999). This growth will accelerate since broadband Internet access for residential households is close and Internet access via schools, libraries, and other public sites is increasingly commonplace.

The Internet has become a way in which individuals gather information about things that are important to them. According to a recent study by the Pew Research Center, the number of Americans who are going online to get their news has close to doubled in the last two years, and the number of well-educated and highly paid individuals using the Internet for news now surpasses those using broadcast TV (Pew, 2000). New tools are making the Internet more user-friendly and easier to navigate, and people will increasingly rely on the Internet to gather information about a whole range of topics.

This revolution in the flow and cost of information can be harnessed to resolve many questions concerning school choice. The fundamental issue is simple: If the Internet reduces costs for shopping for many consumer purchases, can the Internet reduce the costs of choosing a school? Many might object to this comparison, since schools are not cereal and as Hill (1995) notes: "The choice of a school is more akin to the choice of a family doctor or pastor than to the choice of a car dealer or grocery store" (p. 129).

Although on some level this is obviously true, if we explore the shopping process for major consumer products I believe we can easily define a role for the Internet in shopping for schools.

Is Shopping for a School the Same as Shopping for a Car?

As anyone who has shopped for a car knows, gathering information about options, costs, and performance can be time-consuming. Traditionally, consumers would visit showrooms to select a make and model that met their needs and budget. Many consumers, to say the least, obtain imperfect information, putting them at a disadvantage. The Internet has changed this, providing information on options, reliability, and costs across a range of cars at a relatively low cost. In addition, information can be displayed in a comparative fashion, simplifying choice.

There are similarities in shopping for a school: Parents need to gather information to identify the set of schools that meet their selection criteria; they need to gather information about the schools in their choice set; and they need to compare the relative performance of schools in their choice set on the aspects of schooling they value. Data must be presented in a comprehensible and user-friendly manner.

If parents have shopped around and gathered data about schools in their choice set, when they visit the schools they will be more knowledgeable consumers, better prepared to ask questions and evaluate the answers that are given. In addition, comparison shopping on the Internet means they can visit fewer schools.

In short, I believe that the use of the Internet can put parents in firmer control over the choice of schools their children attend. However, just as the rapid diffu-

sion of school choice leads to a set of fundamental research questions, the introduction of modern information technologies, including the Internet, to the
school choice process produces another set of complementary questions:

- Can we design a database that contains the right information to allow
  parents to identify their choice set of schools?
- Can we design a search engine that allows parents to negotiate that database, presenting school performance data in a user-friendly manner?
- Can we design a dissemination strategy so that parents can learn about
  the site and access it?

Perhaps the fundamental issue that researchers must face is the possibility that
parents of different racial, ethnic, and social backgrounds will have different abilities to take advantage of expanded choice, creating higher levels of racial segregation and class stratification. This leads to a fundamental question: Can we design these tools in such a way to minimize differences in the ability of different
types of parents to search for and use information about schools? Let me address
some of these issues.

What Do Parents Want to Know and Can We Give It to Them?

First, there seems to be a consensus among parents about what school conditions
they value. Consider the 1998 Public Policy Forum report on the results of a telephone survey of parents in Ohio and Wisconsin. The list of school choice attributes that the survey identified as being important is fairly representative of most
studies. I re-create their findings in Table 4.3. In general, this list shows that parents want information about fundamental characteristics of schools that we all
are likely to agree are important. However, as they say, the devil is in the details.

Consider the first item. In almost any similar study, most parents list good
teachers as the most important characteristic of education. What should we report
to allow parents to judge the quality of teachers? The number of teachers with advanced degrees? Average salary? Experience level? These questions point to the
more fundamental one: Do we really know what makes a good teacher? Assuming
that we do, what objective indicators point to that? Let's assume that we can agree
on some indicators; the next task is equally difficult: How can we summarize that
data in any way that is easily grasped by parents and that allows school comparison (which of course is the major goal of disseminating information)?

Let us look at another fundamentally important characteristic, one that causes
endless consternation among many administrators: comparative performance
data.

TABLE 4.3   What Information Do Parents Want About Schools?[a]

Item	Percent
Qualifications of teachers/administrators	85
How money is budgeted and spent	78
The results of a financial audit	78
The graduation rate	75
Scores on standardized tests	75
Student attendance rates	73
The curriculum	73
School's governing structure	70
The methods of teaching	66
The mission or philosophy of a school	65
Number of students suspended/expelled annually	61
Teacher turnover	55
Class size	55
Requirements for parental involvement	49
Racial or ethnic makeup of student body	33
Economic makeup of student body	29
Graduate placement	27

[a]This is actually a "surrogate" measure. It is the percentage of respondents who believe that schools should be required to report this information rather than allowing its reporting to be voluntary. However, the response pattern is fairly common to most other studies (see, for example, Schneider et al., 2000, chapter 4).

SOURCE: Adapted from Public Policy Forum (1998), table 7.

Schools differ widely in the characteristics of their student population, and we know that these demographics affect school performance. Since traditional public schools have the least control over the composition of their student population,[8] it follows that traditional public schools are at a disadvantage compared to private schools (both secular and parochial). More recently, and despite evidence that charter schools are at least as representative of local demographics as are traditional public schools (see, e.g., U.S. Department of Education, 1997), some have argued that this disadvantage also exists in comparison to charter and voucher schools.

Regardless of how the debate about stratification across school sectors plays out, we are still faced with the task of somehow standardizing school performance relative to the inputs of the school. There are at least two fundamental dimensions to this task: How do we standardize for different population composition of schools? How do we make sure that we are not unfair to schools that have high value added, even if their absolute level of performance is not high?

The most common way is to define an educational production function and assess how a school is doing relative to its resources, including its population. However, scholars are far from agreement on what to include in a production function (e.g., Clotfelter and Ladd, 1996, use *nine* different measures of school performance to assess performance among fifth-graders in South Carolina, and many of the indicators are not highly correlated). Even if we agreed to a production function to control for differences in student input, there are still difficult questions. How do we communicate this information in a format that parents can understand? Do we report residuals? Do we show them the equation that represented the production function? Do we say, "Trust me, I know what I'm doing"?

There is another possibility: Maybe the emphasis on standardized comparative data is wrong; maybe parents should try to get their child into the highest performing school possible, regardless of the quality of the inputs and the value added. Certainly, many public school officials would fight this position tooth and nail. We struggled with all these issues in our Washington study.

We believe that graphical comparisons are essential for communicating with most parents. We are using a series of questions to help parents narrow down their selection process to a manageable choice set and a set of manageable dimensions by which to compare schools. But there are now technological limits to how dynamic these comparisons can be, and some of our goals could not be realized.

We are also experimenting with different ways to report the equivalent of performance of any school relative to its inputs and over time. But attention spans are limited, and there are limits to how far we can water down technical information to explain how we created the standardized comparisons. This issue has plagued research on the schools and will plague efforts to make information more widely available.

Improving Presentation Techniques

If we can predict that the Internet or some version of it will be around for the foreseeable future, then let's assume that more and more information about schools will be made available by school districts and other providers, and let's also assume that more and more parents will have access to the Internet and use it to search for school information. I believe that we will need to address a newly emerging set of issues.

First, consider the kinds of data on the Internet today. Although I certainly have not visited every schools-based site, I have visited many. There are several types of sites being developed, many of them of uncertain usefulness. Among my favorite examples of what not to do is New York's site [www.nysed.gov/-emsc/info]. Here, huge amounts of data for any school in New York are reported in columns with confusing titles and without any comparative information. Below I repeat a few lines from that report card:

030101060001 1995–96 Grade 4 Science (PET)	Objective Content (of 29) 23.9
030101060001 1995–96 Grade 4 Science (PET)	Objective Skills (of 16) 12.3
030101060001 1995–96 Grade 4 Science (PET)	Manipulative Skills (of 40) 34.4

How this will help anyone shop for a school is beyond me. Of course, I am being somewhat unfair, as the data in those report cards can be downloaded and used for statistical analysis, but how many parents can do this?

Many states and localities, including New York, use another approach for disseminating school data that I also find of questionable value: reproducing printed report cards in a .pdf format. The result here is quite simple—if we can bore people to death with printed school report cards, with minimum effort we can put the exact same information on the Internet and claim credit for outreach and transparency without tapping the interactive nature of the Internet.

Some newspapers have reasonably good sites with some comparative information and interactive capabilities. One of the best that I have discovered is run by *The Washington Post* for schools in the D.C. metro area <www.washingtonpost.-com/wp-srv/local/longterm/library/schools/scores/front.htm>. Although this site is more interactive than most state sites, there are a few problems. First, it is a commercial site and cluttered with advertisements. Second, it is hard to find. Even knowing that the *Post* has the information is not sufficient, as some sites can be frustrating to locate. This leads me to several other points.

Who Should Gather and Report the Information?

Who should be reporting information about the schools? Should it be some public body? If so, which one(s)? Since we can't restrict the proliferation of Internet sites, can we regulate them in some way to make sure the information is correct? Or will it be caveat emptor in cyberspace?

In the Public Policy Forum report cited above, 31 percent of parents surveyed preferred that information be released through a public board consisting of representatives from both private choice and public schools; 25 percent through a state department of education; 11 percent through individual parents rather than an organization; 10 percent through an accreditation agency; and only 8 percent through schools themselves.

If these results are reliable, there is no consensus on this issue among parents, although many parents are obviously suspicious of the schools and local education agencies. This may reflect a fundamental doubt that public schools are really willing to make data available and usable.

Private sources of information, such as *The Washington Post*, were not included in the survey, so we have no idea how parents might feel about the balance between public versus private information providers, but should we rely on these sources to provide this fundamental information?

Differences in Reporting Requirements

There are vast differences in reporting requirements across states and, perhaps more important, across sectors: Private schools are often required to report much less information about performance and demographics than are public schools, and what information is available is often reported in noncomparable formats.[9] This leads to another issue, as yet unresolved: How can we ensure that parents have equal (and sufficient) information about schools in the public, charter, and private sectors to make intersectoral comparisons and choices?

Stratification in the Use of Information

Perhaps the most important issue in the evolution of information sources is once again the stratification issue. Let us assume that the Internet does evolve into a potent force for disseminating information about schools and allows for efficient comparison shopping. Computer literacy and access to computers with fast Internet connections become the entry price for using this tool. Many people who have studied the growth of computer use and the Internet are already concerned about the development of a digital divide between information haves and have-nots. Similarly, in the study of school choice this has been a highly contentious issue. If the Internet becomes an even more common tool for school shopping, to what degree do these issues reinforce each other? I believe that there are several design issues that flow from this basic question.

Site Name and Location

As noted, it is often difficult to locate a site, since the addresses are often arcane. In the D.C. project, we have created a simple domain name: DCSchool-Search.com. We are advertising this domain name widely; for example, we placed public service advertisements in buses and subways, projected information about the site in movie theaters, and engaged in other community outreach activities.

Outreach activities include an extensive mailing about this tool to the intermediaries who are central to the flow of information about schools: the schools themselves, parent organizations, churches, and community organizations. This mailing included a description of the site and the Internet address. We are conducting training and demonstration sessions for parent and community groups. But, as of this writing, we simply don't know which, if any, of these strategies will work (see Schneider and Buckley, 2000, for more on this issue).

Designing the Search Engine

We tried to design a search tool that allows parents to access the database along the dimensions they consider to be the most important. In addition, we believe that the data on the schools in a parent's choice set must be displayed in a comprehensible and comparative framework; that is, once a parent has chosen the dimensions on which she wishes to compare a set of schools, the data must be displayed in a way that allows the parent to see where a school falls relative to others.

This means that the search engine must be able to do several types of searches. For example, we know that location is one of the most important considerations in choosing schools, especially for parents with young children. Let us say that a parent will not consider a school that is more than a mile from her home. The search engine must be able to display a map of every school at the appropriate grade level within that geographic radius. Once this choice set has been defined, the parent must be able to access the database in several ways. For example, she might prefer to point and click on a given school and then get more information on any of the other measures in the database (test performance, demographics, etc.). We also know that parents, especially low-income parents, care about test performance (Schneider et al., 1998b). Thus, a search engine must enable a parent to identify the schools in a set radius and then see their comparative performance, but we were not able to fully implement this dimension in the DC-SchoolSearch site.

The list of possible queries is as long as it is evident. The point is clear: We must make the results of any search accessible and comprehensible to parents, many of whom have low education levels. This is a challenge that I hope we can meet; but, quite frankly, I have had many conversations with computer scientists, and what they call the "machine-human interface" is far from understood and, as noted, we were forced to make many compromises in the actual implementation of the site.

Collecting Demographic Data

Fundamental equity issues in the use of information about schools and the quality of subsequent choice of schools require tracking information about the parents who access the school database. In addition, as will be made clear below, collecting this information is essential for answering a basic set of outcome measures of the effects of choice. People using our site are asked to supply a set of standard demographic data—age, marital status, education level, race, and ethnicity. Plus they are asked to supply information about their prior experience with school choice—have they chosen schools for children before?

How do we know that people are giving us correct information? Recent legislation requires that children get parental permission before divulging any personal information on the Internet. How does this affect research on the use of the Internet as information tool? Similarly, I have run afoul of the human subjects requirement enforced at my university about how to meet informed consent requirements.

Our goal, then, is to see how different parents navigate the site and use patterns of information search as an indicator of preferences and efficiency in search. By tracking patterns of information search on the site (through session transcripts), we will have objective indicators of what parents actually consider important in the search for information (that is, we know what information they access first, second, etc.). We hope to study patterns of search and the implicit ranking of importance of different attributes as a function of demographics and experience with choice. These patterns will then help answer a set of questions about how different types of parents search for information about schools and whether or not certain parents are more or less likely to choose schools on nonacademic values.

Does Better Information Actually Lead to Better Choices?

Many arguments in favor of choice rest on a fundamental assumption: Higher levels of information can lead to better choices and better outcomes for individual parents. I have modified this argument by showing that not all parents need to be informed, and I have argued that we need a better understanding of how parental search processes can lead to enough information to make informed decisions. Even with these refinements, implied in much of this analysis is the idea that through better parental search and better parental use of information, schools and school systems will provide a better product and be more responsive to the needs and interests of an expanded set of informed and empowered parents.

However, even though this final link between better information and better schools remains a fundamental belief for many advocates of school choice, we as scholars still need to provide an empirical foundation strong enough to support such weight.

Setting an Agenda for Schools and Information

I have touched on many issues in this chapter. Here I highlight the most important items for establishing a research agenda on the role of information and the privatization of schools. Consistent with the primary focus of this chapter, I look at this issue primarily from the viewpoint of parents as consumers of information and the people ultimately charged with using information to make choices for their children. However, I do note issues that need to be addressed concerning how schools, other government agencies, and nongovernmental organizations can facilitate this flow of information.

I first consider several questions that are fundamental to any social-science effort to understand the relationship between privatization, information, and choice of public goods. Although I pose these questions in terms of the schools, clearly they are fundamental to a host of policy domains in which government has sought to introduce markets or marketlike mechanisms.

Role of Information

- How much knowledge is enough for parents to choose schools?
- Can parents still choose appropriate schools without pinpoint accuracy? Among the questions that are important here are the following: Do parents have ability knowledge? What heuristics or shortcuts to information do parents use? Who uses different shortcuts and to what effect? If networks are critical in the flow of information about schools, how can we intervene to make them of better quality and more efficient as a means of disseminating reliable information about the schools?
- Does choice actually motivate parents to be more knowledgeable? And if choice motivates only a small set of them, what are the implications of this pattern?

Informed Consumers and Markets

- How many informed choosers does it take to make a market?

- Can we better specify the role of the marginal consumer? Can we identify and measure the ability of a small number of active consumers (and schools of choice) to leverage other nearby schools via the competitive process?

Stratification and Those Left Behind

- Information, like most resources, is differentially distributed; how does this affect the operation of the schools?
- Does privatization increase the levels of segregation and stratification in schools by separating parents into those well-informed who make good choices for their children and those uninformed?

New Information Technologies and Intervening in the Flow of Information

- Can we harness the power of new information tools, especially the Internet, to disseminate information about the schools quickly and cheaply?
- Can we design a database that contains the right information to allow parents to identify their choice set of schools?
- Can we design a search engine that allows parents to negotiate that database, presenting school data in a user-friendly manner?
- Can we construct and present data in such a way as to reflect relative as well as absolute school performance? Here, there are several related questions: How do we standardize for different population composition of schools? How do we make sure that we are not unfair to schools that have high value added, even if their absolute level of performance is not high? How can we present these technical comparisons in a way that parents can understand?

Disseminating Information

- Can we design a dissemination strategy so that parents can learn about the schools and access new information technologies?
- What organizations should be put in charge of disseminating and certifying information about the schools? Or is caveat emptor the watchword for the evolving system of expanding choice?
- Can we somehow convince schools and school systems to participate in the design and dissemination of good and reliable information?

But perhaps the most important question of all is this: *How much of this can we do while making sure that we do not produce a new class of information haves and have-nots and increasing stratification and segregation in the schools?*

Notes

1. Many of the ideas presented in the first sections of this paper were developed during a project on school choice with Paul Teske and Melissa Marschall. We have developed these ideas in more detail in our book, *Choosing Schools: Consumer Choice and the Quality of American Schools*. Princeton: Princeton University Press, 2000.

2. The literature on rationality is voluminous. See A. Lupia and M. McCubbins (1998) for a good recent discussion of the issues associated with the use of rationality in politics and public policy.

3. The four districts were Community School District 1 and District 4 in New York City and Morristown and Montclair, New Jersey. The two central city school districts are similar demographically, but District 4 has a nationally known school choice program, whereas District 1 has only recently (and without much success) introduced choice. In the two suburban districts, Montclair also has a choice program, widely recognized for its quality, and Morristown is committed to residential zones. For more information on these data see Schneider et al. (1999) or Schneider et al. (2000).

4. It was not possible to gather objective data for the child's specific grade level or class, only for the whole school, but since parents choose schools rather than classes, that is probably the most appropriate level of analysis.

5. Although behavioral decision theorists have discussed a wide-ranging set of heuristics that act as shortcuts to decisions, most political science work has focused on interpersonal cues as shortcuts.

6. On the importance of the "marginal consumer" in creating efficiency in schools, see Teske et al. (1993) and Schneider, Teske and Marschall (2000).

7. In fact, they asked me to provide them with the information if I was able to gather it from the schools.

8. We have all heard some version of the following sentiment from public school officials: "If a student screws up in a Catholic school, the student gets kicked out and ends up here. If one of my students screws up, I'm stuck with him."

9. Private schools also seem to be relatively immune to queries from prestigious news organizations. In the January 18, 1999, cover story on outstanding high schools, *U.S. News and World Report* presented results from a study of more than 1,000 high schools in six metropolitan areas. They note, however, that many private schools that aren't in Catholic parochial systems refused to return the survey.

References

Althaus, S.L. (1995, September). *The practical limits of information shortcuts: Public opinion, political equality, and the social distribution of knowledge*. Paper presented at the annual meeting of the American Political Science Association, Chicago.

Anhalt, B.E., DiGaetano, A., Fraga, L.R., and Henig, J.R. (1995, April). *Systematic reform and policy effort in urban education.* Paper presented at the annual meeting of the Midwest Political Science Association, Chicago.

Ascher, C., Fruchter, N., and Berne, R. (1996). *Hard lessons: Public schools and privatization.* New York: Twentieth Century Fund.

Bartels, L. (1996). Uninformed votes: Information effects in presidential elections. *American Journal of Political Science* 40(1), 194–230.

Bickers, K., and Stein, R. (1998). The micro foundations of the Tiebout model. *Urban Affairs Review* 34, 76–93.

Bloch, P., Sherrel, D., and Ridgway, N. (1986). Consumer search: An extended framework. *Journal of Consumer Research* 13, 119–126.

Bridge, G. (1978). Information imperfections: The Achilles' heel of entitlement plans. *School Review* 86, 504–529.

Card, D., and Krueger, A. (1992). Does school quality matter? Returns to education and the characteristics of public schools in the United States. *Journal of Political Economy* 100(1), 1–40.

Caterall, J. (1992.) Theory and practice of family choice in education. *Economics of Education Review* 11, 407–416.

Chubb, J., and Moe, T. (1990). *Politics, markets, and America's schools.* Washington, D.C.: Brookings Institution.

Clotfelter, C. T., and Ladd, H. F. (1996). Recognizing and rewarding success in public schools. In H. F. Ladd (ed.), *Holding schools accountable.* Washington, D.C.: Brookings Institution.

Clune, W., and Witte, J. (eds.) (1990). *Choice and control in American education,* vol. 1. New York: Falmer Press.

Cohen, J., and Chakravarti, D. (1990). Consumer psychology. *Annual Review of Psychology* 41, 243–288.

Coleman, J., Campbell, E. Q., Hobson, C. J., McPartland, J., Mood, A. M., Weinfeld, F. D., and York, R. L. (1966). *Equality of educational opportunity.* Washington, D.C.: U.S. Government Printing Office.

Coles, C. M., and Kelling, G. L. (1996). *Fixing broken windows: Restoring order and reducing crime in our communities.* New York: Free Press.

Coons, J .E., and Sugarman, S. D. (1978). *Education by choice: The case for family control.* Berkeley: University of California Press.

Delli Carpini, M., and Keeter, S. (1996). *What Americans know about politics and why it matters.* New Haven: Yale University Press.

Fiske, S., and Taylor, S. (1991). *Social cognition.* 2d ed. New York: McGraw Hill.

Glenn, C., McLaughlin, K., and Salganik, L. (1993). *Parent information for school choice: The case of Massachusetts.* Report No. 19. Boston: Center on Families, Communities, Schools, and Children's Learning.

Granovetter, M. (1985). Economic action and social structure: The problem of embeddedness. *American Journal of Sociology* 91, 481–510.

Henig, J. (1994). *Rethinking school choice: Limits of the market metaphor.* Princeton: Princeton University Press.

Hess, F. (1999). *Spinning wheels: The politics of urban school reform.* Washington, D.C.: Brookings Institution.

Hill, P. T. (1995). *Reinventing public education.* Santa Monica, Calif.: RAND.

Iyengar, S. (1989). How citizens think about national issues: A matter of responsibility. *American Journal of Political Science* 33, 878–900.

Kardes, F. R. (1994). Consumer judgment and decision processes. In R. S. Wyer and T. K. Srull (eds.), *Handbook of social cognition*. Hillsdale, N.J.: Erlbaum.

Kuklinski, J. H., and Hurley, N. L. (1994). On hearing and interpreting political messages: A cautionary tale of citizen cue-taking. *The Journal of Politics* 56, 729–751.

Kuklinski, J. H., Quirk, P. J., Schwieder, D., and Rich, R. F. (1996, August/September). *Misinformation and the currency of citizenship*. Paper prepared for delivery at the 1996 annual meeting of the American Political Science Association, San Francisco.

Lazarsfeld, P. F., Berelson, B., and Gaudet, H. (1944). *The people's choice: How the voter makes up his mind in a presidential campaign*. New York: Duell, Sloan, and Pearce.

Lodge, M., and Stroh, P. (1993). Inside the mental voting booth: An impression-driven process model of candidate evaluation. In S. Iyengar and W. McGuire (eds.), *Explorations in political psychology*. Durham, N.C.: Duke University Press.

Lupia, A. (1992). Busy voters, agenda control, and the power of information. *American Political Science Review* 86, 390–404.

_____. (1994). Short cuts versus encyclopedias: Information and voting behavior in California insurance reform election. *American Political Science Review* 88, 63–76.

Lupia, A., and McCubbins, M. (1998). *The democratic dilemma: Can citizens learn what they need to know?* Cambridge: Cambridge University Press.

Payne, J. W., Bettman, J. R., and Johnson, E. J. (1993). *The adaptive decision maker*. New York: Cambridge University Press.

The Pew Research Center for the People and the Press. June 8, 1998. *Internet access takes off*. <www.people-press.org/med98rpt.htm>

The Pew Research Center for the People and the Press. June 11, 2000. *Investors now go online for quotes, advice: Internet sapping broadcast news audience*. <www.people-press.org/media00rpt.htm>

Popkin, S. (1991). *The reasoning voter: Communication and persuasion in presidential campaigns*. Chicago: University of Chicago Press.

Price, V., and Zaller, J. (1993). Who gets the news? Alternative measures of news reception and their implications for research. *Public Opinion Quarterly* 57, 133–164.

Public Policy Forum. (1998). *Choice school accountability: A consensus of views in Ohio and Wisconsin*. Milwaukee: Public Policy Forum.

Ravitch, D., and Viteritti, J. (1996). A new vision for city schools. *Public Interest* 122, 3–16.

Rose-Ackerman, S. (1992). *Rethinking the progressive agenda: The reform of the American regulatory state*. New York: Free Press.

Schneider, M., and Buckley, J. (2000). *Can modern information technologies cross the digital divide to enhance choice and build stronger schools?* New York: Teachers College Center for the Study of Privatization in Education. <www.tc.columbia.edu/ncspe>

Schneider, M., Marschall, M., Teske, P., and Roch, C. (1998b). School choice and culture wars in the classroom: What different parents seek from education. *Social Science Quarterly* 79(3), 489–501.

Schneider, M., Teske, P., Roch, C., and Marschall, M. (1997). Networks to nowhere: Segregation and stratification in networks of information about schools. *American Journal of Political Science,* 40:1201–1223.

_____. (1998a). Shopping for schools: In the land of the blind, the one-eyed parent may be enough. *American Journal of Political Science* 42(3), 769–793.

_____. (1999). Heuristics, low information rationality, and choosing public goods: Broken windows as shortcuts to information about school performance. *Urban Affairs Review* 34(5), 729–741.

Schneider, M., Teske, P., and Marschall, M. (2000). *Choosing schools: Consumer choice and the quality of American schools*. Princeton: Princeton University Press.

_____. (1957). *Models of man*. New York: John Wiley and Sons.

Simon, H. A. (1986). Rationality in psychology and economics. In R. M. Hogarth and M. W. Reder (eds.), *Rational choice: The contrast between economics and psychology*. Chicago: University of Chicago Press.

Skogan, W. G. (1990). *Disorder and decline: Crime and the spiral of urban decay in American neighborhoods*. New York: Free Press.

Smith, K. and Meier, K. (1995). *Politics, markets, and fools*. Armonk, N.Y.: M.E. Sharpe.

Sniderman, P. M., Brody, R. A., and Tetlock, P E. (1991). *Reasoning and choice: Explorations in political psychology*. New York: Cambridge University Press.

Sweeney, C. (1999, October 17). In a chat room you can be N E 1." *New York Times Magazine* (late edition—final), sec. 6, p. 66.

Teske, P., Schneider, M., Mintrom, M., and Best, S. (1993). Establishing the micro foundations of a macro theory: Information, movers, and the competitive local market for public goods. *American Political Science Review* 87, 702–713.

Tybout, A., and Artz, N. (1994). Consumer psychology. *Annual Review of Psychology* 45, 131–169.

U.S. Department of Commerce (1998). *The emerging digital economy*. Washington, D.C: Secretariat on Electronic Commerce.

U.S. Department of Education. (1997). *A study of charter schools: First-year report*. Washington, D.C.: Office of Educational Research and Improvement.

Wells, A. S., and Crain, R. L. (1992). *Do parents choose school quality or school status?* Unpublished manuscript, UCLA.

Wilson, J. Q., and Kelling, G. L. (1982). Broken Windows: The police and neighborhood safety. *Atlantic* 249(3), 29–38.

Wilson, S. F. (1992). *Reinventing the schools: A radical plan for Boston*. Boston: Pioneer Institute.

Witte, J. F. (1991). The Milwaukee Parental Choice Program. In E. Rasell and R. Rothstein (eds.), *School choice: Examining the evidence*. Washington, D.C.: Economic Policy Institute.

Witte, J. F., Bailey, A. B., and Thorn, C. A. (1992). *Second year report: Milwaukee Parental Choice Program*. Madison: University of Wisconsin, Robert M. LaFollette Institute of Public Affairs.

Zaller, J. (1992). *The nature and origins of mass opinion*. Cambridge, U.K.: Cambridge University Press.

Preschools and
Higher Education

5

Preschools and Privatization

ELLEN MAGENHEIM

Unlike primary and secondary education, which has been widely held to be a public responsibility, the care of preschoolers has traditionally been viewed as the private responsibility of the family. That perception, by no means universal, has slowly been changing. Although some still hold that the care and education of young children is a private obligation, the belief is becoming more common that there is some public responsibility to ensure that children enter school ready to learn; participation in early childhood education programs can contribute to that objective. This involves a shift in thinking with respect to financing of preschool education; this is reflected in the development of tax credits to lower the cost of purchasing child care, and in public financing of federal and state early childhood education programs. The expansion of the Head Start program, enforcement of state child care regulations, and increasing public financing support for public and private preschool programs all reflect this shift in perception.

The impetus for change has two dimensions, which are explored more fully below. The first arises from the substantial increase in women's participation in the labor force, particularly by mothers of young children. The second, as noted above, is growing recognition that early childhood education programs can contribute to children's development, particularly to their ability to enter grade school ready to learn. These two dimensions highlight the fact that early childhood education is at the nexus of needs among working parents and children. In this context, I examine the questions raised by privatization in the provision of early childhood education.

The Issues

Unlike other types of education, early childhood education and, more generally, child care, have long been provided predominantly through the private sector. E. Kisker et al. (1991) estimate that about one-third of child care centers (including early childhood education programs) are for-profit and two-thirds are nonprofit. Within the nonprofit category, 9 percent are Head Start programs, 8 percent public school programs, and the balance are independent or sponsored (e.g., by a religious organization) programs. In other words, it appears that only 9 percent are definitely publicly provided, and some portion of the Head Start programs may involve public support. Although these categories do not correspond precisely to early childhood education providers, they do give an impression of the composition of the field. Further, the tradition, again with the exception of Head Start and a relatively small number of publicly funded programs, has been for early childhood education to be paid for by parents.

The field offers a range of interactions between private and public sectors; consumers and producers interact along this continuum, from private to public sector. At one extreme are private individuals paying for services provided by private programs. At the other extreme are private individuals whose children participate in public preschools, offered as part of the public education system. In-between are a range of types. First, there are private individuals who receive subsidies through the Child and Dependent Care Tax Credit or Dependent Care Spending Accounts; that is, their purchases of child care or early childhood education activate beneficial tax treatment. Second, there are private service providers operating with funding from public sources or a mix of public and private funds and operating in compliance with local, state, or federal regulations. Third, there are individuals, with vouchers or cash subsidies, choosing from the full range of early education and child care providers that are available in their communities. In each of these three intermediate cases, there are private decisionmakers whose consumption or production decisions are affected by public funds.

Despite the fact that private provision, financing, and parental choice are not new to the field, there are important changes occurring in the provision of early childhood education that make further examination of the implications of privatization important. At the most general level, the issue to be asked is whether the current mix of public and private providers (both for-profit and nonprofit) is optimal. Given the growth in publicly funded prekindergartens in many states, this is an important time to consider whether private and public concerns are well met by the highly fragmented and decentralized system of early childhood education that currently exists. What might be the advantages of having a fragmented, predominantly private system of provision as opposed to a public system? The standard thinking is that there will be more incentives for efficiency, greater responsiveness to consumer desires, and that competition between public and private providers may drive up quality while driving down costs and price. Conversely, public provision would capture economies of scale and help to alleviate variations in quality that are correlated with ability to pay and would, perhaps more importantly, help to overcome issues of accessibility for low-income families. Further, it is easy to apply to early childhood education the same argument that is applied to primary and secondary education; that is, there are positive externalities that are generated when young children participate in good early childhood education programs and that the market (i.e., the decentralized system) will produce less than the optimal quantity of early childhood education services.

Clearly, however, a move toward centralization and public provision of early childhood education through the public school system goes in the opposite direction of the rest of the education sector, meaning privatization. In a sense the early childhood education sector, which is already heavily privatized and, even in an era of increasing public funding, continues to be heavily reliant on private provision and parental choice, provides a laboratory in which many of the arguments made in favor of privatization of education can be tested. Before it is possible to begin to formulate an agenda for research in this area, a profile of what the world of early childhood education looks like is needed.

First, the primary component of such a project requires documentation of who provides the services, who receives them, and how they are financed. Second, it is important to consider what types of providers are most likely to meet the expanding demand for early childhood education programs. The 105th Congress approved passage of Public Law 105-285 (sec. 107) that allows for-profit providers to be Head Start grantees; prior to this amendment, Head Start grantees were either public or private and not-for-profit. In a time of growing demand, it is reasonable to predict that the role of for-profit providers will expand. Third, given this prediction, and given the mix of providers already in place, it is important to consider whether auspices matter. In other words, is there a distinction in terms of efficiency of production, price, and quality of care provided between public and private providers and, within the second category, between for-profit and nonprofit providers? Clearly, to the extent that there are discernible differences, there arise important implications for efficient use of resources expended both privately and publicly. The role of quality differences among providers is a complex and much debated one; there are debates over what constitutes quality (as defined by different constituencies), how to measure quality, and how to measure the effects of early childhood education program participation on children. In this chapter, I will not address in depth the quality debate, except to examine evidence on the relationship between the range of quality characteristics and provider auspices.

Fourth, the implications of financing for parental choice must be considered. Do parents paying for services privately make different choices than parents using vouchers or receiving cash subsidies, all else being equal? As parent subsidies and voucher use become more widespread—as they have through allocation of funds from the Child Care Development Fund (CCDF)—their effects on parental choice and the efficiency of use of resources call for further study. Fifth, it is important to consider whether the current trend (i.e., toward increasing public financing and, in some cases, provision of early childhood education for more children, particularly low-income children) will generate more widespread support for publicly financed and provided prekindergarten for all children, following the example set in a number of European countries. In the United States, there has been widespread acceptance of age five as the appropriate starting point for public education; it must be considered whether in the long run there will be increasing pressure for and acceptance of the appropriateness of universal early childhood education, and then, if so, whether this will be a desirable development.

Before turning to the question of why these topics are important, I would like to define what I will and will not include in the category of early childhood education for this chapter. The term "early childhood education" is sometimes used interchangeably with the more general term "child care," which can be used to include any type of arrangement that is primarily intended to care for children so that their parents can work. Child care encompasses a range of services, including informal care by a relative or unrelated individual in the child's home, family day care centers, child care centers, nursery schools and preschools, and multiple service education programs, the most well known of which is Head Start. Early childhood education programs have traditionally focused on the needs of children rather than on the employment needs of parents. Clearly, this overlaps with some types of child care, such as child care centers with an educational component. E. Zigler and Finn-Stevenson (1996) argue that it would be desirable to eliminate this distinction between child care and early childhood education, but the reality for now is that they meet different needs by, in most cases, providing different services, although, again, there may be overlap.

Working parents might arrange for their children to participate in early education programs as well as child care to cover all the parents' working hours. Children with mothers who are not in the formal labor force may participate in early childhood education programs in order to enjoy the developmental benefits. It is difficult to treat these two types of services as discrete; child care settings, such as centers, may include some developmental activities, even if development is not the primary focus; early childhood education programs may extend to full-day, year-round operation to meet the developmental needs of children and the employment needs of parents simultaneously.

The Head Start program offers a good example of this blurring of boundaries. It is, unambiguously, an example of early childhood education. As parents of children participating in Head Start enter the labor force or training programs, part-time Head Start programs are inadequate to meet the needs of parents for full-day, year-round operation, thus failing to serve early education and child care simultaneously. In this chapter, I will focus most of the discussion on explicitly educational programs, but it must be recognized that the overlap with child care is a complicated one, in terms of definition as well as private and public decision-making. Since different institutions use somewhat different definitions for distinguishing between child care and early education, some of the data presented later in this chapter may appear to be not directly comparable but will, nevertheless, indicate trends in participation in both types of care.

Another way to attempt to distinguish between early childhood education programs and child care programs is by the provider's self-report of the organizations primary objectives. Kisker et al. (1991) report that of center-based programs, 56 percent report that their main goal is to provide a loving environment; 20 percent report the main goal as child development, 13 percent school preparation, and 3 percent compensatory education.

Finally, adding to the complexity of this topic is the fact that the types of care that families choose for their young children follow systematic patterns as the child grows; it is more common for an infant or young child to be in in-home, relative care, or in a family day care home. When a child reaches age three, transitions into formal child care or early childhood education arrangements become more common; for that reason, in this chapter I focus on early childhood education primarily serving three- to four-year-olds. Employment of age three as the lower bound means that this chapter will not engage another area of growing interest and knowledge: the development of children under the age of three. This awareness is reflected in the establishment in 1994 of the Early Head Start program, which targets children younger than three from low-income families. Nevertheless, since the vast majority of early childhood programs focus on three- and four-year-olds, this lower age limit will be used in this chapter.

Why Are These Issues Important?

Study of privatization in early childhood education is important for two reasons: The first is related to the needs of working parents, the second to the needs of children.

The demand for nonparental child care has grown substantially over recent decades, primarily due to the increase in working mothers; in 1997, 61 percent of married mothers with children under the age of six were working (Council of Economic Advisors [CEA], 1998). Between the late 1970s and early 1990s, the number of children under age five with employed mothers being cared for by someone other than their parents rose from slightly over 3 million to nearly 8 million (CEA, 1997). These data provide evidence that it has become increasingly common for mothers of young children to participate in the labor market. Increased work requirements mandated by Temporary Assistance for Needy Families (TANF) is calling forth further increases in child care demand.

Parents solve their child care needs with a variety of options. The Census Bureau (Casper, 1996) reports that in 1993 children younger than five with employed mothers were in the following range of situations: 30 percent attended child care centers (which include center-based child care as well as nursery schools and preschools), 17 percent attended family child care homes, 25 percent were cared for by relatives other than parents, 5 percent were cared for by nonrelatives in the child's home, and 22 percent were cared for by the parents themselves.

Concurrent with growth in demand for all types of child care is the increasing recognition that preschool improves children's development and, more specifically, school readiness. This recognition was manifested in the establishment of the National Education Goals (the Goals 2000: Educate America Act was passed in 1994). Goal 1 ("All children will start school ready to learn") explicitly defines as an objective that "all children will have access to high-quality and developmentally appropriate preschool programs that help prepare children for school" (National Educational Goals, 1998). Further legislative support for educating young children was manifested in the expansion of Head Start (Head Start Amendments of 1994). More recently, Congress passed Public Law 105-285 (sec. 102), which makes explicit that school readiness is one of the goals of the Head Start program (although this was implicit in the prior statement of the goals of Head Start, the rewording stresses this objective). Further, Head Start funding has tripled between the late 1980s and 1998 (General Accounting Office [GAO], 1998). In addition, the Child Care Development Fund, which combines a variety of earlier funding programs including Transitional Child Care and the Child Care and Development Block Grants, provides additional funding for child care in general, some of which is used to pay for participation in early childhood education services.

Evidence that policymakers at the state level are responding to this goal can be seen in the increase in the number of states with publicly funded prekindergarten programs. A. Mitchell et al. (1998) find that thirty-nine states have funds for prekindergarten programs or other educational funding for four-year-olds and only eleven states have no state funds dedicated either to Head Start or other prekindergarten programs.

Data from earlier in this decade suggest that a relatively small portion of three- and four-year-olds participate in early education programs; evidence suggests that attendance is related to a number of family characteristics. According to Department of Education (DOE) data (DOE, 1998), in 1996, 37 percent of three-year-olds and 58 percent of four-year-olds were enrolled in preprimary education; figures jump to a much higher 90 percent for five-year-olds, presumably because of kindergarten enrollment. Preprimary education is defined by the DOE to include Head Start, nursery schools, prekindergarten, and kindergarten. Patterns of enrollment across racial, ethnic, and income groups varied. Specifically, black and white children were equally likely to participate; enrollment rates for Hispanic children were lower. There was a positive relationship between family income and enrollment and between parental educational attainment and enrollment. It is worth noting that participation in early childhood education programs has grown by 50 percent between 1980 and 1996 (Federal Interagency Forum on Child and Family Statistics, 1998).

Earlier evidence also suggests that family characteristics are associated with preschool attendance and that the children likely to enjoy substantial benefits from participation in early childhood education programs are among the least likely to participate. Using data from the 1990 census, the General Accounting Office (GAO, 1994) finds that children from low-income families or whose parents did not graduate from high school were least likely to attend preschool; S. Hofferth et al. (1994), using the National Household Education Survey, reports similar findings. This evidence, too, no doubt helps to support state expansion of prekindergarten funding and service provision.

The policy reaction to the school readiness goal and the recognition that there are income-, education-, and racial/ethnic-related patterns in participation has taken the form of a substantial increase in public financing and, to a lesser degree, provision of prekindergarten. In 1999, Vice President Al Gore, in a speech presenting his presidential campaign agenda, called for all public schools to make preschool education available *(New York Times,* 3/16/99). The range of options offered across the states is substantial: Georgia has a universal program financed by a new lottery; New Jersey will offer services for school districts designated as being in special need of services; and New York allows local districts to use funds to offer early childhood education programs. Services are typically provided through a mix of public and private providers, with some state funds used to expand the existing private early childhood education sector (for more examples, see Kaplan, 1998; Mitchell et al., 1998).

What can be seen clearly is that participation in preschool programs has risen over time and that attendance in programs is not evenly distributed across the population. If these attendance patterns are coupled with an overall increase in demand for child care and with concerns about children's preparedness for school and the ability of good preschool experiences to help with school readiness, then the importance of further examination of these issues can readily be seen. Next we consider the groups that have an interest in these issues and the nature of their concerns.

Who Are the Stakeholders with an Interest in This Issue and What Are Their Interests and Concerns?

The complex mix of consumers, producers, and funders of early childhood education translates into a list of stakeholders representing a range of interests in the current configuration of this sector and in potential changes that might occur with respect to provision and financing. In discussing their concerns, I rely primarily, but not exclusively, on recognition of the fact that these stakeholders are operating in a largely private market for early childhood education services, although one in which the public sector plays a big role with respect to funding and a smaller but still tangible role in provision. The diversity of providers and the ways in which consumption decisions are made and financed raises the potential for competition, a topic that surfaces repeatedly throughout the discussion below.

Who Are the Stakeholders with an Interest in This Issue?

The stakeholders with an interest in the issue of privatization and early childhood education include parents of the children who participate in these programs and parents of children who do not because of problems with accessibility and affordability (or by choice). The providers of early childhood education services, including public and for-profit and nonprofit providers, are interested in parental choices, public policies that will affect the conditions under which they provide their services, and in the actions of their competitors. The same considerations—that is, parental choice, public policies, and competitors' actions—are of interest as well to providers of child care services that are not explicitly educational but that are for some families substitutes for or complements to early childhood education.

Moving away from immediate consumers and producers of early childhood education, another set of stakeholders with an interest in the quantity and quality of early childhood education includes the teachers and schools that will receive these children into their classes and who, in systems that have public preschools, may be involved in the provision of services or the reallocation of resources toward preschools. Finally, policymakers at the local, state, and federal levels are stakeholders in this issue. Local policymakers' interests focus on school readiness issues; state policymakers' interests coincide with those of federal policymakers not only as to educational goals but also the ability of early childhood education providers to support the framework of services necessary to enable parents to work, with a special concern for the needs of low-income parents and those leaving welfare.

What Are the Stakeholders' Interests and Concerns?

The concerns that I list below are related to the current orientation of mixed public and private provision, to likely changes toward increasing privatization, and to the less likely possibility of a move toward more centralized public financing and provision of early childhood education programs.

Parents.   Parents can participate in the early childhood education sector in several ways. They can send their children to prekindergarten programs offered by local public schools; they can pay themselves for their children to attend a variety of types of preschools; they can use vouchers or subsidies to choose child care or early education programs for their children; or they can choose to not participate. Parents who participate have a range of concerns; some they share in common, but others are specific to their situation.

Parents' concerns include the availability, accessibility, quality, and cost of care. These are complicated by the fact, discussed above, that early childhood education can be seen to serve two goals simultaneously: child development and child care. Parents will be concerned with the extent to which early education programs foster children's development and, in some cases, the extent to which these programs enable parents to meet their work obligations. There will be parents, too, who are not committed to the importance of formal early childhood education (or child care more generally) and feel that children should be at home until beginning kindergarten or first grade; for such parents, public funding of prekindergartens may be a concern (see, e.g., *Los Angeles Times*, 3/14/99, on support for expansion of Child and Dependent Care Tax Credit eligibility to include at-home parents).

For parents who do want their children to participate in early childhood education programs, there will be issues of access and affordability. For very low income families, Head Start is an attractive option in that it is generally regarded as being of high quality. Nevertheless, Head Start has historically been unable to meet the needs of all children who are eligible for participation; in 1993, for example, Head Start was able to serve only 29 percent of eligible three- and four-year-olds (GAO, 1995); as Head Start funding has increased this problem has been ameliorated but not eliminated. Furthermore, historically Head Start programs have been part-day, part-year programs and, as a result, do not meet the needs of working parents. Although the number of, and funding for, full-day, year-round programs are growing, they are still limited.

Neither should it be suggested that issues of access, cost, and quality are relevant only to low-income families eligible for Head Start. Families across all groups may experience difficulties locating programs that meet their needs at a price that they consider affordable. Affordability is a complicated topic and raises the possible divergence between what parents say they are willing and what they are able to pay for care. A significant part of this problem of locating care arises from information asymmetries in the child care market that can make it difficult for parents to determine what options are available (Magenheim, 1995).

Discussions of quality of care are complicated in part because parental definitions of "quality care" may not coincide perfectly with expert opinion. For example, parents may put a relatively lower weight than do experts on child-teacher ratios and a higher weight on the program's location or hours of operation. Thus, parents may be concerned as to whether increasing public funding or regulation will lead to more or less care with respect to the characteristics they value.

The relationship between parents' concerns and the issue of privatization arises through the mechanism of competition and choice. Parents face issues of choice because ours is a predominantly private market with a substantial amount of product differentiation (Magenheim, 1995). If the mix of public and private providers facilitates competition, then in theory there should be pressure for providers to offer the types of services that parents want in an efficient (and therefore lower-cost) manner. One organizational alternative, of course, is to have universal, publicly provided early childhood education, with costs spread over all taxpayers and quality determined by educational experts. The trade-offs inherent in a transition to a centralized system are discussed later in this chapter.

Given the current configuration of public and private financing and predominantly private provision, parents may also be concerned about the extent to which their children are segregated in particular programs. The best example of this problem, again, is Head Start; because it must allocate 90 percent of slots to eligible children, Head Start ensures that nearly all the students in the program will be from low-income families. As D. Besharov and N. Samari (1998) note, vouchers—which allow parents to purchase early education services at any provider that will accept the voucher rather than the limited set of providers who have entered into grants or contracts with federal, state, or local governments—may help to reduce segregation. Thus, parents who are eligible for early education subsidies will be concerned with the form that the subsidies take and the extent to which the subsidies enable them to exercise choice.

Finally, it should be noted that some parents who believe that preschool-aged children should not be in any sort of nonparental care may express opposition to expanded availability of preschool programs, either public or private, funded by public dollars. Alternatively, some believe that tax credits, subsidies, and other programs that are available to help parents employed outside of the home to bear the cost of child care should also be made available to at-home parents.

Early Childhood Education Providers and Child Care Providers. I combine the discussion of the concerns of these two groups of stakeholders because they are so intimately related to one another. Before turning to their specific concerns, it is important to note that the diversity of current providers is not likely to be reduced by the increases in state funding for prekindergarten programs; only seven of the thirty-nine states that provide funding for prekindergarten programs require that funds go only to public schools (Mitchell et al., 1998). In addition, CCDF funds can be used to purchase services from any type of child care provider.

The providers of early education services will be most concerned with the extent to which the growth in public financing affects the demand for their services as well as the conditions they must meet in order to offer services and receive public funds. For example, in New Jersey, where early education programs will be offered as an outcome of the *Abbott v. Burke* school finance decision, terms have been specified regarding teacher qualifications and class size that are more stringent than is typical for early childhood education providers (see Barnett et al., 1999). If these requirements are upheld, some providers will have to hire additional and, in some cases, more highly trained teachers to meet the certification and staffing requirements. This, in turn, will put competitive pressure on salaries for teachers and assistants both by increasing demand overall and by increasing demand for more highly trained teachers. The first effect of this will be to raise the cost of production for the early childhood education providers. But as an additional effect, it may help to draw good workers in child care settings to the new, more highly paid opportunities. In turn, this may cause wages to rise in the regular child care setting, which again will lead to higher costs and prices. To put it more directly, by increasing demand for early childhood education and increasing costs through teacher certification and size requirements, costs and prices throughout this sector for both early childhood education and child care can be expected to rise. If public funds cover the additional costs then subsidized providers will be unharmed, but this pattern may cause a reduction in demand by private-pay clients.

A variation on this concern has arisen in New York, where publicly funded preschool services will be provided through public schools as well as through private providers because public provider capacity is inadequate to meet demand. If private providers train their workers to meet certification standards, concerns have been expressed that these newly certified teachers will then leave lower-paying jobs in private centers for higher-paying jobs in public schools (*New York Journal News*, 12/22/98). Although I pointed out earlier that increasing demand for certified teachers likely will drive up wages for teachers, there is no guarantee that they will rise in private programs to the same levels as in public schools. Overall, then, providers are concerned about how expanded public financing, demand, and quality requirements will affect input costs, demand, and their competitive position.

Competition between the range of private providers, both for-profit and non-profit, would obviously disappear as an issue if all early childhood education became integrated into the public school system (a proposal of this type, "The School of the 21st Century," is discussed in the next section). Although some of the child care and early childhood education labor force could be integrated into a public school–dominated system, differences in certification requirements might eliminate opportunities for the many less-educated members of the labor force to find employment in a public early childhood education system. Further, the potential for ownership and control of individual enterprises would be greatly restricted, although, presumably as with private primary and secondary schools, some parents would choose to send their children to private preschools with, perhaps, a particular religious or educational orientation. This discussion does not presume that it is likely that early childhood education will become a predominantly public enterprise; concerns of the type discussed here and in the next section suggest the concerns of stakeholders who might seek to support or oppose political proposals to move toward universal public provision.

Substitution of vouchers for grants and contracts between states and early education providers may also be a cause for concern among providers. If providers who previously had stable contract or grant relationships now have to compete with all providers for consumers, it may represent an unwelcome change in operation. Although increased use of vouchers and, therefore, increased opportunities for parents to exercise choice may have other positive benefits, they will presumably not be seen as desirable by providers who are losing more stable arrangements. In contrast, providers who did not have contracts or grants and who, as a result of vouchers, are accessible to a greater array of subsidized customers will view the move toward vouchers more positively.

Teachers and Schools.   The interests of teachers and schools can be divided into two general categories. First, this set of stakeholders is specifically interested in the extent to which children do enter school ready to learn, the role played by participation in early childhood education programs in meeting this goal, and the potential need to offer special services and supports to children who do not meet this goal when entering school. Second, to the extent that some prekindergarten programs will be offered by public schools, the kinds of issues about quality, adequacy of supply, and staffing considerations discussed immediately above may apply here as well, especially given that demand for resources for prekindergarten programs may be partially drawn away from expenditures on older children. In addition, there may be conflict over whether prekindergarten programs should be under the control of public schools and whether public funding should be provided only to the lowest-income districts, to all districts, or to some other configuration (for anecdotal evidence on these issues see, e.g., *New York Times*, 1/12/99; *Record*, 2/11/99).

One proposal that highlights the magnitudes of these possible concerns is "The School of the 21st Century" (Zigler and Finn-Stevenson, 1996; Finn-Stevenson, Desimone, and Chung, 1999). This program would integrate early childhood education into the public school system and is, in fact, being implemented at several schools now. Although a program of this type would largely solve the problem of accessibility for most parents, it also raises issues of control over resources, financing sources, and the loss of diversity in offerings that currently exists in the noncentralized system.

Policymakers.   Discussion of the concerns of policymakers is complicated by the fact that involvement varies by governmental level. Local governments are involved in implementing and enforcing regulations that affect provision of services and local school districts in providing public education. States' financial involvement in the education market can take a variety of forms. Following the typology developed by Mitchell et al. (1998), states can enable services to be provided in one of the following ways (if they provide state-funded services at all): through public school districts only; through school districts and other agencies by subcontracting with local school districts; and through school districts and other agencies by direct contract from state agencies. Federal policymakers—the third subset among this group of stakeholders—are concerned with allocation of funds to support parental purchases of child care, particularly for parents who need care as part of the welfare reform effort. I will examine a limited set of concerns arising from these policy responsibilities, considering what I think are the most basic issues regarding supply, quality, allocation of resources, and organization.

The question of whether there is adequate supply sounds straightforward enough (e.g., does supply equal demand?); however, it quickly becomes complicated by issues of quality, accessibility, and affordability. Evidence cited earlier indicates that not all children eligible are able to participate in Head Start programs, although they may be able to find places in other programs. Further, it is difficult to know whether parents who place their children in other arrangements—such as family day care homes or child care centers—do so because that is their first choice, because they cannot find an early childhood education program, or because they cannot find one that meets their work schedule. Therefore, if we look at the number of three- and four-year-olds and see how many slots there are in all types of care, that will not necessarily answer the question of whether there is adequate supply.

A common reaction to this phenomenon is that it is not a problem at all—it occurs in the consumption of many types of goods and services. Consumers may not be able to find a car they want or can afford; they may not be able to find affordable airfares for their travel dates. This may be par for the course in consumerism, but the stakes are much higher for early childhood education: school readiness as well as the positive externalities generated by good early childhood programs.

Anecdotal evidence from states establishing early prekindergarten programs suggests that shortages may be encountered (see *Hartford Courant*, 1/31/99). Some of the barriers to Head Start expansion that may be relevant to other types of providers as well are noted in a GAO study (GAO, 1995). These barriers to expansion may be problems only in the short run and will be resolved in the long run, but what is not known is how long this adjustment will take.

Beyond the simple question of quantity of new supply is the question of the quality of new supply. Evidence in the past has shown that for-profit child care providers have been quicker to respond to increases in demand compared to nonprofit and public providers (Magenheim, 1995). Although some researchers find no difference in quality, others report that for-profit providers offer, on average, lower-quality services than do nonprofit and public providers (Helburn, 1995; Whitebook et al., 1990; and Phillips et al., 1992); there may be cause for concern as to whether there will be enough care of appropriate quality or of the quality mandated by state regulations. These studies used child care rather than early childhood education programs as their sample, so caution must be used in interpreting the results. Discussions of quality are further complicated by the fact that parental preferences may not overlap precisely with those of early childhood experts, whose definitions are generally used in expert assessments. As was discussed earlier, for example, parents may put relatively higher weight on hours of program operation and availability of facilities for sick children than do experts; thus supply expansion may be limited by the regulated demands for quality even though parents might prefer aspects of care that would be less of a barrier to supply expansion.

An issue that policymakers need to face is how to allocate funds to subsidize provision of early childhood education. This can be done through grants and contracts between the public funding source and specific providers. This is, of course, the traditional model used for Head Start providers. One alternative, which has grown in popularity for subsidizing consumption of child care by low-income families with CCDF funds, is the use of vouchers. Decisions about how to allocate funds can complicate political decisionmaking about preschools. In one case, despite a state senate's support for prekindergarten programs intended to achieve a school readiness goal, the decision became complicated by one legislator's desire to allocate public funds for prekindergarten through vouchers. The focus of the discussion shifted from the goal of school readiness—for which there was widespread support—to the allocation mechanism, since vouchers were considered so controversial (*St. Petersburg Times*, 1/20/99).

States—or the federal government—can provide cash or vouchers to parents, who then use them to purchase early childhood education services from any provider. Vouchers are already widely used in the allocation of federal funds. Funds from the CCDF can be channeled to families in the form of cash or vouchers; they can also be transferred through grants or contracts directly to child care providers, although this is not typical (U.S. Department of Health and Human Services [HHS], 1998). Besharov and Samari (1998) discuss possible benefits of vouchers. Citing C. Ross and S. Kerachsky (in Besharov, 1996), they note that vouchers enable parents to choose from a greater range of options than if public funds go directly to a small set of providers.

Vouchers are lauded for their potential to facilitate competition, which in theory should lead to improved quality and lower prices. In support of this view, Besharov and Samari (1998) cite D. Osborne and T. Gaebler (1992), who argue that voucher recipients will not consume the services of providers who do not meet the needs of consumers, and will, as a result, drive them out of business. This argument holds, however, only if consumers are well educated about their options and have good information regarding the characteristics of alternative products. As noted earlier, this may not be the case for parents of children participating in early childhood education and child care programs (Magenheim, 1995). Although there are some institutions that serve to facilitate this transfer of information in the child care/early education sector, most notably resource and referral agencies, there is no conclusive evidence regarding the extent to which consumers have good information or the extent to which vouchers drive competition and generate the benefits noted above.

This puzzle is summarized neatly by D. Stoesz (1992), as quoted in Besharov and Samari. He notes that both the public and private sectors yield examples of poor-quality services. The question is how to compare the different outcomes yielded by consumption with vouchers, public provision, and purchases made with cash. Some argue that there are reasons to assume that the integration of early childhood education into the public schools will yield better outcomes (e.g., Zigler and Finn-Stevenson, 1995); others argue that cash or vouchers will be more successful. This is an open question in general and, with respect to purchases of early childhood education in particular, it deserves further study.

Policymakers will want to not only know how vouchers affect parental choices but also consider other effects of vouchers. The standard argument in favor of vouchers is that by allowing parents to exercise choice, lower-quality programs (i.e., the programs that parents do not choose) will have to improve the quality of their services and become more efficient or risk being driven out of competition. Policymakers should want to see whether markets in which vouchers are available encourage, all else being equal, more competition and yield better outcomes.

Besharov and Samari (1998) go further in considering other possible effects of vouchers; specifically, they consider whether use of vouchers in child care (including but not limited to early education programs) can lead to cost increases or distributional distortions. For example, they cite evidence that providers offer discounts to private-pay consumers but charge consumers using vouchers the voucher limit even if it is above their normal fee. Thus, vouchers financed with tax dollars are used to subsidize private consumers; this is a distributional distortion that policymakers presumably did not intend. Further, public costs may increase if CCDF vouchers, which can be used for any type of child care arrangement, may result in relatives and friends—who had previously watched children for no charge—will now be paid for their work. On the one hand, this may simply reflect the monetization of a valuable transaction that would occur anyway without public compensation, but it does mean that more tax dollars will be channeled through vouchers than if these relatives could not now be paid. On the other hand, it is possible that voucher recipients, if prohibited from using the vouchers to pay relatives, might alter the child care arrangement that they use. In total, this suggests that there are many questions that need to be explored regarding the effects of vouchers on child care choices.

Federal and state policymakers dealing with welfare reform issues are likely to be concerned with the extent to which public funds that are used for early childhood education facilitate the labor market activities of former and current TANF participants. As noted above, although the focus in the types of expenditures of concern here is on preparing children for school through early childhood education, programs serve a dual purpose in meeting the needs of children and working parents. Evidence of this duality from a policy perspective is seen in increasing pressure and expenditures to support expansion of Head Start to full-day, year-round operation. Such expansion allows eligible children to enjoy the benefits of participation in Head Start while enabling their parents to work.

To summarize, concerns held by the parents, educators, producers, and policymakers arise from the combination of an existing fragmented and diverse set of early childhood education providers, competing in part with child care services, in a time of growing demand and expanding public finance. The importance of these concerns is amplified by the growing recognition that good early childhood education improves student achievement and the well-being of children and society.

What Types of Studies Might Address These Concerns?

The concerns raised above fall into several general categories dealing with supply, quality, vouchers, and the optimality of a fragmented rather than a centralized early childhood education delivery system. More specifically, the concerns can be restated in the form of the following questions:

1. Is there an adequate supply of early childhood education services? If not, what should be done to generate that supply?
2. How do public and private providers differ? Do they differ in ways that have important implications for the effects of early childhood pro-

grams on children and on public policy toward early childhood education?

3. What are the effects of participation in preschool programs on children?

4. How do vouchers affect parental decisionmaking and behavior of providers?

5. What is the optimal arrangement for delivery of early childhood education services? Is it the current fragmented system or a centralized public system?

6. More specifically, what are the advantages and disadvantages of each type of system?

First, I will review the existing literature that addresses these topics, then consider other types of research efforts that might inform these questions.

Review of the Literature

Before reviewing the existing literature on these topics, it is worth repeating the difficulty in distinguishing between child care and early childhood education services. In some studies the distinction is made clear, but in others it is less well defined. Although it is easy to set aside types of child care for younger children such as in-home care or family day care homes that do not have an explicit educational focus, it is harder to distinguish between formal child care, which may or may not include educational activities, and programs that are explicitly intended to educate preschoolers. When the lines are not clear in the literature reviewed below, the ambiguity will be noted.

Is There Adequate Supply?   As noted above, the question of adequate supply appears to be straightforward but is not. Estimates can be made using population data and information on slots in licensed early childhood education programs, but the complications of the issues discussed above—particularly whether parents can find early childhood education programs that meet their needs—must be considered. Further, there is the question of what characteristics that supply will have. In other words, given the channeling of public funds for prekindergarten through private providers, there may be mismatches between the types of programs that are in excess and for which there is excess demand. As with supply in general, a privatized system in which competition is lively should have market forces take care of mismatches, but this presumes that the market will function as it should.

Finally, it must be asked how quickly supply will respond to changes in demand. If, for example, a voucher system allows parents to increase their demand for certain types of programs, will there be an adequate demand response? Presumably some of the recent or ongoing evaluations of state-funded prekindergarten programs, discussed more fully below, will shed light on this question.

How Do Public and Private Providers Differ?   This issue concerns parents who make individual decisions about child care as well as policymakers who need to consider whether funds are being used to produce quality programs and whether resources are being used efficiently. The question here is whether public and private providers differ in the characteristics of the services they offer; yet economic theory suggests it is important to distinguish between for-profit and nonprofit providers, so it is really a three-way rather than a two-way distinction. One of the economic theories of why nonprofit organizations exist rests on information asymmetries and suggests that nonprofit institutions will arise when product quality is difficult to measure (Hansmann, 1980), as is true in the child care market. Nonprofit status signals that a provider has some objective other than profit maximization and thus may be more trustworthy than for-profit providers. Public providers are hypothesized to face still other incentive structures. Thus, this would lead to the prediction that quality levels may vary across all three types of providers.

Conclusions are difficult to draw, because previous studies present conflicting evidence, and some are not focused specifically on early childhood education programs. S. Helburn et al. (1995) report that there is no difference in quality between for-profit and nonprofit child care centers except in North Carolina, where state regulations allowed low staff training and low staff-to-child ratios. Other studies, however, including M. Whitebook et al. (1990) and D. Phillips et al. (1992), report that nonprofit providers offer higher-quality care compared to for-profit providers. Again, these results were derived from samples of child care centers, not early childhood education providers.

Research on the relative efficiency of different types of providers is also inconclusive. N. Mocan (1995a, 1995b) finds that there is no difference in the efficiency of for-profit and nonprofit providers but does find that providers that receive public funds—and therefore may be required to meet higher quality standards—operate at higher costs. Mukerjee et al. (1990) find that nonprofit providers have higher costs than for-profit providers. They trace these cost differences to the fact that nonprofits are characterized by different inputs and outputs (for example, they pay higher wages, and there is more teacher-student interaction), rather than because of inefficiency. These conflicting findings, coupled with the limitation that these data are not solely from early childhood education programs, suggest that there is no consensus on this issue.

What Are the Effects of Participation in Preschool Programs on Children's Development?   There is a large body of literature examining the effects of participation in early childhood programs. I will not attempt to review this very sizable literature but will mention findings and limitations that are indicative of the literature at large. Studies find a positive association between preschool participation and literacy scores (National Household Education Survey, October 1995), grade retention, social behavior (Barnett, 1995), school competence, and health status (such as immunization rates) (Reynolds et al., 1997). A. Reynolds et al. (1997) and S. Barnett (1995) review many of these studies. Results vary in terms of the magnitude and duration of positive results (Reynolds et al., 1997; Currie and Thomas, 1998). Further, the studies represent a broad range of evaluation techniques, and there are questions as to how informative or comparable some of these evaluations are (GAO, 1997).

An interesting insight into the long-term effects of participation in early childhood education programs, presented by J. Currie and D. Thomas (1998), highlights the need for further and careful analysis of the effects of these programs. They explore the findings from previous work that the positive effect of Head Start participation on black children's test scores disappears more quickly compared to white children. They report, based on their analysis of the 1988 wave of the National Educational Longitudinal Survey, that subsequent to their Head Start participation black children attend schools of lower quality than do white students. Thus, the shorter duration of the gain from Head Start may be associated with attendance at lower-quality schools. This finding suggests that analysis of the longer-term effects of early childhood program participation requires detailed analysis of the educational (and perhaps other) experiences that occur as the children age. This will help in the effort to distinguish between which effects can be attributed to early childhood education programs and which to other life experiences and characteristics.

More insight into this question should be gained in the future from the ongoing National Institute of Child Health and Human Development (NICHD) Early Child Care Study (HHS, NICHD, n.d.). This study follows a large sample of children during their first seven years of life and considers a wide range of child care characteristics, family characteristics, and aspects of child development, including social and language development, and behavior problems. Interestingly, analysis thus far finds that stronger predictors of children's behavior are found in the family, especially in maternal sensitivity, than in child care participation.

More evidence will be reported as the children move through early childhood education programs and enter school.

A related question is which aspects of early childhood education are related to child outcome. In other words, are positive effects associated with group size and staff-to-child ratios or specifically with teacher training? This kind of information, some of which will also be yielded by the NICHD study, will help policymakers to work through the kinds of supply problems that might arise as noted above. If, for example, child outcomes are related only weakly, if at all, to teacher certification levels, then it would not be deleterious to, as New Jersey Governor Christine Todd Whitman has proposed in 1999 (Associated Press, 2/19/99), allow teachers with lower levels of training rather than B.A. degrees to teach in publicly funded early childhood education programs, especially if there are other features present that are shown to be positively associated with child outcomes.

To repeat, this discussion only touches on the very large number of studies that attempt to determine the effects of participation in early childhood programs. This literature clearly demonstrates a positive relationship between a variety of child outcomes and participation in childhood programs; to draw stronger conclusions requires a careful review of this literature to determine exactly what types of programs are included in the sample and to consider methodological issues, particularly whether there are adequate controls incorporated to deal with selection bias problems and to determine how generalizable are results from the particular samples employed.

Potential sources of information on these issues are state program evaluations. Some states are already engaged in evaluation efforts; J. Kaplan (1998) reports that state evaluations generally compare the differences in school performance and behavior between participants in state preschool programs and nonparticipants. Mitchell et al. (1998) report that of the thirty-nine states that allocate funds to at least one type of prekindergarten program, twenty-six have or are conducting evaluations. The types of evaluations cover a broad range, although most focus on measuring the effects of preschool participation on child development, school readiness, and subsequent school performance. For examples of two of what appear to be the most comprehensive evaluations see the High/Scope evaluation of the Michigan School Readiness Program (1997) and the Frank Porter Graham Center at the University of North Carolina evaluation of the North Carolina Smart Start Program (1998).

How Do Vouchers Affect Parental Decisionmaking and Behavior of Providers? As Besharov and Samari (1998) note, very little research has been done on the use of vouchers in child care; a fortiori, little is known about vouchers and early childhood education decisions in particular. Possible effects of vouchers, as raised by Besharov and Samari (1998), have already been noted throughout this chapter, as has the need for future study.

What Is the Optimal Arrangement for Delivery of Early Childhood Education? Although I have treated this as a separate topic, it really is a composite of the earlier questions. In other words, are the benefits of having a fragmented system, in which providers—public, private for-profit, and private nonprofit—coexist preferable to a centralized public system? Given how little is known about the questions I raise above, it is obvious that this one has not been answered analytically; I raise it here as the most general statement of the questions concerning provision of early childhood education programs.

A Recommended Research Agenda

In attempting to answer the questions I pose, the many current state initiatives regarding provision of prekindergarten offer a good laboratory in which to begin. Many of these are being evaluated or soon will be. Although these evaluations may be a good step toward understanding the effects of participation in early childhood education programs, they likely will not focus on all of the concerns raised above. In other words, even though they may shed light on the school readiness of children who do and do not participate in preschool, there will most likely remain some unanswered questions regarding adequacy of supply; the relative attractiveness, effectiveness, and efficiency of different types of programs; the kinds of information parents use to make choices; how vouchers and subsidies affect parental decisionmaking; and how producers respond to competitors' behavior.

How, then, can we determine the answers to the questions above? I propose three projects of varying scope that will help to provide answers.

Project 1: Review Existing Studies and Program Evaluations. A good starting point is to conduct a review to determine what is known about the participation by children in early childhood programs. At the most general level, studies should be included in the review if they address one or more of these questions:

1. Who provides early childhood education programs, and what are the characteristics of the programs offered? Are there systematic patterns with respect to auspices and population served, program characteris-

tics, and efficiency? Which providers respond to increases in demand and/or funding? What are the characteristics of their supply?

2. What are the relationships between program quality variables and child outcomes? Are there tradeoffs discernible between quality variables? For example, can large group size be compensated for by teacher certification or supplemental training?

The review should include both earlier research and recent program evaluations. Earlier research should be included in this review as appropriate, but particular emphasis should be given to recent evaluations that will reflect more up-to-date experience. Study of earlier and current research may offer interesting insight into how early childhood education programs operate, how they are viewed, and how they have changed over time. Inclusion of the more recent evaluations would also provide timely insight into the adequacy of supply. In analyzing the effects of program participation on child outcomes, particular attention should be paid to the validity of the analytical techniques employed and the generalizability of results across samples.

A careful review of this type will allow separation of what is known about child care programs in general as opposed to early childhood education programs in particular. Throughout this chapter I have tried to distinguish between child care and early childhood education; this review will help to further distinguish these categories. As more children are in nonparental care and if demand is growing by parents for educational components in care, the two types of programs, at least for older preschool children, may be converging over time. Insight into this possible convergence may be yielded by this review.

Project 2: Review Literature on Parental Choice and Patterns of Participation. A related project represents an effort to gain insight into the patterns of participation in early childhood education programs. Are the rates of participation across racial, ethnic, income, and education groups attributable to affordability, accessibility, or choice? The information that should be considered in this review includes the kinds of programs that parents choose and the variables that affect their choices. Variables to be considered include the availability of information about programs; whether parents pay the full cost or are subsidized or have vouchers; and the extent to which parental preferences overlap with expert recommendations.

The findings of this review could provide a foundation for the design of policy to increase participation in low-participation populations in which school readiness is inadequate. For example, if the problem is one of information (either about what resources are available or about the benefits of participation in programs) rather than affordability, then parent education programs and expanded activities by resource and referral agencies might be a more effective response than increasing subsidies.

Project 3: Follow, Document, and Analyze the Preschool Program Implementation Process for One or More States.   With Projects 1 and 2 as preparation and background, the next step would be to follow and analyze a state preschool program implementation process. The objective is to answer basically the same questions addressed in Project 1 and 2 but with more control over the collection of information and analysis of data and for programs that are currently being implemented.

The objective here is not to determine the benefits of participation in early childhood education programs. There is substantial evidence that such benefits exist, but more insight is needed into how those benefits are generated and how likely a system that combines public and private financing and provision is to generate those benefits and for whom. The difference is that many studies look at particular programs, rather than the range of programs offered by the system as a whole, or they do not simultaneously address the other market-related variables that should be considered. To summarize, the objective of the proposed project is to determine, for a given state or set of states, whether a largely privatized system of provision yields the desirable mix of program characteristics; which providers are supplying the programs; whether parents are able to access the care that offers these characteristics; and whether different means of allocating public funds (e.g., contracts or vouchers) are more likely to generate the desired mix of providers. By looking at a state's implementation experience, it will be possible to see how the answers to these questions differ in different markets (e.g., how income, population density, and demographic characteristics affect these outcomes).

How can this information be collected? It would be desirable to undertake a study in a large state such as New York or New Jersey that is phasing in a publicly funded preschool program that will include provision by both public and private providers. Data could be collected through surveys, meetings, and interviews. The findings could then be used to develop community profiles that document individual and market decisions with respect to production and consumption. It is interesting, too, to consider the possibility of conducting experiments that allow variation in the kinds of information that parents get, how they pay for the care they choose, and the level of quality standards that providers must meet to see how decisions vary under these different conditions. I do not know, however, how feasible an experimental approach is likely to be.

All of these projects rely on a market-oriented perspective. By addressing issues of supply, efficiency, implication of auspices, effects of vouchers and cash payments, the role of information in decisionmaking, and the other types of issues raised above, these projects will offer answers to somewhat different questions than have been asked in many of the evaluations conducted previously. It appears that these evaluations are intended to determine what the payoff is of participation in early childhood education programs. In other words, policymakers can take the results of these evaluations and conclude that for every dollar that is spent on public preschool, so many dollars in subsequent remedial programs and other expenditures will be saved. A more market-oriented approach would facilitate determination of the relative strengths and weaknesses of offering early childhood education services in a system of different systems and auspices. Further insight can be gained into the costs and benefits of allowing more or less parental choice and of different mechanisms (e.g., vouchers) for facilitating those choices.

Conclusion

After reviewing the characteristics of the public and private aspects of the provision of early childhood education and in arguing in favor of research that will help to determine the costs and benefits of our current fragmented and mixed system of financing and provision, it is reasonable to return to the question asked at the beginning of this chapter: Why are the issues examined in this chapter important? Given the magnitude of problems regarding privatization in primary and secondary education—and of quality of education more generally—that face the United States today, why does it make sense to invest resources in analyzing what is currently a relatively small portion of the education sector? The answer is that this is a time of tremendous growth and change regarding early childhood education. Recognition by parents, educators, and policymakers of its potential contribution to the development and school readiness of children is growing; changes in arrangements (such as full-day rather than part-day programs) that allow it to serve the needs of working parents and children simultaneously are becoming more common and more acceptable; and the particularly important role that it can play in the lives of disadvantaged children and their parents trying to achieve economic self-sufficiency has urgency for these individuals as well as for policymakers.

Given that the current system incorporates such great variety, it offers an opportunity to assess the strengths and weaknesses of the different types of arrangements. At the same time, as more private and, more notably, public funds flow toward early childhood education, it is appropriate to consider whether our current system is using those funds as productively as possible. As more states move toward universal preschool, is it appropriate and desirable to channel funds into our current fragmented, mixed system, or might this be the time to make early childhood education a recognized and standard part of the public education system? To be able to determine what is gained and what is lost—other than in philosophical and political terms—requires answers to the questions posed above. Of course, none of these decisions about provision and financing can be made without ultimately dealing with the complexities of philosophy and politics, but it would be most desirable to begin with an empirical foundation for understanding the strengths and weaknesses of the system we have today.

References

Barnett, S. (1995). Long-term effects of early childhood programs on cognitive and school outcomes. *Future of Children* 5(3), 25–50.

Barnett, S., Tarr, J., and Frede, E. (1995, January 5). *Early childhood education in the Abbott Districts: Children's needs and the need for high quality programs.* New Brunswick, N.J.: Center for Early Education at Rutgers.

Besharov, D. (ed.). (1996). *Enhancing early childhood programs: Burdens and opportunities.* Washington, D.C.: Child Welfare League of America and American Enterprise Institute.

Besharov, D., and Samari, N. (1998, October 2–3). Child care vouchers (and cash payments). Paper presented at the "Vouchers and Related Delivery Mechanisms: Consumer Choice in the Provision of Public Services" conference sponsored by the Urban Institute, the Brookings Institution, and the Committee for Economic Development, Washington, D.C.

Blankenhorn, D., and Carlson, A. (1999, March 14). Commentary: Perspective on child care; give stay at-home parents equity. *Los Angeles Times.*

Bryant, D., Dernier, K., Taylor, K., and Maxwell, K. (1998, June). The effect of smart start child care on kindergarten entry skills. Chapel Hill, N.C.: Frank Porter Graham Child Development Center. <www.fpg.unc.edu/~smartstart/enterred.html>.

Casper, L. (1996). *Who's minding our preschoolers?* Current Population Reports, P–70, No. 53. Washington, D.C.: U.S. Bureau of Census.

Council of Economic Advisors. (1998, February). *The economic report of the President.* Washington, D.C.: U.S. Government Printing Office.

_____. (1997, December). The economics of child care. <www.whitehouse.gov/WH/EOP/CEA/html/childcare.html>.

Currie, J., and Thomas, D. (1998, January). School quality and the longer-term effects of head start. Working Paper No. W6362. Cambridge: National Bureau of Economic Research.

Dublin, L. (1998, December 22). *Journal News.* <www.nyjournalnews.com>.

Federal Interagency Forum on Child and Family Statistics. (1998). *America's children: Key national indicators of well-being.* Washington, D.C.: U.S. Government Printing Office.

Finn-Stevenson, M., Desimone, L., and Chung, A. (1998). Linking child care and support services with the school: Pilot evaluation of the School of the 21st Century. School of the 21st Century Recommended Reading, Yale University Bush Center in Child Development and Social Policy. <www.yale.edu/bushcenter/21C/resource/read/eval.html>.

Fitzgerald, B. (1999, February 11). Preschool providers find NJ plan lacking, *Record.*

Florian, J., Schweinhart, L., and Epstein, A. (1997). *Early Returns: First year report of the Michigan School-Readiness Program Evaluation.* Ypsilanti, Mich.: High/Scope Education Research Foundation. <www.highscope.org/research/michres2.html>.

General Accounting Office. (1994, December 28). *Early childhood programs: Parent education and income best predict participation.* HEHS–95–47.

———. (1995, March 21). Early childhood centers: Services to prepare children for school often limited. HEHS–95–21.

———. (1997, April 15). Research provides little information on impact of current program. HEHS–97–59.

———. (1998, March 31). Head Start programs: Participant characteristics, services, and funding. HEHS–98–65.

———. (1998, June 9). Head Start: Challenges faced in demonstrating program results and responding to societal changes. HEHS–98–183.

Green, R. (1999, January 31). School readiness program falters, preschool initiative short of programs for its $20 million. *Hartford Courant.*

Hansmann, H. (1980). The role of nonprofit enterprise. *Yale Law Journal* 89, 835–901.

Helburn, S. (ed.) (1995). *Cost, quality, and child outcomes in child care centers: Technical report.* Denver: Department of Economics, University of Colorado.

Hofferth, S., et al. (1994). *Access to early childhood programs for children at-risk: National Household Education Survey.* Report No. 973–372. Washington, D.C.: National Center for Education Statistics.

Kaplan, J. (1998). State-funded pre-kindergarten programs. *Welfare Information Network Issue Notes* 2(8).

Kisker, E., Hofferth, S., Phillips, D., and Farquhar, E. (1991). *A profile of child care settings.* Washington, D.C.: U.S. Department of Education.

Magenheim, E. (1995). Information, prices, and competition in the child-care market: What role should government play? In M. Pogodzinski (ed.), *Readings in public policy.* Cambridge: Blackwell.

Mitchell, A., Ripple, C. and Chanana, N. (1998, September). *Pre-kindergarten programs funded by the states: Essential elements for policy makers.* New York: Families and Work Institute.

Mocan, N. (1995a, February). *Quality adjusted cost functions for child care centers.* Working Paper 5040. Cambridge: National Bureau of Economic Research.

———. (1995b, October). *The child care industry: Cost functions, efficiency, and quality.* Working Paper 5293. Cambridge: National Bureau of Economic Research.

Mukerjee, S., Witte, A., and Hollowell, S. (1990, April). *Provision of child care: Cost functions for profit-making and not-for-profit day care centers.* Working Paper 3345. Cambridge: National Bureau of Economic Research.

The 1998 National Education Goals Report. (1998, December). Washington, D.C.: National Education Goals Panel. <www.negp.gov>.

Newman, M. (1999, January 12). Whitman preschool plan puts focus on how to run and expand classes. *New York Times.*

Osborne, D., and Gaebler, T. (1992). *Reinventing government: How the entrepreneurial spirit is transforming the public sector.* Reading, Mass.: Addison-Wesley.

Parello, N. (1999, February 19). NJEA calls for preschools in public school system. *Associated Press State and Local Wire.*

Phillips, D., Howes, C., and Whitebook, M. (1992). The social policy context of child care: Effects on quality. *American Journal of Community Psychology* 20(1), 25–51.

Rado, D. (1999, January 20). Lawmakers wrangle over preschool plan. *St. Petersburg Times.*

Reynolds, A., et al. (1997). The state of early childhood intervention: Effectiveness, myths and realities, new directions. Institute for Research on Poverty. *Focus* 19(1), 1–27.

Ross, C., and Kerachsky, S. (1996). Strategies for program integration. In D. Besharov (ed.), *Enhancing early childhood programs: Burdens and opportunities.* Washington, D.C.: Child Welfare League of America and American Enterprise Institute, pp. 39–40.

Seelye, K. (1999, March 16). Gore offers a more "livable word" with some tinkering. *New York Times.*

Stoesz, D. (1992, July). *Social service vouchers: Bringing choice and competition to social services.* Policy Report No. 16. Washington, D.C.: Progressive Policy Institute.

Svetska, S. (1995, December). Financing preschool for all children. ERIC Digest No. EDO-PS–95–16.

U.S. Department of Health and Human Services, National Institutes of Health. Study Summary of NICHD Study of Early Child Care. <www.156.40.88.3/crmc/secc/summary.htm>.

U.S. Department of Health and Human Services. (1998, March). Child care and development block grant report of state plans for the period 10/01/97 to 9/30/99. <www.acf.dhhs.gov/programs/ccb/programs/plan/exec.html>.

Whitebook, M., Howes, C., and Phillips, D. (1990). *Who cares? Child care teachers and the quality of care in America.* Oakland, Calif.: Child Care Employee Project.

Zigler, E., and M. Finn-Stevenson. (1996). Funding child care and public education. *Future of Children* 6(2), 104–121.

6

Privatization in Higher Education

ARTHUR LEVINE

Privatization is an undeniable reality in higher education today. It is being driven by six forces.

The first driving force is *the rise of an information economy.* Our nation has shifted from an industrial to an information economy. We live in an era in which the new sources of wealth are coming from knowledge and communication rather than natural resources and physical labor, which characterized the United States as an industrial society. Industrial societies have historically been national in focus and put a premium on physical capital—plant, machinery, and the like. In contrast, an information society is global and puts a premium on intellectual capital—knowledge and the people who produce it. As a result, education is fundamental to an information society, which demands higher levels of skills and knowledge of its workforce and its citizenry. The best jobs in our society increasingly require more advanced educational credentials. As a recent report of the NationsBanc Montgomery Securities shows, by the year 2000, 85 percent of U.S. jobs will require education beyond high school, up from 65 percent in 1991. Moreover, eighteen of the twenty-five fastest-growing, highest-paying occupations in the country through the year 2006 will require at least a baccalaureate degree (NationsBanc Montgomery Securities, 1998, p. 60). In this environment, the value of educational credentials is similarly increasing. For example, in 1980, the weekly salary of a college graduate or beyond was 40 percent higher than that of a high school graduate. By 1997, the gap had risen to 73 percent (*The Wall Street Journal Almanac 1999*, 1998, p. 612).

Going hand in hand with the demand for increased levels of education is the need for more frequent education. The half-life of knowledge is shorter in the current environment, and there is increased pressure to remain at the forefront of knowledge use and production. This requires education throughout a career, as well as the rising use of continuing education and professional development. Jim Duderstadt, former president of the University of Michigan, says the emphasis in an information society shifts from "just in case" education to "just in time" education.

The bottom line is that an information society means more higher education, more advanced degrees, more continuing education, and a global marketplace for higher education.

The second driving force behind privatization in higher education is *changing students*. Perhaps the largest change in recent years is who the students are. During the 1980s and early 1990s, the lion's share of college enrollment growth came from students who might be described as "nontraditional." By 1993, 38 percent of all college students were over twenty-five years of age; 61 percent were working; 56 percent were females; and 42 percent were attending part time. Less than one-fifth of all undergraduates fit the traditional stereotype of the American college student attending full-time, being eighteen to twenty-two years of age, and living on campus.

What this means is that higher education is not as central to the lives of many of today's undergraduates as it was to previous generations. Increasingly, it is just one of a multiplicity of activities in which they are engaged every day. For many, college is not even the most important of these activities. Work and family often overshadow it.

As a consequence, older, part-time, and working students, especially those with children, often said (in a national study I conducted of undergraduate attitudes and experiences between 1992 and 1997) that they wanted a different type of relationship with their colleges from what students historically have had. They preferred relationships like those they already enjoyed with their bank, the gas company, and the supermarket.

Think about what you want from your bank. I know what I want: an ATM on every corner, with no lines, and a parking spot right in front. I want my checks deposited the moment they arrive at the bank or perhaps the day before. And I want no mistakes unless they are in my favor. There are also things I do not wish my bank to provide: softball leagues, psychological counseling, and religious services. I can arrange for those things without their assistance or additional cost.

Students are asking for roughly the same thing from their colleges. They want their colleges nearby and operating at the hours most useful to them—preferably, around the clock. They want convenience—easy, accessible parking (in the classroom would not be at all bad), no lines, and polite, helpful, and efficient staff service. They also want high-quality education but are eager for low costs. For the most part, they are very willing to comparison shop—placing a premium on time and money. They do not want to pay for activities and programs they do not use. In short, students are increasingly bringing to higher education exactly the same consumer expectations they have for every other commercial enterprise with which they deal. Their focus is on convenience, service, quality, and cost. They believe that they are paying for their education and that colleges should give them the education they want. They are likely to find appealing distance education, which offers the convenience of instruction at home or the office. They are prime candidates for stripped-down versions of college, located in the suburbs and business districts of our cities, which offer low-cost instruction, high faculty teaching loads, a primarily part-time faculty, limited numbers of majors, and few electives. Proprietary institutions of this type are starting to spring up around the country.

In this regard, the University of Phoenix is instructive. It is now one of the largest private colleges in America, enrolling 70,000 students. Traded on the Nasdaq exchange, this for-profit college is regionally accredited, offering degrees from the associate through masters and soon doctorate. The faculty, who boast traditional academic credentials, are largely part-time, having other forms of primary employment in the fields in which they teach. The equivalent of a full-time faculty member teaches well over ten courses a year. Class syllabi are uniform, being prepared every three years by professionals and practitioners in the subject area. In other words, faculty teach the courses, but they do not prepare or design them. Students attend school at convenient hours as a cohort, taking precisely the same courses in sequence. There are no electives. In recent years, the University of Phoenix has added an online version of their courses to 4,500 students. They offer programs from coast to coast, put an emphasis on assessment of student learning and faculty teaching, and have plans to expand enrollments to 200,000 students over the next decade.

The University of Phoenix is the largest example of proprietary higher education, but it is not unique, and its example is being watched not only by other entrepreneurs but also by Wall Street and venture capital firms. We will see more institutions like it in the future.

Traditional undergraduates are also changing. They are coming to college less well prepared than their predecessors. As a result, there is a growing need for remediation. According to a national survey I conducted in 1997 of student-affairs officers, nearly three-fourths (74 percent) of all colleges and universities experienced an increase within the last decade in the proportion of students requiring remedial or developmental education at two-year (81 percent) and four-year (64 percent) colleges. Today, nearly one-third (32 percent) of all undergraduates reported having taken a basic skills or remedial course in reading, writing, or math. Colleges and universities have a poor reputation in providing effective remediation. A growing number of schools are outsourcing the function to for-profit organizations.

There is another hurdle even more daunting than remediation: the widening gap between the ways in which students learn best and the ways in which faculty teach. According to research by Charles Schroeder (1993) of the University of Missouri–Columbia, more than half of today's students perform best in a learning situation characterized by "direct, concrete experience, moderate-to-high degrees of structure, and a linear approach to learning. They value the practical and the immediate, and the focus of their perception is primarily on the physical world." More than three-quarters (75 percent) of faculty, conversely, "prefer the global to the particular, are stimulated by the realm of concepts, ideas, and abstractions, and assume that students, like themselves, need a high degree of autonomy in their work." In short, students are more likely to prefer concrete subjects and active methods of learning. By contrast, faculty are predisposed to abstract subjects and passive learning. The result, says Schroeder, is frustration on both sides and a tendency for faculty to interpret as deficiencies what may simply be natural differences in learning patterns of students. This mismatch is an invitation to for-profit groups to enter higher education and try to do better.

In addition, the number of eighteen-year-olds is growing at the rate of more than 1 percent a year nationally; however, the growth is disproportionately in the West and South. Plus, an increasing proportion of eighteen-year-olds is attending college: 65 percent of all high school graduates are now attending postsecondary education, up from 42 percent in 1970. The result is that California, for example, is bracing for a tidal wave of a half-million additional college students within the next decade. The state lacks the capacity on existing campuses to accommodate the increase as well as the desire to spend substantial additional resources on higher education or the construction of new campuses. This, too, will invite the private sector into higher education.

The demographics of international students are the wild card. This is a very appealing add-on to the development of new markets for proprietary education in the United States. There is a growing demand for higher education around the world. The American university is thought of as a high-quality source for that education. English is increasingly the world's second language. And because the British Open University has been so remarkably successful in developing an international market, currently administering tests in more than a hundred countries, the possibility of global education seems more achievable to both for-profit and nonprofit colleges.

The third factor is *the cost of higher education.* Between 1980 and 1997 the average price of college tuition, room, and board rose by well over 300 percent (*The Wall Street Journal Almanac 1999,* 1998, p. 607). Today, the common wisdom among admissions officers is that fewer than 5 percent of American families can afford the full cost of a private college education. This is a source of concern to both government and the public. There is a growing belief in the state capitals that the costs of higher education are too high, owing to program redundancy, the proliferation of remedial programs, administrative overhead, physical plant upkeep, the added costs of research, and low teaching productivity. Perhaps the most visible effort in recent years to respond to these perceived difficulties has been the creation by seventeen of the nation's governors of an alternative to traditional higher education, called the Western Governors University. The emphasis is on distance learning. In partnership with fourteen businesses, including IBM, AT&T, Sun, KPMG, Cisco Systems, 3COM, and Microsoft, the new university will not employ faculty or design courses. Instead it is planning a competency-based, online program developed from the offerings of colleges and businesses, domestically and internationally (Marchese, 1998). Toward this end, Western Governors recently developed a newsmaking partnership with the British Open University, the international pioneer in distance education. The possibility of offering higher education at lower cost is also attracting the private sector.

Fourth: *new technologies.* Another force, which may have the greatest capacity to change higher education, is new technologies. Several years ago I had a conversation with the editor of one of the nation's major metropolitan daily newspapers. He said his newspaper would be out of the paper business within the next several decades. Instead, the news would be delivered electronically. Subscribers would be able to design the newspaper they received. They could say they want to begin the day with sports. The headlines and front-page news on their daily paper would accordingly focus on athletics. They could say they have young children and ask that political news be excised. This has enormous import for colleges. It means that the age of textbooks is ending. The days of teaching from the old yellow lecture notes is approaching an abrupt conclusion. Already, private-sector companies are developing products in response, from publishers like McGraw-Hill to new software companies like Blackboard.

In the same vein, I recently read an article that described the travel agency of the future. Through virtual reality, a traveler considering different vacation sites would be able to experience the possibilities. The traveler would be able to smell, hear, feel, and see the different locales. He or she could walk the beaches, climb the mountains, enter the local landmarks, and inspect the restaurants, hotels, and shops. The same might be done with historic locales. One could visit fifth-century Rome, eighteenth-century America, or fifteenth-century Paris. Imagine smelling the smells of fifteenth-century Paris—they must have been putrid—walking the cobblestones, entering the great and not-so-great buildings, and seeing the people on the street. This raises huge questions about pedagogy. How will a stand-up lecture on fifteenth-century Paris compare with the experience of actually being there? As technology advances, we can anticipate dramatic, even revolutionary, changes in the nature of instruction.

For instance, the technology currently exists for a professor to offer a course at Teachers College and for students to take that course in Los Angeles and Tokyo. It is possible for all of them to perceive they are sitting in the same classroom. The student in Los Angeles can electronically nudge her Japanese-speaking classmate, say she missed the professor's last comment, and get the appropriate answer in English. The professor can ask the two students to prepare a project together for the next class. The two students can agree to have tea together after class. If all of this can be accomplished electronically, why do we need the physical plant known as the college?

The American system of higher education was built on the principle of propinquity. The goal was to put a campus in reach of every citizen, to overcome the barrier of geography. Today this has been accomplished for more than 90 percent of the population. Technology makes physical proximity less important than it was in the past; it minimizes the barrier of geography. It also reduces the need to build physical plants. This invites the states to reconsider how they have designed their higher education systems. Why does New York need sixty-four campuses? Why does California need nine public research universities?

The new technologies have the potential to revolutionize higher education. The private sector has greater expertise in this area than the nation's colleges and universities. It also has greater resources to invest in technology than does higher education. And the private sector is likely to move into this area with greater alacrity than higher education.

The fifth force driving privatization in higher education: *changing public attitudes.* Throughout much of the twentieth century, higher education was one of America's sacred institutions, deeply respected and placed on a national pedestal high above the profane aspects of daily life. By the mid-1980s this all changed.

Beginning with a 1984 report by former Secretary of Education William Bennett entitled *To Reclaim a Legacy,* there has been a barrage of publications critical of higher education. There were books with titles such as *Illiberal Education, Profscam, Tenured Radicals, Killing the Spirit, How Professors Play the Game of the Cat Guarding the Cream, The Closing of the American Mind,* and *Integrity in the College Curriculum.* Several volumes made the national best-seller lists. In their aftermath, there were front-page newspaper articles, cover stories on the weekly news magazines, TV shows, and radio broadcasts. They criticized higher education for rising costs, diminishing quality, low productivity, inefficiency, and ineffectiveness. In the aftermath of the private-sector transformation of health care, these perceived weaknesses make higher education a very appealing target, perhaps more easily entered than in the past.

The sixth and final force driving privatization in higher education: *changing attitudes and demands of higher education patrons.* During the late 1980s and 1990s, government support for higher education declined, both financially and politically. This represents a dramatic change in the condition of American higher education. Throughout the twentieth century, colleges and universities were a growth industry. Except during the world wars and two years of the Depression, enrollment rose every year. In the decades following World War II, the biggest and most persistent demand that government made on higher education was to increase capacity—provide college to more and more people. Rising government support was the norm; obstacles to increasing enrollments were swept away. Government's principal role was to expand higher education and increase opportunities for access. More and more faculty were hired. Public institutions of higher education multiplied. Government aid was targeted at private schools to promote expansion. Few questions were asked. This is the lot of growth industries in America.

Government treats mature industries very differently. It seeks to regulate or control them. It asks hard questions about their cost, efficiency, productivity, and effectiveness. It attempts to limit their size and funding. It reduces their autonomy, increases their regulation, and demands greater accountability.

This is precisely what is happening to higher education today. Questions are being asked by government of colleges and universities that have never been asked before. The cost of the enterprise is being scrutinized. The price of higher education is being attacked loudly and continuously. Funding formulas are being reexamined. Financial aid is shifting from grants to loans.

Questions of productivity and efficiency are being raised. How much should faculty teach? What is the appropriate balance between teaching and research? How much should it cost to educate a student? Can campuses and faculty be replaced by new technologies? Should there continue to be lifetime employment or tenure for faculty? Which programs should colleges offer? How much course and program redundancy is necessary? What should be the balance between graduate and undergraduate education?

Questions of effectiveness are being asked, too. Why aren't graduation rates higher? Why should students take more than four years to graduate from college? Why do colleges offer remedial education?

Government is also shifting the terms of the relationship between higher education and the public. The focus is moving from teaching—what faculty do in their classrooms—to learning—what students get out of their classes. The emphasis is moving from process—courses and credits—to outcomes—what students achieve as a result of a college education. In short, the state is demanding greater accountability from higher education.

The effects of these changes on higher education are profound. As a growth industry, colleges and universities could almost count on additional resources annually. "Growth" and "progress" were treated as synonyms. New activities were a matter of addition—the new was simply added to the old.

Today, as resources are stable or declining, this is no longer possible. Change is expected to occur by substitution. If something new is added, something old must be eliminated. If growth is to occur, it can occur only in selective areas. Colleges and universities are being forced to choose limited targets for investment. If colleges are unwilling to do this themselves, government is increasingly willing to help them make the choices. Government is becoming more activist and is very willing to make decisions that were once regarded as the prerogative of the faculty.

The net result is likely to be a "boutiqueing" of higher education. Today, institutions of higher education are being forced to make selections, eliminate overlapping or redundant offerings, and make themselves more specialized. They are moving away from being something akin to full-service department stores toward being more sharply focused boutiques. The common wisdom today is that higher education must do more with less. The reality is that institutions will have to do less with less. In short, higher education has entered a period of fiscal and programmatic constraint. The loss of revenue and the need to contract programming means that colleges and universities are less able to defend against incursions by the private sector.

The bottom line is that in a hot economy, with cash readily available for investment, the private sector has an edge in responding to the changing demands on higher education by the information economy, evolving student needs and wants, rising costs, and new technologies.

The Major Actors

The actors in the higher education scene have responded in very different fashions to these pressures for change.

Colleges and universities have been slow to act. The use of new technology and the option of distance learning is a good example. A report by the U.S. Department of Education (National Center for Education Statistics, 1998) found that only one-third of all institutions were currently offering distance courses and another one-quarter were planning to begin offering distance instruction in the next three years. The scale of collegiate programs has been small. In fact, only 26 percent of colleges and universities with distance programs offer more than twenty-five courses. The focus of collegiate distance programs has been narrowly targeted, almost exclusively undergraduate (81 percent of institutions). With so few colleges and universities offering more than twenty-five courses, this means most schools involved in distance education are offering less than the equivalent of a full undergraduate degree program. They are also far less involved in other areas of education that would seem important in an information society: graduate education (34 percent), professional continuing education (13 percent), other forms of continuing education (6 percent), and adult literacy (2 percent). Additionally, the technology that colleges and universities are employing is not as up-to-date as it might be; only a little more than half (57 percent) are using interactive two-way video. Almost as many (52 percent) are using the older technology of prerecorded one-way video (National Center for Educational Statistics, 1998).

Yet interest, even urgency, regarding the topic is building in higher education. A number of institutions, more public than private and more universities than colleges, have made a serious commitment to distance learning. New York University, for instance, made headlines when it announced the creation of NYU On-Line, Inc., a for-profit subsidiary designed to produce and market online courses and provide client consulting services. In partnership with the Lotus Corporation, the University of Wisconsin system has created a dual for-profit–nonprofit Learning Innovation Center to offer the university's courses and degrees globally. Already 565 courses are available. The University of Nebraska is creating global courses and a degree-vending operation as well. And the University of Hawaii is using two-way video, cable, satellite, and the Internet to offer thirteen degree programs across the state (Marchese, 1998).

However, it is not yet clear to what degree higher education will be a leader in distance learning. What mitigates against it is tradition, cost, the glacial pace of action by higher education governance systems, and faculty attitudes that range from indifferent to hostile.

In contrast, the most aggressive and creative actor in higher education today is the private sector, or business community. The motivation here is profits. The private sector sees higher education as a very lucrative and poorly run industry. As one visitor proposing a partnership with Teachers College recently explained to me, higher education is a $225 billion industry with a reputation for low productivity, poor management, high cost, and low use of technology. He said, "Higher education is going to be the next health care," with similar problems in both industries and equal opportunities for the business community. He went on to say, "We are going to eat your lunch." He reminded me that education was not new to business. There are more than 1,000 corporate universities engaged in training company workforces. In these settings, he believed, instruction was superior and better-assessed than in the typical college.

Also, higher education is seen as a countercyclical industry, meaning college enrollments and revenues increase when the economy is poor. In other words, students are more likely to go to college when there are fewer jobs available and are more likely to drop out when the job market improves. Countercyclical industries are relatively rare and very attractive investments.

Furthermore, higher education has a dependable revenue stream with a good cash flow. Enrollment growth is the norm, and half the customer base makes a two- to four-year, or more, commitment to the product.

In addition, it is a subsidized industry. It has enormous financial aid programs financed by the state and federal governments, and the federal program through recent legislation has become more open to distance learning and nontraditional students.

Add to this one more stunning fact: Education and technology stocks have an incredible record. They have been overwhelmingly outpacing traditional indicators such as the Standard and Poor's index. The story of the University of Phoenix has been everywhere—newspapers, magazines, radio, and television. So both the press and the numbers look wonderful.

The rush to higher education is on in the private sector. Venture capital firms, such as Warburg, Pincus, and Co., are studying the education market. Investment houses, including Legg, Mason, NationsBanc Montgomery Securities, and Merrill Lynch, have developed educational practices. One recent unpublished study found seventy-two significant private-sector firms had already entered the online postsecondary market alone. For example, Michael Milken and Larry Ellison of Oracle are creating a for-profit online university. Caliber Learning Network is offering graduate education with prestigious research universities in health, business, and education. Jones Education Company has put together an electronic catalog offering certificate and degree programs of partnering universities and, through America Online, has developed what it hopes will be a worldwide electronic university. University Access is developing courses to be taken at a distance in the core business subjects by renowned names in the field.

Business brings money to higher education, imagination unimpeded by current practice, and speed in entering the field. It lacks the reputation, accreditation, and inbuilt certification-granting ability of higher education.

There is one more group of actors in education worth noting. They are knowledge organizations—media, publishing, museums, libraries, professional associations, arts organizations, grassroots neighborhood associations, and universities. The activities of all of these organizations are converging. Increasingly, all are in the business of producing and disseminating knowledge. They are all in the field of education. Museums, YMCAs, and libraries are increasingly offering courses. The same groups are entering the publishing business—creating books, monographs, and other educational materials. More and more, they focus on schools, teachers, students, and families.

Not long ago, I visited with the technology division of Simon and Schuster, which I thought of as a book publisher. I learned they are no longer exclusively in the book business; now they are in the knowledge and information business. I asked what this meant. I was told, for example, they are focusing strongly on teacher education and the professional development of teachers. They were involved with thousands of schools via television and computers. Their ultimate goal was to put the Simon and Schuster brand on professional development for teachers. This did not seem like a crazy possibility in that they are involved in more schools than any education school in the country. But I was shocked. I thought this was the work of schools like Teachers College. I never considered a book publisher as a competitor.

I asked where Simon and Schuster obtained the content for the materials it produced for teachers. The answer was they hire "content specialists." I had hoped they would say they worked with university faculty. The only obstacle they faced in doing exactly what colleges and universities do in terms of professional development was accreditation and certification.

Simon and Schuster is unusual in its scale, but it is not unique in direction. For instance, the Public Broadcasting System has with support from the U.S. Department of Education created Mathline, the largest technology-based professional development program for math teachers, now enrolling more than 5,000 teachers. The New York public broadcasting station, WNET, is engaged in similar activities, having developed online courses for schools and professional development programs for teachers.

In sum, we are now entering a new world for higher education in which providers will be expanded to include not only traditional colleges and universities but also for-profit universities, technology companies, publishers, television, education conglomerates, training and consulting firms, professional associations, grassroots organizations, and foundations (see Table 6.1, adapted from Wikler, 1999, p. 18).

The Implications for Higher Education

In the summer of 1999 I met with a well-known business leader who told me about his plans to create a for-profit virtual university. He said the train was leaving the station, and Teachers College needed to get on board. We agreed and disagreed. We both thought the train was indeed leaving the station. The only real difference in our thinking was that I believed the higher education community was driving the train.

Higher education has three critical characteristics. The first is reputation or, in business terms, a "brand" in the field of education. The second is authorization to provide education—accreditation, certification, and licensure. The third element is content. Colleges and universities are in the business of discovering and disseminating content—information and knowledge—and today content is king. Digital technology gives television, telephones, and cable stations the capacity to distribute more and more content, and today there are more channels available to distribute content than there is content to fill them. The fellow I spoke with that summer was just another channel hungry for content.

These attributes may be only temporary advantages to higher education. With regard to reputation, Amazon.com, the online bookseller, showed the fragility of established brand names. In the space of just a few years, it managed to eclipse powerhouse booksellers like Barnes and Noble and Borders and establish a brand name in a new business: online book sales. In the same fashion, online educators may well have the capacity to establish brand names in distance education, distinguishing them from prestigious campus-based colleges and universities.

With regard to authorization, at a meeting of investment houses and venture capital firms, the consensus was that degrees, credits, and accreditation were obstacles, but perhaps only in the short run. They concluded that it would take between one and five years to gain these items in most states. The University of Phoenix was regularly cited as the model of what a tenacious institution can accomplish in overcoming these barriers, even in the face of powerful opposition.

As for content, the story of Microsoft and Encyclopedia Britannica is instructive. Bill Gates invited the most eminent of encyclopedias to develop a CD-ROM edition. Britannica turned him down, worried about losing the market for its tra-

TABLE 6.1   New Participants in U.S. Higher Education

Category	Examples
Virtual universities	Western Governors University, California Virtual University, SUNY Learning Network
Foreign colleges and universities	McGill, Open University, Oxford University
For-profit universities	University of Phoenix, Strayer University, The Graduate School of America
Technology companies	Courseware packagers and distributors, e.g., AT&T, Caliber, RealEducation, ISI, OnlineLearning.net, UOL Publishing, America Online, Jones Education Company; Authoring Software and technology service companies, e.g., IBM, Lotus, Oracle, Collegis
Publishers	Pearson, Houghton Mifflin, Harcourt General
Television companies	PBS, Thirteen/WNET, NBC
Education conglomerates	Sylvan Learning Systems, Knowledge Universe
Training and consulting firms	Times Mirror, Kaplan
Professional associations	National Association of Secondary School Principals, National Council of Teachers of English
Grassroots teachers' groups	Global Schoolhouse, Tapped In
Foundations	The Alfred P. Sloan Foundation

SOURCE: J. Wikler (1999, January). *Technology-mediated higher education: A market map.* Unpublished manuscript, p. 18.

ditional hard-copy edition. So Microsoft bought Funk and Wagnalls and turned it into the digital Encarta. In less than two years, Encarta was the best-selling encyclopedia in the world.

Britannica sales plummeted. Britannica went back to Microsoft and was told it would now have to pay to put its encyclopedia online. The lesson is that if distributors like Microsoft are unable to get content providers to join them, they might as well buy the content or develop the capacity to create content themselves. This is the approach that Simon and Schuster has taken.

The lesson is that colleges and universities have a limited amount of time to decide what role they will play in designing higher education for a new era.

Research Questions

The research on this topic is meager. The critical questions are yet to be answered. I would propose ten research areas are needed to understand, assess, and respond to the privatization of higher education.

1. *What private-sector groups are entering the higher education market? What are they doing?* The number of private-sector organizations coming into higher education is ballooning. Is it important to catalog who they are and what they are doing?

2. *What are the real barriers to entering the market?* This question entails an examination of issues such as accreditation, state licensing, scale, funding, staffing, market acceptance, reputation, and brand name.

3. *What are the actual returns? Is higher education actually a profitable market for the private sector?* The experiences of the Apollo Corporation, DeVry, Kaplan, Princeton Review, and others say yes. But what are the results across the industry in terms of profitability, market penetration, turnover rates, and the like? What are the requirements for success by private-sector entrants into higher education?

4. *What are the differences between the process and the products of traditional higher education and private-sector competitors?* The first assignment is identifying the differences. The second is comparing them and seeking to understand the best practices.

5. *How effective are traditional higher education and the private sector?* This means examining delivery methods, populations educated, content, outcomes, and costs.

6. *What is the desirability and what are the consequences of partnerships between traditional higher education and the private sector?* As in the case of the visitors coming to Teachers College to talk about partnerships, I suspect the number of future joint ventures between higher education and the private sector will boom. In the current environment, colleges and universities really have only three choices.

First, higher education can reject the entreaties of the business community. It might do this on the grounds that it currently has a near-monopoly on the educational content. It could do so on principle, saying a for-profit motive is incompatible with higher education. Or it could do so for reasons of quality, believing that the education ideas being advocated by the private sector diminish educational excellence.

Such a rejection would force the business community to face higher education head-on, much like the University of Phoenix. Under these circumstances, the private sector can be expected to create its own content by hiring the expertise currently found in universities. Profitmakers will do this at lower cost than higher education and seek to reach larger audiences. For instance, a recent proposal I read from a venture capital firm suggested creating a distance learning university that would hire the nation's most eminent faculty at lucrative salaries for short periods of time to create curriculum materials and offer electronic courses intended to reach thousands. In short, the proposal sought to create the equivalent of an academic all-star team found at no other university. Although the salaries paid would be high, they would be far less than the full-time salary of a distinguished tenured full professor. And the enrollments would be many times greater than those found in any college or university course. This is a potentially devastating alternative for higher education financially, especially given the changing expectations of current students.

Second, higher education can attempt to preempt the private sector by developing the technologies, service-delivery capacities, and economies they now offer or at least promise. This seems the least likely alternative, as colleges lack the substantial capital that will be required, particularly in a time of declining government support and the speed of action of the private sector.

Third, higher education can judiciously form partnerships with the private sector.

I have loaded the choices. I see the third as the only reasonable course. The question that needs to be answered is, What is the effect of partnerships on private-sector organizations, colleges, their faculties, their students, and the public? What is lost? What is gained? Do partnerships work?

This leads to several questions:

1. *What is the effect of competition on higher education?* Historically, higher education has been one of the few organizations in which competition has actually raised both costs and prices. It seems unlikely that competition with the private sector would produce the same result. What results does it produce?
2. *What are the consequences of competition for higher education?* Colleges and universities engage in three activities: teaching, research, and service. The private sector is competing in the one profitable area—that is, teaching. If the private sector is successful, what happens to the less profitable research and service functions? What should be done if there is an "unbundling" of the functions of higher education?

3. *What state and federal policies need to be changed to respond to the privatization of the higher education industry?*

4. *What accreditation and other self-regulation policies need to be reexamined?*

References

Marchese, T. (1998). Not-so-distant competitors: How new providers are remaking the postsecondary market. *AAHE Bulletin* 50(9).

National Center for Educational Statistics. (1998). *Distance education in higher education institutions: Incidence, audience, and plans to expand.* Washington, D.C.: National Center for Educational Statistics.

NationsBanc Montgomery Securities. (1998). *The age of knowledge.* San Francisco: NationsBanc Montgomery Securities.

Schroeder, C. (1993). New students—new learning styles. *Change*, September-October, 25 (41), p. 21.

The Wall Street Journal Almanac. (1998). New York: Ballantine.

Wikler, J. (January 1999). *Technology-mediated higher education: A market map.* Unpublished manuscript.

International
Dimensions

7

Privatization Through Vouchers in Developing Countries: The Cases of Chile and Colombia

MARTIN CARNOY AND PATRICK J. MCEWAN

This chapter contributes to the debate on privatizing education by assessing two working voucher plans in Latin America. One is in Chile, the other in Colombia. Their coverage is extensive, and so these two plans can provide useful insight into the effect on educational outcomes of vouchers that smaller experiments, such as those in Milwaukee, Cleveland, and New York, cannot. The plans also represent two different approaches to privatization. Chile's plan covers more than 90 percent of all elementary and secondary pupils; more than one-third attends private schools financed by vouchers. Colombia's plan is targeted only at low-income secondary school students. As a targeted plan, it resembles the experiments in the United States. But it is much larger, covering about 100,000 students, and it is oriented toward expanding access to secondary school through subsidizing private schools rather than substituting for existing public education.

Private schools compete with public education in almost every developing country, but under highly variable conditions (James, 1988). In many, such as in Chile, most parents regard private schools as academically superior to public schools, but this is not universally the case. For example, the Harambee schools in Kenya, largely privately financed and run by communities, are a last resort for students refused entrance to public secondary schools (Knight and Sabot, 1990). Test scores are much lower in such private schools than in the government sector, raising questions about the merits of expanding secondary education by privatizing it (Riddell, 1993). In Colombia, 20 percent of primary and 40 percent of all secondary pupils attend private schools. Although public secondary education is also selective, higher-income parents prefer private schools. But for a typical low-income student, free public secondary education is a desirable option.

In addition to this variability in the relative position of private and public education, governments in most developing countries traditionally have subsidized private education. Since the most pressing problem in these countries is rapidly increasing demand for education under conditions of public resource constraints, the option of expanding education by mobilizing private (i.e., family) resources is attractive. The option is most often exercised at the university level, largely because students at the tertiary level have some capacity to earn income while studying and hence can pay for their education; but tertiary education is also more clearly vocational, leading to increased earnings almost immediately after the educational experience. Many analysts have also argued that those who reach university are much more likely to come from families able to afford to pay (World Bank, 1995).

But privatization is rationalized mainly in terms of saving resources, not so much to extract more resources from families who can afford to pay but because privatization may increase the efficiency of resource use. The original argument for vouchers, as articulated by Milton Friedman (1955, 1962), rests on two claims. The first is that by increasing educational choice and promoting a diversity of schooling options vouchers leave consumers of educational services more satisfied. The second is that by breaking the public sector's monopoly over educational services there are efficiency gains in the delivery of educational services.[1] But vouchers may also induce students to sort themselves among private and public schools, based on income, ability, or other characteristics. If educational outcomes of students are affected by peer characteristics, then vouchers will indirectly affect student outcomes. On the one hand, they could contribute to gains for pupils in schools that are able to attract "good" students. On the other, they could result in the "creaming" of high-ability students from public schools, which would negatively affect outcomes of remaining students.[2]

This makes targeted vouchers particularly attractive. Targeted vouchers for low-income pupils can take advantage of unused capacity in established private schools with a track record. As we will suggest, these schools are most likely to produce achievement gains that are comparable to or higher than public schools. In contrast, we argue, it is much more difficult to sustain the claims by voucher proponents that expanding the number of private schools will lead to achievement gains (although doing so may lower costs).

In the sections that follow, we will review the evidence on the effects of privatizing education through vouchers in Chile and Colombia. In both countries, the objectives of the voucher plans were to increase educational access (especially for pupils from lower-income families) and to improve the effectiveness and efficiency of schooling. Since these are precisely the arguments made for privatizing education in other countries, it is important to assess the available empirical evidence.

Vouchers and Reform in Chile, 1980–1996

The 1980s

At the time of the military coup d'etat in 1973, Chile's education system was one of the most developed in Latin America. It had achieved near-universal enrollment in primary education, a feat that still eludes much of Latin America (Castañeda, 1992; Schiefelbein, 1991). But like other countries in the region, Chile's centralized Ministry of Education assumed exclusive responsibility for administering and financing the entire public school system. A large number of private schools also operated in the country, about half under the auspices of the Catholic Church (Espinola, 1993). Following a long tradition of public support of private education, many received subsidies from the central government that covered roughly 30 percent of costs in 1980 (Larrañaga, 1995).

Upon assuming power in 1973, the military government disbanded the teachers union and fired teachers with leftist views (Parry, 1997). It also initiated an administrative reorganization, dividing the country into thirteen regions, then subdividing those into provinces and municipalities. At each level the president appointed governors and mayors, drawn mainly from the ranks of the military (Stewart and Ranis, 1994). During the 1970s, the Ministry of Education, in addition to other ministries, devolved some powers to Regional Ministry Secretariats (SEREMIs), which were charged with administrative and supervisory duties formerly performed by the central ministry. Despite the apparent move toward decentralization, the system essentially functioned as a military chain of command, organized to implement central government directives (Parry, 1997; Stewart and Ranis, 1994). Mayors of municipalities would not be elected democratically until 1992.

In 1980 the military government initiated a sweeping series of educational reforms.[3] It began by transferring responsibility for public school management from the Ministry of Education to local municipalities. Teachers lost their status as civil servants (with employment reverting to municipal contracts), and school buildings and land were signed over to municipal control.[4] Initial transfers proceeded rapidly, encouraged by financial incentives, and by 1982 approximately 84 percent of schools were operated by municipalities.[5] The process was interrupted by economic crisis in late 1982 when the central government was unable to cover the costs of transfers. By the end of 1986, however, the process was reinitiated, and all schools were transferred soon thereafter (Jofré, 1988).

Once they were transferred to municipalities, schools were placed under the control of one of two kinds of institutions.[6] Most municipalities opted to manage their schools with a Departmento de Administración de la Educación Municipal (DAEM). DAEMs exist under the larger umbrella of the municipal bureaucracy and, as such, are governed by municipal rules. For instance, the head of the DAEM is required to be a teacher, reporting directly to the mayor. Employee contracts must conform to municipal regulations on hiring and salary scales. Instead of DAEMs, municipalities could place schools under the control of a quasi-autonomous "corporation."[7] These corporations are nonprofit organizations that are not subject to direct mayoral control, although the mayor does preside over a governing board. Their operations are generally subject to fewer regulations. In contrast to DAEMs, the corporation head is not required to be a teacher, and corporation employees are not subjected to municipal rules regarding the hiring and remuneration of municipal employees. These features of corporations have led some to argue that they are more effective or efficient in the provision of educational services, although evidence on this issue is conflicting and sparse (Aedo, 1996; Aedo, 1998; Parry, 1997).[8]

Concomitant to public school decentralization, the government drastically altered how public and most private schools were financed. Prior to 1980, as in much of Latin America, school budgets were largely determined by the need to sustain an existing plant of teachers and facilities. If budgets adjusted in response to the level of student enrollments, they did so at a sluggish pace. Under the reform, the Ministry of Education began disbursing monthly payments to municipalities based on a fixed subsidy multiplied by the number of students enrolled in their schools; private schools received equivalent per-student payments if they did not charge tuition. Thus, payments to public or private schools began fluctuating in direct proportion to student enrollments. The law established a base voucher level, which varies according the level of education and the location of the school.[9] Although the real value of the voucher was originally intended to

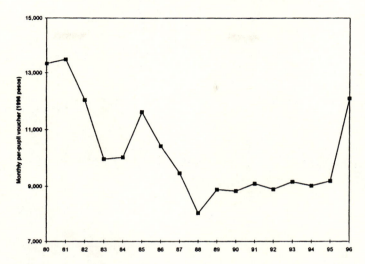

FIGURE 7.1   Monthly Per-Pupil Voucher in Primary
Schools, 1980–1996 (1996 pesos)
NOTE: The base voucher excludes various bonuses and
deductions that vary by municipality and school.
SOURCE: Ministry of Education and authors' calculations.

keep pace with inflation, it was deindexed following the economic crisis of the
early 1980s.[10] Over the course of the 1980s, the real value of the per-pupil
voucher declined precipitously, reaching its lowest point in 1988 (see Figure 7.1).
Despite the falling real value of the voucher, the reform still encouraged a major
redistribution of student enrollments across private and public schools.[11] At the
beginning of the decade, about 14 percent of students were enrolled in private
subsidized schools, almost 80 percent in public schools. By 1990 almost 35 percent of enrollments were in private subsidized schools, an increase that occurred
mostly at the expense of public enrollments (see Figure 7.2). Throughout this period, between 6 and 9 percent of students enrolled in elite private schools that
charged tuition and did not accept vouchers.

The Ministry of Education, in collaboration with the Catholic University, administered several large-scale assessments of student achievement in private and
public schools during the 1980s. Beginning in 1982, more than 90 percent of students in the fourth and eighth grades completed annual tests of Spanish and
mathematics.[12] The results of the Programa de Evaluación del Rendimiento Es-
colar (PER) were intended for wide dissemination among policymakers, principals, teachers, and parents (Espinola, 1993; Jofré, 1988). In practice, however, it is

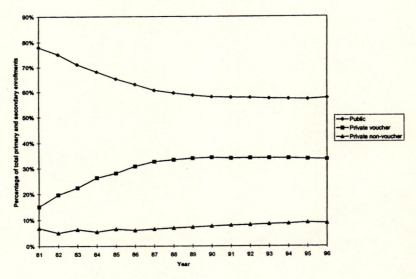

FIGURE 7.2   Enrollment Share in Public, Private Voucher, and
Private Paid Schools, 1981–1996
SOURCE: Ministry of Education.

doubtful whether the distribution of results was that widespread (Jofré, 1988). By
1985, the PER assessment had been discontinued because of budgetary constraints and political pressures from teachers and policymakers who did not want
results to be used to sanction poorly performing schools. The national assessment system was resurrected in 1988, though in modified form. Now called the
Sistema de Evaluación de Calidad de la Educación (SIMCE), around 90 percent
of fourth-graders were assessed in even years, eighth-graders in odd years. Unlike
its predecessor, SIMCE did not begin with the goal of widely disseminating the
results. Classroom averages were delivered to teachers "in a closed envelope."[13]
They were not distributed to parents or published at the level of school averages.
Nonetheless, many schools posted their results or made them available to parents, and by 1994 school results were being published in the Santiago press (Larrañaga, 1995). A recent survey in Santiago suggests that more than 60 percent of
parents are at least aware of what SIMCE is, although fewer can place specific
schools within a range of average scores (Gauri, 1998).

The 1990s

Chile's military ceded power to a democratic government in 1990. Although the
essential form and function of Chile's voucher system were maintained, several

new policies and programs were grafted onto the existing system. The government focused its new policies on improving the quality of primary schools through direct investment, often with aid from international development institutions. The 900 Schools Program, typically called P-900, was targeted at the 10 percent of lowest-achieving schools (Garcia-Huidobro, 1994). Classrooms received a package of basic teaching materials and infrastructure improvements, and teachers received additional in-service training. Funds were also provided to hire and train local secondary graduates as tutors for the lowest-achieving students. In 1992, the Program to Improve the Quality and Equity of Preprimary and Primary Education was initiated with World Bank support (Cox, 1997). More ambitious in scope than P-900, it sought to endow all publicly funded schools (either public or private) with textbooks, libraries, and some infrastructure improvements. Other components of the program were aimed at providing small, multigrade schools with special curricula and pedagogical support; creating a national computer network linking some schools; and rewarding small-scale, school-designed projects with financial grants.

The return to democracy also brought renewed political pressures from teachers seeking improved wages and working conditions. Negotiation between the government and teachers resulted in the passage of the 1991 Estatuto Docente, a national law that subjected the teacher labor market—particularly for public school teachers—to additional regulation.[14] Wage floors were set for teachers with various levels of experience and training; these minimum wages were legislated to vary in lockstep with the voucher's value. Another provision rewarded teachers in some isolated rural schools with higher salaries.[15] Limits on hiring and firing of public teachers were also introduced. Public school teachers could be hired as either tenured or contracted teachers.[16] Tenured teachers were to be hired through public contests in each municipality, and severe restrictions were placed on their firing or reassignment. Contracted teachers had fewer restrictions placed on their hiring and firing and could account for no more than 20 percent of a municipality's teacher workforce. The contracts of private teachers were still governed by the more flexible Labor Code, which permitted greater flexibility in hiring and firing.

Following a vitriolic political debate that pitted the teachers' union against the recently elected centrist government, the 1991 Estatuto was slightly modified in 1995.[17] A new provision relaxed constraints on the firing of public school teachers, allowing municipalities to remove teachers if decisions are consistent with a previously established "Annual Education Plan" (Cox, 1997). Nevertheless, the law stipulates that municipalities are required to first release contracting rather than tenured teachers. Another provision allows for a general system of teacher merit pay, under which every teacher in a given school would be eligible for performance-related awards.

TABLE 7.1   Distribution of Primary Schools and Students Across School Types, 1996

	Percent of Schools			Percent of Enrollment		
	Total	Urban	Rural	Total	Urban	Rural
Public DAEM	55.2	31.5	74.6	40.0	34.7	70.5
Public corporation	12.3	15.5	9.6	18.5	19.4	13.4
Catholic voucher	4.6	9.3	0.8	10.3	11.6	2.8
Protestant voucher	1.2	1.9	0.6	1.5	1.4	1.9
Nonreligious voucher	19.7	26.4	14.3	21.4	23.3	10.9
Private nonvoucher	7.1	15.5	0.2	8.3	9.6	0.6
Total	100	100	100	100	100	100
N (schools or students)	8,393	3,779	4,614	2,015,867	1,716,641	299,226

NOTE: Calculations exclude 163 schools (enrolling 49,537 students) for which data on rural or private status were incomplete.
SOURCE: Ministry of Education and authors' calculations.

A final policy (*financiamento compartido,* or "shared financing") was instituted in 1993. Prior to that law, publicly funded schools were not allowed to charge tuition (although many still found creative ways to circumvent this, such as voluntary fees for parent centers, akin to parent-teacher associations in the United States). The law allowed all private voucher schools—both elementary and secondary—and public secondary schools to charge limited tuition. Voucher payments were to be reduced on a sliding scale that greatly favored charging at least some tuition.[18] By 1996, no more than 2 percent of public schools were participating, whereas 55 percent of Catholic voucher schools and 33 percent of nonreligious voucher schools opted to participate.[19]

Schools and Students Under Vouchers

Table 7.1 shows how primary schools and enrollments are distributed across six different school types. In urban areas, but especially in rural areas, the majority of schools are public. Of these, public DAEMs are the most common management structure. Catholic voucher schools account for 4.6 percent of primary schools nationwide; 1.2 percent of voucher schools are run by Protestant churches. A larger proportion—19.7 percent—is composed of nonreligious voucher schools. Note that Catholic voucher schools and private nonvoucher

TABLE 7.2   Student Characteristics in Public and Private Primary Schools, 1994

	Public DAEM	Public corpor-ation	Catholic voucher	Protestant voucher	Non-religious voucher	Private non-voucher
Female (%)	48.7	48.2	57.2	49.4	46.2	50.5
Years of mother's schooling[a]	7.49 (4.80)	8.97 (2.77)	10.70 (3.45)	9.95 (3.17)	9.28 (2.98)	14.20 (2.26)
Years of father's schooling[a]	7.68 (5.01)	9.44 (2.92)	11.18 (3.56)	10.53 (2.93)	9.64 (3.06)	15.35 (2.36)
Monthly household income[b]	1.65 (2.34)	2.29 (2.23)	3.02 (3.19)	2.61 (1.96)	2.88 (3.11)	11.17 (31.01)
N	16,707	2,740	2,622	227	3,125	1,159

NOTE: Estimates of population standard deviations for continuous variables are in parentheses. Observations are weighted in order to account for their unequal probabilities of selection into the CASEN sample; thus, the distribution of sample observations across school types does not reflect the population distribution.
[a]Means of these variables exclude observations for children whose mothers or fathers are absent from the household.
[b]Variable divided by 100,000.
SOURCE: Encuesta CASEN 1994 and authors' calculations.

schools are much more likely to be located in Chile's urban areas. Even nonreligious voucher schools, which account for 14.3 percent of rural schools, have a proportionally greater representation (26.4 percent) in urban areas. In 1996, eighty-one of Chile's 334 municipalities did not have a single privately run school, although these municipalities, mainly isolated and rural, account for a small fraction of total enrollments.[20]

The students who enroll in each type of school are different in many respects (see Table 7.2). Those attending private nonvoucher schools come from families with much higher incomes, on average, headed by parents with substantially more schooling. The average father of a student in a private nonvoucher school has at least some college, which is not true of any other school type. Differences among students from voucher schools—public and private—are somewhat less pronounced. Nonetheless, the families of students from private—especially Catholic—voucher schools are still of relatively higher socioeconomic status than public school families.

Lessons from the Chilean Voucher Plan

This section explores the impact of the Chilean voucher plan on schools and students, focusing on three questions. First, which families are most likely to choose private voucher schools and which characteristics of schools influence their school choices? Second, are private voucher schools more effective and cost-effective than public schools? Third, did the introduction of vouchers and subsequent expansion of private enrollments increase competition, thereby improving public schools? The following three sections draw on results presented in a series of empirical studies by the authors (Carnoy, 1998; McEwan, 2001; McEwan and Carnoy, 1998, 1999, 2000).[21]

School Choice

Several researchers have shown that Chilean parents with more schooling and higher incomes are more likely to enroll their children in both private voucher and nonvoucher schools, relative to public schools.[22] Although informative, such findings still do not explain why parents have increasingly tended to choose private schools. One method of assessing this is to compare the characteristics of the school actually chosen by parents—whether public or private—to other schools in their choice set. In this fashion, one can examine the revealed preferences of parents for certain school characteristics such as test scores or the socioeconomic background of other parents in the school.

To make this comparison, we estimated conditional logit models of the determinants of parental choice between public, private voucher, and elite private schools where tuition is paid (McEwan and Carnoy, 1998). We find that parents in private voucher schools have higher levels of schooling and income relative to public school parents. Moreover, parental school choice is sensitive to school attributes such as test scores and the educational background of other parents in the school. Stated another way, parents derive satisfaction from increasing amounts of either characteristic and are more likely to choose schools that fulfill those needs. Nevertheless, we find that families have a relatively stronger preference for schools with a higher educated parent clientele. We also find that preferences for school attributes vary strongly in relation to parental education. Less-educated parents, for example, opt for schools with lower test scores and with less-educated parents. The opposite is true of more-educated parents.

The findings are at odds with the hypothesis that less-educated parents respond to the offer of higher-performing, higher-social-class schools to the same degree as do more-educated parents, even when such schools are available in equal numbers and even when their cost is approximately the same. This should not be interpreted as meaning that less-educated parents are "irrational." For example, A. Wells and R. Crain (1992) argue that school choice is governed not only by resource availability but also by access to information and internalized viewpoints associated with social status.

Lower-income parents may not have full information concerning school quality, because such information is costly to obtain or interpret, a sentiment echoed by H. Levin (1991). Existing evidence on Chile suggests that test scores may not be fully disseminated or available to all parents. But even with full information on school quality, members of lower-social-class groups could be "either intimidated by, distrustful of, or resistant to members of the dominant group and therefore [would] remove themselves from competition for seats in the 'best' schools" (Wells and Crain, 1992, pp. 77–78). Lower-income parents might not be as likely to choose higher-performing schools with student bodies exhibiting higher social status even when their children might qualify and they could afford to pay the somewhat higher costs. Their self-perception as not "belonging" in these better public or private schools could explain why the utility functions apparently vary by parental education. Less-educated parents may not be able to escape their position in the social structure to choose higher-status schools. Certainly these explanations must be considered in the Chilean context, where income distribution is highly unequal and class divisions are strong. Schools with educated parents may reinforce these perceptions by dissuading less-educated parents from placing their children there. This would be rational behavior on the part of schools if they believed that lower-status children could affect the school's desirability to other parents, especially those with more education.

The Relative Effectiveness of Private and Public Schools

Which category of school—public or private—produces higher academic achievement among students of a given socioeconomic background? We set out to explore this question using SIMCE achievement data collected by the Ministry of Education between 1990 and 1997 (McEwan, 2001; McEwan and Carnoy, 2000). Since private schools tend to enroll students of a higher socioeconomic status, a simple comparison of average achievement across school types would confuse the distinct effects of schools and families. Thus, both papers make statistical controls for observed student characteristics such as socioeconomic status (SES). Even so, there may be unobserved characteristics of students that lead them to choose private schools more often as well as achieve at higher levels (Murnane, Newstead, and Olsen, 1985). To address this, one of our studies

(McEwan, 2001) makes further statistical corrections for selection bias. In brief, our analyses of these data suggest the following:

At least in recent years (1990–1997), there is strong evidence that nonreligious private voucher schools are not more effective than public DAEM schools, once adequate controls are made for the socioeconomic background of students attending private and public schools (see Table 7.3 for a summary of results, 1990–1996). Despite the consistent pattern of negative and statistically significant effects for nonreligious voucher schools (relative to public DAEM schools), the magnitudes of the effects are not very large. After controlling for SES and school location, achievement in nonreligious voucher schools is around 10 percent of a standard deviation lower than public DAEM achievement.

That being said, one category of private voucher schools may be somewhat more effective than public schools and nonreligious voucher schools: Catholic schools, run either by the archdiocese or by religious orders. The relatively smaller fraction of pupils in such explicitly religious schools (see Table 7.1) has consistently scored higher than students in other voucher schools. Since these Catholic schools are also likely to be selective on student differences that schools can observe but that are not measured in our analysis, their test-score advantage might be overstated. Our attempts to account for such selection bias in the analysis of 1997 data still had Catholic school students scoring slightly higher than public students, although standard errors of the estimates were sufficiently large to prevent strong inferences.

Our results suggest that nonreligious and religious private schools have different effects on student outcomes. The results are consistent with U.S. research that finds positive Catholic school effects on achievement and attainment. Yet results also cast doubt on how useful studies of Catholic schools are in understanding the potential effects of nonreligious private schools that enter the market under a voucher system.

The fact that our analysis of relative student performance in public and private schools begins in 1990, seven years after the initial implementation of the voucher plan, could mean that we are just measuring the positive result of competition between private and public schools. Thanks to vouchers and the public school response to increased competition, the average scores of public students may have increased by 1990 to the point where public-private parity has been achieved. We explore this issue in a separate analysis and briefly discuss it below, but suffice it to say that there is mixed evidence that competition had widespread effects on public school effectiveness.

TABLE 7.3 Fourth-Grade Achievement Differences Between Public DAEM and Other School Types

	Dependent Variable: Spanish Achievement					Dependent Variable: Mathematics Achievement				
	1990	*1992*	*1994*	*1996*	*Mean Effect (90–96)*	*1990*	*1992*	*1994*	*1996*	*Mean Effect (90–96)*
Unadjusted difference:										
Public corporation	0.27	0.22	0.11	0.05	0.16	0.22	0.21	0.10	n.s.	0.13
Catholic voucher	1.11	1.09	1.07	0.99	1.07	1.02	0.98	0.91	0.87	0.94
Protestant voucher	0.40	0.31	0.47	0.39	0.39	0.37	0.22	0.36	0.33	0.32
Nonreligious voucher	0.48	0.40	0.40	0.34	0.40	0.44	0.33	0.33	0.27	0.35
Private nonvoucher	1.93	1.89	1.90	1.61	1.83	1.94	1.75	1.80	1.56	1.76
Adjusted for SES, location:										
Public corporation	-0.04	-0.06	-0.08	-0.08	-0.06	-0.04	-0.03	-0.06	-0.09	-0.06
Catholic voucher	0.31	0.23	0.25	0.27	0.27	0.28	0.19	0.17	0.24	0.22
Protestant voucher	-0.17	-0.21	-0.01	-0.16	-0.14	-0.18	-0.27	-0.09	-0.15	-0.17
Nonreligious voucher	-0.05	-0.10	-0.07	-0.07	-0.07	-0.04	-0.10	-0.08	-0.08	-0.07
Private nonvoucher	0.63	0.61	0.66	0.38	0.57	0.67	0.58	0.65	0.40	0.57

NOTE: n.s. indicates not statistically significant at 5 percent. Unadjusted differences are coefficients from regressions in which achievement is the dependent variable and school type dummies are the only independent variables (omitted category: Public DAEM). Adjusted differences are from regressions that make additional controls for socioeconomic status of students, school location, and other variables. In all regressions, the dependent variable is standardized to a mean of zero and a standard deviation of one.

SOURCE: McEwan and Carnoy, forthcoming.

The Relative Costs of Private and Public Schools

In addition to the achievement of public and private schools, we also compared their relative costs (McEwan and Carnoy, 2000). Because data are limited, we did not systematically estimate private and public school costs using the "ingredients" method suggested by Levin and McEwan (2001). Instead, we used estimates of each school's annual income to proxy total costs in 1996. Public school revenues are derived from five sources: national voucher payments; own-revenue contributions of local municipalities; infrastructure financing from Chile's Regional Development Fund; parent contributions, including parent-center fees and donations; and nationally administered government programs such as the 900 Schools Program. Private voucher schools do without the second and third, although some private schools, particularly those affiliated with the Catholic Church, may receive additional monetary or in-kind resources such as donated infrastructure.[23] Private paid schools, which do not accept vouchers, are entirely funded by private tuition or donations.

We used a variety of data to construct cost estimates, including the national voucher database in 1996, municipal education budgets, and Ministry of Education records. Several particulars are worth noting. Most public schools do not finance infrastructure out of current income from vouchers, whereas nonreligious private schools do. As such, we imputed an annual rental value for buildings and land of public and religious private schools, using a 1996 school infrastructure survey. Furthermore, we calculated private education expenditures for each school type by using a 1997 census of eighth-grade parents, in which parents estimated their monthly expenditures on tuition, parent-center fees, uniforms, and transportation.

Mean per-student costs (in 1996 pesos) are presented in Figure 7.3, divided by school type and location. The costs of public DAEMs and corporations are similar, but there is substantial heterogeneity among voucher schools. Those managed by the Catholic Church are somewhat more costly than DAEM schools (about 14 percent), whereas nonreligious voucher schools are less costly (about 9 percent). Nonvoucher schools, which rely exclusively on private-sector contributions, are by far the most costly alternative of the six. The differences between per-student costs in urban and rural schools are not particularly marked.

We further compared private and public costs using multiproduct cost functions that control for levels of output (achievement) and exogenous "environmental" factors such as student socioeconomic background and school location. Our results suggest that Catholic schools are about as costly as public schools,

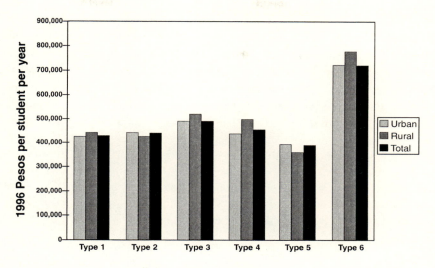

Type 1: Public DAEM
Type 2: Public corporation
Type 3: Catholic voucher
Type 4: Protestant voucher
Type 5: Nonreligious voucher
Type 6: Private nonvoucher

FIGURE 7.3   Mean Annual Per-Student Costs (1996 pesos)
NOTE: Estimates are for 2,945 schools, enrolling predominantly primary students (grades 1–8). They are distributed among school types as follows: 1,278 (Type 1), 386 (Type 2), 125 (Type 3), 21 (Type 4), 766 (Type 5), and 369 (Type 6).
SOURCE: McEwan and Carnoy, forthcoming.

once these factors are taken into account. In contrast, nonreligious schools have somewhat lower costs than do public schools.

The apparent inefficiency of public schools relative to commercial private schools may stem from several factors that are mostly related to the teacher wage bill, the largest share of expenditures. Public schools face a different—and stricter—set of legal constraints regarding teacher wages and working conditions compared to private schools. The result is that public schools are obligated to pay higher wages and have substantially less flexibility in teacher contracting. For example, they cannot fire teachers easily, and hiring of tenured teachers must occur through public municipal contests rather than at the school level. Private schools are much more likely to employ short-term or part-time contractors. In large cities, these schools can easily recruit so-called taxi teachers for shorter-hour contracts among teachers with stable, tenured jobs in the public schools.

To summarize, municipal schools cost more than nonreligious private schools and, hence, the majority of private voucher schools. But as discussed in the previous section, municipal schools are also somewhat more effective. Catholic private schools are both more effective than municipal schools, but they also appear to be somewhat more costly. This raises a number of interesting issues. If we want to maximize effectiveness, public and Catholic education may be a better investment. If we want to minimize costs per unit of output, commercial private voucher schools may be the best option, even if their effectiveness is somewhat lower for a given student. This assumes, however, that as the number of public schools declines, private commercial schools can continue the present practice of recruiting teachers part-time and at lower than public school salaries.

Did Competition Improve Public School Performance?

Milton Friedman suggested that vouchers would "permit competition to develop," thus leading to the "development and improvement of all schools" (1962, p. 93). Despite its importance, the assertion has been little-explored by empirical researchers. The few studies that exist have been conducted in educational systems that do not use vouchers, such as the United States (e.g., Dee, 1998; Hoxby, 1994). The empirical challenge facing researchers is to relate a proxy of market competitiveness—such as the local share of private school enrollments—to outcome measures such as academic achievement. Greater competition, proxied by the enrollment share, is hypothesized to increase achievement, all else being equal. Nevertheless, partial correlations between private enrollments and achievement, even controlling for a wide range of background variables, are not likely to provide unbiased estimates of the effects of competition. There are at least two reasons for this.

First, private enrollments may be correlated with unmeasured determinants of achievement. In Chile, for example, private enrollments tend to be higher in more privileged municipalities; if we do not perfectly control for municipal wealth or socioeconomic status—both likely determinants of achievement—then we confound the effects of competition and unmeasured municipal characteristics. Second, private enrollments and achievement may be simultaneously determined. That is, increasing private enrollments may lead to higher achievement in public schools, but low levels of achievement in public schools may encourage more parents to choose private schools.

To address these biases, we constructed a panel (or longitudinal) data set on public schools between 1982 and 1996 (McEwan and Carnoy, 1999). By differencing the panel data, we were able to control for unobserved determinants of outcomes that might bias estimates of competition effects.[24] Our results suggest that increasing private enrollment shares may be associated with increases in public school achievement for a particular group of schools, namely, those catering to middle-class students in Santiago, a metropolitan area where a very high fraction of students (around 50 percent, on average) attend private schools. Apparently such middle-class public schools, when faced with competition from private schools, are able to respond by raising test scores. But our results also suggest that for public schools enrolling lower SES students, and for those located outside of Santiago, competition may have negative effects.

We suggest at least two potential explanations for the lack of competitive effects. First, some public schools may lack the proper incentives to compete, in spite of declining enrollments and revenues. As one example, V. Gauri (1998) documents how some municipalities faced "soft" budget constraints during the 1980s. When voucher revenues declined, these municipalities lobbied the national government for extra budget allotments instead of improving quality. Second, some public schools may not possess the means to improve quality, even if faced with proper incentives. These schools generally employ the least-qualified teachers and enroll impoverished students who are ill-prepared to succeed in the classroom. When these schools are faced with declining enrollments, they may simply lack the pedagogical tools that are necessary to raise achievement. As partial evidence of this, we found that P-900—implemented by the national Ministry of Education—was quite successful in raising achievement in poor schools (McEwan and Carnoy, 1999). P-900 targeted poor schools with a minimal package of inputs, including teacher training and textbooks.

Targeted Vouchers in Colombia

The voucher program in Colombia was initiated in the fall of 1991 with objectives somewhat different compared to Chile's plan. First, the Colombian plan was directed at expanding secondary education by taking advantage of underutilized private school infrastructure. With overcrowding in public secondary schools, the primary goal was to give vouchers to students who would otherwise not go to secondary schools and to low-income students wishing to transfer from overcrowded public schools. Like most voucher plans, this one was immersed in a rhetoric of providing more choice and increasing efficiency through increased competition among secondary schools (Calderón, 1996).

The Colombian plan was introduced as part of the 1992 Decentralization Bill that transferred decisionmaking and financial resources directly to departments and municipalities and provided for greater autonomy for schools.[25] As part of a general move to restructure the Colombian economy, the government proposed to give municipalities control over local school management, with money supplied through bloc grants from the central government. These bloc grants implied cuts in central government spending. In this same proposal, departments would be in charge of technical support and teacher training, and schools themselves would have autonomy over managing and selecting school personnel. To increase choice for parents and competition among schools, vouchers were to be created for poor students, and private education expansion was to be encouraged.

The debate in the Constitutional Assembly over the reform package showed that municipal governments viewed the decentralization proposal as motivated mainly by a desire to reduce central government spending on education. The municipalities wanted larger monetary transfers and smaller local responsibilities for raising resources in return for taking on the job of providing educational services. Ultimately, the central government did increase the resource transfer package as part of the new constitution, even though it meant raising the fiscal cost of the reform. But once the constitution was enacted, the Congress had to propose specific legal changes in the way education was run, and this brought on a new round of opposition from the teachers' union (Montenegro, 1995). The union drafted its own legislation in direct opposition to the reform. After a lengthy and painful debate, both Reform Laws were approved. As a result, full responsibility for schools was transferred only to departments and the larger municipalities. Moreover, schools did not get the autonomy to select, hire, fire, and sanction teachers and administrative personnel, and the evaluation of student achievement was to become a part of the reform but was not to be a basis for teacher promotion. Finally, vouchers were approved for poor students, and the pay of teachers and education managers was guaranteed to come out of the central government transfers to the departments and larger municipalities (Calderón, 1996).

Colombian schools do not have the autonomy of Chilean schools, and the bureaucracy in the Colombian system remains greater. Yet the problems faced by the poorest and lowest technical capacity municipalities in Chile are less likely to occur in Colombia, where departments can still maintain much of the responsibility for making educational decisions for municipalities. Also—due in part to municipality and teacher union protests—Colombian schools get relatively more public funds than did Chilean schools during the 1980s decentralization, and privatization evolved more slowly, perhaps allowing public schools to adapt more effectively. The confrontation—particularly teacher-union resistance to a reduction of funding for public schools—ensured that the voucher plan was limited to low-income students.

In its final configuration, then, the compromise resulted in a voucher plan restricted to students from low-income families entering the sixth grade and who previously attended a public primary school. Parents can document their low income by showing a utility bill that indicates the relative wealth of the household neighborhood. Only families in the bottom two (of six) strata are eligible for vouchers (Calderón, 1996). In municipalities where demand for vouchers exceeds supply, officials are supposed to hold a lottery among applicants. The voucher can be renewed upon the completion of each academic year until graduation. Students who fail a grade automatically lose their voucher.

Because of the nature of the 1992 reform, the voucher program is also a "partnership between the central government and local governments" (King et al., 1997, p. 9). Municipalities choose to participate in the program, although this choice is influenced by policies at the department level. If a municipality does participate, it must pay 20 percent of the voucher's cost against the central government's 80 percent. Municipalities are more likely to participate in the program when they have a higher unmet demand for secondary school places and have greater private secondary school capacity.[26] Private schools in those municipalities participating in the voucher program also can choose to take vouchers or not. Nonprofit schools are more likely to take vouchers than for-profit schools, and academic schools are less likely to participate than nonacademic technical or vocational schools.

As expected, schools that serve low-income pupils are more likely to participate, and so are schools with lower tuition fees. The average monthly fee in a participating private school is 40 percent lower compared to a nonparticipating school. But this fact hides a more complex relationship between fees and participation. Nonparticipating schools include those with very high fees, for whom the voucher is far too small to induce accepting low-income students, as well as relatively low-tuition schools, already most affordable to low-income students and perceived to be of lower quality than public schools (and, hence, unlikely to be attractive to voucher recipients).

The number of vouchers has increased from an initial 18,000 in 1991 to 49,000 in 1992 to 89,000 in 1995 and the targeted 100,000 in 1996. This represents about 10 percent of the total increase in secondary enrollment in the period 1991–1995 but only 1 percent of all students in secondary school and 2.6 percent in private secondary schools (Calderón, 1996; King et al., 1997, p. 16). Most of the increase in the program occurred between 1992 and 1994. At its peak, in 1995, 216 municipalities and 1,800 private schools participated. Since then, the number of new vouchers has decreased sharply, from about 30,000 in 1994 to about 5,000 in 1996, and although the maximum value of a voucher rose from US$128 to US$177 between 1992 and 1996, apparently this was too small an increase to meet large increases in tuition costs in 1996 (King et al., 1997, p. 21). Both facts suggest declining support for the voucher plan in the central government; indeed, the Ministry of Education is limiting the number of new vouchers to those funded by the World Bank loan project that provides 5,500 vouchers annually to selected municipalities.

Lessons from the Colombian Voucher Plan

Research on the Colombian plan is far more limited than in Chile, but we can draw a few inferences from it regarding the benefits to low-income recipients and the likely supply responses from private schools to vouchers for low-income students.

King et al. (1997) compare average test results for *all* students (voucher and nonvoucher) in private participating, private nonparticipating, and public schools for 1992–1993, the first year in which a significant number of voucher recipients entered private secondary schools in the seventh grade. The average math and language mastery levels of students in the seventh grade do not differ significantly between private participating and public schools but are significantly higher in nonparticipating schools.[27] Students in the lowest decile in voucher schools score about the same as students in lowest decile in public and nonparticipating private schools, and those in the highest decile in voucher schools do as well or better than those in the highest decile in public schools but not nearly as well as those in nonparticipating private schools.

In a recent evaluation of Colombian vouchers, World Bank researchers studied a sample of 1995 and 1997 voucher applicants from Bogotá and a sample of the 1993 applicant cohort from Jamundi, a Cali suburb (Angrist et al., 2000). The results showed that voucher winners were about 16 percent more likely to attend private school than those not chosen in the voucher lottery. Winners were also likely to complete more schooling, mainly because they were less likely to repeat a grade. Results of a test given by the researchers to a separate, non-random sample in Bogotá indicate that winners had marginally higher reading scores.

The study suggests that winning a voucher does provide financial inducement to attend private schooling. More important, the voucher has a positive impact on student attainment, in part because it motivates students to do better academically to avoid repeating a grade and losing the voucher. As Angrist et al. (2000) note, however, private schools are also induced to reduce repetition among voucher holders, since losing the voucher might mean that a student leaves the school. The results do not show that private schooling is necessarily more effective than public. Voucher winners seem to do better than losers even when both attend private schools, and might also do better than losers in public schools if they could use the voucher there and the same rules applied.

It is also telling that, according to King et al. (1997), by the ninth grade, with much higher dropout rates in both private and public schools, the differences in both math and Spanish in the average mastery level percentages among the three types of schools are smaller or not significantly different from zero.

Like the Chilean voucher plan, the targeted plan in Colombia suggests that the academic performance of low-income students is not very different in public and private schools. But the two cases also suggest that private voucher schools may produce relatively higher achievement when they are established and not-for-profit (such as Catholic schools in Chile). For-profit schools that are formed in response to vouchers seem less likely to provide greater achievement than public schools (and, as the Chilean results suggest, they may produce even less achievement). It is telling that in 1995 the Colombian government restricted vouchers to nonprofit schools. This action was taken because a number of for-profit schools, created in response to the voucher plan and with voucher students as their sole clientele, had real difficulties (Calderón, 1996).

This reinforces yet another lesson to be drawn from such voucher plans. Even when the plan targets low-income students, the supply of private education can be a major constraint on the quality of overall educational provision. This is why prevoucher econometric comparisons between existing private and public education can be so misleading even when student characteristics are adequately controlled. The underlying assumption of such comparisons is that the effectiveness of current private schools will largely be replicated by new market entrants after the introduction of vouchers. In Colombia, this problem was partially solved by providing vouchers to fill unused capacity at existing private schools. But those schools are concentrated in areas (mainly cities and larger towns) with a sufficient lower-middle- and middle-class clientele to support tuition schools. In poor areas without such schools, even within large cities, the supply of new voucher schools may have produced very different results. Similarly, in Chile, the new schools created to profit from vouchers are, on average, relatively less effective than public and Catholic schools.

Conclusion

Chile's national voucher plan led to a rapid growth in private enrollments, driven by the expansion of nonreligious, for-profit schools. Evidence suggests that these schools are somewhat less effective (but also more efficient) than public schools in producing academic achievement. In contrast, established Catholic schools are more effective (but similarly efficient) than public schools. Increasing competition from private schools may have improved public school achievement for a subset of middle-class students in Santiago, but not nationwide. In Colombia, a targeted program awarded secondary scholarships to poor students. It appears to have succeeded in expanding access to secondary education, although there do not appear to be large differences in the quality of public and participating private schools. However, the existing comparisons are limited to private schools that existed at the beginning of the program; some anecdotal evidence suggests that new private schools were of lower quality (Calderón, 1996).

For U.S. researchers and policymakers, the results have important implications. It is misleading to predict the impact of large-scale voucher plans in the United States by relying on current comparisons of public and Catholic schools.[28] Vouchers will probably lead to the creation of many new private schools and the modification (or closure) of existing public and private schools. The objectives, resources, constraints, and outcomes of new private schools (especially nonreligious and for-profit schools) may bear only a passing resemblance to those of existing Catholic schools. Our theoretical and empirical understanding of these differences is regrettably limited. Rather than continue to churn out comparisons of Catholic and public schools, it would be more interesting to focus research on emerging charter school reforms that encourage the creation of publicly funded and privately managed schools.

The evidence in Chile and Colombia also provides a cautionary tale. It suggests that voucher plans that are comprehensive in coverage are less likely to benefit the poor. The best-quality voucher schools in Chile are operated by the Catholic Church; however, these schools enroll higher SES students than do nonreligious voucher schools and charge higher tuition copayments. Most poor students attend public or nonreligious voucher schools. Furthermore, the majority of private schools are still located in urban areas with higher-income and better-educated families. Despite twenty years of voucher reform, public schools are still the only option for an important fraction of primary students. Finally, competition appears not to have improved the achievement of the poorest public school students. In contrast to Chile's plan, Colombia's targeted voucher plan was able to provide greater benefits to the poor, largely because it was explicitly limited to poorer families.

Notes

1. Voucher proponents have claimed that private schools are more effective and efficient than public schools because they produce higher achievement and attainment in similar kinds of students at lower cost. Much of the evidence in the United States has focused on achievement and attainment in Catholic schools (for reviews, see Neal, 1998; Witte, 1992; Witte, 1996). Studies in Colombia, the Dominican Republic, the Philippines, Tanzania, and Thailand have purported to show that private education produces higher achievement at lower per-pupil cost even when corrected for the socioeconomic background differences of pupils in private and public schools and for selectivity bias (Cox and Jimenez, 1990; Jimenez et al., 1991; Jimenez, Lockheed, and Wattanawaha, 1988; Jimenez, Lockheed, and Paqueo, 1991). Similarly, a recent study of 900 eighth-grade students attending schools in Lucknow, Uttar Pradesh, India, shows much higher cost-effectiveness of fee-paying private schools (Kingdon, 1996). For a summary of the evidence on private school effectiveness in developing countries, see E. Jimenez and M. E. Lockheed (1995). For a more critical review, see A. R. Riddell (1993). A growing literature attempts to assess how increasing competition from private schools affects public school outcomes (Arum, 1996; Couch, Shughart, and Williams, 1993; Dee, 1998; Hoxby, 1994).

2. Studies of peer effects are generally of two types. Many empirical studies test for the existence and magnitude of peer effects (e.g., Henderson, Mieszkowski, and Sauvageau, 1978; Summers and Wolfe, 1977). Other researchers have incorporated peer effects in models of communities or schooling markets and examined the effects on efficiency and equity (e.g., Arnott and Rowse, 1987; Epple and Romano, 1998; Nechyba, 1996).

3. For a detailed account of the reforms, see V. Gauri (1998).

4. Gauri (1998) and T. R. Parry (1997) describe how property and equipment were leased at no cost to municipalities for ninety-nine years.

5. Municipalities received an overhead grant of 3–5 percent on total municipal wages and salaries as an inducement to begin administering schools (Parry 1997; Winkler and Rounds 1996).

6. For further details, see C. Aedo (1996), V. Espinola (1993), or Parry (1997).

7. After 1988 a legal ruling closed this option to municipalities. Although the creation of new corporations was ruled unconstitutional, existing ones were permitted to operate (Aedo, 1996).

8. Gauri (1998) recounts that the corporation of one large city, Antofagasta, typically ran large deficits and employed excessive numbers of school administrators.

9. Chilean law specifies a factor by which the base voucher is adjusted for students at every grade level. Furthermore, selected municipalities receive "zone assignments" to compensate for high poverty or isolation. It should be noted, however, that adjustments are largely ad hoc and may not reflect true variation in educational costs. Since 1987, rural schools within municipalities have received upward adjustments. See Parry (1997) for further details.

10. After indexation was suspended, the nominal value of the voucher was occasionally increased in accordance with wages of other public sector employees, which still fell significantly short of inflation (Gauri, 1998).

11. Growing private enrollments in the context of plummeting revenues suggests that other factors were in flux such as costs. The levels of teacher salaries—the largest proportion of costs—declined 40 percent in real terms between 1981 and 1990 (Rojas, 1998).

12. Several criteria were used to exclude schools from participation in the testing process, including primary enrollments and the physical isolation of the school. A smaller percentage of students (around 10 percent) completed assessments in other subjects such as science.

13. See Espinola (1993, p. 161).

14. Law 19.070 of 1991. See Rojas (1998) for additional details.

15. The rural bonus also applied to private voucher schools. Although paid out to municipalities and *sostenedores* along with the standard voucher payments, the bonus was earmarked for teachers.

16. Chilean Spanish makes the distinction between *titulares* and *contratados*.

17. Gauri (1998) describes the political circumstances leading up to the modifications.

18. Discounts to vouchers are applied progressively. If the tuition charge is less than half the level of the current voucher level, no discount is applied. Tuition charges between one-half and one voucher incur a 10 percent deduction. Charges between one and two vouchers incur a 20 percent deduction. C. Cox (1997) provides additional details. Ninety-three percent of schools that opted to participate in shared financing in 1994 had either a zero or 10 percent deduction (Aedo, 1996).

19. Author's calculations with data from the Ministry of Education.

20. Author's calculations with data from the Ministry of Education.

21. In this paper, we only provide brief summaries of methods, data, and findings. For further details, we encourage interested readers to consult the published works, or to contact us for copies of unpublished papers.

22. See Table 7.2 in this chapter, as well as Aedo and Larrañaga (1994), Gauri (1998), and Winkler and Rounds (1996).

23. U.S. Catholic secondary schools, for example, receive about 25 percent of their annual income from nontuition sources (Guerra 1995).

24. We initially first-differenced the data (akin to including "fixed effects," or dummy variables, for each school). First-differencing controls for unobserved determinants of outcomes that are constant across time for individual schools. We then differenced the data a second time using a "difference-in-difference" approach that controls for unobservables that have a constant time-trend.

25. In Colombia the department is roughly equivalent to the state as a unit of administrative organization.

26. See E. King et al. (1997), table 7.

27. Mastery level is the proportion of students in each type of school who have mastered levels 3 and 4 of the criterion-referenced achievement tests. Level 3 is the test items that should be mastered by at least one-half the students; level 4 is the test components that should have been mastered by at least one-quarter of the students (King et al., 1997, p. 34).

28. Derek Neal concludes in his review of Catholic school effectiveness that "we cannot confidently expect positive outcomes for [voucher] program participants if the program is large in scale. . . . Large school voucher programs would likely mean the expansion of many existing private schools and the entry of many new private schools. How would this expansion and entry affect the quality of private schools or the quality of remaining public schools? We do not know, and available data shed little light on this question" (1998, p. 84).

References

Aedo, C. (1996). Calidad de la educación y elementos de mercado. In *Educación en Chile: Un desafío de calidad*. Santiago, Chile: ENERSIS.

———. (1998). Differences in schools and student performance in Chile. In W. D. Savedoff (ed.), *Organization matters: Agency problems in health and education in Latin America*. Washington, D.C.: Johns Hopkins University Press.

Aedo, C., and Larrañaga, O. (1994). Sistemas de entrega de los servicios sociales: La experiencia Chilena. In C. Aedo and O. Larrañaga (eds.), *Sistema de entrega de los servicios sociales: Una agenda para la reforma*. Washington, D.C.: Banco Interamericano de Desarrollo.

Angrist, J. D., Bettinger, E., Bloom, E., King, E., and Kremer, M. (2000). *Vouchers for private schooling in Colombia: Evidence from a randomized natural experiment*. Washington, D.C.: World Bank (mimeo).

Arnott, R., and John Rowse, J. (1987). Peer group effects and educational attainment. *Journal of Public Economics* 32, 287–305.

Arum, R. (1996). Do private schools force public schools to compete? *American Sociological Review* 61, 29–46.

Calderón, A. (1996). Voucher programs for secondary schools: The Colombian experience. HCO Working Paper 66. Washington, D.C.: World Bank.

Carnoy, M. (1998). National voucher plans in Chile and Sweden: Did privatization reforms make for better education? *Comparative Education Review* 42, 309–337.

Castañeda, T. (1992). *Combating poverty: Innovative social reforms in Chile during the 1980s*. San Francisco: ICS.

Couch, J. F., Shughart, W. F., and Williams, A. F. (1993). Private school enrollments and public school performance. *Public Choice* 76, 301–312.

Cox, C. (1997). *La reforma de la educación chilena: Contexto, contenidos, implementación*. Santiago: Programa de Promoción de la Reforma Educativa en América Latina (PREAL).

Cox, D., and Jimenez, E. (1990). The relative effectiveness of private and public schools: Evidence from two developing countries. *Journal of Development Economics* 34, 99–121.

Dee, T.S. (1998). Competition and the quality of public schools. *Economics of Education Review* 17, 419–427.

Epple, D., and Romano, R.E. (1998). Competition between private and public schools, vouchers, and peer-group effects. *American Economic Review* 88, 33–62.

Espinola, V. (1993). *The educational reform of the military regime in Chile: The system's response to competition, choice, and market relations*. Ph.D. diss., University of Wales, U.K.

Friedman, M. (1955). The role of government in education. In R.A. Solo (ed.), *Economics and the public interest*. New Brunswick, N.J.: Rutgers University Press.

———. (1962). *Capitalism and freedom*. Chicago: University of Chicago Press.

Garcia-Huidobro, J. E. (1994). Positive discrimination in education: Its justification and a Chilean example. *International Review of Education* 40, 209–221.

Gauri, V. (1998). *School choice in Chile: Two decades of educational reform*. Pittsburgh: University of Pittsburgh Press.

Guerra, M. J. (1995). *Dollars and sense: Catholic high schools and their finances, 1994*. Washington, D.C.: National Catholic Educational Association.

Henderson, V., Mieszkowski, P., and Sauvageau, Y. (1978). Peer group effects and educational production functions. *Journal of Public Economics* 10, 97–106.

Hoxby, C. M. (1994). Do private schools provide competition for public schools? National Bureau of Economic Research Working Paper No. 4978.

James, E. (1988). The public/private division of responsibility for education: An international comparison. In T. James and H. M. Levin (eds.), *Comparing public and private schools*, vol. 1. New York: Falmer Press.

Jimenez, E., and Lockheed, M. E. (1995). Public and private secondary education in developing countries: A comparative study. World Bank Discussion Paper 309. Washington, D.C.: World Bank.

Jimenez, E., Lockheed, M.E., Luna, E., and Paqueo, V. (1991). School effects and costs for private and public schools in the Dominican Republic. *International Journal of Educational Research* 15, 393–410.

Jimenez, E., Lockheed, M.E., and Paqueo, V. (1991). The relative efficiency of private and public schools in developing countries. *World Bank Research Observer* 6, 205–218.

Jimenez, E., Lockheed, M.E., and Wattanawaha, N. (1988). The relative efficiency of public and private schools: The case of Thailand. *World Bank Economic Review* 2, 139–164.

Jofré, G. (1988). El sistema de subvenciones en educación: La experiencia chilena. *Estudios Públicos*, no. 32, 193–237.

King, E., Rawlings, L. Marybell Gutierrez, M., Pardo, C., and Torres, C. (1997). Colombia's targeted education voucher program: Features, coverage, and participation. Working Paper Series on Impact Evaluation of Education Reforms, No. 3. Washington, D.C.: World Bank.

Kingdon, G. (1996). The quality and efficiency of private and public education: A case-study of urban India. *Oxford Bulletin of Economics and Statistics* 58, 57–82.

Knight, J. B., and Sabot, R. H. (1990). *Education, productivity, and inequality: The East African natural experiment*. New York: Oxford University Press.

Larrañaga, O. (1995). Descentralización de la educación en Chile: Una evaluación económica. *Estudios Públicos*, 243–286.

Levin, H.M. (1991). The economics of educational choice. *Economics of Education Review* 10, 137–158.

Levin, H. M., and McEwan, P. J. (2001). *Cost-effectiveness analysis: Methods and applications*. Thousand Oaks, Calif.: Sage Publications.

McEwan, P. J. (2001). The effectiveness of public, Catholic, and non-religious private schooling in Chile's voucher system. *Education Economics* 9, no. 2.

McEwan, P. J., and Carnoy, M. (1998). Choice between private and public schools in a voucher system: Evidence from Chile. Unpublished paper, Stanford University.

_____. (1999). The impact of competition on public school quality: Longitudinal evidence from Chile's voucher system. Unpublished paper, Stanford University.

_____. (2000). The effectiveness and efficiency of private schools in Chile's voucher system. *Educational Evaluation and Policy Analysis* 22, 213–239.

Montenegro, A. (1995). An incomplete educational reform: The case of Colombia. HCO Working Paper 60. Washington, D.C.: World Bank.

Murnane, R. J., Newstead, S., and Olsen, R. J. (1985). Comparing public and private schools: The puzzling role of selection bias. *Journal of Business and Economic Statistics* 3, 23–35.

Neal, D. (1998). What have we learned about the benefits of private schooling? *Federal Reserve Bank of New York Policy Review* 4, 79–86.

Nechyba, T. J. (1996). Public school finance in a general equilibrium Tiebout world: Equalization programs, peer effects, and competition. National Bureau of Economic Research Working Paper No. 5642.

Parry, T. R. (1997). Achieving balance in decentralization: A case study of education decentralization in Chile. *World Development* 25, 211–225.

Riddell, A. R. (1993). The evidence on public/private educational trade-offs in developing countries. *International Journal of Educational Development* 13, 373–386.

Rojas, P. (1998). Remuneraciones de los profesores en Chile. *Estudios Públicos,* 121–175.

Schiefelbein, E. (1991). Restructuring education through economic competition: The case of Chile. *Journal of Educational Administration* 29, 17–29.

Stewart, F., and Ranis, G. (1994). Decentralization in Chile. Human Development Report Occasional Papers No. 14.

Summers, A.A., and Wolfe, B.L. (1977). Do schools make a difference? *American Economic Review* 67, 639–652.

Wells, A.S., and Crain, R.L. (1992). Do parents choose school quality or school status? A sociological theory of free market education. In P.W. Cookson (ed.), *The choice controversy*. Newbury Park, Calif.: Corwin Press.

Winkler, D.R., and Rounds, T. (1996). Municipal and private sector response to decentralization and school choice. *Economics of Education Review* 15, 365–376.

Witte, J.F. (1992). Private school versus public school achievement: Are there findings that should affect the educational choice debate? *Economics of Education Review* 11, 371–394.

_____. (1996). School choice and student performance. In H. F. Ladd (ed.), *Holding schools accountable: Performance-based reform in education*. Washington, D.C.: Brookings Institution.

World Bank. (1995). *Priorities and strategies for education: A World Bank review*. Washington, D.C.: World Bank.

8

Privatization in Industrialized Countries

GEOFFREY WALFORD

Although privatization has become a major aspect of change in the educational systems of many industrialized countries, the concept of privatization in education is far from easy to define. The concept covers a range of activities and goes beyond the simple ownership of schools by for-profit companies. Moreover, when considering privatization within a range of industrialized countries, it is important to recognize that there are considerable differences in what might be considered as privatization among educational systems. These differences are not simply due to disputes about definition but relate to the great diversity in how educational systems have developed within industrialized societies.

The concept of privatization implies a starting point from which various activities lead to changes within the structure and nature of educational provision in a given country. But over the centuries, various countries have developed different, and often complex, ways of funding and managing schools and other educational programs. The starting points before privatization occurs are different, so the nature of the interventions that may be promoted under the banner of privatization differ, as do the effects of privatization measures. Thus, for example,

The research reported in this chapter was made possible in part by a grant from the Spencer Foundation. The data presented, the statements made, and the views expressed are solely the responsibility of the author.

within the Netherlands, some 70 percent of schools are officially private yet fully funded by the Dutch government on exactly the same basis as schools that are owned and managed by the state. In contrast, in England most private schools receive no direct funding from the state, but Roman Catholic and Church of England schools (which are still owned and largely governed by the churches) are considered to be part of the state sector. In two such different contexts, there is a broad similarity between the nature of the privatization measures, with less similarity between the effects of changes brought on by privatization. What becomes immediately obvious is that any evaluation or comparative study of the nature and effects of privatization must adopt a broad definition of "privatization." Further, it must focus on the conditions and constraints under which specific privatization changes occurred, rather than the fact of privatization itself. Privatization cannot be labeled "good" or "bad" in the abstract. What is important is the ways in which the state and others have acted to structure the privatization process and the ways in which schools can subsequently operate.

It is not clear whether privatization is best seen as an example of "policy borrowing" or of globalization. Both concepts are useful in describing the forces behind specific examples of privatization in industrialized countries. Since the early 1980s what has come to be known as "educational policy borrowing" has greatly increased. Government ministers, civil servants, and educationalists have looked for transportable solutions to perceived problems in their own educational systems (Walford, 1995a; Halpin and Troyna, 1995). One prominent example can be seen in the British City Technology Colleges (CTCs), which, at least in part, were justified by American magnet school programs (Green, 1993). A more recent example is the 1993 Education Act for England and Wales, where policy borrowing from the Netherlands played a part in legitimizing legislation that made it easier for existing private Muslim, fundamentalist Christian, and other faith-based schools to become state-funded (Walford, 1997a). Alternatively, an explanation that focuses on globalization would consider trends in worldwide economic, political, and social factors that led to increased privatization of goods and services as a response. This model would certainly help us understand the broad similarities in policy among various countries, but it is deficient at the micro level: It can be shown that countries at very different stages of industrial development have initiated changes that might be considered to be based on privatization.

Whichever broad framework one adopts, looking at the educational systems of other countries and observing what works has an obvious appeal to politicians and policymakers looking for rapid solutions to perceived difficulties or those wishing to legitimize changes of direction within their own systems. However, in practice, wrenching policies from their historic, economic, political, and cultural roots can result in unanticipated consequences. As D. Phillips (1992) argues, it is the sociocultural setting that keeps a country's educational policies in place; the rather different sociocultural setting of the borrower country provides resistance to the implantation of ideas from other systems. Although it is highly instructive to examine the ideas and structures of other countries, superficial comparisons are likely to mislead. In-depth comparative studies are required that take account of the different historic, economic, political, and cultural situations. Such comparisons would not give instantly transportable solutions but would help us to rethink our own assumptions and clarify our aims and ideas.

The title of this chapter is "Privatization in Industrial Countries," but I am immediately forced to admit that it is impossible for me to write about all industrialized countries. This is not simply a problem of space limitations or lack of knowledge on my part (although I admit to a great deal of that), but simply that we do not know about the nature and effects of privatization policies across all industrialized countries. Although there is much more systematically gained evidence about the nature and effects of privatization in the countries of Western Europe, even here we have fundamental gaps in our knowledge. Further, despite studies of individual countries, I know of no systematic comparative studies that have examined more than two or three countries at a time. A full comparative study of several Western European countries is a vital necessity if we are to begin to understand how privatization policies are impacting education and the potential that various privatization measures might bring.

Thus, this chapter will give examples of privatization in just two countries of Western Europe. Given the complexity and diversity of privatization processes, I make no apology for using England, Wales, and the Netherlands as my examples. This is where I have the greatest knowledge, having researched and written about privatization in England and Wales for the last decade or more, and having a current research interest in the Netherlands. Moreover, England and Wales provide excellent examples of the diversity of policy forms that can be considered as part of privatization processes, and the Dutch system provides a contrasting example that might be seen as having been privatized for the last eighty years. I also make no apology for restricting my discussion to schools. Although there are some interesting examples of privatization in higher education, preschool education, and vocational training, it would be a mistake to attempt to cover all of these areas in this chapter.

Privatization in England and Wales

As in several other European countries, privatization in education in England and Wales must be understood alongside other privatization policies. Privatization was one of the major policy priorities of successive British Conservative governments between 1979 and 1997. The term now applies to a number of apparently disparate government policies. Most obviously, it refers to the sale of government-owned monopolies and trading companies to shareholders, but privatization can be said to have occurred in residential homes for the elderly, bus deregulation, the sale of council houses, the establishment of private prisons, and changes to pensions, health, and social services. In all of these cases there has been a shift away from state provision (although not necessarily state subsidy), and a corresponding encouragement of the private sector. Writing in a pamphlet published by the right-wing Adam Smith Institute, M. Pirie (1985) described privatization as a general approach that can generate and focus policy ideas. He illustrated this diversity through a list of about twenty different methods by which privatization has been introduced: selling the whole or the part, charging for services, contracting-out, buying out existing interest groups, encouraging private institutions, encouraging exit from state institutions, and divestment. All of these aspects can be found in recent changes in England and Wales.

Within education, privatization has similarly taken many different forms. R. Pring (1986) discussed these in terms of the government's two main thrusts of (1) supporting and encouraging many aspects of the private sector while (2) gradually decreasing its support for the state-maintained sector. Thus, while the state-maintained sector has seen contracting-out of services, with increasingly inadequate levels of state funding (and a consequent growing need to raise additional support from industry, parents, and the local community), the government has given positive encouragement to alternative private institutions and contracting-out of services through its ideological and financial support and has encouraged exit from state institutions.

From very early on in Margaret Thatcher's first Conservative government in 1979, a series of separate yet interlinked policies were introduced to support and encourage private-sector education while gradually decreasing support given to the state-maintained sector. There has been a gradual blurring of the boundaries between the two forms of education provision and a growth in competition among schools.

The first Conservative legislation to give support to the private sector was the Assisted Places Scheme of 1980. As with several other Conservative Party policies, this scheme was linked to ideas of academic selection of children for different types of school (Walford, 1997b). Under this scheme academically able children were given means-tested scholarships so that they could attend certain private schools. In practice, T. Edwards, J. Fitz, and G. Whitty (1989) have shown that a large proportion of the children benefiting from the scheme have been from families able to play the system. Those families sufficiently knowledgeable about the procedures and able to negotiate the choice and selection processes have been re-warded with staffing and facilities. The scheme acted as a direct financial support for selected high-status private schools, but, perhaps more important, it also gave ideological support to the whole private sector. The implication of the scheme was that private schools are "better" than the state sector and that the government had little faith that its own schools were the right place for aspiring parents to send their children.

At first sight, this scheme might not be considered as a privatization measure at all; indeed, there is debate about its role in the broader privatization process (Whitty et al., 1998). However, examined within its historical, economic, political, and social context, it becomes clear that such a designation is appropriate. At a simple level, the scheme can be seen as allowing the private sector to run part of a service previously provided by the state and thus exemplifies one of the elements of privatization identified by D. Heald (1983). But the words of Stuart Sexton (1987), one of the main architects of the Assisted Places Scheme and educational adviser to two secretaries of state for education, made it clear that a fully privatized education service was his long-term aim. According to him, the Assisted Places Scheme could be seen as the first step in a gradual plan toward the "eventual introduction of a 'market system' truly based upon the supremacy of parental choice, the supremacy of purchasing power"(p. 9). The scheme was extended and modified several times by successive Conservative governments. However, when it returned to power in 1997 the Labour Party had a manifesto commitment to abolish it, and support is now being phased out.

The second, and most clearly significant, development of educational privatization in England and Wales occurred in 1986, when the central government announced that it intended to work with sponsors to establish a pilot network of twenty City Technology Colleges. CTCs were intended to provide free, technology-enhanced education to selected children within particular inner-city areas. They were to be private schools run by independent charitable trusts, with the sponsors having a major influence on the way in which the colleges were managed. These sponsors were also intended to provide substantial financial and material support. A key element of the CTCs is that they were established as private schools, and the expectation was that the CTCs would be funded at a higher level than other schools through contributions from both the state and private sponsors. Private school status also allowed the CTCs considerable flexibility in staffing, curriculum, and management issues (Walford, 1991). Again, selection was a central feature of the plan. In this case selection of children is not based on academic ability—a spread of abilities is required by law—but the method of selection still closely resembles that of the Assisted Places Scheme. Families need to know about the CTCs and be able and prepared to negotiate the entrance procedures (which usually include a test and interview). The children have to agree to work a longer school day and longer terms and intend to stay at school until age eighteen.

As is well known, there were considerable difficulties in attracting sufficient sponsorship and in finding appropriate sites for the CTCs (Walford and Miller, 1991; Whitty, Edwards and Gewirtz, 1993). A recurring feature of both Conservative and, more recently, Labour privatization is that private industry and commerce have been reluctant to become involved in education in the ways that the government intended. Although industry and commerce were encouraged to be centrally involved in the establishment and running of the CTCs, they were not allowed to make any profits. The program foundered at fifteen CTCs, with about 20 percent of capital funding having been provided by sponsors and the bulk of the capital expenditures (and practically all of the current expenditures) being provided by the central government.

The 1986 announcement of the CTCs thus marked a break with the traditional pattern in England and Wales that all state-funded schools should be financed and managed through the local education authorities. The 1988 Education Reform Act's introduction of grant-maintained schools made the break decisive. The development of grant-maintained schools can be seen to be closely linked to privatization. Although these schools were nonprofit, they frequently had businesspeople on their boards of governors and had considerable independence of action. They were free to contract-out various services and to supply services to others. Entrepreneurship was encouraged.

In contrast, even as the Conservative government gave strong financial and ideological support to grant-maintained schools, the local authority–maintained sector was at the receiving end of various negative elements of privatization. In particular, spending on education overall did not keep up with the necessary demands made on it. A succession of Her Majesty's Inspectorate (HMI) reports throughout the 1980s and 1990s cataloged the neglect of physical bricks and mortar, and it became commonplace for parents to paint and decorate classrooms in order to ensure an appropriate environment for their children. Many parents now pay for what were once regarded as the essentials of education (Pring, 1987), and their donations have become increasingly important in maintaining the quality of service and facilities. In addition to providing funds for school trips, new computers, decoration of premises, and new equipment, many schools now rely on parents to fund actual staff. It is now common for some teachers and additional auxiliary staff to be dependent on voluntary donations for their salaries (Leach, 1997). Payment has become a ubiquitous necessity for those parents who demand high standards; the problem is that not all parents are able or willing to contribute, leading to inadequate funding in some schools.

Although fund-raising for schools occurred well before 1988, the act's establishment of grant-maintained schools and local management of all schools meant that schools became far more responsible for their own financial situation. Seeking private industrial or commercial funding has become an important part of many headteachers' jobs. In some schools companies now pay to have advertisements sited within the buildings (£5,000 per year for ten billboards; Whittaker, 1998); in other schools companies sponsor cultural or artistic events in return for brand advertising. When supermarkets such as Tescos and Sainsbury's offer computers or other equipment to schools if parents shop at their stores, many schools actively encourage parents to do so. One recent campaign involved collecting tokens from junk food such as crisps and newspapers such as *The Sun,* which could be collected through the schools and exchanged for books. If sufficient tokens are collected, some 2 million books could be provided. Although the addition of more books must be approved, there are clear ethical problems about schools acting to encourage such a diet. Moreover, the problem with all such schemes is that some parents are more able or willing to donate than others, and some schools have better links with industry than their neighbors. Schools that serve children from poor homes are unlikely to be able to generate much additional funding from either parents or sponsors, whereas schools serving more affluent families may do well soliciting from both. Consequently the inequalities among schools may gradually increase.

School-based management, coupled with government requirements for local authorities to seek competitive contracts for services, has also led to further privatizing measures. Before 1979 practically all school meals were provided by the schools themselves through the local education authority. Grant-maintained schools were given the right to organize their meal service as they wished, and by 1998 about 22 percent of grant-maintained schools used private caterers (Midgley, 1998). Additionally, some 16 percent of Local Education Authority (LEA) schools were supplied by the private sector, as their LEA had contracted out this responsibility. This change was controversial, as school meals in England have traditionally been considered part of the welfare state. They were an attempt to ensure that all children received at least one nutritious meal each day, and children from poor households received free school meals—which is still used as the major indicator of poverty in educational research. Free school meals remain, but the quality of the meal is dependent on how tightly the contract was drawn in individual cases.

School-based management has also led to another, somewhat unexpected, privatization process. Before 1988, when a teacher was absent it was possible for schools to contact their local education authority and request a supply or substitute teacher. The local education authorities had a list of such teachers, paid on a standard daily rate by the LEA. Quite rapidly, this system has been largely replaced by agreements made between schools and individual supply teachers or, more commonly, through schools' use of supply agencies. A large number of private, for-profit companies now guarantee to find a replacement teacher at short notice. Rather than the school having to make numerous telephone calls to find an available substitute teacher, one call ensures success (Morrison and Galloway, 1994). The agencies are strong in London, where schools often found it difficult to obtain teachers at short notice. Some London agencies specialize in Australian teachers who, it seems, are particularly able to deal with some children who provide difficulties for English teachers.

The delegation of funding to schools has also led to a variety of private consultants and trainers within schools. The 1988 Education Reform Act made it compulsory for all schools to provide regular training days for teachers while students are on vacation. Some of these days are organized in-house, but it is now common for schools to call in consultants and trainers to provide specific knowledge about curriculum, management, preparation for inspection, and specific programs such as assertive discipline (Rigoni and Walford, 1998). Again, these services would once have been provided by the LEAs but are now often provided by for-profit organizations and individuals.

Privatization Measures in the 1990s

The 1992 Education Act made great changes to the way in which schools were inspected. It established the Office for Standards in Education (Ofsted), and the post of chief inspector for schools in England, the holder of which is charged with ensuring that all schools are regularly inspected by teams of registered inspectors every four years. Registered inspectors are individuals who have successfully completed a training course and are free to bid to inspect schools when the chief inspector determines that they should be inspected. In practice, as inspections require several registered inspectors, many for-profit agencies bid for contracts and then staff inspections with freelance inspectors. In the original Bill, schools were to choose the inspectors they wished from those groups that submitted a bid, but this rather strange proposal was changed before the legislation was passed. The chief inspector for schools now makes the decision. Yet competition between agencies has led to a swift decline in the costs of each inspection. In the early days following the act inspectors could expect to get about £5,000 for each week's inspection, but fees have recently fallen to about £2,200—and there is a growing concern about the quality of inspections as experienced inspectors are rapidly leaving for better-paying work (Magowan, 1999).

There are several aspects of the 1993 Education Act and subsequent government announcements that include elements of privatization. The act allowed voluntary aided and grant-maintained schools to apply to the secretary of state for education for a change to their governing instruments and articles to include sponsor governors and become CTCs. This was later extended to local-authority schools. Schools that already have a strong and planned commitment to technology, science, and mathematics were expected to be able to find sponsorship from industry in return for these places on the governing body. These sponsors have to make a financial commitment of £100,000 per school and are expected to have meaningful involvement in the school's operations. There is no question of business ownership of such schools, but the sponsors are expected to have places on the governing body. Once this support has been obtained, three extra sources of funding are available: an initial capital grant for furniture, equipment, and associated building work; an enhanced annual capital formula allocation intended to contribute toward replacement and upgrading of enhanced equipment; and additional revenue funding above their normal funding designed to "assist with the extra costs of operating an enhanced, technology-rich curriculum" (DFE, 1992, p. 10). The intent is that these colleges be funded (initially and thereafter) at a higher level than other schools, predicated on the idea that some children should be selected to benefit from schools funded at a higher level, whereas other children are left in schools that presumably are not funded at a level sufficient to provide an up-to-date technology experience.

The 1993 Education Act also encourages diversification of schools through the establishment of new sponsored grant-maintained schools that support particular religious or philosophical beliefs. These schools may aim to foster, for example, Islamic, Buddhist, or evangelical Christian beliefs or wish to promote unique educational philosophies. Existing faith-based private schools were able to apply to become reestablished as grant-maintained schools. At first sight this aspect of the policy would appear to be the very opposite of privatization, as existing private schools are being taken into the state sector. In practice, the policy's implementation demonstrates that it is best considered as having elements of privatization (Walford, 1997a, 2000).

The important difference between these new sponsored grant-maintained schools and existing grant-maintained schools was that sponsors had to pay for at least 15 percent of costs related to providing a site for the school and its buildings. The booklet by the Funding Agency for Schools (FAS; *Guidance for Promoters*) made it clear that this 15 percent was a minimum and that potential sponsors should not assume that the agency would fund 85 percent of the project:

A major factor for the Agency is whether the proposals represent value for money. If you are able to contribute a higher proportion of the capital costs of a project, any capital grant we pay will represent better value for money for the public and we will therefore be better placed to give overall support for the proposal. (FAS, 1995)

The legislation came into operation in April 1994. In the period leading up to the general election of May 1997, seven schools in England were granted sponsored grant-maintained status. All seven schools had religious foundations—six Roman Catholic and one Jewish—and all gave substantially more than 15 percent of the capital costs. A further seven schools in England have been given grant-maintained status under the Labour administration. Although there are some interesting contrasts between the schools granted sponsored grant-maintained status by the Conservative government and those granted the status under Labour, one would not expect a complete discontinuity. As the new government wished to restructure the whole schooling system, no further applications were accepted after May 1997, so the Labour government was making decisions on applications that had been put forward under the Conservative government. However, the most recent applications were made in the expectation that a Labour government would be returned and that they would have had little chance of success under a Conservative government. The Labour decisions marked some dramatic changes in policy. Although all of the successful schools under the Conservative government were either Roman Catholic or Jewish and thus showed no decisive break with the past, the Labour government granted four applications that may be of considerable political and social significance: one Seventh Day Adventist secondary school, two Muslim primary schools, and one small community school, each of which serves a particular minority population (see Walford, 2000). In all but one case, these seven schools made substantial contributions to capital costs. For example, the trust that runs one of the existing private Muslim schools in Birmingham is paying 50 percent of the capital costs of a new building for more students. The state is thus benefiting from private funding for an expanding Muslim population as well as delegating the task of management to private trusts.

The Conservative government's Private Finance Initiative took many years to come to fruition. This was an attempt to reduce capital expenditures on schools (and other public buildings) with the intent that LEAs would rent purpose-built accommodation rather than build their own. As the Labour government is also keen to reduce capital expenditures, this policy has been encouraged and extended since Labour took power (Department for Education and Employment [DFEE], 1998). The first such school—a small primary opened in Hull in January 1999—and the second—a large, well-established secondary in Dorset—

moved to new buildings in September 1999. The buildings were the first to be designed, built, financed, and operated by private-sector companies, which will receive revenues for a contracted period of twenty-five years (Thornton, 1998). Here, there is a strict separation between running the building and being involved in schooling itself. The owing companies are responsible for the physical maintenance of the buildings and will provide such services as required according to the contract, but they will not be involved in teaching or staffing matters.

Privatization Under Labour?

Privatization was a key Conservative policy for almost two decades, but the current Labour government has tried to distance itself from the concept. Indeed, Secretary of State for Education and Employment David Blunkett has denied that new educational developments should be considered as privatization. Perhaps so under a very narrow definition of the concept, but it is evident that several recent policies have important privatization features.

The 1988 School Standards and Framework Act was multifaceted but included aspects that increased inspection powers and put into place remedies for failing organizations. It extended the powers of inspection of the Office for Standards in Education such that whole LEAs could be inspected as well as schools. If an LEA is found to be performing badly, the act gives powers to the secretary of state to take control of that LEA. He can ask other LEAs—or any nonprofit or for-profit organization he chooses—to take on the responsibility. In an important speech, David Blunkett stated that he did not exclude the possibility of a for-profit company being invited to take over such a failing LEA (Rafferty, 1999).

Schools that are found to be failing in their Ofsted inspections may be taken over by private for-profit companies. The first case was King's Manor, where the Surrey LEA decided to close the school and invited bids to reopen and operate it under a private company. At one point Edison was going to make a bid but did not. However, one for-profit company (Nord Anglia) and two nonprofit companies (Centre for British Teachers and 3Es) submitted bids to take over the school. In the end the contract was awarded to 3Es, which is the business arm of the first City Technology College, Kingshurst in Birmingham (Walford and Miller, 1991). The result is now being put forward as "an imaginative twinning arrangement" rather than a privatization (Pyke and Ghouri, 1999).

Education Action Zones (EAZs) represent another ambitious policy development under the 1998 act. EAZs are designed to develop programs that help raise educational standards in deprived inner cities or rural areas. Typically, an EAZ comprises between 15 and 25 primary, secondary and special schools, working in partnership with local parents, Early Years Providers, businesses, the LEA, community organizations, TEC(s), careers service, colleges, other statutory agencies (such as health authorities, the youth service and the police) and other. The strategic direction of the zone will be set by an Action Forum. (DFEE, 1999, p. 5)

The basic idea behind EAZs is that schooling in certain deprived areas could be improved by targeting greater financial and human resources and by involving a variety of local people and organizations in a new partnership. The details of the policy have changed slightly since their original announcement in the 1997 Green Paper (DFEE, 1997), and the first twenty-five EAZs are now in operation. Each receives up to £1 million extra funding a year for five years, of which the government provides £750,000. The additional £250,000 has to be found from sponsors who are able to contribute with cash or in-kind. This need for sponsorship is linked to the way in which EAZs are selected. Rather than identify target areas of deprivation where EAZs are thought to be necessary, the government has left it to local initiative to develop proposals for EAZs and to submit bids for funding. Schools have to agree to be part of an EAZ before any bid can be made.

One critic (Chitty, 1998) has already labeled EAZs as "test-beds for privatization," but such a designation is not straightforward. It is certainly true that business and industry are expected to play major roles in EAZs. For example, it is stated that "businesses can provide leadership, or management expertise, or enter into radical new contracts to provide services" (DFEE, 1999, p. 1). But it is also clear that

business contributions, whether in cash or kind, should be unconditional, i.e., they must not be pledged against future purchase of goods, equipment or services from the donor, or other arrangements with financial benefit to the donor. They must carry no loss-leading commercial advantage to the donor. (DFEE, 1999, p. 25)

Thus there might be said to be increased privatization of the management of schools—but there can be no direct profit. However, Chitty is also concerned with the ideology that such an emphasis on private business supports, as well as with the various ways in which business can influence the curriculum, aims, and purposes of schooling. This is also one of several concerns expressed by R. Hatcher (1998).

The EAZs have been given various exemptions from the legal requirements under which all other state-maintained schools operate. First, they do not have to teach the National Curriculum, which both Hatcher and Chitty believe could lead to a limited and more directly work-related curriculum for some children in disadvantaged areas. Second, teachers do not need to be paid on the national salary scale. The intent here is that teachers in the EAZs will be paid more, but there are concerns that this could be another step toward local wage bargaining. Third, the EAZs may put private consultants in management positions within schools, and they need not be trained teachers.

EAZs are still at an early stage. Unexpectedly, most have been led by LEAs, but such household names as ICI, British Telecom, McDonald's, Shell, IBM, American Express, and Cadbury Schweppes are at the forefront of these developments. Although the government denies that the EAZs are privatization measures, it is evident that some commentators see them as a part of a wider privatization process. The facts that the British government should be so emphatic in its denial, and that they might not be seen in this light in other countries, is further evidence that privatization can be researched and understood only within a wider study of the social, historical, economic, and political context in which policies are developed and put into practice.

Privatization in the Netherlands

In terms of privatization, the Netherlands provides a direct contrast to England. For supporters of a greater diversity of state-funded schools, the Dutch system presents several features that appear to be highly desirable. The most significant are that state-owned and private schools are financed by the state on an equal basis, and that about two-thirds of all primary and secondary pupils are taught within private schools. It is open for any group of parents and others to apply to the Ministry of Education and Science to establish new schools; if the relevant criteria are met, these new schools become state-funded. This means that in addition to the state schools organized by the state municipalities the Netherlands has Roman Catholic and Protestant Christian schools, as well as Islamic, Hindu, and Jewish schools. There are also several private secular schools that promote educational philosophies such as Montessori, Dalton, Jenaplan, and Freinet schools (Ministerie van Onderwijs en Wetenschappen [MOW], 1996).

But aspects of the Dutch system that are so attractive to supporters of diversity cannot be understood in isolation. The nature and structure of Dutch education must be examined in the context of the wider historical, religious, and political features of Dutch society. Indeed, E. James (1989) argues that "the evolution of the Dutch system of primary and secondary education is unique in the Western World" in that it moved from a relatively secular state monopoly at the beginning of the nineteenth century to a highly pluralistic, largely religious-based system by the beginning of the twentieth century.

Geographically, the Netherlands has few natural boundaries on the east and south, and the current political boundaries follow the defeat of Napoleon, the creation of the kingdom of the Netherlands in 1814, and the subsequent withdrawal of Belgium from the kingdom in 1839. This division left Belgium relatively homogeneous religiously but divided linguistically, the Netherlands relatively homogeneous linguistically but divided religiously (Andeweg and Irwin, 1993). The basic cleavage between the Roman Catholic and Protestant denominations became more complex during the nineteenth century as divisions within the Dutch Reformed Church occurred and, led by such people as Abraham Kuyper, groups of orthodox Calvinist Protestants broke away from the theologically liberal Dutch Reformed Church to form their own churches. These "little men" (*de kleine luyden*), who were often small shopkeepers, clerks, artisans, and the like, eventually formed the Rereformed (Gereformeerde) churches. These three religious groups eventually became associated with political parties and, with the addition of a further party that developed from the socialist workers' movement and another based upon the relatively affluent Liberals (who held power until universal suffrage), still form the basis of the five current main political parties in the Netherlands.

Although Roman Catholics had never been banned, they were given the right to establish their own schools only in 1848, and the church hierarchy was reestablished only in 1853. The Catholics then joined with the growing number of Gereformeerde churches to seek state support for religious schools on an equal basis with state-supported schools. The funding of such schools became one of the two major issues in the nineteenth-century Netherlands and was finally resolved by the new 1917 constitution when a Catholic-Calvinist majority coalition led to the so-called Pacification, which introduced social reform, universal suffrage, and the right to state funding for religious schools.

The fact that such a change to the education system should be intertwined with issues of social justice and universal suffrage is an indication of the "pillarization" of Dutch society that existed at the time and thrived until the late 1960s. The minority groups were not simply linked to the five political parties; they were organized social groups or subcultures that affected many aspects of everyday life. At its strongest (for Catholics in the 1950s, for example), the "pillar" included separate hospitals, social services, television channels, newspapers, schools, universities, trades unions, and employers' organizations. A Catholic "would have lived his or her life within the confines of a homogeneous Catholic subculture and its organizational infrastructure" (Andeweg and Irwin, 1993, p. 29).

But pillarization is no longer the strength that it was. Increasing secularism and materialism, along with a greater internationalism, have meant that since the late 1960s there have been great changes in Dutch society. In particular, the importance of religion has waned. By the late 1980s some 30 percent of Dutch people stated that they had no belief in God, and only some 40 percent claimed to attend a church service at least once a month. In Britain the comparable figures were 20 percent and 23 percent (Inglehart, 1990, p. 188). Except for those in the Gereformeerde churches, religion no longer has such a strong hold. Moreover, pillarization is no longer encouraged by the Dutch elite, leading to greater linkages among different providers of social services, education, and so on. Greater social and geographical mobility has led to a diminution of social divisions based on the pillars.

This outline history shows that the principle of state support for private schools where there should be separate-but-equal school systems was the direct result of a society of minorities that was already sharply segmented along religious lines. The stability of the society as a whole is dependent upon the degree to which the various religious groups hold to a collection of fundamental shared assumptions and values about the nature of society. This situation has considerable differences from those pertaining to present-day England, where some of the religious groups wishing to open their own schools adhere to beliefs that challenge the mainstream.

In a sense the Netherlands can be said to have encouraged a privatized schooling system since 1917, but the nature of that privatization is heavily constrained by the state. Schools are run by local governing bodies that have considerable autonomy over whom to employ and how to organize the school, but in return for full state funding private schools accept and work within many constraints. These constrains largely link to issues of equity about which the Dutch government has long been concerned. Particularly at the primary (basic) school level, considerable attempts are made to ensure equity of treatment for all children in all schools. Central government control of class size, teacher numbers, subjects of study, and inspection, in particular, are designed to ensure that significant differences do not develop among schools. Thus, for example, private schools are forbidden to charge any but small, specific fees to parents; neither are they able to use donations or sponsorship to improve the teacher-student ratios. They are heavily constrained in all issues that relate to equity among the typical student's daily experiences (aside from faith or philosophy, of course). Although these constrains are considerable, private groups have largely been prepared to accept them. The number of private schools not receiving state support is minute, largely limited to foreign national and international schools not wishing to follow the Dutch curriculum.

Another significant aspect is that in the Netherlands schooling, rather than education, is compulsory. It is not possible for parents to teach children themselves in their own homes. Thus, the growth in home schooling that has occurred in England, the United States, and Australia (to name a few) has not happened in the Netherlands (Webb, 1990; Thomas, 1998). This particular form of privatization is outlawed.

It is not, of course, that the Dutch have been entirely successful in maintaining equity between schools. One current problem that has educators and politicians concerned is ethnic segregation. The growing ethnic minority population is unevenly distributed geographically, such that in some areas, particularly in the four largest cities of Amsterdam, The Hague, Rotterdam, and Utrecht, the concentrations of ethnic minority children can be high. S. Karsten (1994) claims that at a time when the Netherlands is becoming increasingly multicultural the schools are, paradoxically, becoming less integrated. Once the proportion of ethnic minority children exceeds about 50 percent, many Dutch parents use their freedom to avoid schools where non-Dutch children form a substantial proportion. This has led some urban schools to become ethnically divided (Louis and van Velzen, 1990/1991). White Dutch parents have been found to be much more "mobile" in their choices than most ethnic minority groups and are prepared to take their children to schools outside their neighborhood (Karsten, 1994). In particular, because the majority of ethnic minority children are enrolled in state schools, some private religious schools are now seen as providing "safe havens" for white pupils. They can perform this function because, although they cannot discriminate in admissions on the basis of ethic origin, they can refuse entry to children on religious grounds.

This phenomenon of white flight is seen as a problem on both academic and social grounds. Several studies suggest that ethnic segregation has adverse effects on minority and majority students (Tesser and Mulder, 1990, quoted in Karsten, 1994) and hampers social integration. Although the Dutch school legislation makes it difficult to decrease segregation, several municipalities have made significant attempts to do so (Karsten, 1994). Change in the composition of existing schools is, however, only part of what is increasingly seen as a problem of ethnic segregation in schools, for there has been a growth in the number of newly formed Muslim schools (now nearly thirty) and Hindu schools. Thus, within the Netherlands the right to found new schools is no longer seen as having unambiguous merit; it is now viewed as having potential weaknesses as well as benefits.

Setting the Research Agenda

In the two major examples described in this chapter, I have attempted to illustrate the diversity of policy changes that might be seen as being linked to privatization. I have also tried to show that these changes can be understood only within a framework of knowledge of the social, historical, economic, and politic context in which they were developed and put into place. Attempting to investigate all industrial countries as if they present a homogeneous group is to simplify reality; what is interesting and of wider relevance and usefulness would be lost. Detailed studies of the processes of privatization are required so that we can better understand the effects of policies and learn from the experience of other countries. A multistage research process is required. I have also argued that any evaluation or comparative study of the nature and effects of privatization must adopt a broad definition of "privatization." To narrow the focus to just one predefined activity is potentially to lose the possibility of analyzing much of the promise and problems of privatization. Further, any research must focus on the conditions and constraints under which privatization changes occurred, rather than the fact of privatization itself. Privatization cannot be labeled "good" or "bad" in the abstract. The two examples illustrate the importance of how the state and others have acted to structure the privatization process and the ways in which schools can subsequently operate.

Stage 1

The first stage of any research agenda focusing on privatization within industrialized countries is, of necessity, a mapping process. There is a need to document the nature and extent of privatization in its many forms in a variety of countries. In practice, a small number of countries will have to be selected for detailed study to illustrate the potential range of possible privatization measures and the level of constraint under which privatization measures operate.

This stage of the research would be possible through a series of commissioned literature reviews of a sample of countries. These reviews would be best conducted by active academics who are nationals of each of the countries concerned. But there would be a need to carefully coordinate these reviews and to develop a common framework for discussion that allowed each country's review author to cover the full range of privatization measures. One or more coordinating meetings of authors and some visits to the selected countries by the project coordinator would be necessary.

The selection of the focus countries is not as straightforward as it might seem. It would be instructive to obtain reviews that investigate the extent and nature of privatization in a diversity of countries, but some of the most interesting countries may be difficult to investigate. For example, there is great interest and activity in privatization in Eastern Europe and the Baltic republics (Beresford-Hill, 1998). A full review of educational privatization in the Czech Republic (Svecová, 1998) or Poland (Laciak, 1998) would be highly instructive. However, due to the developing state of educational research in those countries and the difficulties of language, it may be necessary to restrict reviews to countries where English is the first or a major language of research communication. Obvious contenders (outside the United States) include: England and Wales, Scotland, New Zealand, Australia, Canada, the Netherlands, Finland, Norway, Germany, Spain, and Greece. All of these countries present different and potentially illuminating examples of policy changes that might be considered as privatization.

Stage 2

Having obtained a broad understanding of the situation in selected countries, there would be a need to undertake specific research case studies of particular policies. In each of these case studies it will be necessary to examine what policymakers put forward as the intended outcomes and assess the extent to which these outcomes have been met. There has now been a series of evaluations of educational policy in Britain that have attempted to assess outcomes against intentions (e.g., Edwards et al., 1989; Walford and Miller, 1991; Fitz et al., 1993; Whitty, Edwards, and Gewirtz, 1993), and a similar broad research strategy could be followed. Additionally, there is a need to assess the effects of any privatization measure against the criteria of efficiency, effectiveness, excellence, and equity. Not only are these criteria commonly used in promoting privatization changes; they might be considered as closely linked to any evaluation of services for the public in a democratic society.

If the research in England and Wales is typical, what is remarkable is that the main thrust of research has focused on equity; issues of efficiency, effectiveness, and excellence have until recently largely been forgotten. Although equity is relevant, it is also necessary to investigate the efficiency, effectiveness, and excellence that result from policy changes, for increasing them was often the intent of policymakers. Thus, for example, there has been considerable research on the equity effects of the changes brought about by the 1988 Education Reform Act, where researchers such as S. Gewirtz et al. (1995), R. Glatter et al. (1997), G. Walford

(1994), S. Carroll and G. Walford (1997), and P.A. Woods et al. (1998) have shown that some aspects of privatization and increased choice encouraged by the act have led to greater class, ethnic, and gender inequities in schooling. But there has been practically no comparable research that has examined the other effects of the changes (one example is Anderson and Bush, 1999).

The choice of case studies needs to be considered with care, and it probably will be possible to make choices only after the initial mapping process has been undertaken. For example, it might seem obvious that insights could be gained by looking at the privatization inherent within the changes to the English inspection service for schools or the involvement of private businesses in Education Action Zones, but far greater insight could be gained if comparable policies have been initiated in other countries. Ideally, we need comparative studies of selected similar policies within two or more countries. Although it is instructive to examine the educational ideas and structures of other countries in isolation, rigorous and systematic comparative work is likely to be most rewarding. There is a need to go beyond superficial comparisons, which are likely to mislead, and conduct in-depth comparative studies that take account of the different historic, economic, political, and cultural situations.

This second stage of the research would thus investigate the ways in which two or three systems support or inhibit privatization strategies, with a focus on the role of the state and the constraints that it sets on such strategies. Detailed comparative study will shed light on the substantive issues and seek to answer such questions as:

- What is the established policy of each state toward privatization in education?
- How has this policy evolved over time?
- What are the principles on which privatization measures are considered?
- What kind of financial and other support is provided?
- What constraints and regulations are imposed?
- How has the system responded to recent privatization changes?
- What are the current tensions in the system?
- How do various participants seek a resolution to these conflicts?
- Have privatization policies increased efficiency?
- Have privatization policies increased effectiveness?
- Have privatization policies led to greater excellence?
- Have the results of privatization policies been equitable?

References

Anderson, L., and Bush, T. (1999). Educational standards and grant-maintained schools. *Educational Management and Administration* 27(1), 17–27.

Andeweg, R. B., and Irwin, G. A. (1993). *Dutch government and politics.* London: Macmillan.

Beresford-Hill, P. (ed.) (1998). *Education and privatisation in Eastern Europe and the Baltic Republics.* Wallingford, U.K.: Triangle.

Braster, J.F.A. (1993). School struggle, pillarization, and the choice of public and private schools in the Netherlands. In J. Dronkers (ed.), *Education and social change, vol. 3: International perspectives on education and society.* Greenwich, Conn.: JAI Press.

Brown, F. (1992). The Dutch experience with school choice: Implications for American education. In P. W. Cookson Jr. (ed.), *The choice controversy.* Newbury Park, Calif.: Corwin Press.

Carroll, S., and Walford, G. (1997). Parents' responses to the school quasi-market. *Research Papers in Education* 12(1), 3–26.

Chitty, C. (1997). Privatisation and marketisation. *Oxford Review of Education* 23(1), 45–62.

_____. (1998). Education action zones: Testbeds for privatisation? *Forum* 40(3), 79–81.

Cox, C., and Marks, J. (1979). *Education and freedom: The roots of diversity.* London: National Council for Educational Standards.

Department for Education (U.K.). (1992). *Choice and diversity: A new framework for schools.* London: DFE.

_____. (1993). *Technology Colleges: Schools for the future.* London: DFE.

Department for Education and Employment (U.K.). (1997). *Excellence in schools.* London: DFEE.

_____. (1998). *Investing for excellence: Guide to the structure and financing of the education and employment sectors.* London: DFEE.

_____. (1999). *Meeting the challenge: Education Action Zones.* London: DFEE.

Dronkers, J. (1995). The existence of parental choice in the Netherlands. *Educational Policy* 9(3), 227–243.

Edwards, T., Fitz, J., and Whitty, G. (1989). *The state and private education: An evaluation of the Assisted Places Scheme.* London: Falmer.

Faasse, J. H., Bakker, B., Dronkers, J., and Schijf, H. (1987). The impact of educational reform: Empirical evidence from two Dutch generations. *Comparative Education* 23(3), 261–277.

Fitz, J., Halpin, D., and Power, S. (1993). *Grant maintained schools: Education in the market place.* London: Kogan Page.

Flew, A. (1991). Educational services: Independent competition or maintained monopoly? In D. G. Green (ed.), *Empowering the parents: How to break the schools monopoly.* London: Institute of Economic Affairs.

Funding Agency for Schools. (1995). *Guidance for promoters.* York, U.K.: Funding Agency for Schools.

Gewirtz, S., Ball, S. J., and Bowe, R. (1995). *Markets, choice, and equity in education.* Buckingham, U.K.: Open University Press.

Glatter, R., Woods, P. A., and Bagley, C. (1997). Diversity, differentiation, and hierarchy: School choice and parental preferences. In R. Glatter, P. A. Woods, and C. Bagley (eds.), *Choice and diversity in schooling.* London: Routledge.

Green, A. (1993). Magnet schools, choice, and the politics of policy borrowing. *Oxford Studies in Comparative Education* 3(1), 83–103.

Halpin, D., and Troyna, B. (1995). The politics of education policy borrowing. *Comparative Education* 31(3), 303–310.

Hatcher, R. (1998). Profiting from schools: Business and Education Action Zones. *Education and Social Justice* 1(1), 9–16.

Heald, D. (1983). *Public expenditure: In defence of reform.* Oxford: Robertson.

Inglehart, R. (1990). *Culture shift in advanced industrial society.* Princeton: Princeton University Press.

James, E. (1989). The Netherlands: Benefits and costs of privatized public services—lessons from the Dutch educational system. In G. Walford (ed.), *Private schools in ten countries: Policy and practice.* London: Routledge.

Karsten, S. (1994). Policy on ethnic segregation in a system of choice: The case of the Netherlands. *Journal of Education Policy* 9(3), 211–225.

Karsten, S., and Teelken, C. (1996). School choice in the Netherlands. In G. Walford (ed.), *School choice and the quasi-market.* Wallingford, U.K.: Triangle.

Laciak, B. (1998). The development of non-public education in Poland. In P. Beresford-Hill (ed.), *Education and privatisation in Eastern Europe and the Baltic Republics.* Wallingford, U.K.: Triangle.

Leach, E. (1997, May 2). Car raffle aims to pay for teacher. *Times Educational Supplement,* p. 7.

Louis, K. S., and van Velzen, B.A.M. (1990/1991). A look at choice in the Netherlands. *Educational Leadership* 48(4), 66–72.

Magowan, C. (1999, January 29). Fall in fees threaten inspections. *Times Educational Supplement,* p. 10.

Marks, J. (1991). *Standards in schools: Assessment, accountability, and the purposes of education.* London: Social Market Foundation.

Meighan, R., and Toogood, P. (1992). *Anatomy of choice in education.* Ticknall, Derbyshire, U.K.: Education Now.

Midgley, S. (1998, November 13). Taste of control over schools lunches may turn sour. *Times Educational Supplement,* p. 5.

Ministerie van Onderwijs en Wetenschappen (MOW). (1996). Personal communication from Public Informer, MOW, Zoetermeer, the Netherlands.

Morrison, M., and Galloway, S. (eds.) (1994). *The supply story: Professional substitutes in education.* London: Falmer.

Phillips, D. (1992). "Borrowing Educational Policy." *Oxford Studies in Comparative Education* 2(2), 49–55.

Pirie, M. (1985). *Privatization.* London: Adam Smith Institute.

Pring, R. (1987). Privatization in education. In R. Rogers (ed.), *Education and social class.* Lewes, U.K.: Falmer.

Pyke, N., and Ghouri, N. (1999, February 12). Councils deny selling out. *Times Educational Supplement,* p. 9.

Rafferty, F. (1999, January 8). Private firms to take over councils. *Times Educational Supplement*, p. 14.

Rigoni, D., and Walford, G. (1998). Questioning the quick-fix: Assertive discipline and the 1997 Education White Paper. *Journal of Education Policy* 13(3), 443–452.

Robertson, D. B., and Waltman, J. L. (1992). The politics of policy borrowing. *Oxford Studies in Comparative Education* 2(2), 25–48.

Svecová, J. (1998). Education and ideology in the Czech Republic during transition and after. In P. Beresford-Hill (ed.), *Education and privatisation in Eastern Europe and the Baltic Republics.* Wallingford, U.K.: Triangle.

Sexton, S. (1987). *Our schools—a radical policy.* Warlingham, Surrey, U.K.: Institute for Economic Affairs Education Unit.

_____. (1992). *Our schools—future policy.* Warlingham, Surrey, U.K.: IPSET Education Unit.

Tesser, P., and Mulder, L. (1990). Etnische Scheidslijnn in het Amsterdamse Basisonderwijs, een Keuze? [Ethnic dividing lines in Amsterdam primary education]. *Migrantenstudies* 2(6), 31–45.

Thomas, A. (1998). *Educating children at home.* London: Cassell.

Thornton, K. (1998, September 4). Deals on funding the future. *Times Educational Supplement*, p. 8.

van Laarhoven, P., Baker, B., Dronkers, J., and Schijf, H. (1990). Achievement in public and private secondary education in the Netherlands. In H. K. Anheier and W. Seibel (eds.), *The third sector: Comparative studies of nonprofit organizations.* Berlin: Walter de Gruyer.

Walford, G. (1990). *Privatization and privilege in education.* London: Routledge.

_____. (1991). City Technology Colleges: A private magnetism. In G. Walford (ed.), *Private schooling: Tradition, change, and diversity.* London: Paul Chapman.

_____. (1994). *Choice and equity in education.* London: Cassell.

_____. (1995a). Faith-based grant-maintained schools: Selective international policy borrowing from the Netherlands. *Journal of Education Policy* 10(2), 245–257.

_____. (1995b). The Christian schools campaign—a successful educational pressure group? *British Educational Research Journal* 21(4), 451–464.

_____. (1995c). *Educational politics: Pressure groups and faith-based schools.* Aldershot, U.K.: Avebury.

_____. (1996). Diversity and choice in school education: An alternative view. *Oxford Review of Education* 22(2), 143–154.

_____. (1997a). Sponsored grant-maintained schools: Extending the franchise? *Oxford Review of Education* 23(1), 31–44.

_____. (1997b). Privatization and selection. In R. Pring and G. Walford (eds.), *Affirming the comprehensive ideal.* London: Falmer.

_____. (1998). Durkheim and the growing diversity of schools in England. In G. Walford and W. Pickering (eds.), *Durkheim and modern education.* London: Routledge.

_____. (2000). A policy adventure: Sponsored grant-maintained schools. *Educational Studies* 26, (2), 269–284.

Walford, G., and Miller, H. (1991). *City Technology College.* Buckingham, U.K.: Open University Press.

Webb, J. (1990). *Children learning at home.* London: Falmer.

Whittaker, M. (1998, February 27). Advertisers offer £5000 a year for corridor space. *Times Educational Supplement*, p. 3.

Whitty, G., and Edwards, T. (1984). Evaluating policy change: The assisted places scheme. In G. Walford (ed.), *British public schools: Policy and practice.* London: Falmer.

Whitty, G., Edwards, T., and Gewirtz, S. (1993). *Specialisation and choice in urban education. The City Technology College experiment.* London: Routledge.

Whitty, G., Power, S., and Edwards, T. (1998). The Assisted Places Scheme: Its impact and its role in privatization and marketization. *Journal of Education Policy* 13(2), 237–250.

Woods, P. A., Bagley, C., and Glatter, R. (1998). *School choice and the public interest. Markets in the public interest?* London: Routledge.

Charter Schools

9

Assessing the Growth and Potential of Charter Schools

PEARL ROCK KANE AND CHRISTOPHER J. LAURICELLA

Charter schools touch the core of our nation's most pressing educational problems: equity and excellence. As public school reform efforts have moved to the front of the newspaper and above the fold, it is clear that both the media and the general public demand creative solutions to these problems. In this highly visible context, the charter school movement has enjoyed tremendous growth for almost a decade, growing from two schools in 1992 to 2,036 schools in 2000.

Few reforms in the history of schooling have spread so quickly. Growth alone attests to the popularity of the charter school concept, but it is not a measure of school success. Neither should the movement be celebrated with one or two schools that stand out as shining stars, or damned by one or two abysmal disappointments. Careful study of the direct impact of charter schools on constituents and the indirect impact on the wider system is a responsibility of the educational research community.

This chapter seeks to set a foundation for this research. It begins with a brief overview of the charter school movement and the most current charter school demographics available. It then discusses the assumptions of the charter school concept and sets an agenda of further research questions on the validity of these assumptions.

Charter Schools: Early History

The term "charter" first appears in the language of educational reform in *Education by Charter*, a 1988 book by educator Ray Budde. He envisioned an educational system in which school districts granted charter agreements to teachers who wished to create new curricula. Fashioned loosely after the contracts granted to early explorers by trading companies and monarchies, these charters would add elements of exploration, risk-taking, and competition to the educational system. After strategies and plans were approved, chartered teachers would be given the necessary supplies and a specific time frame to achieve the goals articulated in the agreement. They would then be held accountable to the school district, with the renewal or revocation of the charter based on periodic evaluation of performance by an outside agency.

Albert Shanker, then the president of the American Federation of Teachers, expanded upon Budde's original thinking, proposing that "local school boards and unions jointly develop a procedure that would enable teams of teachers and others to submit and implement proposals to set up their own autonomous public schools within their own school buildings" (as quoted in Budde, 1996). In 1988, Shanker and Sy Fliegel, an innovative New York educator who had created a teacher-run school in East Harlem's District 4, spoke at an education conference sponsored by a Minneapolis foundation. In his speech, Shanker supported Fliegel's ideas concerning charter schools and their role in school reform. Inspired by this endorsement, Ember Reicghott Junge, a Democratic Minnesota state senator, proposed the charter concept to the Minnesota legislature, and a citizen's league was created to study the concept.

The Charter School Concept

In Minnesota, the charter school concept evolved once again. Rather than being *dependent* schools that are part of a district, charter schools could be *independent* of the local school district, thereby stimulating systemic reform through competition and market forces. Ted Kolderie (1990, p. 2) framed the following key assumptions underpinning the revised charter school concept:

- School restructuring—"site-based management" or "self-governing school"—has limited potential. It provides no incentives for systemic change. Although inspired leadership has transformed some schools, fundamental improvement in public education will not come one school at a time.

- The school districts' exclusive monopoly on public education is the heart of the problem. This is what makes local school boards more responsive to the interests of the adults in the educational system—administrators and teachers—than to children, who are compelled by law to attend school. According to Albert Shanker, president of the American Federation of Teachers, our school system "takes its customers for granted."
- The [states] are the critical actors in revitalizing public education, because only they can withdraw the districts' exclusive franchise. Until that is done, districts will have no incentive to change—and will face no real penalty for failing to change.
- A competitive school system can best be achieved if a variety of public agencies are free to charter new schools: existing districts, colleges, local governments, the states, and perhaps even the federal government.
- *Lastly,* [the charter school movement] *looks beyond creating new public schools to an even more radical reform option—divestiture, or allowing the districts to get out of running and operating public schools altogether.* Divestiture would also establish a contract relationship between the local school boards and the schools it presently owns.

From Concept to Reality

Spurred along by a reform-minded climate, the charter school concept made a quick transition from educational theory to public policy. J. Nathan (1996) offers an operative definition of charter schools that accurately describes the key characteristics of these and subsequent charter schools:

- Autonomy for Accountability. Reduced reliance on rules and regulations in exchange for educators accepting responsibility for demonstrating increased student achievement.
- Choice among public schools for families and their children.
- Innovation. Entrepreneurial opportunities for educators and parents to create the kind of schools they believe make the most sense.
- Carefully designed competition in public education.
- Use of the central ideas of public education: equal access, nonsectarian curriculum, no tuition charged, and no admissions test.

After Minnesota passed charter school legislation in 1991, California, Colorado, Georgia, Massachusetts, Michigan, New Mexico, and Wisconsin added similar legislation to their state educational plans, and a total of sixty-four charter schools were operating in the country by 1992. In the ensuing years, the charter school movement exploded. As of this writing, thirty-six states and the District of Columbia have passed charter school legislation, and 2,036 schools are currently chartered. It is this rapid expansion that lends gravity to the charter school movement, giving hope to those who feel it promises reform—and troubling those who feel it does not (CER, 2001).

Although Kolderie's assumptions and Nathan's definition can serve as conceptual frames for charter schools, there is no monolithic Charter School per se. Certain generalizations can be made, but each charter school is individually shaped by complex interactions among students, founders, trustees, teachers, the local educational district, and the state education department, as well as previous reform efforts and a host of other factors.

Factors That Inhibit or Stimulate Charter School Growth

The Center for Education Reform (CER), a charter school advocacy group, has developed criteria for determining whether a state charter school law is expansive or restrictive in terms of the ability to create and operate charter schools. Since there is no "typical" charter school law, these criteria provide a framework for comparing and ranking state legislation, and they are often cited in the literature on charter schools. There are ten factors that determine whether a law is expansive (which CER considers to be "strong" legislation) or restrictive (which CER considers to be "weak" legislation):

1. The number of schools allowed to operate in the state;
2. whether charters can be granted by multiple authorities;
3. the number of eligible charter applicants based on the state's criteria for eligibility;
4. whether newly created charter schools are allowed;
5. the availability or absence of automatic waivers from state and district laws;
6. whether schools may be started without evidence of local support;
7. the amount of per-pupil funding granted to the charter school;
8. the amount of legal/operational autonomy that charter schools are granted;
9. the amount of fiscal autonomy that charter schools are granted; and
10. whether the charter school is exempted from collective bargaining.

Expansive Laws

Approximately 70 percent of charter schools are found in seven "expansive law" states (Arizona, California, Colorado, Florida, Michigan, North Carolina, and Texas). These states generally foster the development of genuinely independent charter schools. The state with the most expansive law is Arizona: There is no cap on the number of charters that can be granted, almost all individuals or organizations are eligible to apply for a charter, and three different public bodies are authorized to sponsor charter schools. Moreover, Arizona charter schools receive full funding from the state and are legally and financially autonomous as well as exempt from state laws and regulations, district policies, and collective bargaining agreements. There are currently 417 charter schools operating in Arizona (CER, 2001).

Restrictive Laws

Less than 1 percent of charter schools are found in the eight "restrictive law" states (see Tables 9.1 and 9.2). The most restrictive state is Mississippi: Only six charters are allowed to be granted by the state board of education, and only existing public schools that want to convert to charter status are eligible to apply. Moreover, Mississippi charter schools are not legally or fiscally autonomous and are not exempt from collective bargaining agreements. There is currently only one charter school operating in Mississippi.

Charter School Demographics

This section provides a brief demographic overview of the growth of the charter school movement since 1991. Since 1992, an average of five charter school laws have been passed per year. Five additional states (Maine, Maryland, Nebraska, Tennessee, and Washington) are currently considering charter school legislation.

The growth of charter schools has been rapid since 1992, but the precise number of schools is difficult to ascertain. Enrollment figures are in constant fluctuation as new schools open or add grade levels. Current estimates suggest that nationally charter schools are serving a population of 433,797 children (CER, 2000. See Figure 9.1). The median enrollment per school is approximately 137 students, and the majority of charter schools include elementary grades (RPP, 1999).

TABLE 9.1   Charter school legislation and operation as of January 2001

State	Expansive/ Restrictive Legislation	Charter School May Be Managed or Operated by For- Profit Organization	Year Passed	Schools in Operation
Alaska	Restrictive	No	1995	17
Arizona	Expansive	Yes	1994	417
Arkansas	Restrictive	No	1995	4
California	Expansive	Yes	1992	274
Colorado	Expansive	Yes	1993	79
Connecticut	Expansive	No	1996	16
Delaware	Expansive	Yes	1995	7
District of Columbia	Expansive	No	1996	36
Florida	Expansive	Yes	1996	152
Georgia	Restrictive	Yes	1993	38
Hawaii	Restrictive	No	1994	6
Idaho	Restrictive	No	1998	9
Illinois	Expansive	No	1996	22
Kansas	Restrictive	No	1994	15
Louisiana	Expansive	Yes	1995	23
Massachusetts	Expansive	Yes	1993	41
Michigan	Expansive	Yes	1993	184
Minnesota	Expansive	Yes	1991	68
Mississippi	Restrictive	No	1997	1
Missouri	Expansive	Yes	1998	21
Nevada	Restrictive	Yes	1997	7
New Hampshire	Expansive	No	1995	0
New Jersey	Expansive	Yes	1995	55
New Mexico	Restrictive	No	1993	11
New York	Expansive	Yes	1998	23
North Carolina	Expansive	Yes	1996	90
Ohio	Expansive	Yes	1997	70
Oklahoma	Expansive	Not addressed	1999	6
Oregon	Expansive	Yes	1999	12
Pennsylvania	Expansive	Yes	1997	65
Rhode Island	Restrictive	No	1995	3
South Carolina	Expansive	No	1996	8
Texas	Expansive	No	1995	159
Utah	Expansive	Yes	1998	8
Virginia	Restrictive	Yes	1998	2
Wisconsin	Expansive	Yes	1995	87
Wyoming	Restrictive	No	1995	0
Total: 35	Expansive: 25 Restrictive: 12	Yes: 21 No: 15 Other: 1		2036

SOURCE: The Center for Educational Reform (January 2001). *1999 Charter School Highlights and Statistics* <http://edreform.com/pubs/chglance.html>.

TABLE 9.2   State Charter School Legislation Since 1991

Year	Number of States Passing Charter School Legislation
1991	1
1992	1
1993	5
1994	3
1995	10
1996	6
1997	4
1998	5
1999	2
2000	0

SOURCE: The Center for Educational Reform (January 2001). *1999 Charter School Highlights and Statistics.* <http://edreform.com/pubs/chglance.html>.

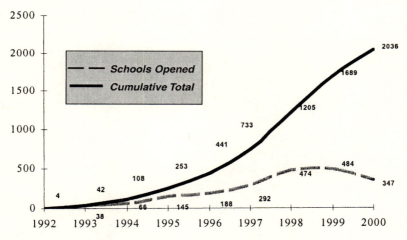

FIGURE 9.1   Charter School Growth as of January 2001
SOURCE: The Center for Educational Reform. (1999, March 11). *1999 Charter School Highlights and Statistics.* < http://edreform.com/pubs/chglance.html>; Updated: The Center for Education Reform (January 2001). *National Charter School Directory 2001, 7th Edition.* Forthcoming. Washington, DC: CER.

Charter Schools as a Potential Reform

This section considers the assumptions of the charter school concept and assesses relative strengths and weaknesses. An agenda of questions for further study follows each discussion.

Accountability

Charter school advocates tout accountability as a core benefit of the charter school concept. Indeed, most state charter legislation stipulates that the contractual agreement between the school and the sponsoring agency must spell out clear outcomes that the school is obligated to achieve in order to retain its charter. In theory, if these outcomes are not met, the school will have its charter revoked. Charter school advocates believe that such performance mandates provide a compelling incentive for charter schools to articulate goals for student outcomes and success and then measure success relative to those goals. This process of articulating and assessing desired educational outcomes, coupled with periodic review by the sponsoring agency, is seen as a radical departure from the traditional public district school model of accountability, which is largely based on regulated inputs such as student attendance (Kolderie, 1990; Nathan, 1996; Manno et al., 1997).

The push for accountability is not reserved for charter schools. Accountability plans are at the forefront of most every state's reform policy. These plans generally rest on seven basic elements: state standards; tests to measure whether schools have met these standards; summary report cards of individual schools' performance; a ranking system to determine performance thresholds; targeted assistance to help schools improve; performance-based rewards; and the authority to take over, close, or reconstitute schools (Olson, 1999). In many states, charter schools are a complementary component of accountability-based reform policies.

Beyond contractual accountability, charter schools are also perceived to be client-driven organizations that are ultimately accountable to market forces. A charter school's primary constituents—students and parents—choose the school because it offers benefits beyond those offered by other local schools. If the charter school fails to deliver, clients are free to leave for other educational options. To prevent this, charter schools must create and maintain relationships with students and parents and have an incentive to be innovative. Theoretically, such relationships and innovations are rooted in the maximization of the client's benefit by delivering a demonstrably high-quality educational program, thereby building a reputation within the local market as an attractive option. But are charter schools really more accountable to the state for educational outcomes than traditional public district schools? The answer to this question varies greatly from state to state as a result of a variety of factors.

The Definition of "Accountability."   Student achievement is the likely criterion most states will use to assess charter schools. To measure it, most states require charter school students to take the standardized achievement tests used in districts; much of the early research on the effectiveness of charter schools suggests that charter school students perform at about the same level as students in district schools (Cheung, Murphy, and Nathan, 1998; Mulholland, 1999). However, as states begin to debate curriculum standards as well as the validity of the assessments to measure those standards, charter and district schools are finding that assessing student outcomes is complex and difficult to measure. For example, California recently switched its standardized assessment exam, effectively nullifying specific benchmarks written into charters predicated on the old assessments (Wells, 1998). Moreover, many charter schools have used their autonomy from state regulations to develop educational programs tailored to the needs of their clients; some programs do not easily lend themselves to standardized assessments or comparisons to district norms.

No Clear Mechanisms for Public Oversight.   Some states, like Arizona and Michigan, have purposefully taken a hands-off approach to charter school accountability; others, such as Massachusetts, have codified and implemented vigorous oversight programs (Schnaiberg, 1998). Some states, such as New Jersey and California, are ambiguous about how, and by whom, charter schools are going to be monitored (Kane, 1998; Wells, 1998). This variability of oversight is problematic for states as well as charter schools, as it weakens the enforceability of the charter contract and the inherent incentives to maintain quality academic programs.

Several states are relying on market forces to provide a regulatory mechanism. Depending upon competitive scale, however, these market forces may be nonexistent or slow to react. In two such states, Arizona and Michigan, negative public attention has already been focused on schools that were substandard or found to be financially malfeasant. These schools were closed only after long delay and repeated state efforts, and local charter school operators fear the resulting negative attention may erode public support for charter schools (Mulholland, 1999; *U.S. News and World Report*, 1998).

Vague Goals.   Theoretically, charter schools and their sponsors are responsible for creating clear performance contracts with demonstrable goals that can be assessed over a defined time frame. The degree to which clear articulation actually happens is mixed (Nathan, 1998). Many charters are abstract proposals, and some contain performance goals that may be vague and difficult to measure, such as "enabling pupils to become self-motivated, competent, and life-long learners" (as quoted in Wells, 1998, p. 21). Further, many of these goals are stated in absolute terms, rather than presenting a range of acceptable levels or benchmarks that students are expected to achieve (Nathan, 1998).

It is possible that some less-than-optimal charters have been ratified by expansive-law states in order to create a critical mass of charter schools that will rapidly inject market forces into public education. If this is indeed the strategy that legislators are using to create change, it may ultimately be a double-edged sword. If states are capable of chartering a critical mass of schools, they may realize enough market forces to create competitive change. If, in so doing, the state allows too many substandard schools to be created, public and political support of the charter school movement may be seriously undermined. Other states, such as Massachusetts, have taken a slower approach to implementing the charter school concept, opting to grant and vigorously oversee a relatively low number of charters per year.

Will Charter Schools Be Allowed to Fail?   Given the number of new charter schools and the possibility that some may have been approved not on their merits but to stimulate competition, it seems reasonable to expect that some charter schools may fail. According to the most recent national estimates provided by the Center for Education Reform, as of December 2000, the number of failed charter schools is 86, or 3.0 percent of the overall number of charter schools ever opened. There are four major reasons for charter school closing: financial inequities, including low enrollment (37.6 percent); general mismanagement (37.6 percent); failure to carry out an acceptable academic plan (16 percent); and, the inability to secure a viable facility (8 percent). These figures do not include an additional 26 charter schools that consolidated into their local districts and approximately 50 schools that, for a variety of reasons, never opened (CER, 2001). This relatively low number may reflect states' willingness to allow charter schools a grace period to adjust to the inherent challenges of starting a new venture. However, it may also reflect the political popularity of the charter school movement and reluctance on the part of sponsoring agencies to close schools, lest they damage the entire movement. If this is the case, states and charter school operators run the risk of circumventing the very feedback mechanism upon which the charter school concept is founded.

How Accountable Are Charter Schools to Market Forces?   Charter schools are probably very accountable to market forces, but the market may be more likely to hold them accountable for factors involving school culture rather than academic effectiveness. Market forces are ultimately contingent on the context of the market and the level and nature of competition within the market. In districts with many educational choices, charter schools may have to be more responsive to their constituents because they can choose many other options. In districts with fewer choices or increasing enrollments, market arguments carry less weight. In these cases, a mediocre charter school might present the best option in that district, and swelling enrollment would mean a steady supply of new students to charter schools and district schools.

Charter school studies often focus on parent satisfaction as a key indicator of market accountability. These studies report that a majority of charter school parents are "very satisfied" with their schools (Vanourek et al., 1997; Kane, 1998). Low mobility rates—the number of students who leave a school during the year—are also cited as indicators of student and parent satisfaction, especially when contrasted against urban district populations that have high mobility rates.

Although client-based accountability is a real phenomenon in charter schools, the relationships between families and schools are not based solely on academic programs. Other factors—safety, discipline, structure, school philosophy, and the like—are also reflected in the benchmarks mentioned above. It is believed that the creation of public schools that have individual, client-based visions—rather than schools that are part of a larger, more generally focused, systems-based vision—is the major strength and innovation of the charter school movement (Brigham and Associates, 1998; Kane, 1998; Kolderie, 1990, 1992).

It must also be stressed, however, that client-based accountability does not ensure that a charter school academic program will be better compared to a district school. Early data suggest that the academic performance of charter schools is on par with (or only slightly better than) district schools (Mulholland, 1999; Nathan, 1998). Therefore, the fact that many charter schools have large pools of applicants eager to enroll suggests that culture is as attractive as academics. This may be especially true of for-profit charter schools that offer a range of tangible extras such as take-home computers and new facilities.

Research Questions: Accountability

The following research questions on accountability need to be addressed:

- How are states assessing student performance in individual charter schools?
- What defines "best practices" among assessments? Can best practices be described and disseminated?

- How, and by whom, is the overall program of operating charter schools evaluated at the state level?
- How, and by whom, are new charter contracts evaluated at the state level?
- What are the states' criteria and motivation for granting charters? Are these criteria consistently upheld?
- What are the criteria for revoking or maintaining a charter?
- Are market forces closing poorly performing charter schools, or are other forces preempting charter school failure?
- Does client-based accountability assure high-quality charter schools as measured by state assessments?
- What effect, if any, does increased client-based accountability in charter schools have on district schools?
- Do for-profit charter schools have an advantage over nonprofit charter schools in their ability to offer perceived benefits that attract and retain students?

Autonomy

Autonomy is the flip side of accountability. Charter school advocates argue that autonomy allows charter schools to operate more efficiently and provides the freedom to be innovative and fulfill charter obligations. The specter of parents who vote with their feet is seen as a clear incentive to innovate and make charter schools accountable to parents and educators rather than to a central school bureaucracy (Shanker, 1988; Kolderie, 1990; Nathan, 1996). Has autonomy empowered charter schools to be more efficient and/or effective in delivering educational programs? The answer to this question varies greatly from state to state, and it involves a variety of factors.

"Autonomy" Is a Relative Term.   Charter schools report varying levels of autonomy from external sources, and they often run into bureaucracies in dealing with funding applications and paperwork. In general, states either allocate funds to charter schools directly (and consider charter schools to be independent school districts or local educational agencies) or indirectly through the local school district (Government Accounting Office [GAO], 1998). As independent public schools, charter schools are often the sole agency responsible for supplying information to the various state and federal agencies that require it. However, administration at charter schools is so lean—usually one or two administrators and minimal support staff—that the paperwork can quickly become daunting. For

example, a recent report on federal funding for charter schools reports that two-fifths of charter schools surveyed did not apply for Title I funds; one-third did not apply for funds under the Individuals with Disabilities Education Act. Operators cited lack of time and resources needed to complete applications among several barriers that prevented them from applying for such funding (Kane, 1998; Wells, 1998; GAO, 1998).

Individual states are able to grant charters that exempt schools from state and local regulations. However, states have no authority to grant the same autonomy with respect to federal regulations. J. P. Heubert (1997, p. 303) sees this as a potential liability for charter schools:

> Public charter schools and charter school boards are subject to all the rules and procedures of federal disability law to which traditional public schools are bound. . . . Public charter schools, particularly those independent of local school board control, may paradoxically have greater obligations than most traditional public schools to serve students with disabilities.

Ironically, schools operating under the strongest state charter school laws may be the most vulnerable to federal disability laws.

Autonomy Can Be Isolating.   Charter school directors report feeling isolated from their local educational communities, and they often do not have the benefit of professional networks and services that other schools offer (Weiss, 1997; Brigham and Associates, 1998). As a result, federal and state government agencies are taking measures to increase technical support to charter schools (GAO, 1998). Without such deliberate support mechanisms in place, the ongoing development and dissemination of new practices and ideas between and among charter and district schools will continue to be difficult. This poses a problem if charter schools are supposed to drive innovation and reform.

Although autonomy can empower, it also requires charter schools to create entirely new organizational structures. Practitioners report that this sense of newness is both exhilarating and terrifying. A director in a New Jersey charter school explains, "Things you take for granted are not there. I go reach for the policy book, or the curriculum guidelines and they are not there. We have to create these things" (Kane, 1998). Early data suggest that creating new governance structures and policies is a major barrier to effectively implementing educational plans (RPP International, 1998; Weiss, 1997). Although this is to be expected, the ultimate burden of autonomy may be the sense of the job's enormity in the face of so little resources. In the words of one charter school principal, "It's like being given a hammer and a forest and being asked to build a house" (as reported in Brigham and Associates, 1998).

Independent or Dependent Charter Schools?   Some states allow multiple chartering sponsors, whereas others stipulate that local educational districts are the sole chartering entity. Schools chartered by local school districts can be thought of as *dependent* schools because they rely on the district for support and funding. Dependent charter schools are directly accountable to the local school board and are often existing schools that have been converted. Schools that are chartered by an entity other than the local school board—for example, the state or a university—are often thought of as *independent* charter schools because they are not dependent on the local district and are often newly created.

Large urban districts often view dependent charter schools as part of a large move toward comprehensive school reform. In these districts, a charter school's internal autonomy—hiring, curriculum, testing—may be constrained by the district. For example, in New York City some early plans for the recently enacted charter school law include creating a charter school district that would oversee and administer charter schools. This district would provide the schools with "relative autonomy" from the New York City Board of Education while ensuring that they were still generally aligned with that board's goals. As of this writing, it is unclear what form and shape this relative autonomy may take (Personal Communication, New York City Board of Education, 1998).

Funding.   Early data suggest that charter schools enjoy a significant amount of fiscal flexibility while being constrained by low per-pupil allocations (Wells, 1998; WestEd, 1998). Many state laws stipulate that charter schools are to receive a portion—usually 80–90 percent—of either the local district's or the state's average per-pupil allocation. The remaining monies are held to reimburse the district or the state for providing services such as transportation and oversight. In most states, because charter schools do not have the power to issue construction bonds, this limited per-pupil funding must also pay for capital costs (RPP International, 1998; Kane, 1998; Wells, 1998).

This financial burden increases charter schools' reliance on private funding sources and limits their operating budgets (RPP International, 1998; Wells, 1998). Financial constraints may strengthen the incentive to be entrepreneurial and efficient with available funds. For example, charter schools throughout the nation enter into partnership agreements with local public institutions such as museums and libraries to offer educational resources that the schools could not otherwise afford (Brigham and Associates, 1998; Kane, 1998; Mulholland, 1999;

RPP International, 1998). Limited public funds may also motivate charter schools to seek private money. Charter schools often create booster organizations and write grant proposals to supplement additional programs. However, for disadvantaged populations charter schools may encourage schools to tap sources of private capital that heretofore have been ignored.

Lean charter school budgets, however, expose obvious liabilities that impact facilities, staff salaries, and programs. A common theme in the current literature is that underfunded autonomy may force charter schools to rent or buy facilities that are not suited for the educational needs (e.g., Brigham and Associates, 1998; Kane, 1998; Mulholland, 1999; RPP International, 1998). Many states have relaxed zoning requirements for charter schools, allowing schools to operate in a diversity of nontraditional structures. Although this is an obvious short-term solution, many sites will need costly renovations, including changes to comply with the Americans with Disabilities Act, to sustain the schools' long-term growth.

This lack of facilities funding may give well-funded for-profit management companies a competitive advantage as they seek out clients. However, it also raises interesting questions in states that allow charter schools to become legal entities that can own property. In these states, for-profit corporations may be able to mortgage buildings and then meet monthly payments with a portion of their per-pupil allocation. In effect, this may mean that public monies can be used by for-profit companies to purchase buildings and build equity.

As increasing numbers of charter school students make use of public institutions such as libraries and museums, some of the institutions have expressed concerns that they may be unable to meet these increased demands (Mulholland, 1999). Reliance on private funds may also prove to be a weakness if these funds become a major proportion of a school's operating budget, forcing charter schools to devote already limited school resources to a constant cycle of fundraising and grant-writing.

Nonetheless, one of the more positive immediate effects of autonomy is budget flexibility. For example, in Los Angeles charter schools are able to create programs with reduced class size that would be impossible under current district regulations. These same schools also report that they were able to shorten the time it normally takes to purchase education-related materials and to negotiate more efficient contracts with food-service providers and technology consultants (WestEd, 1998).

Research Questions: Autonomy

The following research questions on autonomy need to be addressed:

- Is there a proper balance between support and autonomy that will allow charter schools to develop while sustaining incentives to produce quality programs and innovate?
- How are charter schools using their financial flexibility?
- What changes are occurring over time to states' funding formulas?
- What percentage of charter schools' programs comes from private sources?
- How much are charter schools spending per pupil when all sources of revenue are factored into their allocations? How does this compare to district spending? Do these comparisons suggest national trends?
- How do various state laws approach for-profit building purchases and property issues?
- What are the similarities and differences between dependent and independent charter schools?
- How do these two models interact with local district schools?
- What implications do these two models have for district-level reform?
- State charters alleviate some state and local regulations but do not have the authority to absolve obligations to federal guidelines. What is the impact of these federal guidelines on charter schools?

Innovation

Advocates claim that charter schools, freed of bureaucratic regulations, will stimulate innovative practices. This begs the question of precisely what constitutes an "innovation."

A recent study of charter schools suggests that an innovation is something that effects change and that satisfies the criteria of being relevant, transferable, and effective (Brigham and Associates, 1998). Another study suggests that educational innovation is assessed best in context: "Where progressivism reigns as local orthodoxy, a back-to-basics school signifies innovation—and vice versa. Where traditional age-grading is the norm, multi-age grouping appears to be revolutionary—and vice versa" (Manno et al., 1998). As such, another study defines innovation as "a practice that is distinctly different from the practices of other public schools in the charter school's surrounding district(s) or region," encompassing the broad areas of educational programs, governance models, financial arrangements, personnel practices, approaches to parent and community participation, or school operations (RPP International, 1998). Regardless of whether "innovation" is interpreted narrowly or broadly, an assessment of a particular school's innovative practice appears to require research at the school site and in the neighboring community.

As a group, most charter schools share characteristics that distinguish them from most district public schools. In this respect, the charter school, as a discrete entity, may be considered an innovative practice. These innovative characteristics include: mission focus; governance; personnel practices; and parental involvement.

Mission Focus.   A *mission statement* distills a school's purpose, goals, and core beliefs. Once written, a mission statement provides the focal point for a planning process involving careful deliberation, weighing alternatives, and arriving at a consensus—a kind of reflective practice useful for all schools. In every state, the act of applying for a charter requires detailed planning on the part of prospective founders. Many states have applications that require an extensive written plan in which applicants must specify the school's purposes and goals, target population, curriculum, assessment methods, budget, school calendar, daily schedule, teaching staff qualifications, and parental involvement plans. Founders often collaborate with the director they have hired, devoting months to preparing the application. Properly executed, the planning process is likely to result in a cohesive school program that reflects a clearly articulated sense of purpose.

In a 1998 study of New Jersey charter schools (see Kane, 1998), every charter school director interviewed was able to clearly articulate the school's mission; furthermore, the missions were often narrowly defined and geared to the specific needs of the target population. With few exceptions, teachers in New Jersey charter schools could also describe their school's mission and how the mission shaped practice (Kane, 1998). Some states do not demand New Jersey's level of mission planning as part of the application process for new or conversion schools, but the strong mission orientation of New Jersey charter directors and teachers suggests that these states may be missing an opportunity to drive school reform.

Governance.   Most charter school legislation requires schools to establish a governance structure led by a board of trustees, but much legislation does not specify rules regarding the composition of the board or the selection process for trustees. A school's charter is granted to the board, and the board assumes responsibilities for fiscal and managerial oversight, including the hiring and (when necessary) firing of the principal. Moreover, in many states, charter schools operate as nonprofit organizations or corporate entities that legally require the oversight of a voluntary board.

Most charter school boards act solely as policymaking bodies, delegating full responsibility for educational programming and day-to-day operations to the principal and staff (Kane, Ballen, and Atkins, unpublished study, 1997). Boards may also raise additional money for the school, and some schools set up nonprofit corporations as a way to ensure appropriate procedures and channels for fund-raising.

Charter school boards differ from public school boards in that they concentrate solely on a single school rather than many schools within a district. Similar to private independent schools, charter schools often have a high number of board members who are parents of current students. This ensures a degree of parental involvement and a vested interest in the school's success (Kane, 1992). However, there are potential problems associated with high parent representation, including decisionmaking strategies that emphasize short-term benefits while ignoring the long-term perspective and the potential to micromanage daily administration.

There are also potential problems associated with start-ups that require the board's attention to pressing short-term problems, such as faculty hiring and budgeting. Different skills sets may be appropriate for different phases in the charter school's development, and skills that were initially strengths may become weaknesses as the school matures and requires a longer-term policy focus. There is an indication that initial board problems abate in subsequent years, but more research is needed to document the utility of school-site governing boards (RPP International, 1998).

Personnel Practices.   State laws give charter schools latitude in hiring noncertified teachers to attract talented professionals who are experts in their fields (including scientists, mathematicians, and artists). However, most charter schools employ traditionally certified teachers. A 1997 report of 552 charter school teachers suggests that they are already certified or working on obtaining certification. Charter schools have attracted a small number of professionals new to teaching, and one-fourth of the teachers in charter schools say they would be doing something other than teaching if they weren't working in a charter school (Vanourek et al., 1997). Attracting professionals to charter schools from outside the regular teaching ranks may help alleviate some of the strain of the impending teacher shortage predicted for the next ten years (*Education Week*, 1999). Early findings indicate that the charter model may also be a factor in teacher retention. Only about one-third of charter school teachers said they would work in a district public school if they weren't teaching at the charter school (Vanourek et al., 1997).

The role teachers play in decisionmaking and the relative increase in working hours raise questions about whether charter schools enhance or diminish teacher professionalism. Studies show that teachers in charter schools take on multiple roles and work longer hours than do teachers in district schools (WestEd, 1998).

Charter school teachers spend many hours planning and making decisions about curriculum and instructional approaches that district school teachers may not be required to undertake (Kane, 1998). Critics of charter schools thus regard increased workloads and demands on teachers as a blow to teacher professionalism. Others question whether teachers can sustain their level of commitment and whether the increased workloads will lead to burnout and high turnover (Wells, 1998).

The initial studies show that charter schools tend to encourage and attract staff who want to play a greater role in decisionmaking and developing programs and services for students (WestEd, 1998). Despite long hours, teachers and administrators appear content with their jobs in charter schools. Teachers in the New Jersey study participated in developing curriculum and setting policies for the school, and many teachers are involved in hiring decisions (Kane, 1998).

Parental Involvement.   According to one study (see Vanourek et al., 1997), more than three-fourths of all parents indicated they were very satisfied with the opportunity for parent participation. Parents choose charter schools because they are perceived to be nurturing environments that have a strong value system, small class sizes, high standards, an educational philosophy or vision that fits their child, greater opportunities for parental involvement, and better teachers (RPP International, 1998). This list often reflects parents' dissatisfaction with local district schools and specific concerns about academics, school culture, safety, and parent accessibility (RPP International, 1998). This concern was reflected in a recent Gallup poll on public education in which 46 percent of Americans gave their local public schools an overall grade of C or lower (Gallup, 2000); a 1995 Public Agenda report describes a "public poised for flight" from schools that do not provide an education that is safe, reflects high standards, and has a sense of order (Johnson, 1995).

Parents' dissatisfaction with public education is a major factor in the creation of charter schools. Parents often partner with educators and community organizations to realize an alternate vision for schooling or to serve the needs of a special population of children. These needs are often expressed in several themes: a quality academic program with high standards; a supportive environment often based on small school size; and a flexible approach to education or—conversely—a highly structured school environment (RPP International, 1998).

Parental involvement in charter schools continues well beyond the start-up phase. For example, in New Jersey, over half of all parents report volunteering their time to work in the schools or to serve on committees, and all parents said they attended parent-teacher association meetings (Kane, 1998). Such involvement may reflect a move away from the notion that schools are best run exclusively by a system of professional educators, as well as a return to local control over neighborhood schools. However, for some families whose time and financial resources are limited, this emphasis on parental involvement may in fact be a barrier to enrolling their children in charter schools.

Research Questions: Innovation

The following research questions on innovation need to be addressed:

- What role does a mission focus play in shaping coherent programs and the resulting outcomes in student achievement?
- How do we best track the evolution of board behavior in charter schools and analyze on the composition, structure, commitment, and effectiveness of charter boards?
- What are the qualifications and characteristics of those attracted to teach in charter schools?
- What factors are associated with turnover and retention rates in charter schools?
- Are teachers in charter schools forging a new professional identity, or are they diminishing the profession by abandoning hard-won benefits for improved working conditions?
- Will parental involvement in charter schools continue as charter schools mature?
- Is the emphasis on parental involvement discouraging or preventing families from enrolling in charter schools?

Choice

The concept of public education as the great equalizer of American society still looms in the hearts and minds of most people. The common school, invented in the nineteenth century, was intended to provide a basic education *common to all children*. The state, not the family, would assume responsibility for educating the nation's children, promising equal opportunity regardless of family circumstance. School would be the institution of the state where children would learn the skills essential for effective and productive citizenship in democratic society.

Despite the historic failure of our nation's schools to fulfill that promise for certain populations, particularly children of color and children of the poor, the ideology of the common school persists. Since school attendance is determined by geographic residence, affluent families have had the benefits of choosing communities that provide good schools for their children. Historically, families of limited means did not have such choices and were left to patronize neighborhood schools, many of which have continually failed to adequately educate students. Relatively new to the American scene is the notion that all families—not just the affluent—should be given the opportunity to choose the school their children will attend. The charter school movement builds on this idea, providing a mechanism for families to create schools if they do not otherwise exist.

Making the family, not the state, the agent of the child's education is a departure from the original notion of the common school. In that sense, it is a form of privatization. Yet family choice is not a new idea; for decades magnet schools, alternative schools, home schools, and private schools have increased families' options. However, these systems of choice have not significantly increased access to quality schooling for groups that have been ill-served by public schools (Fuller, Elmore, and Orfield, 1996).

Researcher Brett Lane of Northwest Laboratories underscores that the question for policymakers and analysts is not whether there should be choice (since choice already exists) but what kind of choice system is most equitable. Policies must focus on the strategies and mechanisms needed to ensure that the basic intent of the choice movement and charter schools—addressing historic inequities—is realized (Lane, 1998).

In order for choice to be an effective reform strategy, families need viable choices. Excluding vouchers, which have only been tried on a limited scale, charter schools have gone farther than any previous reform in giving families true educational options. These options carry associated risks, both real and ideological, as well as potential benefits for improving the quality of education for disadvantaged students. Most salient are concerns about discrimination and equity of access.

Discrimination.　　Before the existence of charter schools, the desegregation of public schools in the United States, driven by geographic mobility of households and their choice of neighborhoods, was clearly demonstrated (Hoxby, 1996). Within the traditional district framework, the concern that charter schools will become bastions of segregation and produce other forms of discrimination, including failure to serve students with disabilities, persists. Some fear that charter schools will select only certain students even though state laws prohibit discrimination based on race, ethnicity, and disability and prohibit charter schools from charging tuition or establishing a sectarian school. Moreover, selection is by lottery.

Legislation in many states does not mandate that a school's composition be representative of a charter's sponsoring district, but a government study shows no evidence of discrimination (RPP International, 1998). As a group, U.S. charter schools mirror the racial distribution of students in all public schools (RPP International, 1998). It is estimated that six out of ten charter schools are not racially distinct from their surrounding district, and three out of ten are much more likely to enroll students of color and low-income students compared to other public schools in their surrounding district (RPP International, 1998). The higher proportion of students of color can be problematic, particularly in states that mandate that charter schools reflect the racial makeup of the local area. Consider the case of Healthy Start Academy in Durham, North Carolina:

> Healthy Start Academy in Durham, North Carolina is a year-old charter school with a remarkable record of student achievement. The kindergarten class scored in the 99th percentile on the Iowa Test of Basic Skills, up from the 42nd percentile a year ago. Second-graders are in the 75th percentile, up from the 34th percentile. But Healthy Start is in danger of having its charter revoked because state law requires charters to reflect the racial and ethnic composition of their communities after the first year. Healthy Start is 99 percent Black. Under the state's quota system the school is supposed to be only 45 percent Black.
>
> The director of the state's largest teacher's union claims the school is segregated and wants the State Board of Education to close the school down despite no evidence of discriminatory admissions practices. Vernon Robinson, a Winston-Salem alderman, who lobbied for a state charter school law, argues that the goals of those who seek integration at all costs are laudable but misguided. "At some point, we must let our people go to the schools they want to attend rather than where someone else wants them to go." (*Wall Street Journal*, July 6, 1998)

Another fear of discriminatory practice focuses on serving students with special needs. A government study found that the percentage of students with disabilities at charter schools (8 percent) is somewhat less than for all district public schools (11 percent); the percentage of students with limited English proficiency in charter schools (13 percent) is about the same as in district public schools (RPP International, 1998). In a study of California charter schools and their nearby public schools (Wells, 1998), the differences regarding socioeconomic status, special education, and limited English proficiency were small overall, but there were large ranges on a school-by-school basis where start-ups were involved.

For-profit charter schools present a more complicated picture. A study of for-profit charter schools in Massachusetts—a state with a high percentage of for-profits—contains surprising findings. The schools serve far fewer percentages of students with complicated disabilities compared to neighboring district schools. Additionally, substantial numbers of students with disabilities—"mostly those with more complicated disabilities and expensive needs"—have left the for-profit charter schools and returned to local district schools (Zollers and Ramanathan, 1998, p. 229). In Arizona for-profit charter schools, special education students account for only 3 percent of total enrollment, a figure far below the normal 10–13 percent in district schools. Another study of for-profit charter schools indicates that 20 percent of special education students who came from other schools legally dropped their special education designation when they enrolled. Some parents signed legal waivers relinquishing their child's entitlement to all or some special education services (Dykgraaf and Lewis, 1998).

Whether students have been counseled out of schools in Massachusetts and Arizona is a matter of conjecture. Charter school proponents sometimes contend that public schools overidentify students with disabilities and that charter schools' inclusion plans "can facilitate the removal of the disability label" (Zollers and Ramanathan, 1998, p. 229) For example, officials at the Edison Corporation, which sponsors the Boston Renaissance School, claim that many parents "hid the fact that their children were classified as learning disabled in the hope of letting them make a fresh start" (Chubb, 1998, p. 208).

Equity of Access.   Many state laws are designed to favor granting charters to schools that serve disadvantaged populations. For example, Nevada and Texas have no limits on the number of charters granted to schools that focus on populations of at-risk students. Most legislation also specifies procedures designed to ensure equity of access; the most common is a lottery process for choosing among applicants.

It is left to individual charter schools to develop outreach programs and admissions procedures aimed at recruiting target populations. The level of advertising or recruiting may reflect the energy, knowledge, and resources of various schools, but some schools may be deliberately limiting access through their admissions practices. For example, A.S. Wells found that charter school administrators exercised greater power compared to district schools in choosing students through recruitment efforts (including information dissemination and publicity), as well as through student academic requirements, discipline/expulsion practices, and parental involvement (Wells, 1998).

Norman Atkins, codirector of the Northstar Academy Charter School in Newark, New Jersey, suggests that some charter schools try to get a good fit by holding meetings for prospective families to clarify the school's program and their expectations of students and families (Personal Communication, February 5, 1999). Many schools ask parents to sign voluntary contracts that explicitly state school expectations about student behavior and family responsibility for student performance. Contracts include expectations such as volunteering for parents and attendance, discipline, and homework for students (WestEd, 1998). The high degree of satisfaction expressed by parents in most attitudinal studies may be a result of clarifying expectations, but these requirements may also limit access to like-minded families and fail to meet an explicit purpose of the school to serve disadvantaged families.

Wells (1998) also demonstrates that the availability of transportation may shape the nature of charter school communities. Areas not served by public transportation or school busing may be accessible only to families that have the means for private transportation. Critics of charter schools also see discrepancies between those who exercise choice and those who do not. They claim that choice serves the interests of the already privileged and increases the gaps between those who are already successful at manipulating the system and those who are not (Moore and Davenport, 1990).

Moreover, when active families leave a school there may be ramifications for the school community. Sociologists James Coleman and Thomas Hoffer (1986) emphasize that the departure of involved families from the neighborhood school may benefit the immediate family, but it can have consequences for the schools and families left behind. School-involved families have "social capital" that serves to enforce social norms and sanctions that aid the school in its task. When a family departs from a community school, other persons may experience losses by the severance of relationships. The exercise of choice may, therefore, benefit certain individuals at a cost to society, and it may diminish the experience of families and students most in need. Still, charter schools can break the cycle of failure for groups of students who have been resistant to educational achievement.

Research Questions: Choice

The following research questions on choice need to be addressed:

- What will demographic data reflect in regard to the racial and ethnic composition of students enrolled in charter schools, and what will longitudinal studies reflect in regard to retention patterns?
- Should charter schools be obliged to reflect the composition of the local district, particularly when charter schools are serving students from disadvantaged populations?

- Some critics contend that charter schools may resegregate public education: Is this a valid assertion? Given the relatively small size, uniqueness of mission, and geographic locations of charter schools, how can a legitimate study be designed?
- How can we best design longitudinal studies that will track students with disabilities who enter charter schools, as well as those whose disabilities are discovered at the charter school site, to gauge their mobility rates and the adequacy of programs designed to accommodate them?
- How do we compare the number of special needs students served by charter schools and neighborhood schools?
- How are state funding formulas impacting charter school services for children with exceptional needs?
- How do we conduct studies to ascertain admissions and recruitment practices in charter schools and the effects of those practices on prospective applicants?
- Which families are most likely to take advantage of charter schools? Which are not?
- What are the effects of the departure of charter school families from neighboring schools?
- In what geographic areas are charter schools being located? Do certain types of charter schools cluster to certain demographic areas? To what extent does the physical location of charter schools affect enrollment and admissions?

Competition

The first schools in this country used private funding or a combination of public-private funding; since the advent of universal free education, however, district schools have enjoyed a monopoly on no-cost education. One of the underlying tenets of charter school legislation is to introduce the forces of market competition that threaten this monopoly. Policy advocate Ted Kolderie (1992) calls this "withdrawing the exclusive franchise" of public schooling. Kolderie says that the intent of charter school legislation is not only to provide good schools for a few children but also to drive educational improvement in district schools for all children. Others have argued similarly: By injecting competition into the school environment, the quality of education will improve (Chubb and Moe, 1990). The hope is that charter schools will force district schools to adopt curriculum and organizational reforms, making the schools better suited to adopt practices that meet individual needs. Preliminary findings on the initial success of charter schools in providing the impetus for change are equivocal.

Districts' Reactions to Charter Schools.   In her study of ten districts in California, Wells (1998) found that regular public schools in districts with charter schools felt little or no pressure from the charter school to change the way they operate. Leaders at the district schools noted that the charter schools in the study received supplementary funding from the government and private sources, creating "an uneven playing field." Arguably, the opportunity for additional funding may spur district schools to compete for similar funds, but Wells postulates the opposite. The effect, she believes, is to make educators in the district unresponsive to competitive forces in the manner that economic theory would predict.

Resentment toward charter schools appears to increase when funding flows through the district to the charter school. In states such as New Jersey, district superintendents often expressed animosity toward charters for taking "dollars off the budget" (Kane, 1998). Superintendents perceived that they had less money to work with and little reduction in expenditures, for it costs as much to run a class for twenty-one students as it does for twenty-six. Similarly, a charter school study in Massachusetts found negative effects on the district because leaders perceived that the loss of resources would make it even harder to innovate (Brigham and Associates, 1998).

Institutional inertia may also keep district schools from responding to increased competition from outside sources. Consider the responses of two Massachusetts superintendents who were asked about adopting their local charter schools' innovations (Brigham and Associates, 1998, p. 19):

- Two teachers in a class is an excellent idea. They even have some certified teachers as second teachers because there is a glut of teachers. They also have a longer day. But we can't do that because of costs and unions. It is a luxury to set the work day, but it can't be replicated.
- We're a regional school. We have to get our budget through five towns, all determined to whittle it down. The charter school faces only its board, which is already favorably disposed to everything they want to do.

It seems that by framing new procedures and practices in old ways, these district school leaders may be missing the point. Independent charter schools are not so much about pedagogical programs or discrete innovations as they are about a whole new way of organizing and thinking about schools (Kolderie, 1990). To effect such a wholesale paradigm shift on the part of district schools may take the intervention of compelling competitive forces.

There is some indication, however, that districts are being nudged into small change. More hopeful findings of the effects of markets on schools are found in a study of eight states and the District of Columbia. Researcher Eric Rofes (1998) reports that most districts have responded to charters slowly. However, only one-quarter of school districts have made significant changes (e.g., opening schools organized around a specific philosophy or theme or creating add-on programs such as an after-school program or all-day kindergarten) in their educational offerings.

Marketing Schools.   One explanation for the juxtaposition of the expansive growth of charter schools and the modest response of districts to charter schools is marketing. Charter school operators are dependent upon marketing and public relations to create interest in their schools; this is a relatively foreign concept to most district schools. Newspaper articles, print and TV advertisements, and outdoor billboards are some of the strategies used by charter schools to attract students and create public awareness. For-profit management companies may be especially savvy at marketing, as they have both the budgets and experience to launch effective campaigns.

It may be this increased public focus on local schools—rather than a fear of losing students—that creates the sense of urgency needed to force some district schools to change. A central district administrator in Michigan frames this urgency nicely:

> There's definitely a psychological effect. It's a moral issue in terms of the staff. At first they have some initial fear: is the government out to destroy public schools? Then there's the urgency. People recognizing we're in a competitive market. When you visit a staff room in a building located near a charter school, you sense an immediate change in psychology: now we're in competition with the charter. We have to market our schools (quoted in Rofes, 1998, p. 8).

For charter as well as district schools, it remains an open question whether marketing means improved academic performance. However, the most immediate downside of marketing can be the damage it does to meaningful communication between charter schools and district schools. The following reaction of an Arizona district school teacher illustrates the downside of competitive marketing:

> I've found great division in the community. I've found that teachers who have been here any length of time are very resentful of the type of advertising the charter is doing and the type of comments that are made about the traditional public schools.

Teachers resent the fact that we are being discussed as a below-average school, a school that doesn't teach anything. (quoted in Rofes, 1998, p. 17)

Marketing rhetoric may also get in the way of empirical studies and truly reflective practices. As of this writing, few practices in charter schools have been documented. There is also little evidence of systematic, formal self-evaluation at this time, making it difficult for district schools to contemplate replication. Much of the charter school literature is politicized and focuses on policy-level issues or descriptive analysis rather than the study and improvement of practice. Another explanation for the failure of charters to drive change through competition may be that sharing teaching practices is not part of the culture of schooling, even among teachers in the same district or within the same school. Teachers are unaccustomed to talking about practices that are successful and those that are not. In light of increased public scrutiny and polarization in some districts, any expectation that this behavior will change because a new school is introduced may be unrealistic.

Market Forces.   Market forces operate only when there is real competition. Education economist Caroline Hoxby (1996) predicts that a school district would have to lose between 6 percent and 9 percent of its enrollment for school districts to feel pressure to compete, a concentration that no district has yet achieved. Moreover, demographic figures indicate that the increase in overall school population in recent years may be balancing or surpassing the loss of students to charter schools.

Ironically, market principles designed to influence district schools appear to have the greatest impact on charter schools. District schools—even schools marked by years of failing student achievement—have little fear they will be closed. Charter schools, in contrast, have no captive population, and there are direct consequences for not meeting state achievement outcomes or not pleasing parents who can vote with their feet. The limited terms of the charter and the political challenges schools confront in most districts make charter schools feel vulnerable. Although the growth and stability of charter schools may eventually accelerate reform for school districts, for the time being market forces seem to be operating most effectively among charter schools themselves.

Research Questions: Competition

The following research questions on competition need to be addressed:

- Studies need to be conducted to gauge the effect of competition on district schools: How do district schools respond to charter schools? What are the nature of changes that are prompted and what are the implications of those changes?

- What is the effect of marketing schools on public perceptions of education? How do these public perceptions affect district and charter schools?

- What is the nature of market forces within districts? What can we learn from districts that have a significant population of charter schools within their geographic boundaries?

- Are there differences in the way for-profit charter schools and nonprofit charter schools react to competition and market forces?

- What is the public perception of companies profiting from public education? Do these attitudes change if a for-profit company provides a demonstrably better education than a local education agency?

References

American Federation of Teachers. (1994). *AFT resolution on charter schools*. Anaheim, Calif.: AFT.

_____. (1996). *Charter schools: Do they measure up?* Washington, D.C.: AFT.

_____. (1997). *Is education Wall Street's next high-flyer industry?* Washington, D.C.: AFT.

Budde, R. (1996). The evolution of the charter concept. *Phi Delta Kappan* 78 (1), 72–73.

Center for Educational Reform. (1998). *Charter school legislation: A heartening show of bipartisan support*. <http://207.86.17.180/laws/Bipartisan.htm>.

_____.(1998, Fall). *Charter school legislation: State rankings*. <http://edreform.com/laws/ranking/.html>.

_____. (1999). *Charter schools: A progress report, part 2: The closures*. <http://edreform.com/pubs/CharterClosures99.html>.

_____. (2000). *National charter school directory 2000, 6th edition*. Washington, D.C.: CER.

_____. (2001). *National charter school directory 2001, 7th edition*. Washington, D.C.: CER.

_____. (2001a). *Charter schools today: Changing the face of American education, 2000*. An update of chapter 2. Washington, D.C.: CER, 1-16.

Cheung, E., Murphy, J., and Nathan, S. (1998). *Making a difference? Charter schools, evaluation, and student performance*. Minneapolis: Hubert H. Humphrey Institute, University of Minnesota.

Chubb, J. E. (1998). Edison scores and scores again. *Phi Delta Kappan* 80 (3), 205–212.

Chubb, J. E. and Moe, T.M. (1990). *Politics, markets, and America's schools*. Washington, D.C.: Brookings Institution.

Coleman, J., and Hoffer, T. (1986). *Public and private high schools: The impact of communities*. New York: Basic.

Cuban, L. and Tyack, D. (1995). *Tinkering toward utopia: A century of public school reform*. Cambridge: Harvard University Press.

Dykgraaf, C. L. and Lewis, S. K. (1998). For-profit charter schools: What the public needs to know. *Education Leadership*, 56 (2), 51-53.

Engler, J. (1994). Let's revolutionize public education. *Wall Street Journal*, Letters to the Editor, p. B4.

Fulford, N., Raack, L., and Sunderman, G. (1998, January). *Charter schools in our midst: Charter schools as agents—will they deliver?* Oak Brook, Ill: North Central Regional Educational Laboratory.

Fuller, B., Elmore, R. F., and Orfield, G. (1996). *Who chooses? Who looses? Culture, institutions, and the unequal effects of school choice*. New York: Teachers College Press.

Government Accounting Office. (1998). *Charter schools: Federal funding available but barriers exist*. Report No. 98–84. Washington, D.C.: U.S. General Accounting Office.

Goodnough, A. (1988, March 19). Whitman shows support for criticized charter schools. *New York Times*, p. A34.

Heubert, J.P. (1997). *Harvard civil rights—civil liberties law review*. Report No. 2, vol. 2. Cambridge: Harvard University Press, pp. 301–353.

Hoxby, C.M. (1996). Are efficiency and equity in school finance substitutes or complements? *Journal of Economic Perspectives* 10(4), 51–72.

_____. (1999). Where should federal education initiatives be directed? In M.H. Kosters (ed.) *Financing college tuition: Government policies and educational priorities*. Washington, D.C.: The AEI Press.

Johnson, J. (1995). *Assignment incomplete: The unfinished business of educational reform*. New York: Public Agenda.

Kane, P.R. (1992). *Emerging issues in K-12 independent school governance*. AGB Occasional Paper 14. Washington, D.C.: Association of Governing Boards of Universities and Colleges.

_____. (1998). *New Jersey charter schools: The first year*. New York: Teachers College, Columbia University.

Kane, P. R., Ballen, M., and Atkins, N. (1997). *Charter school governance: A national survey*. Unpublished report, Teachers College, Columbia University.

Kolderie, T. (1990). *Beyond choice to new public schools: Withdrawing the exclusive franchise in public education*. Saint Paul, Minn.: Center for Policy Studies.

_____. (1992). Chartering diversity. *Equity and Choice* 9(1), 28–31.

Lane, B. (1998). *Choice matters: Policy alternatives and implications for charter schools*. Portland, Ore.: Northwest Regional Educational Laboratory.

Lewis, S. K., and Dykgraaf, C. L. (1998, October). For-profit charter schools: What the public needs to know. *Educational Leadership* 56(2), 51–53.

Manno, B. V., Finn, C. E., Bierlein, L. A., and Vanourek, G. (1997). *Charter school accountability: Problems and prospects—charter schools in action*. Final report, pt. 4. Washington, D.C.: Hudson Institute.

_____. (1998). Charter schools: Accomplishments and dilemmas. *Teachers College Record* 99(3), 537–558.

Matthews, J. (1999, March 7). The differences are elementary; regular, charter D.C. schools. *Washington Post*, p. C1.

Moore, D. R. and Davenport, S. (1990). School choice: The new and improved sorting machine. In W. L. Boyd and H. J. Wahlenberg (eds.) *Choice in education: Potential and problems*. Berkeley: McCutchan Publishing Corporation, 187-223.

Mullholland, L. A. (1999). *Arizona charter school progress evaluation*. Tempe, Ariz.: Morrison Institute for Public Policy.

Nathan, J. (1996). *Charter schools: Creating hope and opportunity for American education*. San Francisco: Jossey-Bass.

_____. (1998). Heat and light in the charter school movement. *Phi Delta Kappan* 79(7).

Nathan, J., and Power, J. (1996). *Policy-makers view the charter school movement*. Minneapolis: Center for Policy Studies, Hubert H. Humphrey Institute, University of Minnesota.

Olson, L. (1999, January). Shining a spotlight on results. *Education Week*, Quality Counts 17, pp. 8–10.

Rofes, E. (1998). *How are school districts responding to charter laws and charter schools?* Berkeley: Policy Analysis for California Education.

Rose, L. C., and Gallup, A. M. (2000). The Thirty-Second Annual Phi Delta Kappa/Gallup Poll of the public's attitudes toward the public schools. *Phi Delta Kappan* 82(1), 41–57.

Rosenblum Brigham and Associates. (1998). *Innovation and Massachusetts charter schools*. A report for the Massachusetts Department of Education. Boston: Rosenblum Brigham and Associates.

RPP International. (1998). *A national study of charter schools*. Report No. 2. Washington, D.C.: Office of Educational Research and Improvement, U.S. Department of Education.

_____. (2000). *The state of charter schools 2000: National study for charter schools*. Fourth-year report. Washington, D.C.: Office of Educational Research and Improvement, U.S. Department of Education.

Schnaiberg, L. (1997, December 10). Firms hoping to turn profit from charters. *Education Week*. <www.edweek.org>.

_____. (1998, June 10). Charter schools struggle with accountability. *Education Week*. <www.edweek.org>.

Schroeder, J. (1998). Update on passage of changes in the federal charter school grant program legislation. <www.chaterfriends.org/federal.html>.

Shanker, A. (1988). Restructuring our schools. *Peabody Journal of Education*, 65, 88–100.

Toch, T. (ed.). (1998, April). The new education bazaar. *U.S. News and World Report*. <www.usnews.com>.

Vanourek, G., Manno, B.V., Finn, C.E., and Bierlein, L.A. (1997). *Charter schools as seen by those who know them best: Students, teachers, and parents—charter schools in action*. Final report, pt. 1. Washington, D.C.: Hudson Institute.

Weiss, A. (1997, March). *Going it alone: A study of Massachusetts charter schools*. Boston: Institute for Responsive Education. <www.csus.edu/ier/IRE_Report.html>.

Wells, A. S. (1998). *Beyond the rhetoric of charter school reform: A study of ten California school districts*. Los Angeles: UCLA Charter School Study.

WestEd. (1998). *Cross-site report—the findings and implications of increased flexibility and accountability: An evaluation of charter schools in Los Angeles Unified School District*. San Francisco: WestEd.

Winerip, M. (1998, June 14). Schools for sale. *New York Times Magazine,* pp. 42–49.

Zollers, A. K., and Ramanathan, N. J. (1998). For-profit charter schools and students with disabilities. *Phi Delta Kappan* 80(4), 297–304.

10

Privatization and Charter School Reform: Economic, Political and Social Dimensions

AMY STUART WELLS AND JANELLE SCOTT

In this chapter we make the argument that charter school reform—possibly the most popular educational reform movement that exists today—is at the forefront of privatization in public education. We came to this conclusion based on our study of California charter schools and our reading of the growing body of research on the thirty-six state charter school laws and the nearly 1,800 charter schools across the country (U.S. Department of Education, 1999). Our analysis has led us to believe that in most instances charter school laws allow—and sometimes prod—these autonomous schools to become more private in several economic, political, and social dimensions of their existence. Furthermore, we learned that this shift toward privatization, as it is taking place in hundreds of

Amy Stuart Wells is the principal investigator of the UCLA Charter School Study. Research associates are Ligia Artiles, Sibyll Carnochan, Camille Wilson Cooper, Cynthia Grutzik, Jennifer Jellison Holme, Alejandra Lopez, Janelle Scott, Julie Slayton, and Ash Vasudeva.

charter schools across the country, may have very disparate effects on schools in wealthy versus low-income communities.

At the same time, however, we argue that the relationship between privatization and charter school reform is highly complicated and multifaceted, as different charter schools, operating in different local contexts, adopt different privatization strategies based on their needs and what is available to them.

In the first section of this chapter, we briefly describe the multiple meanings of the term "privatization" and provide an overview of charter school laws as they help shape privatization within this reform movement. In the second section, we discuss the various privatization strategies that charter schools employ, including relying heavily on private resources; employing educational management organizations (EMOs) to run day-to-day operations; contracting-out with private firms for individual services; and restricting who applies, who gets in, and who has a voice within the school community. Within the context of these economic, political, and social dimensions of privatization, we demonstrate the ways in which charter schools in disparate communities (e.g., wealthy versus low-income) are differentially affected by the shift toward privatization.

In the final section of this chapter, we discuss the implications of what we know about charter schools and privatization thus far, namely, what these various forms of privatization within charter schools mean for the public system, who should care about these phenomena, and why. Finally, we suggest areas of further research that would enhance our understanding of these complex but extremely timely issues.

The Multiple Meanings of Charter School Reform and Privatization

Both "charter school reform" and "privatization" are elusive terms with multiple meanings. In this section, we examine several definitions of these two phenomena so that we can better explore the intersection between them. We also briefly describe our study of California charter schools, the source of much of our data and insights.

The Economic, Political, and Social Meanings of Privatization

The term "privatization" as used in the context of education describes a range of practices, some of which are long standing and some of which are more recent developments (Henig, 1990). For instance, public schools have, for many years, privatized various aspects of their operations by contracting with for-profit companies to provide cafeteria services, transportation, and maintenance. Some also contract with private companies for special education services (Ascher, Fruchter, and Berne, 1996).

But the recent shift toward privatization in education goes even farther and touches more aspects of the educational system than ever before. In fact, as we noted above, we argue that currently there are at least three overlapping and intertwined dimensions of privatization in education: economic, political, and social.

Since 1980, much of the policy debate on privatization has centered around economic and political dimensions (e.g., allowing public money to flow to schools that operate outside the government-run system). This focus relates to several dominant themes in educational reform, namely, the call for greater deregulation and more competition and market-driven change in the educational system. For example, M. Carnoy (1993) argues that "*privatization* means that individual schools—whether publicly owned, privately owned and secular, or privately owned and religious—would operate with equal access to public resources and largely independent of public controls, in a free market for educational services" (p. 164).

Meanwhile, J. Murphy (1996) presents a slightly broader typology of different forms of privatization, which includes *volunteerism, contracting,* and *deregulation.* Volunteerism is when voluntary associations provide services traditionally offered by a government agency. Contracting is when a government agency purchases service from for- and not-for-profit groups in the private sector. Deregulation is the removal of governmental oversight and legislation to allow market forces to operate more freely (Murphy, 1996, pp. 20–34).

Although Murphy's (1996) typology expands the discussion of privatization, it is still limited primarily to issues of funding and regulation. Yet we argue that it is important to consider the social dimensions of privatization in education as well, because they can have a profound impact on students' opportunities. For example, in our study of California charter schools, we saw how some charter schools could restrict who learned about them and thus who had access to them—aspects of privatization that have more to do with issues of association. One of the main differences between public and private schools is that private schools have far more control over who enrolls and who remains enrolled. Thus, charter schools display aspects of privatization when they limit who can enroll through subtle mechanisms such as selective recruitment, applicant interviews, stricter discipline codes, and parental involvement requirements.

Furthermore, voice and governance are, theoretically, different in public versus private schools because private schools are generally governed by a board of trustees who are appointed, whereas public schools are governed by elected boards who are at least somewhat responsive to their constituencies. Thus, a discussion of the shift toward privatization in public education should include attention to issues of association, including student access and who has a voice in the governance of the school (which is an obvious political dimension of privatization as well).

Indeed, as we explain below, all of these overlapping and intertwined dimensions of privatization—economic, political, and social—are present in charter school reform.

The Diversity of Charter School Reform Versus the Narrow Legislative Agenda

Likewise, the term "charter school reform" is difficult to define because it encompasses a range of actors with highly divergent political agendas and beliefs about schools. The diverse political support for charter school reform was apparent at the birth of the movement, which grew out of the global phenomenon of deregulating, privatizing, and marketizing public education and the distinctly American phenomenon of recurring demands for local and community control of schools (see Nathan, 1996; Tyack and Cuban, 1995). Given its dissimilar political roots, charter school reform has come to symbolize different things to different people, which applies as well to state policymakers who propose, pass, and implement the legislation (see Wells et al., 1999).

For instance, charter school reform clearly intersects with the more economic and political dimensions of privatization, especially in the minds of those who advocate charter schools as market-based reform. Indeed, many supporters of charter schools fervently believe that the public education system is beyond repair and that competitive, market-based strategies are its only hope (Chubb and Moe, 1990; Lieberman, 1989). Rather than seeking public school reform, they advocate deregulation of the bureaucratic oversight.

Thus, what makes the charter school reform movement so unique is that it unites people who support such a conservative, market-based agenda with people who consider themselves to be much more liberal and opposed to privatization, at least in principle. Despite this diversity of views within the charter school movement, our data and the work of other researchers show that the ways in which charter school laws have been written leave room for a great deal of privatization, and in some cases they actually leave charter school educators no choice but to head down the privatization path.

Charter School Laws: Framing Privatization.   In this section we examine some of
the ways in which legislation helps create situations in which charter school
founders—even those who oppose privatization—must turn to the private sector
if they intend to start and operate financially viable institutions.

First of all, in terms of the economic and political dimensions of privatization,
there is ample evidence that charter schools lack sufficient funds. In fact, most
major studies have found that a lack of adequate resources was the primary im-
pediment to implementing charter school reform (UCLA Charter School Study,
1998; U.S. Department of Education, 1998; SRI International, 1997; RPP International and the University of Minnesota, 1997).

For example, in California, where public funds for charter schools are, in most
cases, routed through the local school districts, charter schools are supposed to
receive public funding equal to the "base revenue limit"—or the maximum
amount of state and local general-purpose revenue that a district receives—multiplied by the number of students enrolled. In addition to basic (general) funds,
charter schools are entitled to receive state and federal categorical funds—for example, Title I or special education—for their students who qualify (see, for example, Slayton, 1999).

But beyond these general operating funds, charter schools are not entitled to
any additional public money, such as capital funds, to help cover the cost of
buildings and maintenance. This is particularly problematic for start-up charter
schools that have no existing infrastructure to build upon. They must then turn
to the private sector for economic and political support.

In contrast, most conversion charter schools—those that were converted from
existing public schools—often received the same level of support from their districts as they did before, including the right to continue using—generally at no
cost—the building in which the school was housed. This occurs in part because
conversion charter schools tend to be less politically independent from their districts; in fact, they continue to rely on their school district administration for various services, including payroll, insurance, and legal services (see UCLA Charter
School Study, 1998).

Start-up charter schools, in contrast, tend to be much more independent
from their districts, both politically and financially. Generally, they are on their
own to find their buildings and basic materials. Furthermore, the more independent a charter school is from its school district, the fewer services it will receive directly from the district and the more it will spend out of its own budget
for everything from liability insurance to legal services. The cost of freedom
from district bureaucracy, therefore, can be quite high, forcing charter schools

to rely more heavily on private resources wherever they can get them, for example, from parents, local foundations, or corporations (UCLA Charter School Study, 1998).

Thus, the organizational structure of a charter school and its relationship to its charter-granting agency also affect the cost of running a school and the school's ability to meet those costs. For instance, size can dictate expense in charter schools. Student enrollment in charter schools, particularly start-ups, tends to be much smaller than in comparable public schools (Scott and Holme, 1998; U.S. Department of Education, 1998). The start-ups in our study, with the exception of the home schooling and independent charter schools, tended to be small schools, with student enrollment ranging from a low of sixty students to a high of 180 students. In such schools, the per-pupil funding is often insufficient to pay for capital expenses, staff salaries and benefits, curricular materials, and administrative overhead.

In terms of the more social aspects of privatization, charter schools are technically schools of choice, but access to these schools varies by state and especially the local context. For instance, the laws in twenty-nine states allow charter schools to have enrollment requirements or admissions criteria. In fact, only nine of the twenty-nine state laws stipulate that criteria shall *not* be based on "intellectual ability" or measures of achievement or "aptitude."[1] In California, for instance, charter schools are allowed to have admissions criteria "if applicable." Such criteria could include anything from evidence of prior achievement, to contracts requiring parents to volunteer for a specified number of hours, to specific codes of conduct.

As we discuss in more detail below, these aspects of the legislation give charter school founders and educators great control over enrollments and with whom they will associate. Start-up charter schools in particular have control over who is recruited and admitted, for they must recruit a student body from scratch, whereas conversion schools generally continue to enroll—at least in the short run—many of the same students who were there before.

Meanwhile, nine charter school laws, including that in California, state that charter schools should reflect the racial makeup of the school districts in which they are located. Still, we found no evidence in California that this stipulation was being addressed, monitored, or enforced (see UCLA Charter School Study, 1998). Furthermore, nineteen of the thirty-six state laws say nothing about racial balance requirements. In this way and others, charter school legislation allows autonomous schools greater control over who does and does not enroll—a form of social privatization.

The UCLA Charter School Study

In 1992, California became the second state, after Minnesota, to pass charter school legislation. By the mid-1990s, California was second only to Arizona in number of charter schools, and by 1997 it had the largest number of students (more than 50,000) enrolled in charter schools. Thus, the story of charter school reform in this huge and diverse state is salient and timely. Our goal in conducting qualitative case studies of ten California school districts and their charter schools was to understand how policy, with its diverse political base, interacts with different local communities.

Accordingly, we sampled school districts for diversity and, using purposive sampling, selected ten districts that differed on several key factors, including: size; racial and socioeconomic diversity; position in an urban, rural, or suburban community; geographic location in Southern, Central, or Northern California; and number, percentage, and types of charter schools in the district. Our sample consisted of five large urban districts; three districts that were mostly rural but also had some suburban housing; and two districts that were mostly suburban, although one included a rural section. These ten districts housed thirty-nine charter schools, or almost one-third of all that existed in the state at the time.

We selected the seventeen charter schools within these districts by, once again, sampling for diversity along various dimensions, for example: dependent versus independent relationships with districts; grade levels served; size and demographics of the students; type or format of the school, including home schooling and independent study charters; philosophy of the school; and duration of the charter. The final sample included two suburban, five rural-suburban, and ten urban charter schools. Eight of the seventeen were conversion charter schools, and nine were start-up schools. Three of the charter schools were home schooling/independent study schools that spanned grades K-12; three schools were high schools serving students in grades 9–12; and four were middle/junior high schools with some combination of grades 5–8. One school was a K-8 charter school, and six of the charters were elementary schools serving some subset of grades K-6.

From spring 1996 through spring 1998, we conducted three site visits to each of the eight larger school districts in our study and two site visits to the two smallest districts. Data collection included 462 semistructured interviews with district officials; charter school founders, leaders, teachers, parents, governance council members, and community supporters; and educators at nearby public schools. We also conducted observations of district and charter school meetings and classrooms in charter schools. Finally, we collected hundreds of district and charter school documents. This qualitative methodology allowed us to examine the many ways in which charter school reform intersects with various forms of privatization in education.

The Intersection of Charter School Reform and Privatization

Over the years we have studied charter school reform from several standpoints—including those of policymakers,[2] educators, and parents—and it has become increasingly clear that this is a multifaceted reform and that different people engage in it for a host of reasons (see Wells et al., 1999). Yet as we mentioned above, we learned that even charter school founders who are adamantly opposed to privatization in education heavily rely on private resources simply for their very survival. Furthermore, although we see charter schools at the forefront of privatization in public education, we also learned that no two charter schools are drawing on the private sector or employing private school strategies in quite the same way.

In the next sections, therefore, we discuss the various privatizing strategies charter school founders and educators employed, noting that some charter schools engaged in all of these strategies while others only used one or two. Furthermore, these strategies are not mutually exclusive—for instance, there are overlaps between the private management practice and contracting-out, as some charter schools contract out for their management. Generally, however, most of the charter schools we and other researchers have studied engage in at least one of the following practices.

Relying on Private Resources

In their efforts to start and maintain charter schools, founders and operators often rely heavily on private resources for basic day-to-day operations. As we mentioned above, charter schools—particularly start-ups that must secure a site and pay rent or mortgage out of their operating budget—frequently operate with a lower level of public funding than do traditional public schools.

We found, therefore, that for some charter schools fiscal survival often depends on the ability to acquire additional private support. We also learned that charter schools in wealthy communities are better able to garner such support compared to those in low-income communities, which raises serious questions related to equity and privatization in public education (UCLA Charter School Study, 1998; Scott and Holme, 1998).

Thus, below we discuss the ways in which charter schools are garnering private support and which schools are in the best position to do so; this is the central economic and political dimension of privatization within charter school reform. Although we acknowledge that regular public schools have shown an increased reliance on supplemental private resources acquired through voluntary contributions and fund-raisers (Brunner and Sonstelie, 1996), charter schools' need for such resources can be particularly acute, leading to an acceleration of such activities.

Private Fund-Raising.   The need to tap private sources of funds—be they community-based, corporate, or foundation sources—is tremendous, especially for start-up charter schools. In fact, one charter school in our study draws only 60 percent of needed revenue from public coffers. The remainder of the school's money comes from corporate donors (Scott and Holme, 1998). Although this school is an extreme example, every school in our study sought funding from such private sources. Yet the person responsible for this activity varied from school to school. For instance, some wealthier charter schools employed fiscal or business managers who often had connections to people and organizations with money. Other charter schools employed professional grant-writers, many of whom were also well connected. In addition, these wealthier charter schools relied upon parent volunteers to help write grants.

Meanwhile, the parents of charter students at lower-income schools generally had less time and fewer social networks. Thus, the already overburdened administration and teaching staff at the low-income schools wrote grants and solicited funds in addition to their instructional responsibilities.

Yet even in wealthy charter schools, where grants have funded many programs, teachers expressed concern about the sustainability of this type of financial support, as most grants cannot be extended once they are used. Also, charter school educators sometimes complained that grants can be too prescriptive—for example, providing funding only for a specific activity—which often whittled away at the autonomy they cherished. In other words, as charter schools educators they had become less beholden to school districts, but in some ways they had become beholden to private funders.

In addition to grants from corporations and foundations, some charter schools in our study, particularly suburban and wealthy charter schools, were able to raise more grassroots money within their own school communities. These wealthier charter schools relied upon parent volunteers to fund-raise—either within the community or through their wider connections. In some sites, parent organizations raised staggering amounts of money for school programs. For instance, at one charter school we studied, parents were able to raise hundreds of thousands of dollars each year.

Other schools did not draw upon parents for fund-raising. For instance, we found that charter schools in low-income communities tended to be much more reliant on outside sources—especially corporations—to raise enough private resources to maintain their programs. This meant that when low-income charter schools received donations they were more likely to be beholden to corporations and other outside donors, forcing them to be more responsive to the demands and interests of those funders. For example, one charter school received a large cash donation from a major bank; in exchange, the school agreed to teach its mostly poor African American and Latino elementary students a banking curriculum—complete with information about how to use a checking account.

This relationship between generous donors and cash-strapped charter schools needs to be examined through further research exploring the degree of autonomy poor schools have from corporate funders. It could be that in such instances charter schools are trading autonomy from their bureaucratic school districts for dependence on corporate donors.

Also, based on an evaluation of charter schools in Texas (Taebel et al., 1998), it appears that reliance on private resources is not specific to California. For instance, the study found that more than three-quarters of charter schools in Texas receive some kind of support from community and business organizations. The study also found that parent participation in these charter schools is high and that parents are most frequently involved in fund-raising activities (Taebel et al., 1998).

Volunteerism and In-Kind Resources. In addition to fund-raising for economic and material support, parents and teachers can use their professional connections to attract additional resources. In some of the wealthier schools we visited, we witnessed parents—or friends and colleagues of parents—teaching courses, assisting teachers in the classrooms, performing administrative work, and serving on governing boards.

Thus, parents with medical, legal, technological, or fiscal expertise shared their skills with the charter schools. Although there was some variation within schools in terms of parental support, in wealthy schools parental resources helped the schools academically. A teacher at a charter school in a wealthy community noted, "I have a couple of parents who have just been God-sent. One is an amateur astronomer, she got her degree in physics and she does computers now. . . . She did our Mars web page." This teacher described another parent who used her training in microbiology to conduct science experiments with the children.

In contrast, less-educated parents, particularly in charter schools in low-income communities, were less likely to help in the classrooms and more likely to work on maintaining the facilities: cleaning bathrooms, laying concrete sidewalks, cutting grass. In one school we studied, parents were there every day to clean the school's only bathroom. Such volunteerism saves the poor charter schools money in maintenance, which is especially helpful when they do not have the budget to hire full-time custodial services.

But it was clear to us that the volunteer experiences of charter school parents vary from one school to the next, depending on the most urgent needs of the school and the ways in which the educators perceive the expertise of the parents. This raises important issues not only about the differential experiences of parents with children in charter schools but also about the differences in the types of in-kind resources available to charter schools.

For instance, we asked a governing board member at a charter school in a very wealthy community whether her school had a distinct advantage over other charter schools—particularly those in a nearby urban area—because of the scientists, computer experts, and mathematicians the school had recruited to teach the K-8 students' elective courses in such topics as anatomy and computer programming. Her response was that the parents in the inner-city charter school could always teach courses on topics for which they have some expertise, such as ham radio operation. The differences in terms of socially valued cultural capital—not to mention employable skills—between taking a class in computer programming versus ham radio operation did not appear to occur to her.

We realize that regular public schools, particularly those in wealthy communities, also experience high levels of parental involvement and benefit from the sophisticated social networks of families. Still, charter school reform seems to take volunteerism and in-kind resource donation to a higher level as parents of all social backgrounds participate either by contract or choice. Also, the fact that charter schools enjoy greater autonomy from the public system means they can use parents and colleagues instead of certified educators as instructors for some courses.

Private-Public Partnerships.   There is yet another way to make up for lost revenue: Some charter schools have launched partnerships with universities and corporations or affiliations with national educational reform groups. For example, two of the schools in our study were formally associated with universities, which provided facilities, consultants, and public visibility. An administrator at Directions High School talked about the benefits of his school's partnership with a university: "We get full access to their media center, so pretty much unlimited use of VCRs, LCD projectors, monitors, microphones, so we don't have to buy any of those, we just use theirs—they're fully serviced—as well as unlimited use of the computer labs during the day."

Other charter schools received substantial financial support through partnerships with major corporations in the banking, computer, and entertainment industries. For example, one of Academic Charter School's corporate partners gave it more than $1 million at the time of our study. In addition, an executive from the corporation served on the school's board of trustees, flying to town once a month to see to the business of the school. According to this executive, "My job is to chair the business of the school, and the board is just like any board in charge of fiscal accounts, fiscal and legal management of the institution."

In this case, as in the case of other charter schools with university or corporate partnerships, the connections help the charter schools strengthen powerful social connections and garner greater support throughout the business and academic communities. This in turn assists them in raising even more private donations.

Private Management of Charter Schools: The Proliferation of Educational Management Organizations

Yet another way in which privatization overlaps with charter school reform is through a new development in educational governance and operations known as education management organizations. Even though most EMOs run charter as well as traditional public schools, the rapid growth in the number of these private for-profit and nonprofit organizations since 1990 has coincided with the growth in the charter school movement. Furthermore, charter schools managed by EMOs appear to be the high-growth sector of the diverse charter school movement, and the percentage of charter schools run by EMOs appears to be growing (Moore, 2000).

Some of the best-known EMOs include Edison Schools; Advantage Schools, Inc.; Beacon Management; The Tesseract Group; Sabis Educational Systems; and the School Futures Research Foundation. Despite some controversy and opposition from groups such as teachers' unions, there has been growing political support for the private for-profit management of charter schools (Parry, 1997; Carnoy, 1998).

Washington, D.C., Massachusetts, Wisconsin, Arizona, and Michigan all allow either private schools to convert to charter schools or allow for-profit companies to start charter schools. For instance, L.M. Rhim (1998) writes that Massachusetts is ripe for contractors because of its permissive legislation, high per-pupil allocation, and support for public-private partnerships in state government. Her study also suggests that officials in the upper echelons of state government in Massachusetts supported privatization.

An evaluation of charter schools in Michigan, where the law is very permissive in terms of EMOs, reported that during the 1998–1999 school year a full 70 percent of the state's charter schools were contracting with either for-profit or nonprofit EMOs to provide a range of services, from helping the schools secure a site, to employing the teachers, to handling all aspects of accounting and budgeting (Horn and Miron, 1999). Some of these EMOs work with several schools across the state; others work with only one or two local schools.

In other states, the charter school laws are not always clear on the issue of for-profit firms, but there are often ways around the ambiguity. For instance, California's charter school legislation does not permit private schools to convert into charter schools; neither does it allow charter schools to charge tuition. But the legislation does not exclude for-profit firms from operating charter schools. In practice, once a school has been granted a charter, it can then contract out for EMO-provided services. This contracting-out is often described as a partnership.

Thus, the specifics of the legislation in terms of EMOs do not seem to matter: Once a nonprofit group obtains a charter, it can hire a for-profit firm to run it. And although for-profit firms are not yet operating a large number of charter schools in California, they are beginning to emerge as a major presence in the charter school movement. In particular, many of the newest charter schools to be approved in California are operated by for-profit companies. For instance, Edison Schools operates nine charter schools in California. Bolstered by a hefty $25 million donation from The Fisher Family Foundation, as well as publicly traded stock, Edison Schools now has the capital to expand and is in the process of developing many new schools across the country (Guthrie, 1998).

The possibility of partnering with an EMO may be particularly attractive to grassroots charter schools in high-poverty communities of color. In these environments—where many of the public schools are failing miserably—educators and community leaders may seek to break away from the school district bureaucracy and obtain autonomy over curriculum and school philosophy, yet they find themselves limited in management expertise and in the ability to raise and sustain resources for capital expenses.

For instance, one of the urban charter schools in our study was started by a nonprofit EMO. Representatives from the EMO wrote and presented the charter to the school board, secured a building in which to house the school, recruited students with the assistance of a community organization, and paid for the re-modeling of school facilities. In addition, the foundation hired the faculty, selected the members of the governing council, and chose the curriculum. None of the school's staff and only one parent served on the governing council.

We also interviewed educators at another school that petitioned its district to end its charter due to conflicts with the school's EMO partner over control and decisionmaking. In light of the activities undertaken by the EMO in establishing and managing the first school, and the overpowering role that the EMO held over the second school, we have questions regarding the degree to which these schools were actually in "partnership" with private entities. Were they being run by members of the private sector? The implication of poorer schools and communities contributing to the profits of EMOs needs to be discussed more fully in the research and policy debates about the future of publicly funded education.

Moreover, we argue that more research is needed concerning the politics of private management of public charter schools and the educational environments that can be created by it. For instance, the study mentioned above (Horn and Miron, 1999) found that charter schools in Michigan, 70 percent of which are managed by EMOs, spend more on support services compared to nearby school districts. This finding raises important questions about the efficiency claim regarding market-based reforms such as charter schools.

Even though formal research is just beginning to emerge on the private management of public charter schools, the issue has received much more attention from the media. There is no clear picture emerging from media accounts of EMO-managed schools (Moore, 2000), but some articles have begun to document that charter schools operated by for-profit management firms make promises to parents when trying to attract students (and capital) and then often fall short of expectations (Toch, 1998; Winerip, 1998). For instance, T. Toch (1998) reports that while there are some high-quality charter schools, abuses abound in privately managed ones. For example, he writes:

Nearly half of Arizona's charters are high schools, the majority run by chains such as PPEP TEC High School, Excel Education Centers Inc., and the Leona Group. These companies take advantage of the fact that Arizona requires high school students to attend only four hours of school a day. They target kids on the margins of traditional public schools—low achievers, discipline problems, truants—with pledges of swift and simple routes to graduation. And many of the companies increase their revenues by running two or three four-hour sessions a day and substituting self-paced computer instruction for a regular teaching staff" (1998, p. 37).

Toch also describes distressingly low academic standards for some high school students enrolled in EMO-run charter schools, including some schools that give course credit for students working in fast-food restaurants.

Other articles have documented the disturbing trend of some for-profit management companies to discriminate against students perceived to be problems. For example, the Boston Renaissance School, managed by Edison Schools, was sued for its treatment of a special education student (Vine, 1997).

Conversely, at least one article has reported test-score gains for some schools run by EMOs (Steinberg, 1997), but the measurement problems involved in evaluating progress make such arguments less credible. For instance, the availability of baseline data, or even the assurance that charters will use the state standardized test, is not guaranteed (UCLA Charter School Study, 1998). The Study of Student Achievement in Edison Schools found mixed results. It also pointed to the need for consistent, reliable data. In July 2000, Edison Schools announced that the RAND Corporation would conduct an independent analysis. Yet, many EMOs use prepackaged curriculum, such as Success for All. Thus, it is unclear if any progress or regress is to be attributed to the management of the school, the curriculum, or the ability to exclude students (Rothstein, 1998).

Thus, the picture is a cloudy one. Although EMOs have brought charter schools needed resources, particularly in high-poverty communities, it is less clear if there are meaningful opportunities for community involvement in the governance of these schools. Additionally, media accounts have raised questions about student access and achievement in privately managed schools, particularly those that are run on a for-profit basis. These issues relate directly to our discussion on the social dimensions of privatization.

Contracting-Out with Private Firms for Specific Services

As we noted earlier, charter schools can be fiscally dependent or fiscally independent in relation to the charter-granting school district. Generally, if they are dependent they utilize district administrative services and oversight; fiscally independent schools, in contrast, manage all aspects of their administrative and budgetary infrastructure and sometimes receive their funding directly from the state. Although some of these schools flock to EMOs that handle many of the logistics, others contract out with private, often for-profit, firms to perform specific services such as payroll and accounting.

To meet this growing demand, a cottage industry of entrepreneurs anxious to capitalize upon charter school reform is springing forth. Thus, consulting agencies, payroll and insurance contractors, food-service providers, maintenance companies, and curriculum specialists have all focused in on charter schools, often providing services formerly handled by school district bureaucracies. Obviously, this practice of contracting-out for specific services overlaps with the EMOs discussed above. However, EMOs tend to provide each school with an array of services and are more involved in day-to-day management. Contracting-out usually happens on more of a piecemeal basis, with charter schools contracting-out only one or two services or contracting with more than one firm.

Also, as we mentioned, traditional public schools have long contracted out with for-profit and nonprofit firms for such services as transportation, food services, and special education, as well as building maintenance and custodial care. C. Ascher et al. (1996) write that this history of public-sector contracting-out for ancillary services has "a complicated balance sheet" (p. 89). They note that many school systems have been victims of fraud, overcharging, and other forms of corruption.

Now charter schools are taking the concept to a new level by contracting-out for many more of their regular services, saving money by avoiding the hiring of unionized public employees. For instance, in one school we studied the principal had chosen not to hire district personnel and instead contracted with a private landscaping firm to cut the grass and trim the trees on the school's property (which was still owned by the school district). The workers for the private firm were paid less than the district employees and were not members of a union. The local union representing classified staff in the district sued the charter school, arguing that it must use district employees. The charter school won the case by successfully defending its right, as an autonomous school, to hire the less expensive private company to conduct gardening and maintenance. Given that school district maintenance is often provided by minority workers who enjoy the protection of unions with regard to compensation and safe working conditions, this trend raises questions about the future of those employees' working conditions, as well as working conditions for employees in private nonunion companies.

Furthermore, we learned that many schools in our study used the same payroll or insurance company, but such services were not always provided with the same quality. For example, a low-income charter school in our study had contracted with a payroll company that had reportedly made serious errors in bookkeeping and had overcharged the school. This was an especially poor school serving low-income students of color that did not have a functioning heater during the winter. Thus, it was not surprising that the principal had no time to oversee the payroll company's bookkeeping. Thus, the underresourced schools were at a greater disadvantage in terms of contracting-out; they had the weakest bargaining position and had neither the time nor the resources to oversee contractors.

Privatizing Association: Restricting Who Applies, Who Gets in, and Who Has a Voice

Although the privatization practices described above mainly impact the economic and political dimensions of charter school operations, we also learned from our study and subsequent studies that charter schools also engage in the more social dimensions of privatization. We learned, for instance, that it is common for charter schools to state in their proposals a desire to be inclusive in communities where all children are welcome and all parents and community members are actively involved in shaping the school; yet many charter schools use mechanisms to limit enrollment to certain students and make sure that only certain parents and community members have a voice in how the school is operated. Although these are not issues of funding or school management—the typical issues in privatizing education—they impact the degree to which charter schools operate more like private than public schools.

We do acknowledge, however, that in traditional public schools attendance is usually bounded by residential geography, which is also fraught with racial and social class discrimination. Still, we see charter schools as taking this concept farther, refining the art of excluding the unwelcome. Through various mechanisms—enrollment, recruiting, and requirements—charter schools have more power than most public schools to shape their educational communities.

Recruitment and Enrollment.   Charter schools tend to have more control over who enrolls compared to traditional public schools. This is true even when charter school operators state that they serve students on a first-come, first-served basis, because the enrollment process begins with targeted recruitment and dissemination of information; in addition, very few parents in a given community or district know that a charter school even exists. For instance, few of the charter schools we studied sent out information using district-wide brochures, as do other public schools of choice such as magnet schools.

Other charter schools simply posted flyers in their local communities or sent out mailers to nearby families. A couple of charter schools placed ads in the newspaper, and others sent representatives to attend various meetings and public forums to make presentations. Finally, several charter schools in our study relied solely on word of mouth to attract students and parents. Often, these efforts were targeted toward certain audiences based on geography, racial/ethnic composition, language proficiency, and even at-risk characteristics (Lopez et al., 1998). Such targeted recruitment gives the saying "first-come, first-served" a new meaning: Those who arrive first are the children of a small, interconnected group.

Beyond stacking the deck in recruiting students, charter schools employ subtle admissions requirements and processes that allow them to control enrollment. For instance, many of the charter schools in our study operate on a first-come, first-served basis, yet they granted priority to certain students (e.g., they attended the school before it was converted to a charter school, they have siblings at the school, their parents work at the school).

In addition to these admissions priorities, several charter schools require some sort of parent and/or student meeting with school officials before the student can enroll. These mandatory meetings range from informal discussions where the school culture is described to more of an interview designed to assess the student's abilities and interests as well as the parents' level of commitment to education and volunteer service. Charter school operators described how such meetings/interviews are often used as opportunities to ensure there is a "fit" between the charter school and the family. Students may be steered to apply or not apply, based on whether they meet the behavioral and/or academic standards of the school or whether their parents can meet the school's expectations.

These admissions requirements and processes are highly valued by charter school operators who see them as a mechanism through which they can filter applicants to ensure that they share the same values and beliefs about education. Charter school operators stated that having admissions criteria and an application process in place creates an environment in which most everyone is committed to the school's goals and rules. For example, a counselor at one of the charter high schools commented, "I guess what makes [the charter] a little bit better is just the fact that you have to go through an application process and do these things. It makes it more of a commitment on both the parent's and the student's part. And that ultimately helps the school and helps everybody."

In their study of charter schools in California, SRI International (1997) found that 44 percent of the ninety-eight charter schools surveyed cited students' and/or parents' lack of commitment to the school's philosophy as a factor for being denied admission. For start-up charter schools the number was 50 percent; for conversion charters it was 39 percent.

Student and Parent Requirements.   In addition to recruiting and enrollment strategies, the charter schools we studied often stated explicit expectations and requirements in their charter proposals and policies. Students were held to standards of academic performance, effort, and behavior; parents were expected to be involved in the school. Unlike other public schools, charter schools are legally able to enforce such requirements, mainly through the use of contracts and discipline/expulsion policies.

All but four of the charter schools we visited had specific requirements, policies, and/or contracts in place for students. These requirements ranged from attendance policies to dress codes to specific conduct codes. Educators can even ask students to leave the school if they or their parents do not live up to the charter or the contract. In other words, students who were not trying hard enough, were frequently tardy or absent, wore the wrong clothes, or misbehaved (as defined by the school's conduct code) could be kicked out. As one parent at a charter school we studied commented, "It is nice to have some 'teeth' when you need 'teeth' as far as discipline and having children be accountable for themselves and the work" (see also Lopez et al., 1998; Wells, Holme, and Vasudeva, 2001).

Charter schools frequently specify expectations and requirements of parents and are able to enforce them, mainly through the use of contracts. The SRI International study (1997) found that 75 percent of California charter schools required parents to sign a contract upon enrolling their children. For start-up charter schools it was 86 percent; for conversion charters it was 64 percent. Seven of the charter schools we visited required parents to sign contracts asking them to conduct a variety of tasks, including reading to their children, going over homework, and encouraging appropriate student behavior in accordance with school codes.

Yet the most common requirement was that parents volunteer and participate in school activities, usually for a certain number of hours per school year. Many of the charter schools reserved the right to ask families to leave if parents did not meet requirements specified in the contract. They also denied families admission to the school if parents did not agree to fulfill the requirements of the charter (Lopez et al., 1998; UCLA Charter School Study, 1998). SRI International (1997) reported that 32 percent of charter schools in its study had denied families admission due to parents not being able to fulfill a parental involvement requirement. This was more likely to have occurred in start-up charter schools (37 percent) versus conversion schools (27 percent).

Our data also indicate that some parents had difficulty meeting requirements because they did not have the time. Parents who lived far from the school, for instance, had more trouble getting to campus. Thus, even when charter schools were serving low-income communities and attracting students from poor families, to the extent that these schools had parent contracts they were likely to attract only the most involved and efficacious parents within those communities (Lopez et al., 1998; UCLA Charter School Study, 1998).

Also, as we noted above in the section on in-kind resources, there was a range of activities that parents were encouraged to participate in, and there appeared to be a relationship between the status and social class of the parents and the tasks charter schools asked them to conduct. In general, low-status parents are more likely to be cleaning, not helping with academics. Although this may be true in most public schools with high levels of parental involvement, the contracts mean that these issues are more prominent because parents are forced to do the type of volunteer work the school requires (Lopez et al., 1998; UCLA Charter School Study, 1998).

Thus, contractual requirements consistently helped to define who belonged at the schools and who would be better off elsewhere. We clearly see this as a form of privatization of education, for charter schools are better able to control who is associated with their schools and thus how open and "public" these schools actually are.

Governance and Voice. Another area reflecting the social and political dimensions of privatization is governance and voice within charter schools. There was a tendency at the charter schools we studied to seat only the most powerful and best-connected parents and community members on the governing councils. For instance, we learned that some charter schools use the governing council specifically as a way to attract resources. In other words, council members were often recruited, appointed, and selected to serve based upon what they could bring to the table.

In fact, many schools in our study, including some in low-income communities, appointed individuals simply because of their connections, expertise, and resources. Of course, many advisory boards for nonprofit organizations (and even traditional public schools) are chosen with similar goals in mind. But such activity is more problematic in charter schools because reform is often presented as a means to offer local control, and yet few charter school communities actually elect governance council members. For example, at a charter school in a well-to-do community, one governance council member described the selection process, saying, "And there were people who were . . . recruited, who were commandeered, really, people wanted them."

The members of this governance council have, in turn, used their connections to garner resources for the school, resulting in grants for technology and curriculum materials. As with the EMO-run charter schools discussed above, those who are handpicked to govern are not always those with the most vested interest—parents and educators. Instead, they are the ones with the most money, expertise, and connections.

The question of who has a voice in the governance of charter schools needs further exploration. How the answers relate to privatization needs to be considered. As we have argued here, privatization is not only about resources and dollars but also about more social and political aspects of schools, including association and voice.

Implications and Further Research

In this final section, we discuss the implications of what we know about charter schools and privatization thus far, namely, what these various forms of privatization within charter schools mean for the public system, who should care, and why. Finally, we discuss what type of further research should be conducted to help enhance our understanding of the issues.

Implications and Audience

In our research on charter schools in California and our reading of studies of charter schools in other states, we find several implications that are worthy of further study and public debate. First, given that charter school reform has a diverse constituency and that many supporters either oppose or favor privatization in public education (see Wells et al., 1999), the various forms of privatization apparent within charter school reform need to be made more public and debated more openly. Only then can the successes and failures, as measured by student outcomes or greater efficiency, be discussed in terms of the trade-offs (e.g., more selective recruitment and admissions policies and more reliance on private as opposed to public resources).

For instance, if charter schools over the next four or five years outperform public schools on standardized tests, should anyone be surprised given that many schools selectively recruit and enroll students? To the extent that some charter schools are open to all and perform well academically, other schools should be able to learn from those experiences. And if some charter schools are hailed as models of innovation, should the fact that they acquired a leg up on others through corporate largesse dampen our enthusiasm for their model? Perhaps most important, will the success of privatized charter schools be enough to overcome the fear that increased private-sector involvement in public education will undermine the democratic principles on which it was formed? As one researcher points out, "It is ironic that the same people who complain about the government's imposition of standards and regulations invite corporations with anonymous shareholders and highly paid executives to devise and deliver educational values" (Vine, 1997, p. 14).

But perhaps the most interesting aspect is the way in which privatization is subtle and discrete, particularly as to the public that pays to support these schools. Distinctions between charter schools and traditional public schools are not well known. In our interviews with non–charter school principals, for instance, educators generally had little information about operations at nearby charter schools. Oftentimes, their only interaction occurred when charter students were expelled and sent to the traditional public school (UCLA Charter School Study, 1998). Thus, it occurs to us that the public needs to be better informed about the types of privatization; the implications need to be discussed, particularly as additional reports on the success or failure of charter schools emerge.

Parents of school-age children enrolled in traditional public schools and the educators in those schools have the most at stake. They will be most affected by a broader move toward privatization. Thus, to the extent that they and others are firm believers in public schools and oppose corporations making money by running public schools, they would be interested in privatization in charter schools.

But we think there are other audiences, including civil rights and child advocacy organizations as well as policymakers and the general tax-paying public. Issues of equity, including unequal access to private in-kind and material resources and selective recruitment and admissions policies, should be of great interest to organizations that fight for the rights of low-income students and students of color. Furthermore, policymakers and the general public will want to know the outcomes of various forms of privatization (e.g., whether or not they make the schools more efficient or more productive and, if so, at what cost to the larger education system). If charter schools are creating yet another layer of stratification within a stratified education system, is that simply considered the price that society pays for innovation? These are important public policy questions.

People anxious to invest in the business of school management or service provision should also be a target audience for future research and information on privatization and charter schools. This audience will certainly want to know how much money is and can be made in the new frontier of capitalist expansion—publicly funded education. In addition, members of the private sector may want to avoid some of the pitfalls other companies have experienced with regard to equity and access for all students.

Further Research

As with any complex set of public policy issues, further research is needed to enhance our understanding of the promises and threats of privatization as it interacts with charter school reform. Yet some research—designed in such a way as to ignore many of the issues we raise in this chapter—could be more damning than helpful. For instance, like so much of the research on school choice, studies that simply look at student outcome data (sometimes after only one year of the choice program) and compare schools of choice—in this case charter schools—to "comparison" public schools nearby are not helpful. We argue, based on many of the issues we raise in this chapter, that such comparison studies, decontextualized from the policies and practices that shape the different communities of the schools being compared, cannot control away critical variables that make test scores higher in one school than the other. For instance, even when two schools—one a choice school, the other a neighborhood school—enroll students of similar race and social class, there remain subtle but significant differences among families who actively choose a school of choice and those who do not (see Wells and Crain, 1997). Thus, research that emphasizes test-score differences without accounting for other issues—screening and selective recruitment of students, for example—only distorts the discourse.

We advocate studies that combine quantitative and qualitative methodology to paint a larger picture coupled with in-depth examination of how these practices impact daily lives. Thus, we argue that more quantitative data is needed to determine the frequency of the various privatization practices we have described. For instance, it would be helpful to have both national and state-level figures as to the percentage of charter schools run by for-profit EMOs, their total number, and which services are most likely to be contracted out to private firms by charter schools as well as public schools. In addition, we need more national and state-level data on student access to charter school opportunities. For instance, we need data on selective recruitment and enrollment; on parent and student contracts; and on the issues of governance, voice, and private fund-raising. But researchers also need to spend time in charter schools and nearby public schools to better understand how people experience privatization on a daily basis and how they make meaning of their choices.

Although student achievement data are important, we believe, based on our study of charter schools in ten school districts in California, that student achievement data, especially if measured by standardized test scores, cannot be examined in isolation of the major shifts in funding, management, enrollment, and governance within a complex reform movement such as charter schools.

Conclusion

Because charter school reform is at the forefront of many efforts to privatize education in the United States, research on this movement should be integral to a research center designed to examine current trends and issues in privatization.

Yet we believe, based on our research on charter schools in California, that attention must be paid to the multifaceted economic, political, and social dimensions of privatization as they interact with charter schools in American communities. As we have demonstrated here, there are several strategies charter schools employ toward greater privatization: relying on private resources, private management of charter schools by EMOs, contracting-out with private firms, and privatizing association. In a few cases all four types of privatization are present in a single school, but more often individual schools will adopt one or more of the above practices but not all. Still, in many charter schools privatization has affected the economic, political, and social dimensions of the schools' existences.

This individualized yet broad-based impact of privatization within charter school reform calls for very careful and thoughtful exploration in different local contexts. We believe that the Center for the Study of Privatization in Education has an important role to play in conducting and disseminating such careful and thoughtful research.

Notes

1. This finding is based on a thorough analysis of charter school laws in thirty-six states and the District of Columbia conducted by Jennifer Jellison Holme and Alejandra Lopez.

2. Prior to our study of the ten school districts, several researchers on our team conducted more than fifty interviews with state-level policymakers in six states on the reasons why they supported charter school reform (see Wells et. al., 1999).

References

American Federation of Teachers (2000). *Trends in student achievement for Edison Schools, Inc.: The emerging track record.* <www.aft.org/research/edisonschools/2000edison.pdf>.

Ascher, C., Fruchter, N. and Berne, R. (1996). *Hard lessons: Public schools and privatization.* New York: Twentieth Century Fund Press.

Brunner, E., and Sonstelie, J. (1997). *Coping with Serrano: Voluntary contributions to California's local public schools.* Proceedings of the 89th Annual Conference on taxation. National Tax Association.

Carnoy, M. (1993). School improvement: Is privatization the answer? In J. Hannaway and M. Carnoy (eds.), *Decentralization and school improvement: Can we fulfill the promise?* San Francisco: Jossey-Bass, pp. 163–201.

_____. (1998). *Do vouchers improve education?* Paper presented at the Ford Foundation Constituency Building for School Reform Initiative, New York.

Chubb, J. and Moe, T. (1990). *Politics, markets, and America's schools.* Washington, D.C.: The Brookings Institution.

Guthrie, J. (1998, October 18). The Fisher King. *San Francisco Examiner Magazine*, pp. 6–13.

Henig, G. (1990). Privatization in the United States: Theory and practice. *Political Science Quarterly* 104(4), 649–670.

Horn, J., and Miron, G. (1999, Jan.). *Evaluation of the Michigan Public School Academy Initiative.* Final Report. Kalamazoo: Evaluation Center, Western Michigan University.

Lieberman, M. (1989). *Privatization and education choice.* New York: St. Martin's Press.

Lopez, A., Wells, A. S., and Holme, J. J. (1998). *Creating charter school communities: Identity building, diversity, and selectivity.* Paper presented at the annual meeting of the American Educational Research Association. San Diego.

Moore, A. (2000, January 2). ABCs of managing an education—the for-profits see charters paying off. Will the plan work? *Philadelphia Inquirer.* <www.philly.com/newslibrary>. Article ID: 0001050065.

Murphy, J. (1996). *The privatization of schooling: Problems and possibilities.* Thousand Oaks, Calif.: Corwin Press.

Nathan, J. (1996). *Charter schools: Creating hope and opportunity for American education.* San Francisco: Jossey-Bass.

Parry, T. R. (1997). How will schools respond to the incentives of privatization? Evidence from Chile and implications for the United States. *American Review of Public Administration* 27, 248–270.

Rhim, L. M. (1998). *Franchising public education: An analysis of charter schools and private education management companies.* Paper presented at the American Education Research Association, San Diego.

Rothstein, R. (1998). Charter conundrum. *American Prospect* 9(39), 46–60.

RPP International and the University of Minnesota (1997, May). *A study of charter schools: First-year report.* Washington, D.C.: U.S. Department of Education, Office of Educational Research and Improvement.

Scott, J., and Holme, J. J. (1998). Private resources, public schools: The role of social networks in California charter school reform. AERA Conference Paper. San Diego.

Slayton, J. (1999). School funding in the context of California charter school reform: Legislation versus implementation. Ph.D. diss., University of California, Los Angeles.

SRI International (1997). *Evaluation of charter school effectiveness.* Report prepared for the State of California Office of Legislative Analyst. Written by J. Powell, J. Blackorby, J. Marsh, K. Finnegan, and L. Anderson. Menlo Park, Calif.

Steinberg, J. (1997, December 17). Edison Project reports measurable progress in reading and math at its schools. *New York Times.*

Taebel, D., Barrett, E. J., Chaisson, S., Kemerer, F., Ausbrooks, C., Thomas, K., Clark, C., Briggs, K. L., Parker, A., Weiher, G., Branham, D., Nielsen, L., and Tedin, K. (1998, December). *Texas open-enrollment and charter schools: Second year evaluation.* Arlington: School of Urban and Public Affairs, University of Texas–Arlington.

Toch, T. (1998, April 27). Education bazaar. *U.S. World and News Report* 124(16), pp. 34–46.

Tyack, D., and Cuban, L. (1995). *Tinkering toward utopia: A century of public school reform.* Cambridge: Harvard University Press.

UCLA Charter School Study. (1998). *Beyond the rhetoric of charter school reform: A study of ten California school districts.* Los Angeles: UCLA Charter School Study.

U.S. Department of Education. (1999, May). *The state of charter schools: Third-year report, 1999.* National Study of Charter Schools. RPP International. Washington, D.C.: U.S. Department of Education. <www.ed.gov/pubs/charter3rdyear/title.html>.

U.S. Department of Education. (1998). *A national study of charter schools.* ISBN 0-16-049751-5. Washington, D.C.: Office of Educational Research and Improvement.

Vine, P. (1997, September 8–15). To market, to market . . . The school business sells kids short. *Nation* 265(7), 11–17.

Wells, A.S., and Crain, R. L. (1997). *Stepping over the color line: African American students in white suburban schools.* New Haven: Yale University Press.

Wells, A. S., Grutzik, C., Carnochan, S., Slayton, J., and Vasudeva, A. (1999). Underlying policy assumptions of charter school reform: The multiple meanings of a movement. *Teachers College Record* 100, 513–535

Wells, A. S., Holme, J. J., and Vasudeva, A. (2001). Charter school reform and the future of public education: The promises and threats embodied in one charter high school. In B. Fuller (ed.), *Charter schools and the paradox of radical decentralization.* Cambridge: Harvard University Press.

Winerip, M. (1998, June 14). Schools for sale. *New York Times Magazine,* pp. 42–48, 80, 86–89.

Perspectives of Stakeholders

11

Vouchers, Privatization, and the Poor

GARY NATRIELLO

Vouchers—payments of public funds given to families to secure education for their children—and other forms of privatization of educational services have been advanced as strategies to enhance the educational opportunities available to poor children in the United States (Hill, 1996). The arguments offered for greater privatization of the education of the poor are a special case of the more general arguments put forward in support of privatization of education overall (Chubb and Moe, 1990). Moreover, the arguments regarding privatization and the education of poor children are in some ways a response to one of the criticisms of such initiatives, that is, that privatization (and particularly vouchers) would be most injurious to and least beneficial for the educational opportunities of poor children (Natriello, McDill, and Pallas, 1990).

In this chapter I address five general issues regarding the impact of vouchers on the education of poor children in the United States. First, I consider ways in which the concepts of privatization and vouchers have been discussed as avenues for improving the education of poor children. Second, I identify the major stakeholders (i.e., those with an interest in the use of privatization and vouchers to provide education for poor children). Third, I describe the interests and concerns of the stakeholders. Fourth, I specify the types of studies that might address stakeholders' concerns regarding privatization, vouchers, and the poor. Fifth, I briefly review the studies that have been conducted to date and assess what we have learned from them.

Framing the Issue

One recent study (Greene, Peterson, and Du, 1999) identifies three mechanisms whereby privatization can lead to improved schooling. First, privatization can encourage competition among providers and lead to reduced costs and/or improved quality. Second, it can result in improved matching of consumer preferences and services supplied. Third, it can allow providers to more easily engage the participation of families in the education process.

Each mechanism can be analyzed for its implications regarding the education of poor children. There is more than sufficient evidence to suggest that in many cases public schools are not competing to educate poor children. In fact, urban public schools have been observed to push poor students away, encouraging them to drop out prior to graduation (Garibaldi and Bartley, 1988). Thus, the prospect of a system in which schools would actually compete to attract poor children and educate them holds interest. However, it is worth noting that such competition for students can result in what H. Levin (1998) refers to as "cream skimming," or the tendency of schools to choose students from more desirable backgrounds (e.g., less poor, higher prior achievement, etc.), and we might anticipate such a process operating even within a pool of largely poor families.

There is also evidence of a disjunction between the culturally shaped patterns of preferences of families—particularly families of limited means and nonmajority ethnic group status—and the programs offered by most public schools. Public schools geared to majority, middle-class culture are often not attuned to the inclinations of certain groups of parents outside the mainstream, as many poor parents are (Natriello, McDill, and Pallas, 1990). The privatization of educational services available to families may lead to a more diverse set of educational options more aligned with parental tastes.

Despite efforts to involve poor parents—indeed, all parents—in the education of children through various parental participation strategies, it is often difficult to secure their genuine participation to facilitate student learning. Efforts to encourage poor parents to participate in education face barriers beyond those confronting educators working with nonpoor parents. If private educational options lead to greater parental participation in the educational process, that participation could be an important component in a more powerful educational experience for poor children.

Of course, in addition to the likely advantages of vouchers and privatization for the education of poor children, a host of concerns has been raised. Some of these concerns directly parallel the advantages outlined above (see Greene, Peterson, and Du, 1999); others move beyond. There is a question as to whether providers of educational services will actually seek the business of poor families and their children, particularly if they also have the option of providing educational services to wealthier children in situations where achieving desired outcomes is less problematic. So, one concern is whether providers will engage in competition leading to improvement of outcomes or reduction of costs.

Two other concerns grow out of what J. P. Greene et al. (1999) see as another advantage of privatization: the closer matching of schools with consumer preferences expressed through choice among alternative providers. If consumer preferences do drive the design of schools and the content of programs, then there is some question whether a voucher-based system will result in the establishment and growth of schools that are not in the national or community interest. Although this concern pertains to voucher programs in general, it takes on special significance in the case of poor children who may come from families outside the mainstream culture. A second, related concern is the prospect that voucher systems will lead to increased segregation of children from different backgrounds, with poor children being excluded from the schools dominated by their wealthier peers. Of course, there is already substantial segregation along various lines in public schools in the United States (Orfield et al., 1997).

Still other worries have been raised about vouchers and the education of poor children in the United States. There is concern that voucher programs will lock in the kind of severe inequities that characterize the current U.S. system of public education, that they will fail to respond to the greater needs of disadvantaged and disabled students, and that they will lead to less expensive but not more effective education for poor children.

One of the driving forces behind serious consideration of voucher plans by more than just the most devoted advocates is the continued poor performance of schools serving high proportions of poor children, particularly in U.S. inner-city areas. The dismal state of public schooling available to poor children has caused some to argue that voucher programs ought to at least be tried for poor children. Thus, voucher programs may be targeted at poor children as a desperate strategy to improve educational outcomes for them (Viteritti, 1996).

Table 11.1 summarizes the major advantages thought to be associated with a move toward vouchers and privatization in the education of poor children as well as the major concerns about such a move.

TABLE 11.1   Advantages and Concerns Connected with the Use of Vouchers and Privatization for the Education of Poor Children

Advantages	Concerns
Encourage competition and lead to reduced cost and/or improved quality	Question of whether there will be sufficient quality providers for poor children
Improved matching of consumer preferences and services supplied	Development of schools not in the community or national interest
Engage families more fully in the education process	Possible increased ethnic and class segregation
	Possibility of locking in current inequalities

Major Stakeholders

There are at least eight major groups with some interest in the issues surrounding vouchers and privatization of schooling for poor children. Three of these are groups of professionals whose work involves poor children at least some of the time. Educational professionals who staff the public schools include administrators, teachers, and teachers' aides. Some members of this group work in public school systems serving large numbers of poor children. A second professional group includes members of the social welfare profession, individuals who staff welfare agencies as managers or social workers as well as those who work as advocates on behalf of poor children. The members of the civil rights establishment represent a third stakeholder group; included here are civil rights leaders, civil rights lawyers, and civil rights workers.

Providers of educational services outside of the public sector, including private school educators and educational entrepreneurs, also have a clear stake in the outcome of the debate about vouchers and privatization. Political leaders who have historically opposed public provision of services are a fifth group with an interest in the voucher and privatization debate. Local community leaders are yet another group with a stake. Poor children and their families are a seventh major group with an interest in the debate. Finally, individuals in the research and policy analysis sector have an interest in the debate, if not its outcome.

Stakeholder Interests

Each of the eight stakeholder groups identified above has a set of interests around which behavior is organized. Clearly, each of the three professional groups has reasons to be wary of any attempt to dislodge the public school monopoly. Professional educators who have built their careers working in public school bureaucracies are the most directly challenged by any move toward privatization of educational services. These individuals—those providing instruction directly as well as those managing schools and school districts—have adapted their personal and professional lives to the habits of large, state-run, publicly supported enterprises. They have been attracted to the profession by the security of government enterprises and the lifetime employment guarantees associated with tenure. For professional educators, the prospect of vouchers and privatization represents a direct threat.

Somewhat less directly challenged are professionals in the field of social welfare who work to provide support to poor children and their families. Like professional educators, individuals in these positions have chosen and adapted their lives to government employment. Unlike professional educators, the work lives of social welfare professionals are not directly threatened by a move toward privatization, as education presumably could be turned over to the private sector while social welfare services remained a function of government agencies. However, social welfare professionals who deal with poor children and their families have been able to count on the public provision of education as they go about their work with families. If vouchers and other privatization initiatives relying upon more active parental participation and decisionmaking are implemented, welfare professionals may have new tasks supporting and encouraging parents' efforts. This could represent a substantial change, a change that may be resisted.

Civil rights professionals have also configured their work with the assumption that public schools would be the major avenue for educational opportunity in the United States. Members of this group, which include lawyers and various advocacy organizations operating on behalf of poor families and children, have worked for decades to reduce racial and social-class isolation by using the courts to desegregate schools and promote equitable school funding and, most recently, to advocate adequate support for the education of poor children. The strategy of this group has been to work for improvements in public education. This strategy, which has proven more successful in some venues than in others, is compromised by efforts to move children out of the public schools through the use of vouchers and other privatization strategies. The attempt to reduce racial and social-class isolation can be frustrated by policies that allow families to choose where to send their children to school, as many families can make choices that intensify such isolation. The attempt to argue for equity within the public sector from community to community can be compromised by injecting new, less comparable schooling arrangements into the debate, particularly since at least some of the these alternative private arrangements carry lesser costs.

Educational service providers operating outside the public sector include those operating private and parochial schools as well as those delivering particular educational services short of a complete schooling package. The interests of many of the individuals in this group would at first seem to be in fostering vouchers and other forms or privatization. Thus, private school educators, parochial school educators, and corporate entities considering entry into the schooling market might welcome policies that open up that market for competition with the public-sector schools.

However, other members of the group of nonpublic providers might find their interests best served by the maintenance of the public school monopoly. Those who sell goods and services necessary for the educational process may prefer to sell those items to government bureaucracies instead of to private providers who compete with each other on the basis of cost and quality. For example, publishers of textbooks may prefer to sell to public bureaucracies in markets regulated at the state and federal levels rather than to large numbers of individual providers in the private sector.

Political leaders opposed to public services also have a stake in the movement toward vouchers and privatization. These individuals may recognize efforts to privatize education as part of a larger movement to reduce the role of public agencies in the provision of goods and services in U.S. society and so welcome them. Clearly, if privatization efforts prove successful in some sense, it would enhance arguments for the reduction of government bureaucracies in general.

Local community leaders in areas where poor children are concentrated have an interest in the education of those children. However, the interests of these leaders are likely to be complex and in some cases conflicting. Community leaders would seem likely to give first priority to whatever educational system offers the highest-quality option to the children in the community. This may indeed be the case in communities where there are sufficient resources to respond to other needs. The situation may be quite different in communities where basic resources are insufficient to meet those other needs. For example, in communities where the public school system is the primary provider of adult employment, community leaders may balance the need of poor children to be educated against the need of their equally poor parents and neighbors to hold employment.

Adults in very poor communities often find employment as service workers and aides in local public schools; these jobs carry security and benefits that may not be available from lower cost private providers of education, and private providers may see little incentive to hire adults in poor communities.

Poor children and their families have an obvious direct interest in the system of education provided to poor children in a community. Perhaps because of this direct interest, there is no uniform interest in the privatization question among poor families. Some poor families have participated in efforts to improve public schools in their communities, including efforts to desegregate schools and ensure that they have adequate resources as guaranteed by law. Other poor families have taken steps to develop and participate in private schooling options within their communities, often in reaction to the perceived inadequacy of local public schools.

Finally, researchers and policy analysts make up an interest group of their own on the issue of vouchers and privatization. Members of this group (including this author) participate in the debate over privatization and school reform as part of our professional activities. Our interests are in opportunities in research, publication, and consulting. Such interests are best served by a vigorous debate in which the answers, if they do appear, are not revealed easily or quickly. In fact, if the answers did appear, we would be unemployed, at least in this area, and so would be forced to move on to some new dispute. Thus, we have an interest in the fight and in appearing to win from time to time.

Table 11.2 summarizes the stakeholders with an interest in the education of poor children and their likely interests in the debate over privatization of educational services for those children.

Studies to Address the Concerns of Stakeholders

The concerns of the eight stakeholder groups suggest varied lines of research. The concerns of education professionals regarding their own careers suggest a somewhat broader agenda of research on the prospects for staffing public and private schools in the future. Whether the educational system remains organized as a public bureaucracy or is transformed into an open market of private providers, presumably there will need to be instructional staff. The current model of public bureaucracies staffed by career teachers with job security and relatively undifferentiated rewards arose at a time when the options open to talented women were severely limited. Now and in the foreseeable future educational organizations will have to compete for talent against other public and private employers. Although the immediate concern of educational professionals leads us to focus on the tran-

TABLE 11.2   Stakeholders in the Debate over Vouchers and Privatization in the Education of Poor Children

Stakeholders	Position	Explanation
Educational professionals	Opposed	Interest in protecting the current institutional arrangements and careers
Social welfare professionals	Opposed	Interest in maintaining stability and avoiding additional work
Civil rights professionals	Opposed	Interest in protecting the hard won gains for access and equity
Educational service providers outside the public sector	Mixed	Providers of total schooling packages favor privatization while providers of components of schooling favor public provision to concentrate buyers and maintain margins
Political leaders opposed to public services	Favor	Interest in using education sector to demonstrate the superiority of private provision of services
Local community leaders	Both	Interest in quality education for poor children is balanced against an interest in quality jobs for poor adults in the community
Poor children and their families	Mixed	A very direct interest in quality schools causes individuals in this group to seek multiple paths to achieve them
Researchers and policy analysts	Mixed	Interest in maintaining the controversy and expanding opportunities for research, publication, and consulting

sition of these individuals from careers in public service to employees in the competitive private sector, the longer-term issues concern the optimum arrangements for identifying, recruiting, and retaining talented individuals in teaching, particularly in high-demand positions associated with the education of poor children. Thus, any research agenda on vouchers and privatization should include studies of the impact of such new organizational arrangements on staffing.

The concerns of social welfare professionals accustomed to working (or not working) in conjunction with public schools suggest a second, somewhat broader category of inquiry that might be initiated as part of a research agenda into the prospects and pitfalls of vouchers and privatization. There is increasing consensus that to educate poor children effectively we must coordinate educational services with a host of other social welfare and support services. In general the public schools have not done this consistently, although there are notable exceptions in the form of pilot programs and special initiatives (Natriello, McDill, and Pallas, 1990).

If we can agree that the education of poor children will require coordination of education and other social services, then a key area of inquiry will require studies that assess the prospects for coordination by private providers in contrast to the spotted history of public bureaucracies. We need to know whether private providers of education will be more effective than public bureaucracies in making effective use of social welfare and other support services. At first glance we might imagine that public school bureaucracies would be more effective in working with other government agencies. However, private providers may have a greater incentive to involve social welfare agencies in the educational process if such moves are effective ways to shift some costs to public agencies.

The interests of civil rights professionals call our attention to the issues of access and equity that have motivated their work over the last generation. Clearly, any research agenda on the issues of vouchers and privatization should include efforts to understand the potential of such reforms to allow poor children to participate in schooling without the racial and social-class isolation that characterizes many schools attended by poor children in the United States. Just as clearly, the agenda should include studies that assess the access a system of education affords poor children to educational resources and the adequacy of those resources for meeting educational needs. The current bureaucratic system of public schools does not guarantee either equitable or adequate educational opportunities to poor children as evidenced by the large number of legal challenges to the current system for failing on one or both counts. The question for an agenda of research on vouchers and privatization is whether such options offer more or less hope for realizing such goals.

I have described the interests of educational service providers outside the public sector as mixed: Providers who wish to operate entire schools find privatization and vouchers to their liking; those who provide goods and services to schools find it easier and more profitable to sell to government bureaucracies than to many more private providers locked in competition. These mixed interests raise a host of interesting and important research issues regarding the provision of education for poor children. If we think of schools as delivery systems and the things they provide as educational goods and services, then we can ask what combination of public and private delivery systems and goals and services will result in the highest-quality education for poor children. Would poor children be best served by a public delivery system (school) and a public supply of goods and services (curriculum, instruction, materials, etc.), a direction we seem to be moving toward under the banner of systemic reform? Or would poor children be best served by a public delivery system (school) and a private supply of goods and services, a pattern that characterizes at least some aspects of U.S. schooling in the past? Or would poor children be best served by a private delivery system (school) and a public supply of goods and services, a pattern operating when private schools are mandated to implement a state curriculum? Or would poor children be best served by a private delivery system (school) and a private supply of good and services?

The interests of policy leaders opposed to public provision of services seem rooted in claims of greater efficiency in the private sector as well as concerns about the growing power and size of the government and its potential to curtail individual liberty. The efficiency claim suggests the need for research to better understand the actual costs and benefits of public bureaucracies versus private providers, research that might need to be considerably more fine-grained in its analysis than has been typical of studies of school resource utilization in the past. As this particular issue pertains to the education of poor children, it may depend on what the actual state of knowledge is regarding the technical means for delivering high-quality education on a mass basis to the large population of poor children. Private-sector providers staffed with technical specialists may be in a better position to deliver educational services efficiently in situations where the technical means to achieve desired outcomes are well developed, whereas government bureaucracies staffed with professionals may be better suited to operating in situations where extensive research and development remains to be done and where the chances of success are remote.

If there is any validity to this position, then the current interest in beginning our national experiment with vouchers and privatization as a remedy for the dismal performance of bureaucratic school systems in our major urban centers may be exactly the wrong place to start. Such a strategy may fail to reveal the real potential of privatization efforts to address other educational needs. An alternative strategy might be to move aggressively to privatize educational services for middle-class and wealthy families outside the urban centers as a way to drive down educational expenditures in those areas, thereby permitting a massive transfer of educational resources to develop government-run, high-powered, research and development–based educational and social welfare initiatives in urban districts serving poor children and their families.

The liberty claims of political leaders opposed to public services raise other interesting questions for a research agenda on vouchers and privatization. The argument that reducing the role of government in all aspects of the lives of citizens has enormous emotional appeal given the history of the United States and our commitment to individual initiative and opportunity. Indeed, many if not most citizens can advance farther along a range of dimensions if they are left to compete for goods and services through individual exchange processes in private markets. The question regarding the provision of quality educational services for poor families and children is whether those who have not fared well in the private marketplace in general will fare better in that same market when armed with publicly generated resources to purchase educational services. Beyond the actual outcomes in terms of quality of educational services, however, is the impact that greater control over educational decisions may have on these same individuals, as well as the subjective benefits that may accrue. Investigating these kinds of processes will require fine-grained research regarding the experience of participating in the market for educational goods and services with various levels of public resources.

The interests of local community leaders in areas where poor families are the majority in the community suggest additional research on the broader impact of vouchers and privatization initiatives. The concerns of local leaders in communities where poor families are the majority suggest additional research on the broader impact of vouchers and privatization initiatives. The concerns of local leaders that a movement away from public bureaucracies toward private providers for the delivery of educational services will reduce the number of stable, well-paid public-sector jobs in a community suggest research to examine the current contribution of public bureaucracies to employment in poor communities, as well as research to monitor the contributions of private-sector alternatives.

The presumption that government bureaucracies will provide more jobs for adults in poor communities should be examined. Public school bureaucracies may be the largest employers in many poor communities, but such employment is typically at the level of support personnel; higher-paid professional teachers and administrators live elsewhere. Private providers may hire the same kinds of support staff from local communities, and if private providers develop approaches to the provision of educational services that rely less upon professionals for instruction, they may actually hire more people from the local community either as additional support personnel or as less highly credentialed and more technically oriented instructional staff. Moreover, a market for the private provision of educational services may engender entrepreneurial activity among at least some members of the local community. All of these possibilities might be considered in a research agenda on privatization.

The interests of poor children and their families in seeking a quality education, and the reliance of any system that enhances parental choice in a marketplace of private providers on such quality-seeking interests, raises the question of what constitutes "quality" for parents and children, particularly poor parents and their children. Parents and children may have various interests in schooling and so may seek different experiences and outcomes. Some may pursue the kinds of academically oriented outcomes increasingly reflected in state and federal policy initiatives. Others may seek affiliation with particular groups, and still others may view schooling as a way to pursue other agendas. Understanding the variety of parents' and students' conceptions of "quality" is an important building block for any studies that seek to assess the extent to which vouchers and privatization lead to higher-quality education. Similarly, understanding the conceptions of quality that motivate public educational bureaucracies and the professionals who staff them is an essential starting place for the design of studies of the comparative processes and outcomes of public and private educational services.

The interests of researchers and policy analysts suggest that it be treated as a case from which both communities might take more general lessons. This indicates the need to apply well-articulated theoretical perspectives from the social sciences to frame research on vouchers and privatization, as well as the need to understand how such initiatives fit into a more complete set of policy options for dealing with the poor.

Social-science theories of various sorts might be employed to guide research on vouchers and privatization. Without identifying specific theories, let me suggest that our current understanding of how voucher and privatization initiatives might work in the education sector is sufficiently underdeveloped that multiple theoretical perspectives could profitably be considered. For example, to investigate the relationship between the organization of the education sector and individual action, we might apply exchange-based theories as well as theories that consider the impact of molar organizational features on individual affiliation and commitment. Similarly, to study the potential of school organizations to operate effectively under different environmental conditions we might consider both rational theories of resource dependence as well as social theories of institutional identity.

Framing studies of vouchers and privatization initiatives with a more fully developed set of policy options for addressing the plight of poor families and children in U.S. society might lead to a richer discussion of possible courses of action. Rather than posing the question of vouchers and privatization as a contest between these private-sector strategies and the existing public school bureaucracies, it might be more fruitful to raise some broader questions. For example, if we specify that the only private venue for education is the family, then we can ask the following question: When is it advantageous to address the social and educational needs of poor children through public rather than private means? In other words, when should society direct investments through public as opposed to private means to address the growing disparities in the social conditions of children and the continuing negative impact on educational performance of students with limited access to social and human capital? This kind of question could take a number of forms. For example, we could consider whether increased public investment in public efforts would improve outcomes for youth or whether the increased tax burden on poor families would destabilize at least some families and result in deterioration in the human and social capital available to children. Addressing this question would involve both the anticipated productivity gains from increasing public resources and the anticipated additional burden for families at different income levels in light of current and proposed revenue mechanisms.

Once we determine which educational activities are best organized through public means we can ask two additional questions: When is it advantageous to address the social and educational needs of poor children through public means that are governmental in nature? And when is it advantageous to address the social and educational needs of poor children through public means that are corporate? Casting the questions in this sort of framework suggests the possibility of a system of education that is more mixed in its organization than the current public-versus-private debate seems to allow.

Table 11.3 summarizes the elements of a research agenda on vouchers and privatization in the education of poor children derived from stakeholders' perspectives.

Existing Research

It is difficult to assess the existing research in light of the agenda outlined above because the available research was not designed with such an agenda in mind. However, reviewing the existing research will indicate the base upon which to build the new lines of research I have suggested. One way to characterize the existing research on vouchers and privatization is to say that we have studies of dubious relevance, focusing on outcomes we might not care much about, under

TABLE 11.3   Elements of a Research Agenda on Vouchers and Privatization in the Education of Poor Children

Stakeholders	Research Agenda Element
Educational professionals	Studies of the relationship between system arrangements and the recruitment and retention of talent
Social welfare professionals	Studies of the relationship between system arrangements and the prospects for coordination of services
Civil rights professionals	Studies of the relationship between system arrangements and the equitable and adequate distribution of educational resources
Educational service providers outside the public sector	Studies of what combination of private and public delivery system (school) and goods and services leads to the highest quality schooling for poor children
Political leaders opposed to public services	Studies of the costs and benefits of participating in the private market for educational goods and services (efficiency claims)
Local community leaders	Studies of the impact of privatization initiatives on both the educational opportunities for children and the employment opportunities for adults in local communities
Poor children and their families	Studies of what constitutes "quality" education for poor children and their families
Researchers and policy analysts	Studies which apply or develop more general theories from the social sciences or frame issues within a larger set of policy options

conditions we do not fully understand and so from which we cannot generalize, leading to results where the interpretation depends more upon the proclivities of the analysts than the strength of the patterns in the data.

There seem to be two kinds of research. First, comparisons are made between educational experiences in the public and private sectors, often by using available national data sets (e.g., Bryk et al., 1993; Chubb and Moe, 1990; Coleman and Hoffer, 1987; Coleman, Hoffer, and Kilgore, 1982; Evans and Schwab, 1993; Jencks, 1985; Wilms, 1984, 1985). From this work we can reach various conclusions. Second, the impacts of trial programs are examined to determine whether they show some advantage when compared to some form of traditional public education (e.g., Beales and Wahl, 1995; Moe, 1995; Witte, 1992). Again, various conclusions are possible. As one study observes (Greene, Peterson, and Du, 1999), neither of these research traditions has provided a definitive answer regarding the comparative efficiency of private and public schools.

Conclusion

As we seek to develop a research agenda for examining the prospects of privatization initiatives in the education sector, we should be wary of the ease with which we may secure resources for research. It is clear that there is a great deal of interest in supporting efforts to examine alternatives to current schooling arrangements. However, it is not clear how much of this interest is in finding answers to difficult questions and how much is simply directed at sustaining the debate. As we move ahead in our work on vouchers and privatization we must constantly ask ourselves whether we are being enlisted as researchers or rhetoricians.

References

Beales, J. R. and Wahl, M. (1995). *Given the choice: A study of the PAVE Program and school choice in Milwaukee.* Policy Study No. 193. Los Angeles: Reason Foundation.

Bryk, A. S., Lee, V .E., and Holland, P. B. (1993). *Catholic schools and the common good.* Cambridge: Harvard University Press.

Chubb, J. E., and Moe, T. M. (1990). *Politics, markets, and American schools.* Washington, D.C.: Brookings Institution.

Coleman, J. S., and Hoffer, T. (1987). *Public and private schools: The impact of communities.* New York: Basic.

Coleman, J. S., Hoffer, T., and Kilgore, S. (1982). *High school achievement.* New York: Basic.

Evans, W. N., and Schwab, R. M. (1993). *Who benefits from private education? Evidence from quantile regressions.* College Park: University of Maryland, Department of Economics.

Garibaldi, A. M., and Bartley, M. (1988). Black school pushouts and dropouts: Strategies for reduction. *Urban League Review* 11, 227–235.

Greene, J. P., Peterson, P. E., and Du, J. (1999). Effectiveness of school choice: The Milwaukee experiment. *Education and Urban Society* 31, 190–213.

Hill, P. T. (1996). The educational consequences of choice. *Phi Delta Kappan* 77, 671–675.

Jencks, C. (1985). How much do high school students learn? *Sociology of Education* 58, 128–135.

Levin, H. M. (1998). Educational vouchers: Effectiveness, choice, and costs. *Journal of Policy Analysis and Management* 17, 373–392.

Moe, T. M. (1995). *Private vouchers.* Stanford: Stanford University Press.

Natriello, G., McDill, E. L., and Pallas, A. M. (1990). *Schooling disadvantaged children: Racing against catastrophe.* New York: Teachers College Press.

Orfield, G., Bachmeier, M. D., James, D. R., and Eitle, T. (1997). Deepening segregation in American public schools: A special report from the Harvard Project on School Desegregation. *Equity and Excellence in Education* 30(2), 5–24.

Viteritti, J. P. (1996). Stacking the deck for the poor: The new politics of school choice. *Brookings Review* 14(3), 10–13.

Wilms, D. J. (1984). School effectiveness within the public and private sectors: An evaluation. *Evaluation Review* 8, 113–135.

_____. (1985). Catholic school effects on academic achievement: New evidence from the "High school and beyond follow-up study." *Sociology of Education* 58, 98–114.

Witte, J. F. (1992). Private school versus public school achievement: Are there findings that should affect the educational choice debate? *Economics of Education Review* 11, 371–394.

12

Teachers and Privatization

CAROLINE HODGES PERSELL

This chapter considers some of the issues that privatization raises for teachers and teaching. The term "privatization" as used here means more than simply nongovernmental control of education. In general, the term refers to the turning of public nonprofit activities into private for-profit activities, usually paid for with public monies.[1] What is distinctive about privatization is its focus on market principles, rather than professional principles, as a way of organizing work and service delivery. Under this definition, making a profit is no longer considered an illegitimate element in education.

It is important to understand relationships between teachers and privatization for several reasons. Teachers are the carriers of educational programs, curriculum, content, and standards. They are the primary (sometimes the sole) interface between educational institutions and students and often parents as well. They represent a major portion of the personnel involved in education, as well as a significant part of the cost of education, because education as it has been traditionally practiced is a labor-intensive enterprise. For all of these reasons, it is important to examine potential issues concerning privatization and teachers.

Who Are the Stakeholders and What Are Their Concerns?

Besides teachers, key stakeholders include students, parents, educational administrators, school alumni, community members, the public, future employers in business, government, nonprofit enterprises, and the state. Two newly emergent sets of stakeholders appear to be investors seeking to develop for-profit educational enterprises and persons seeking to reduce the power of the state by substituting private for public control of education. What are the interests or concerns of these stakeholders and audiences and why, especially with respect to privatization?

Teachers

Teachers' interests and concerns include retaining jobs, remuneration, benefits, working conditions, tenure, being able to work successfully with young people to prepare them for their futures, and, in higher education, conducting and publishing original scholarship to advance knowledge. Like others, teachers are concerned about being treated with respect, and with receiving recognition and appreciation for the value of what they are doing. Many teachers are also concerned about providing equal educational opportunities for all students. Teachers tend to see educational goals as complex, multidimensional, and difficult to measure. Many include ideas about personal development, perhaps character, as well as academic goals in their conception of valued educational outcomes. They see risks in using simple achievement-test scores as the only indicators of educational success. Teachers are often reluctant to accept proposals to link merit increases for individual teachers with measurable improvements in performance. Thus, incentives and remuneration are often concerns of teachers.

Teachers' Unions

The interests and concerns of teachers' unions include maintaining membership and keeping the gains obtained for their members in pay and benefits. Because unions see privatization as likely to circumvent the higher wages and better working conditions negotiated through collective bargaining contracts, they tend to be opposed to efforts at privatization (Ascher et al., 1996, p. 101).

Students

Students' interests and concerns include developing knowledge and skills that will prepare them for their future roles as citizens, family members, earners, community members, and pursuers of leisure; having fun; spending time with their peers; making friends; developing their personal values and identities; and having an equal opportunity regardless of their race, ethnicity, gender, social class, or other social attributes.

Parents

Parents' interests and concerns include having their children be safe and healthy; seeing their children learn what they need to know to function in their future roles; seeing their children achieve recognition for some form of achievement (academic, athletic, musical, artistic, and so forth); seeing their children happy; seeing their children either develop their own values or learn the values the parents hold; having their children stay out of trouble; seeing their children treated with respect and even caring; and having their children prepared to enter the next level of education and, ultimately, be prepared for life. Some parents are concerned that schools may undermine the values they seek to instill in their children. Some parents desire to be involved in school activities of various kinds. They may favor equal opportunity for all students regardless of their socioeconomic background, especially if such a goal does not limit their child's opportunities. Parents also value educational stability, that is, knowing that the school their child attends will not "go out of business" in the middle of the year or over the summer.

Educational Administrators

Educational administrators' interests and concerns include recruiting and retaining good teachers; having enough resources to run what they consider to be an effective school; avoiding serious problems whether with students, teachers, parents, community members, or board members; and having their school respected by others. Many administrators are concerned about providing equal educational opportunities for all students regardless of their social backgrounds. In private schools administrators need to be concerned about attracting enough students and contributions, balancing their budget, and making their payroll.

School Alumni

School alumni interests and concerns include the reputation of the school they attended, the friends they made there, what they learned, whether it is possible for their children to attend the school, and whether or not they continue to be in contact with the school.

Community Members

Community members' interests and concerns include the reputation of the school; whether the school is effectively preparing young people for adult life in the community; whether the school is a source of problems or pride; whether the school's reputation enhances or diminishes the value of residential real estate in the area; and whether the school helps to solidify community identity and cohesiveness (as is often the case in small towns).

General Public

The general public's interests and concerns include the costs of education (especially in keeping school taxes down); whether the school is teaching important knowledge, values, and skills; and whether the school is preparing young people to be responsible, considerate citizens, earners, and family members.

Employers

The interests and concerns of future employers in business, government, and nonprofit enterprises include the knowledge, values, habits, and skills being taught by the schools and whether the schools are preparing young people to be responsible workers. They may also care whether schools are teaching people how to work in teams and teaching them "soft skills" such as communication and teamwork, as well as writing, mathematics, and other skills.

State

The state's interests and concerns include having future citizens understand the language, culture, history, political values, and forms of governance in the country. This is particularly important in nations with large numbers of immigrants or great cultural diversity. In democratic states there is a concern with teaching young people how to participate in political discussions and decisionmaking; how to follow procedures of due process; how to operate within the rule of law; how to adjudicate differences without resorting to force or violence; how to effect change peacefully; and how to protect the rights of minorities. Traditionally, schools have been seen as major vehicles for achieving these citizenship goals.

Investors

Investors seeking to develop for-profit educational enterprises have additional interests and concerns. Their economic interests include cutting costs; producing rapidly growing revenues and possibly even profits; seeing their stock become publicly traded; seeing their stock price rise; and perhaps selling out to a larger company or other investors. They argue that education as an institution is currently inefficient and costly. They may have educational concerns as well, such as seeing knowledge and skills taught effectively and having achievement measured in a way that can be quantified, made visible, and serve as evidence of success or failure. They may seek to cut costs by substituting educational technologies for teachers, by replacing teachers with lower-paid aides, by eliminating tenure for teachers, by eliminating teachers' unions, or through other cost-cutting measures that may create alarm and resistance among teachers, parents, students, and other stakeholders.

Of all these stakeholders, teachers (and administrators) probably spend the most time and have, potentially, the most continuity over time. One could argue that teachers and students are the two most important participants in the educational enterprise and that other stakeholders should be doing everything they can to facilitate and support effective teaching and learning. Teachers may sometimes come to see other stakeholders as having concerns that may not support the teaching-learning nexus and may even be antagonistic to it. At other times, teachers forge productive alliances with other stakeholders, whether administrators, parents, employers, or others. More research is needed to examine variability in the relationships among stakeholders and the possible effects of those relationships on teaching and learning.

Previous Work on Privatization

Three types of existing work bear on teachers and privatization, namely, empirical studies, conceptual work that seeks to identify and clarify issues, and polemical writings that advocate or attack privatization. Each type is worth examining for what it can reveal about questions and needs for further research, conceptualizing, and theorizing.

Empirical Studies

Empirical research on privatization has been conducted at the societal level and at the institutional level. At the societal level, T.P. Gerber and M. Hout (1998), for example, studied the effects of privatization in Russia from 1991 to 1995. They discovered a tremendous amount of conversion of public property into private wealth. They also saw a great deal of merchant capitalism, with a scramble to capitalize immediately rather than an emphasis on efficiency-oriented productivity that rewards human capital for its productivity over the long term. Education, from the viewpoint of many stakeholders, is a long-term proposition, not one that is improved by a short-term merchant-capitalism orientation. Another societal accompaniment to privatization in Russia noted by Gerber and Hout (1998) was greatly increased economic inequality. This finding suggests that possible consequences of privatization for inequality need to be considered.

At the institutional level within the United States, C. Ascher et al. (1996) assessed existing examples of privatization at the elementary and secondary levels with respect to five critical issues in education: student outcomes, costs, parental voice, accountability, and equity. However, they focused very little on teachers. They do comment that to the degree that privatization or the charter school movement is antiunion and aims to lower teachers' salaries it "makes a profession that is struggling to compete with others to attract qualified individuals even less competitive" (Ascher et al., 1996, p. 22). This comment suggests the importance of studying how privatization may relate to the supply of qualified teachers.

S. Doughty (1997) examines the experience of four school districts that entered contracts for the private management of public schools. In Dade County, Florida, there was almost no opposition to Education Alternatives Inc. (EAI) in the new South Pointe Elementary School because EAI built a strong coalition of community support among all major stakeholders, including teachers, for its presence. South Pointe was a new school, and EAI helped to select the personnel, "thus assuring that the educational philosophies of the program implemented by the company and the philosophies of the school staff were compatible" (Doughty, 1997, p. 3). Presumably teachers who had doubts about the program or private management were excluded from the outset. Another very important element in the Dade County experience was that school board members and the local teachers' union were involved in the early stages of the contracting process. Indeed, EAI's first proposal—specifying that they would have school management authority—was rejected. Thus, Doughty (1997) found that some forms of opposition did exist and that the terms of EAI involvement were negotiated by key participants in the situation.

D. L. Edwards (1997) also studied the Dade County experience, with an eye to its educational consequences. She reports that the Dade County Office of Educational Accountability compared South Pointe to a demographically and geographically similar public school with no EAI presence and found no difference in student academic achievement at the two schools. Edwards (1997) did find, however, improved attendance, higher levels of parental and community involvement, and favorable staff attitudes. Interviews (she doesn't say with whom) revealed a surprising lack of distrust or fear of privatization, which appeared to be due to EAI's advisory role, its independent fund-raising (which paid EAI's fee so there was no perception that the company was taking money intended for use in educating children), and the limited contract period (five years). EAI was not seen as threatening a school takeover. One member of the teachers' union said that an indication that the program "had worked" was that "when the bell rings, the kids don't run out the door."

Studies by Edwards (1997) and T. H. Peeler (1995) identify some of the distinctive ways that teaching and learning was organized in South Pointe. Low student-staff ratios (12:1) were achieved through differentiated staffing, that is, by using teaching assistants and paraprofessionals. There was one certified teacher and one paraprofessional (who were third- and fourth-year college students serving as interns) for every twenty-four students. The school was organized into four communities of 144 students each, with twenty-four students in each grade, producing a "feeling of family and cohesiveness" (Edwards, 1997). Teachers sought to use "state of the art teaching/learning strategies" (Peeler, 1995). Their role was that of "coach, model, facilitator, listener and guide" rather than that of a teacher who conducted lessons for all classes (Peeler, 1995). The goal was to put the active learner on center stage and to use frequent cooperative learning activities. EAI needed certain concessions from the United Teachers of Dade, including contract waivers for teacher selection, teacher responsibilities, and work requirements. For example, more teacher training was required by EAI (up to fifteen days before school began), but the teachers were paid for that additional time. EAI conducted the staff training. In addition, more staff meetings were required throughout the year.

One issue the research was not able to address was the possibility that positive outcomes observed may have resulted from the so-called Hawthorne effect. Observed in experimental studies, the Hawthorne effect is an improvement in morale (and sometimes productivity) that occurs when any change is made, regardless of what the change is (e.g., raising the light levels, lowering the light levels, changing the color of the walls, rotating work, and so forth).

L. Jackson's (1997) evaluation of the Minneapolis school district's three-year contract with a private company, Public Strategies Group (PSG), made very little mention of teachers, except to say the "company did not receive payment for unsatisfactory negotiation of the teachers' contract." What the result was, and what would have been considered a satisfactory negotiation, are not specified. Teachers' unions were not involved in the contract negotiations undertaken by the school board. However, the PSG president was a person widely known and respected in the community.

In Baltimore, teachers' unions and other stakeholders were left out of the decisionmaking, which was hastily conducted during the summer. Some teachers heard about the decision from the news, a condition that did not enhance their support for the approach, according to Doughty (1997, p. 4).

In Hartford, Connecticut, EAI faced the strongest opposition. Although the school board narrowly voted to enter into the EAI contract, the support base was very weak. "EAI's proposal to cut the number of teaching positions was not supported by the school board" and "only escalated an already tense situation" (Doughty, 1997, p. 6). The teachers' union offered strong opposition to EAI. Doughty (1997, p. 8) also observed the importance of documenting expectations between both parties in the contract and specifying the strategy for evaluation to be used to assess whether the venture was meeting those expectations.

In her report on the Hartford experience, P. Cazares (1997) notes that the

> teachers union, as well as other unions, opposed private management from the onset, possibly at least in part because they viewed EAI as a vehicle for reducing teaching jobs. Opposition reached its peak when EAI submitted a budget proposal for school year 1995–96 that would have eliminated a substantial number of teaching positions. EAI wanted to cut teacher costs and use the savings to help fund technology initiatives specified in the contract, as well as invest in clean and safe schools, implement site-based management, and improve instruction. However, most school board members would not support the reduction in teachers. EAI believed the reductions were warranted, claiming that teacher pupil ratios, determined by the district's contract with the teachers' union had resulted in a system that was "overstaffed by millions of dollars of personnel." According to Hartford, the cuts would have resulted in massive violations of class size limitations contained in the district's agreement with its teachers' union. (Cazares, 1997, pp. 9–10)

The five-year contract with EAI was terminated after a year and a half. "EAI is credited with improving access to educational technology and making school repairs (concentrated in six schools) and helping the school district secure a zero increase in teachers' salaries for one year" (Cazares, 1997).

G. Vanourck et al. (1997) studied fifty charter schools in ten states enrolling 16,000 students. They do not say how they sampled the schools, the states, the teachers, and the students, so we can't assess the generalizability of their results. They also do not say how the various charter schools were organized (i.e., whether within the public sector, the private nonprofit sector, or the private for-profit sector). They collected survey data on 521 teachers but do not specify the sampling method used. They report that more than 90 percent of the teachers are very or somewhat satisfied with the philosophy, fellow teachers, and size of the schools. Some of the things we do not know from this study include the following: What is the average size of these schools? How does that compare with other public schools? How does the level of teacher satisfaction compare with that of teachers in similarly sized public or private schools?

Of the teachers surveyed, 72 percent were certified in the state where they were teaching; many had public school teaching experience, although only 23 percent had taught the year before in a public school; 76 percent were not members of a teachers' union (how does that compare with public and private school teachers in those states?). Regarding salary, 38 percent said their salaries were lower at the charter school (than at the last job they had held), 35 percent said they were higher, and 28 percent said they were about the same. What is the age, gender, and race of these teachers? Are these relevant characteristics? How long do the teachers stay? Do their reasons for choosing the schools differ from the reasons other teachers give?

In a study of students in for-profit postsecondary institutions (proprietary schools) compared to similar students in public nonprofit community colleges, C.H. Persell and H. Wenglinsky (unpublished manuscript) found that students in the for-profit schools show less civic participation on a variety of measures, even when prior levels of civic participation, family socioeconomic status, age, gender, and other characteristics were controlled. Teachers concerned about developing such attitudes in their students might find such results discouraging.

Studies of privatization of other state-supported functions and health care are also relevant to the study of education. J. Goldstone (1998), for example, found that prison riots in for-profit prisons tended to be more violent, bitter, and result in more deaths compared to riots in nonprofit prisons. He suggests that privatization seems to undermine the legitimacy of the authority structure in the prison. There was greater anger (e.g., over bad food) because prisoners thought that they were being deprived so that the owners could make a profit.

Other human services with a long history of involvement in for-profit enterprises are medicine, health care, and nursing home care. There have been numerous examples of abuse in for-profit nursing homes in New York and perhaps in other states as well. Other forms of medical treatment also provide comparisons between for-profit and nonprofit providers. For example, two-thirds of all people with kidney failure are now treated in for-profit dialysis centers in the United States. They were 20 percent more likely to die and 26 percent less likely to be referred for kidney transplants than were patients using nonprofit facilities (*New England Journal of Medicine*, November 25, 1999, reported in Grady, 1999). Earlier work found many more reported instances of infections resulting from reusing the plastic tubing (which is meant to be used only once) and shorter time on dialysis machines in the United States compared to European countries, where dialysis is not done on a fixed-fee basis in for-profit centers. Such results suggest that the context within which health care providers are embedded may affect their behavior in ways that are not always in the patient's best interest. Such studies in medicine direct attention to the importance of studying whether changing the context of education to one organized on for-profit principles changes the conduct of teachers and, if so, how.

Some health maintainance organizations (HMOs) have gag rules preventing doctors from telling patients about treatments or expensive medicines not covered by their health plans. Some also require doctors to obtain clearance from the insurance provider for every treatment they propose before it can be performed. At least one HMO, UnitedHealthcare, has proposed allowing doctors to treat patients without interference (Whitaker, 1999). The problem of cost containment remains. One strategy companies may use is to analyze doctors' practice patterns over the year, both to ensure they are following their profession's best practices and to identify doctors who may be using "needlessly expensive or inappropriate care," possibly dropping them from the preferred list of providers (*New York Times*, Nov. 28, 1999). A second strategy is to pay doctors a fixed fee for each patient, regardless of the amount of care required. Both of these options place the burden of juggling costs and care more directly on physicians. These examples from medicine suggest some of the conflicts between professional norms and cost pressures that teachers might face in privatized situations.

When such health care providers as National Medical Enterprises and Humana bought up community hospitals, they often changed personnel practices, an issue that relates clearly to teachers. Managers of individual hospitals are held to strict financial performance goals. One way to meet those goals was by firing the most experienced nurses first (Lindorff, 1992, p. 80). As one researcher reports:

> A National Institutes of Health study of for-profit medicine reported a 1986 survey conducted by the [American Medical Association] in which, though gross nursing staff levels varied little between for-profit and non-profit chains in the aggregate, only 48 percent of physicians whose primary hospital was part of an investor-owned chain thought their facility's nursing support was better than at other hospitals with which they were familiar. At hospitals owned by non-profit chains or consortiums, the figure was 60 percent. (Lindorff, 1992, p. 82)

One reason for their perceptions may be the increased use of registry nurses, people who work for an agency not the hospital. Agency nurses have new patients in a new environment every day, preventing continuity of patient care and creating more stress for nurses, a factor that may affect the quality of patient care they can provide. The experience of the health care industry suggests that privatization in education may translate into reductions in permanent professional staff, growing use of temporary help, and greater differentiation of staff. The implications of such potential changes for teacher recruitment and retention and for educational processes need to be carefully studied. The growing use of adjuncts in higher education has certainly increased faculty differentiation. It also means less faculty availability for curriculum development, advisement, recommendations, committees, governance, and scholarly productivity. Finally, it creates increasingly unattractive career prospects for the brightest, most motivated young people who may reject academic careers in favor of other careers (see Finkelstein, Seal, and Schuster, 1998).

Conceptual Work

Important conceptual work has been done by several authors who raise important questions that need to be considered in relation to teachers. One research team (Feigenbaum, Henig, and Hamnett, 1999, pp. 131–132), for example, asks: Is privatization a pragmatic adjustment in a depoliticized milieu, or does it become invested with a partisan content? Is it a managerial response to fiscal constraint, to be debated in technical and economic terms, or it is a matter of social philosophy and political goals? They note, "Privatization initiatives are political because they redistribute costs and benefits among diverse and competing groups" (1999, p. 172). Teachers may fear they will be called upon to bear more of the costs while the benefits accrue to absent shareholders. If they are right that privatization may be used "to reshape the interest group environment," then the resistance of teachers and teachers' unions is not surprising.

Another set of conceptual issues is assessing teacher quality. How can parents assess whether a teacher is good? On what basis would contractors assess teacher quality? (See, e.g., Hill, Pierce, and Gutherie, 1997, p. 235.) Pondering teacher qualifications, for example, J. R. Henig (1994) wonders whether teachers should be required to have graduate degrees in education or in a subject field. Should they be required to have a college degree? Should they be required to take a competency test? Who designs the test? Should they be subject to background checks for criminal records? Should there be any requirements for teachers that are deemed unacceptable or illegal, for example, should schools be free to require teachers to belong to a particular religion, sign a national loyalty oath, submit to mandatory drug testing, join (or not join) a union? Can they reject applicants who are homosexuals or lesbians? No research, to my knowledge, has been done on the hiring practices of privatized schools, with the small exception of the study on South Pointe in Florida. All we know from that study is that EAI selected the teachers. We do not know on what basis they selected them.

C. H. Persell (2000) and J. A. Weiss (1990) identified different values and forms of control within which education may be embedded. Most germane to our discussion here is a comparison between using markets to organize education and using professionalism as the dominant value and mode of control. Most of the critics of public education complain about political and/or bureaucratic forms of organization. What is remarkable is that their response is to suggest that the market, rather than a professional model, is the solution (see Table 12.1 for an explication of some distinctions between markets and professions). Market and professional models reveal different orientations toward recipients, bases for deciding what to do, goals, views of service, and ways of seeking recourse. This awareness underscores the importance of studying how market or professional values and control affect the conduct of education and the behavior of teachers. What happens when these values and norms conflict? What forms of market regulation might be needed in education? Would regulations come from political bodies—as has begun to happen in health care—or from professional concerns? How would regulations be enacted and enforced? These issues are not yet explored in any research on teachers and privatization that I found, but clearly they warrant further research.

Advocacy Writings

The third type of literature—polemical, or advocacy, writings on teachers and privatization—reveals something about the assumptions upon which various perspectives rest. Identifying such assumptions can raise new questions for investigation.

Articulate supporters of privatization include Chester E. Finn Jr.; Benno C. Schmidt Jr., president of the Edison Corporation; and Christopher Whittle, president of Whittle Communications. Their proposals for privatization are based on certain claims and assumptions. They assert that current schools are ineffective; that achievement is too low; that education is mediocre; that education's "bureaucratized management values uniformity and process over initiative and results"; that education "lacks clear standards, sound assessments, and effective accountability mechanisms"; and that "reform efforts over the last 13 years have been generally unproductive" (Finn, 1996). There is the assertion that "the nation is at risk because our children are receiving such poor education" (Finn, 1996, p. 6), although such an assertion is at odds with survey data showing that most par-

TABLE 12.1   Distinctions Between Market and Professional Structures

	Market Structure	*Professional Structure*
Orientation toward recipients	Customer	Client, patient, learner
Basis for deciding what to do	What the customer wants	What is in the best long-term interests of the recipient Professional standards
Goal of activity	Profit	Quality service or care
View of service	Private consumer good	Both a public and a private good
Recourse	Choice, alternatives; exit	Professional peers; due process; voice

ents feel that the schools their children attend are doing a good job. There is also the implicit assumption that education is a private consumer good, like a home, clothes, or dinner. Another assumption is that educational performance is measurable with tidy quantitative test results. Finn proposes a new paradigm of school reform that he calls "reinventing public education." His paradigm would

> welcome diverse strategies and dissimilar schools organized and run by teacher co-operatives, parent associations, private corporations, community-based organizations, and religious institutions. Students and families would choose the schools best suited to them in a system that requires little bureaucracy and few regulations. The new "reinvention" paradigm of school reform is not incrementalist, top-down, or uniform. The new paradigm welcomes decentralized control, entrepreneurial management, and grass-roots initiatives, within a framework of publicly defined standards and accountability. (Finn, 1996)

He also claims that under the current system employees wield the most power, rather than "customers" (p. 2), but he says nothing about how standards and accountability get "publicly defined" and nothing about what issues would be the focus of the "few regulations." He assumes that teachers are a problem because in the current system they wield more power than customers, but he says nothing specific about what teachers' shortcomings are or why they should not have a power advantage relative to their clients.

Writing in *School Administrator*, Whittle (1997) suggests that the "development of national school companies could significantly improve career opportunities for teachers, principles, and administrators" who could move seamlessly within a national system (p. 9). They could also be part of a rapidly growing enterprise. Moreover, because such companies have access to more mainstream capital sources, they could do more educational research and development.

This access to more mainstream capital sources is not a factor that Finn (1996) considers when he suggests that grassroots educational innovations might be started by teacher cooperatives or parent bodies. Surely the relative access different groups have to capital resources is a factor affecting the likelihood that teacher cooperatives could be a major source of innovation.

Writing in *Educational Leadership*, Schmidt (1995) stresses that the Edison Project's plan to redefine public education has great teachers at its heart. Edison will invest in teacher preparation and professional development, for example, with a "residency" program for beginning teachers and continuous opportunities for veterans to stay current. Nowhere does he consider how market and professional norms might conflict or indicate how such conflicts might be resolved: areas in need of further research. It is interesting that both Whittle and Schmidt are appealing to teachers' sense of professionalism in their writings.

Myron Lieberman (1995), author of *Public Education: An Autopsy* and *The Teachers' Unions: How the NEA and AFT Sabotage Reform and Hold Students, Parents, Teachers, and Taxpayers Hostage to Bureaucracy,* argues that public education is no longer fostering basic skills, scientific and cultural literacy, civic virtues, and desirable habits and attitudes toward our society and its institutions. The reason is lack of competition for the consumer's dollar, government red tape, and the powerful special-interest lobby of the teachers' unions. Like other advocates for privatization, Lieberman (1995) asserts, without documentation, that public education is a uniform failure. D. C. Berliner and B. J. Biddle (1995) counter this and other myths about public education by providing evidence that is missing from Lieberman's assertions. The assertions by proponents of privatization do underscore the importance of considering educational outcomes, however. This focus raises questions about what outcomes are important, how those outcomes are measured, and the possible unintended consequences of measuring some but not all desired outcomes.

Several authors have written strong critiques of practices such as devolution, decentralization, and site-based management, especially in Canada and Australia. Some of the tendencies observed in the context of those changes are assumed to be likely if privatization occurs. For example, R. Bates (1995) sees efforts at privatization as an assault on the value premises of both government and education. Is the role of government simply to increase wealth, or does it also have a role in strengthening the character of citizens? Bates (1995) also notes that the preoccupations with economies, markets, and money are moving into education, with a push toward financial flexibility, functional flexibility, and numerical flexibility (p. 15). Financial flexibility involves cost-cutting or reducing the size of the educational workforce. For example, devolution of public schools has occurred in Alberta, Canada, where more than 1,000 teachers were redeployed in a round of restructuring, as were a similar number in Victoria, Australia (Robertson, 1995, p. 13, cited in Bates, 1995, p. 15). The term "functional flexibility" "refers to the more efficient use of permanent full-time employees through quality control, working smarter and continuous production" (Robertson, 1995, p. 13, cited in Bates, p. 15). The term "numerical flexibility" "involves the close tailoring of the size of the workforce to the use of part-time, contractual and temporary personnel. Within Australia a number of proposals have surfaced directed towards the development of a smaller but more highly paid 'core' of labour force teachers, supplemented by a tiered periphery made up of expendable semi-skilled and cheaper labour: parents, student teachers and teacher aides" (Robertson, 1995, p. 13, cited in Bates, 1995, p. 15; cf. Ashenden, 1992). This is similar to what D. Lindorff (1992) notes occurred when hospitals were privatized, namely, a great increase in temporary help, a general reduction in the size of core staff, and a reduction in the number of more experienced professional staff. Although some would argue that parents prefer continuity and community in the schools attended by their children, it is not clear that parental preferences will necessarily prevail. No doubt patients would also prefer continuity of nursing care, but at least so far they do not always obtain the preferred form.

A second change noted by S. I. Robertson (1995) involves the way teachers' work is redefined and intensified while new forms of collegial surveillance emerge. A further theme within the self-managing school arises as a result of the compression of time and space. Teachers are expected to confer on a raft of administrative details as a result of the displacement of state responsibilities down to the local level. In a study of the impact of devolution on teachers in western Australia, teachers reported that: they were required to constantly attend meetings for administrative or collegial purposes; accountability pressures had escalated; they were expected to be more entrepreneurial within the school and the local community; and the increasing scarcity of resources had led to greater conflict as a result of intense politicization. All of these activities took considerable time. In order to meet their commitments, teachers worked longer hours during the day and more days during the week. Moreover, the contrived collegiality that resulted disguises a more sinister motive, a means whereby individuals are able to engage in surveillance of others as a form of self-regulation leading to workplace control for increased productivity (Robertson, 1995, p. 13, cited in Bates, p.

15). It is an empirical question whether such trends would also occur under privatization.

Proponents of privatization might see such outcomes as highly desirable ways of increasing teacher effort and productivity. Clearly there is a need for research by ideologically neutral scholars that could consider whether such changes in time allocation affect the effort and attention teachers put into direct education of children and whether peer surveillance increased or decreased collegial support and norms of professionalism.

Another passionate critic of privatization is Alex Molnar, author of *Giving Kids the Business: The Commercialization of America's Schools* (1996). He is critical of many aspects of privatization, but for this chapter his comments on teachers are most relevant. He describes the movement as "teachers in private practice" who "want to work as entrepreneurs rather than employees." The movement calls for greater professionalism of teachers, who could be "free to work when and where they want and even free to set their own fees" (Molnar, 1996, p. 163). It promises liberation from union restrictions and the possibility of greater rewards for the most talented teachers. Although it is appealing to some educators, Molnar (1996) suggests that

> the ability of professionals to set their own fees depends on how many others are competing in the marketplace. Since the money available for public education is tightly constrained, it is most likely that cost, not competence, will often be the most important factor in whether someone is hired. . . . If school districts are given the opportunity to hire teachers as private contractors without regard to union contract provisions, they will have a financial incentive to hire as many as possible on that basis. Furthermore, if teachers are private contractors, school districts won't have to provide them with fringe benefits, meet work rules negotiated by a union, or guarantee job security. (p. 163)

If contractors were responsible for providing fringe benefits, that does not mean that such benefits would necessarily be provided. The experiences of nurses suggests otherwise (Lindorff, 1992).

If a movement toward private contracting is attractive to significant numbers of teachers and/or parents (and it is by no means clear that it would be widely accepted), there is a need to research the reasons why it is attractive. Do union contracts create particular kinds of work restrictions? Are there conflicts between professional values and union contracts? If so, what forms do such conflicts take, and what effects do they have in education? Do more professionally oriented teachers find such contractual limitations frustrating?

Needed Research

Needed research on teachers and privatization can be considered in five areas: relationships among stakeholders including teachers; teacher recruitment, retention, and qualifications; possible value conflicts for teachers; research on other professions and state services with an eye toward seeing their relevance for education and the role of teachers; and institutional forms, stability, and their effects on teacher behavior. Each of these is discussed below, with the goal of generating research questions.

Relationships Among Stakeholders

Under what conditions do various stakeholders form what types of alliances? More research is needed to examine variability in the relationships among stakeholders and the possible effects of those relationships on teaching and learning. For example, when does significant opposition to privatization occur, and when do all the existing stakeholders in education—parents, students, teachers, administrators, communities, future employers, and states—accept the addition of new stakeholders, namely, investors seeking to make a profit? Are existing stakeholders willing to either spend more or earn less so that new participants can make a profit? Teachers, at least when they are organized in unions, have generally been opposed to the introduction of for-profit firms into school systems. Are nonunion teachers less likely than unionized teachers to oppose privatization? Why?

In Dade County there was little opposition to privatization at least partly because EAI conducted independent fund-raising that paid EAI's fee. Teachers did not see their own paychecks shrink or see EAI being paid from funds diverted from educational purposes. Is such an enlargement of the general pie a necessary condition for reducing opposition to privatization?

All of the stakeholders in Dade County were involved in planning the new school from the outset. Is opposition to privatization reduced when all stakeholders are involved and reasonably satisfied? Does getting all stakeholders involved and satisfied require that limitations be placed on privatization? What types of limitations have been deemed necessary? Further case studies of how privatization is implemented are needed to understand the relationships among stakeholders.

Teacher Recruitment, Selection, and Retention

Studies are needed on teacher characteristics, recruitment, selection, and retention in differently organized work settings. Do for-profit educational enterprises seek and hire different types of teachers compared to nonprofit private and public schools? Are privatized schools less likely than public schools to have certified teachers? What kinds of qualifications do the teachers have? What kinds of candidates do they reject? More research is needed on the educational backgrounds, experiences, age, gender, race, and other relevant characteristics of teachers in public and private for-profit schools. How might privatization affect the supply of qualified teachers? How are teacher qualifications assessed in different types of schools? Are those differences consequential for teaching and learning? Do they affect teacher persistence? Do teachers perceive different career trajectories and rewards in one rather than another setting? We know from comparing teachers in private nonprofit schools with those in public schools that private school teachers are often paid less (Chambers, 1988), but they have fewer students to teach and may be governed more often by professional values and norms than by bureaucratic ones. Are teachers who want to work effectively with students drawn to settings organized around professional norms? What organizational conditions nurture professional norms? Finally, is privatization related to changes in teacher staffing patterns and greater staff differentiation? If so, what are the consequences of such changes, for example, for teacher recruitment, retention, and for educational processes and outcomes?

Possible Value Conflicts for Teachers

Potential conflicts for teachers between different values and control—whether bureaucratic, professional, market, or other—have been noted. This is an important area in need of further research.

Another potential value conflict for teachers concerns the educational goals of equity and equal opportunity. What are the effects of privatization on equity and equal opportunity? In general, we know that markets tend to increase inequalities because they benefit those who begin with more resources. Where have efforts at privatization occurred? What populations of students have experienced them? What have been the effects on social and economic inequalities?

What are the effects of privatization on special education? Are legislated mandates being met? In health care, HMOs and insurance companies (unless there are regulations governing them) seek to serve the healthiest people they can find because sick people cost much more. Similarly, in education one of the biggest costs is special education. An important question for at least some teachers is, How does or will privatization handle special education, and with what effects?

Research on Other Professions and State Services

Does research on other professional fields—like health care—or another state service—such as prisons—suggest further research issues on privatization and teachers? Managed health care is facing increasing political reactions to its efforts to contain costs, for example, legislation mandating the number of days of hospital care required after giving birth. Does increasing the operation of market principles in the setting of professional practices ironically increase the likelihood of political reactions and rules? Both economic and political controls may undermine the operation of professional values, norms, and responsibilities. What are the likely consequences for teachers of such changes in education? We need research on the effects of for-profit and nonprofit systems of education for the professional behavior of teachers in schools. For example, do the roles played by professional peers vary in different settings? Does the way teachers spend their time change in different institutional settings? If so, how, and with what consequences?

Deregulation of the U.S. airline industry, electric utilities, and the rapid growth of HMOs both reveal instances where cost imperatives may take precedence over client needs. Proponents of privatization see no inherent contradiction or conflict between professional standards and market exigencies. However, an awareness of potential conflicts between them highlights the need for research on how market or professional values and control affect the conduct of education and the behavior of teachers. What happens when the values conflict? Does organizing education according to market principles put teachers (and administrators) in situations where they have conflicts of interest between what they see as the best interests of the child and their cost and profit targets? More important, does being in a market context change their conduct? For example, does more grade inflation occur in educational institutions that experience greater market dependence, as Persell and Wenglinsky (1993) found? Clearly we need research on whether privatization affects the values and norms governing teacher behaviors and practices.

Research on prison riots in public and privatized prisons suggests the need for research on how privatization might affect the legitimacy of teachers' authority and the authority structure of an entire school. Privatization could lead to questioning of the motives of both teachers and administrators by students and parents. They might begin to wonder whether a teacher or administrator is doing something simply to make money. At a time when the legitimacy of many schools' authority is being seriously questioned, the possible consequences of privatization for perceived educational legitimacy are worth investigating.

Institutional Forms, Stability, and Their Effects on Teacher Behavior

Do for-profit educational enterprises hold different values and promote different educational goals compared to nonprofit educational institutions? As a result, does the conduct of teachers in these settings differ and, if so, how? Do those differences matter? We need more case studies of the consequences of privatization for teachers and learners.

Related to the goals of different institutional forms, have any companies actually made money in any educational privatization ventures thus far? If so, how? If not, does that suggest anything about the potential problems of wringing a profit out of education? If the major profits are obtained from positive changes in the stock prices of educational companies, what are the implications of such a situation for the work of teachers? Would short-term concerns about stock performance put new constraints on teacher behavior? What happens when educational companies are sold? These are areas that have not been researched at all.

In a related vein, research is needed on the issue of institutional continuity. Are privatized schools less stable because they depend more on exit than voice for self-correction compared to public schools? (See Hirschman, 1970.) What consequences does the collapse or closing of a school in the middle of the year have for teachers and children?

If privatization is about the redistribution of costs and benefits among diverse and competing groups, then it is ultimately about the struggle for power. Part of that struggle will be over the power to define how issues will be framed, to measure how well education is doing, and to judge whether the market is an appropriate mechanism for delivering education. For example, how do schools, communities, states, and societies arrive at a framework of publicly defined standards and accountability? Who sets the standards, and how is their attainment assessed? These ideological struggles are reflected in the intensity of the claims made and rhetoric used by both advocates and detractors of markets. Research and theorizing on social movements might be very relevant to the study of efforts to redefine education and the role of teachers.

Notes

1. R. C. Hunter (1995) notes at least six ways that governments can privatize: (1) sale of government enterprises (not something that has been advocated in education); (2) user fees, whereby the government provides services and the public pays for them; (3) competition, whereby the government owns the sites and allows private companies to

produce goods and services in competition with each other (e.g., sanitation or vehicle repair services); (4) vouchers that enable consumers to make purchases, with the state reimbursing all or part of the costs; (5) loadshedding, whereby the government withdraws from funding and providing certain services and leasebacks which permit for-profits to build or buy public facilities and then lease them to public agencies under mutually agreed-upon terms; and (6) contracting-out, for example, where the production of education is transferred to a private for-profit provider. Local districts retain the responsibility of providing education and other services, but private for-profit organizations actually do it. This may require government regulation to ensure competition.

References

Ascher, C., Fruchter, N., and Berne, R. (1996). *Hard lessons: Public schools and privatization*. New York: Twentieth Century Fund Press.

Bates, R. (1995). *A socially critical perspective on educational leadership*. Paper presented at the Flinders University Conference on Educational Leadership. Adelaide, South Australia, Australia. ERIC Document Reproduction Service No. ED 413 645.

Berliner, D. C., and Biddle, B. J. (1995). *The manufactured crisis: Myths, fraud, and the attack on America's public schools*. Reading, Mass.: Addison-Wesley.

Cazares, P. (1997). The private management of public schools: The Hartford, Connecticut, experience. Paper presented at the annual meeting of the American Educational Research Association, Chicago. ERIC Document Reproduction Service No. ED 407 738.

Chambers, J. G. (1988). Patterns of compensation of public and private school teachers. In T. James and H. M. Levin (eds.), *Comparing public and private schools, vol. 1: Institutions and organizations*. New York: Falmer, pp. 190–217.

Doughty, S. (1997). The private management of public schools: lessons learned from the experience of four school districts. Paper presented at the annual meeting of the American Educational Research Association, Chicago. ERIC Document Reproduction Service No. ED 407 741.

Edwards, D. L. (1997). The private management of public schools. Paper presented at the annual meeting of the American Educational Research Association, Chicago. ERIC Document Reproduction No. ED 407 704.

Feigenbaum, H., Henig, J., and Hamnett, C. (1998). *Shrinking the state: The political underpinnings of privatization*. Cambridge, U.K.: Cambridge University Press.

Finkelstein, M. J., Seal, R. K., and Schuster, J. H. (1998). *The new academic generation: A profession in transformation*. Baltimore: Johns Hopkins University Press.

Finn, C. E., Jr. (1996). *Different schools for a better future*. Indianapolis: Hudson Institute.

Gerber, T. P., and Hout, M. (1998). More shock than therapy: Market transition, employment, and income in Russia, 1991–1995. *American Journal of* Sociology 104, 1–50.

Goldstone, J. (1998, March 27). *Prison riots as revolutions: A test of theories of social order*. Presentation given in the "Power, Politics, and Protest Workshop," Department of Sociology, New York University.

Grady, D. (1999, November 25). Treatment of kidney failure is flawed, 2 studies suggest: Death rates and transplant referrals cited. *New York Times*, p. A18.

Henig, J. R. (1994). *Rethinking school choice: Limits of the market metaphor*. Princeton: Princeton University Press.

Hill, P. T., Pierce, L. C., and Guthrie, J. W. (1997). *Reinventing public education: How contracting can transform America's schools.* Chicago: University of Chicago Press.

Hirschman, A. O. (1970). *Exit, voice, and loyalty: Responses to decline in firms, organizations, and states.* Cambridge: Harvard University Press.

Hunter, R. C. (1995). Privatization of instruction in public education." *Education and Urban Society* 27, 168–194.

Jackson, L. (1997). *The private management of public schools: The Minneapolis, Minnesota, experience.* Paper presented at the annual meeting of the American Educational Research Association, Chicago. ERIC Document Reproduction Service No. ED 407 737.

Levin, H. M. (1987). Education as a public and private good. *Journal of Policy Analysis and Management* 6, 628–641.

Lieberman, M. (1995). *Public education: An autopsy.* Cambridge: Harvard University Press.

———. (1997). *The teachers' unions: How the NEA and AFT sabotage reform and hold students, parents, teachers, and taxpayers hostage to bureaucracy.* New York: Free Press.

Lindorff, D. (1992). *Marketplace medicine: The rise of the for-profit hospital chains.* New York: Bantam.

Molnar, A. (1996). *Giving kids the business: The commercialization of America's schools.* Boulder: Westview Press.

New York Times (1999, November 28). Managed care's future, Section 4, p. 10.

Peeler, T. H. (1995). *South Pointe Elementary School assessment project. A special issues report.* Greensboro, N.C.: SERVE: SouthEastern Regional Vision for Education. ERIC Document Reproduction Service No. ED 387 918.

Persell, C. H. (2000). Values, control, and outcomes in public and private schools." In M. Hallinan (ed.), *Handbook of research in the sociology of education.* New York: Plenum, pp. 387–407.

Persell, C. H., and Wenglinsky, H. (1993, August). *Privatization, market logic, and educational experiences: The case of proprietary schools.* Paper presented at the annual meeting of the American Sociological Association, Los Angeles.

———. (2000). *The civic consequences of attending public and for-profit post-secondary schools.* Unpublished manuscript.

Robertson, S. I. (1995). "Fast" capitalism and "fast" schools: New realities and new truths. Paper presented at the annual meeting of the American Educational Research Association, San Francisco.

Schmidt, B. C., Jr. (1994). The Edison Project's plan to redefine public education. *Educational Leadership* 52(1) 61–64.

Vanourck, G., Manno, B. V., Finn, C. E., and Bierlein, L. (1997). *Charter schools as seen by those who know them best: Students, teachers, parents.* Indianapolis: Hudson Institute.

Weiss, J. A. (1990). Control in school organizations: Theoretical perspectives. In W. H. Clune and J. F. Witte (eds.), *Choice and control in American education, vol. 1: The theory of choice and control in education.* London: Falmer, pp. 91–134.

Whitaker, B. (1999, November 28). Changing of the managed-care guard. *New York Times,* Section 3, p. 11.

Whittle, C. (1997). Lessons learned: The Edison Project founder's musings on American schooling. *School Administrator* 54(1), 6–9.

Evaluation Designs

13

Criteria for Evaluating School Voucher Studies

DAVID E. MYERS

School choice initiatives come in many packages. There are privately and publicly funded programs, intra- and interdistrict programs, public school choice programs, and programs that include private schools. For some families and children, the ability to choose a school has long been taken for granted; for many others such an option has not been available. In the past few years, however, legislative proposals giving families the option of selecting from a wider range of schools have been introduced in Congress and in many state legislatures. Some of these proposals offer families vouchers so that they can choose among private as well as public schools.

Many states have gone beyond proposing legislation, having already initiated school choice programs. In 1998, for example, eighteen states had large-scale public school choice programs, and eleven states had school choice programs operating in at least some school districts. Two of the better-known school choice programs are operated in Milwaukee and Cleveland. In 1990, the Wisconsin legislature enacted a pilot program giving public school students access to secular private schools in Milwaukee; the program was expanded in 1996 to include religious schools. The Ohio legislature established a similar program in Cleveland in

I would like to thank Mark Dynarski and Julia Kim for their thoughtful comments and review of this chapter.

1996. Other programs, which are privately funded, are operating in many communities throughout the nation, including San Antonio, Albany, Washington, D.C., Indianapolis, New York City, and Dayton, Ohio. In addition, a national program run by the Children's Scholarship Foundation offered about 40,000 privately funded scholarships to low-income families in more than forty cities in 1999.

Although many states are considering, or already conducting, school choice programs, and privately funded programs are on the rise, the debate about the efficacy of voucher programs as the means for reforming the nation's system of education continues. On the one hand, critics of school choice argue:

- Perceived gains of students in private schools result from the selected nature of private school families;
- Low-income families will not make good choices because they are likely to select schools on the basis of location, religious affiliation, and sports programs rather than educational quality;
- School choice will further segregate students on the basis of income and race; and
- Vouchers will take money away from neighborhood schools and the community.

On the other hand, supporters of school choice contend:

- Children learn more in private schools;
- Private schools use their resources more efficiently than do public schools;
- Choice increases socioeconomic and racial integration; and
- Competition among schools for students will improve the nation's schools and students' educational achievement.

As one public school official recently described in a personal communication, the debate about school choice is "a dumb debate as long as we don't have credible information about the effects of school choice and vouchers." Although the results of many studies comparing public and private schools have been published, such work has generally been criticized for comparing different populations of students (see, e.g., Bryk, 1981; Coleman, Hoffer, and Kilgore, 1981, 1982; Coleman and Hoffer, 1987; Chubb and Moe, 1990; Greene, Howell, and Peterson, 1998; Murnane, 1981; Witte, 1991; Witte, Bailey, and Thorn, 1992). Currently, several studies of school choice are under way, and new studies of school choice are sure to be conducted in the next few years (see, e.g., Peterson et al., 1999; Metcalf, 1999).

In this chapter I present some criteria for evaluating school voucher studies. I do not address studies that explore the effects of charter schools or magnet schools, or other forms of public school choice. Furthermore, I focus only on studies that assess the impact of vouchers on students and families and not the impact of vouchers on schools. I consider three criteria we can use to evaluate voucher studies: (1) construct validity—explication of the constructs underlying the measurements made in voucher studies; (2) internal and statistical conclusion validity—the ability to make causal statements about the impact of vouchers on students and families; and (3) external validity—generalizing the findings from specific voucher studies to a broader policy context.

I have organized the chapter as follows. First, I describe different ways to frame the policy question about the impacts of vouchers. Second, I discuss the criteria for evaluating studies of voucher programs. Third, I present an illustrative report card for two ongoing voucher studies.

Framing the Policy Question

Policymakers, educators, and parents would like to answer a question: What effects will vouchers have on children and the nation's system of education? Researchers, in turn, have sought to answer this through a variety of designs, including random assignment and regression-based approaches. Unfortunately, each design has been used to address different aspects of the same general question. For instance, if we approach the question from the perspective of the impact of vouchers on families and students (the demand side of the school voucher issue), then we must necessarily address the following additional questions:

- What are the impacts of vouchers on families and children when they are *offered* a voucher?
- What are the impacts of *using* a voucher?
- What are the impacts of *attending* a private school?

Studies using random assignment (a lottery) to construct a voucher group and a control group have typically addressed the first two questions, and regression-based approaches have been used to answer the third question.[1] However, answers to all three questions can be estimated from a well-implemented, randomized experiment. Answers to the first question tell us not about the impact of school choice itself but about the impact of *offering* vouchers to families, some of whom will use them while others will not. For instance, imagine a policy that offers vouchers to all families or all low-income families in a school district. We might expect that some families would be motivated to move their children from a public school to a private school either because it is a better match for the child, or because of concerns about the current school environment. We might also expect other families to keep children in a public school because they are satisfied with the school's curriculum and resources, or because transporting their children to another school may be too difficult. Studies that seek to answer the second question show the program's impact on those who actually use vouchers and not the more general group of eligible families who were offered vouchers.[2] Answers to the third question give us insight into the impact of attending a private school, that is, a school that operates in a market economy and competes for consumers of educational services.

Few studies have examined the impact of vouchers from the supply side of the issue (see, e.g., Hoxby, 1996; Peterson, Myers, and Howell, 1999). Although supply-side studies are not the focus of this chapter, many of the criteria I describe for evaluating voucher studies that examine impacts on families and children could be applied to these studies as well. Questions posed from this perspective may include the following:

- Do schools and school systems compete for children when vouchers are available?
- Do children who attend public and private schools, on average, experience educational gains when all schools must compete for educational consumers?
- Can private schools increase capacity and maintain a quality education?
- Do schools become more academically segregated? Do schools become more racially segregated? Do they become more stratified in terms of family income?

Criteria for Evaluating School Voucher Studies

The criteria for evaluating studies of school voucher programs should be the same criteria used for evaluating any empirical study: construct validity, internal and statistical conclusion validity, and external validity (see Cook and Campbell, 1979). These criteria are defined below in terms of how they would be applied in studies of school voucher programs.

- *Construct validity*—the explication of theoretical constructs that will be used to study the impact of vouchers and the methods that will be used to measure the constructs.
- *Internal and statistical conclusion validity*—the ability to make causal statements about the impact of vouchers on family and student outcomes. This includes concerns about processes that may produce bias between the experimental group and the comparison or control group, as well as processes that may make for imprecise impact estimates and therefore obscure real differences between groups when conducting tests of statistical significance.
- *External validity*—the ability to generalize findings to some larger population, or to another setting or time.

Weaknesses in any of these areas can cast doubt on the validity of study results. In the following discussion of these criteria, I describe how each might be threatened. Although T. D. Cook and D. T. Campbell (1979) give a long list of potential threats to each, I focus on those that may be most germane to voucher studies.

Construct Validity

Explication of Constructs. Voucher studies can include three kinds of constructs: (1) the policy variable—vouchers and attending a private school; (2) long-term outcomes; and (3) intermediate outcomes/constructs that help us explain the relationship between vouchers and the outcomes. As I described above, a voucher policy can be evaluated from several viewpoints. We can look at the impact of offering a voucher and of using a voucher, and we can look at the impact of attending a private school. Although information on the impact of each aspect of voucher policy can be useful to policymakers, the three are not equivalent and so must be *explicated* when designing an evaluation of vouchers and when interpreting findings about impacts. In other words, evaluators should not confuse the impact of one with the impact of another.

Besides explicating the policy variable in voucher studies, researchers must also explicate the constructs treated as outcomes and ensure that all aspects of the expected outcomes of a voucher policy are measured or that the limitations in the measurement are clearly noted. Two outcomes most often associated with voucher studies are the parents' satisfaction with their child's school and students' educational achievement. Two other possible outcomes are racial and socioeconomic segregation of the child in the school and in the classroom.

Of all these outcomes, achievement (or learning) is particularly difficult to measure; however, when assessing the impacts of vouchers it is the outcome that is often given the most weight by consumers of voucher studies. As some have commented, the impact of vouchers and private schools on students' achievement is the litmus test for school choice. Most studies rely on standardized reading and math tests to measure achievement, but such tests focus on the acquisition of general knowledge and facts, tending to overlook the development of higher-order thinking and affective skills. Some may believe that state and local assessments are more appropriate than standardized tests; however, one should be cautious using such assessments because of state-specific exclusion policies and the often limited potential to link test results over several years for individual students.

Other constructs that may be considered in a voucher study are those that can be used to explain a relationship between vouchers and the outcomes. These explanatory constructs include class size, parental involvement, and school environment. Most voucher studies have not included these mediating constructs, focusing instead on the total impact of vouchers or private schools on student and parent outcomes. However, should impacts be identified, we must work to understand how these impacts come about.

Mono-Operation Bias.   The term "mono-operation bias" refers to the use of singular operations to measure the constructs being tested. Perhaps the best example of this phenomenon is specifying the key experimental variable, that is, the size of the voucher being offered to families. Most privately funded demonstrations use vouchers that do not cover the complete cost of private school tuition, fees, and uniforms. This so-called partial voucher may affect a family's responses to the program. For example, when a large gap exists between the value of a voucher and the cost of attending a private school, families that are better off financially may be more likely to take advantage of the voucher offer than might be expected if the voucher program covered all costs of schooling. This means that the results of an evaluation of a demonstration with relatively small vouchers may not be indicative of the impact of programs that offer larger vouchers. As we will see later, this is an example of a factor that may affect a study's external validity.

Mono-Method Bias.   Most recent studies of voucher programs rely on survey data collected from parents and students and on a single test of students' academic performance. Although these studies also have rigorous research designs for estimating the impact of voucher programs, they generally have limited resources for collecting data from a range of respondents. For example, when trying to explain the effect of vouchers on achievement-test scores, one may want to know about differences in school environment, curriculum, and the delivery of instruction. Ideally, we would measure these constructs directly or through surveys of teachers and school administrators instead of relying on parents' and students' perceptions. Data on school environment and related concepts are available in some observational studies (see, e.g., those conducted by Coleman and his colleagues, 1981, 1982, and 1987; and by Chubb and Moe, 1990). However, these studies of private schools have been plagued by self-selection biases that may have been confounded with the effects of attending private and public schools. Although it may be desirable to collect school-related information directly from the schools, experience suggests that public school systems may refuse to provide the information or to allow teachers and school staff to participate as respondents in evaluations (this has been true of privately funded voucher experiments). Publicly funded voucher programs, as in Florida, may provide researchers better access to this information since schools may be required to provide the data to outside evaluators.

Internal and Statistical Conclusion Validity

Selection Effects. The term "selection effects" refers to the situation in which the groups being compared are different in terms of two or more dimensions, including the difference in treatment status. This is probably the most pervasive threat to internal validity in studies of school vouchers in which nonrandomized experiments are used to compute program impacts. (For examples of particularly problematic selection effects, see the earlier studies by Coleman and his colleagues, 1981, 1982, and 1987; and by Chubb and Moe, 1990, who used extant data.) Other examples include the more recent studies of voucher programs in Milwaukee and Cleveland, where researchers compared scholarship students attending private schools with public school students who were similar on a variety of observed characteristics (see Witte 1991; Witte, Bailey, and Thorn, 1992; Greene, Howell, and Peterson, 1998).

Although evaluators have focused extensively on statistically adjusting for differences in the characteristics of the families and children who self-select into the experimental and comparison groups in voucher studies, one must also be concerned about selection biases that may be related to the systematic loss of observations (families and children) because of missing information. Information could be missing for two reasons. First, there may be systematic attrition of families and children from the study sample (families refuse to participate or cannot be found for follow-up surveys and testing). Second, some respondents will not complete all items in a survey or will fail to complete an achievement test (missing values). Both problems are present in all voucher studies, and one must be on guard when analyzing data and interpreting results from such analyses. Some biases that result from differential attrition by families in the voucher group and the control group can be checked by comparing the baseline characteristics of the two groups who remain in the sample at the end of the experiment, but subtle forms of selection bias nonetheless may affect the outcomes.

Resentful Demoralization of Respondents.   Families and students assigned to a control group may react negatively to their control status. For example, low-income families in a control group may feel that they have never gotten a chance and that they will always lose; this feeling becomes reinforced by not winning a voucher in a lottery. These negative attitudes may be expressed in what parents report about their child's school and in how children respond when given an achievement test. To the extent that families who did not win a voucher in a voucher experiment respond more negatively than they would normally when asked about their schools in the absence of a voucher experiment, one may overestimate the impact of school vouchers.

Imprecise Estimates of Program Impacts.   Selection effects and resentful demoralization of respondents involve biases that may result between the treatment and control/comparison groups, independent of the intended effect of the intervention. In addition to these two threats to internal validity, imprecise estimates may also cause one to draw the wrong conclusion about the impact of vouchers. An impact can be measured imprecisely when the sample sizes for the treatment and control groups are small and the probability of detecting an impact, when one exists, is very low. This means that even though a study may do a good job of removing biases that may exist between the treatment and control/comparison group by using techniques such as random assignment, it is still possible to conclude that no impact is present when one is present.

   To see the implications of using small sample sizes, I have computed the probability of detecting a small impact on students' achievement-test scores when using a random assignment study design with different-size samples (see Figure 13.1).[3] Most researchers would consider a probability of detecting a significant impact of 0.8 or larger as ideal. This means that eight out of ten times that we conduct an experiment we would conclude that a statistically significant impact existed when an impact was, in fact, present in the population. Figure 13.1 shows that at about 1,300 children should be in the voucher group and 1,300 children should be in the control group if we want a sufficiently large chance of detecting

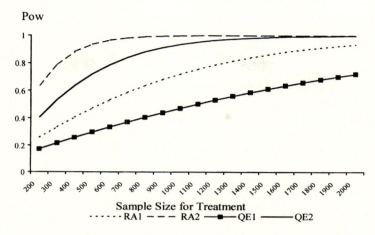

RA1—random assignment design and an effect size of .10
RA2—random assignment design and an effect size of .20
QE1—quasi-experimental design (e.g., using regression adjusted estimates
    or selection modeling procedures) and an effect size of .10
QE2—quasi-experimental design and an effect size of .20

FIGURE 13.1   Probability of Detecting an Impact with Alternative Designs

a very small impact (effect size = 0.10).[4] If we expect to find small impacts (effect size = 0.20 standard deviations), then a sample of about 400 voucher students and 400 control group students is sufficient.[5] Samples with fewer children give us a small chance of detecting a meaningful impact.[6]

I also present results that we can expect from a quasi-experimental design in which statistical models are used to reduce the selection bias that results from observed and unobserved heterogeneity between treatment and comparison groups (see, e.g., Maddala, 1983). Theoretical computations and empirical findings from another study (Fraker and Maynard, 1987) suggest that when statistical models are used to adjust for selection effects, then samples that are two or more times larger than those used in a random assignment design may be needed to achieve the levels of precision achieved through random assignment.[7] I show the implications of the results in Figure 13.1. Here, the probability of detecting an impact may be very low when applying quasi-experimental designs to adjust for selection effects. Even with samples of 2,000 children in the treatment group and 2,000 children in the comparison group, the probability of detecting a very small, significant impact is unacceptably low (effect size = 0.10).

External Validity

Interaction of Selection and Treatment.   Analyses of extant data—from High School and Beyond and the National Education Longitudinal Study, for example—give researchers an opportunity to compare public and private school students and to make comparisons for particular subgroups, including low-income and middle-income families. Other groups that can be considered when analyzing such data include students with limited English proficiency and students with in-school behavior problems (for other examples of relevant subgroups, see Coleman and Hoffer, 1987). As I have noted, analyses based on extant data are susceptible to selection effects. More focused studies, such as the ongoing evaluations in New York City, Dayton, and Washington, D.C., use experimental methods to construct the treatment and control groups; however, the respondents in these studies are low-income families and predominately African American or Hispanic families, and the ability to look at differential treatment effects is limited by the variability on these key dimensions.

Interaction of Setting and Treatment.   When evaluating school voucher studies, one should consider the context in which the voucher program is operating. For example, does good public transportation exist so that students have easy access to private schools? In cities with poor transportation to and from schools, fewer families may use the vouchers, and the impacts obtained for these families may differ from those obtained for a representative sample of families.

In addition to transportation, another factor affecting the interpretation of the impacts of a voucher program is the difference between the amount of the voucher and the actual cost of sending a child to a private school. Some voucher experiments offer stipends of about $1,000 per year, others offer $1,400, and some offer as much as $3,400 up to $4,000 per year. Clearly, a family's ability to pay the difference between the voucher and the cost of schooling could affect whether they use a voucher and the length of time they can remain in the voucher experiment. Each of these conditions can affect the ability to draw general conclusions about what we might expect to see from a state or federal policy concerning the use of vouchers for school reform.

Summary of Criteria and Illustrative Report Card

A checklist of the criteria for designing and reviewing voucher studies and for analyzing study data is shown in Table 13.1. This list, which summarizes the discussion in this chapter, is not intended to prescribe what a voucher study must in-

TABLE 13.1   Summary of Criteria for Evaluating Voucher Studies

Construct Validity	Internal and Statistical Conclusion Validity	External Validity
Explication of the policy question: (1) the impact of offering a voucher, (2) the impact of using a voucher, and (3) the impact of attending a private school.	Substantive self-selection biases confounded with true program impacts. Selection biases that arise from missing data patterns.	Interaction of selection and treatment—subgroup analyses for children with special needs, middle-income children.
Outcomes for voucher studies—students, parents, schools, and communities.	Demoralization of the respondents because they were not selected for a voucher.	Interaction of setting and treatment—size of the voucher offer, availability of transportation, information about choice schools.
Intermediate outcomes used to explain the impact of vouchers.	Sample size needed to detect meaningful impacts.	
The use of single or multiple operations to measure constructs.		
The use of single or multiple methods (sources) to measure constructs.		

clude. Instead, I have attempted to provide consumers of these studies with a basis for assessing the credibility of particular studies and, hence, their value to the debate about the efficacy of using vouchers for reforming the nation's system of education. The first row of the table shows the three basic criteria I have described in this chapter. Below each of the criteria are more refined approaches for evaluating voucher studies.

An illustrative report card for two studies is shown in Table 13.2. The two examples I have used are Milwaukee and New York City. These evaluations used distinct methods for computing program impacts and as a result answer somewhat different policy questions.

TABLE 13.2 Illustrative Report Card for Two Recent Voucher Studies

Study	Site	Treatment Group	Control/ Comparison Group	Construct Validity	Internal and Statistical Conclusion Validity	External Validity
Witte et al.	Milwaukee	Choice students	Random sample of Milwaukee public school students	Policy question focuses on the impact of private schools on students' achievement and related outcomes.	Large samples used with comparison group methodology. Moderately good chance of detecting impacts, but selection biases may still be affecting outcomes.	Moderately large, urban school district. Hoxby (1998) shows that Milwaukee ranks 16th in terms of percent of students attending private schools. Only three voucher schools operated during the period of the evaluation.
Peterson et al.	New York City	Randomly selected choice students	Randomly selected control group of eligible program applicants	Policy question focuses on the impact of being offered a voucher, using a voucher, and of attending private schools.	Random assignment used to construct voucher group and control group. Moderately large samples used, and small effects have a high probability of being detected if they are present (1,000 treatment families and 960 control families). High response rate for surveys and tests. Potential negative reaction by control group families.	New York city has a high percent of students attending private schools, and there is a large supply of choice schools to choose among. Modest voucher offered to students ($1,400).

Notes

1. Besides using different research designs to answer questions about the impacts of vouchers and private schooling and possibly confounding method effects with substantive effects, a review of the literature suggests that all or almost all studies concerning private school impacts rely on high school students' experiences and that voucher studies focus on children in elementary school.

2. When interpreting the impacts of a voucher under a randomized design, it is important to realize that some families in the control group may find a way to finance attending a private school even without the assistance of a voucher. If some families in the control group attend private schools, then the impacts we compute show the effect of a voucher offer or the use of a voucher above and beyond what families might normally do in the absence of a voucher (e.g., attend a private school).

3. J. Cohen (1988) suggests that impacts of less than .2 standard deviations (effect sizes) are small, those of about .4 are medium, and effect sizes of more than .8 are large. In most education settings, impacts of about .2 or less are expected.

4. To construct the power curves, I made the following assumptions: (1) the effect size of a "very small" effect is 0.10 and the size of a "small" effect is 0.20; (2) the probability of rejecting the hypothesis of no impact by chance is 0.10 for a two-tailed test; and (3) the size of the control group equals the size of the treatment group. The power curves were computed using the following expression:

$$ Z_\beta = \left(\sqrt{\left(\frac{1}{N_T} + \frac{1}{N_C} \right)} \times I \right)^{-1} - Z_\alpha $$

where Z_α is the critical value that corresponds to the probability of rejecting the hypothesis of no impact by chance alone, N_T is the size of the treatment group, N_C is the size of the control group, and I is the true size of the impact. The quantity we compute from this expression, Z_β, can be used to compute the probability that we will reject the hypothesis of no impact when an impact of size I or larger actually exists; this is accomplished by using the cumulative normal distribution and computing the probability that Z_α is greater than Z_β (see Snedecor and Cochran, 1989). This is just an approximation because it ignores the tail at the other end of the null distribution.

5. If the voucher study plans to compare impacts for subgroups of families or children, such as children from very low income families, then larger samples may be required.

6. Many voucher experiments randomly assign families to the voucher and control groups. In doing so, cluster effects will be present when analyzing student outcomes such as achievement test scores. When cluster effects are present and standard statistical techniques designed for the analysis of simple random sampling are used, standard errors of the impact estimates that are too large will be computed. To better approximate the correct standard error, one should adjust the standard errors computed under the assumption of simple random sampling by taking into account the design effect or by using direct methods of computing standard errors such as the bootstrap method.

7. To compute power curves with quasi-experimental designs, an adjustment factor is included to reflect the fact that there will generally be a correlation between an indicator of participation in a voucher program and one or more covariates that are used to statistically control for observed and/or unobserved selection effects.

References

Barrow, B. S., Cain, G. G., and Goldberger, A. S. (1981). Issues in the analysis of selectivity bias. In E. Stromsdorfer and G. Farkas (eds.), *Evaluation studies review annual*, vol. 5. Beverly Hills, Calif.: Sage.

Bryk, A. S. (1981). Disciplined inquiry or policy argument? *Harvard Educational Review* 51, 497–509.

Chubb, J. E., and Moe, T. M. (1990). *Politics, markets, and America's schools.* Washington, D.C.: Brookings Institution.

Cohen, J. (1988). *Statistical power analysis for the behavioral sciences.* 2d ed. Hillsdale, N.J.: Lawrence Erlbaum.

Coleman, J., and Hoffer, T. (1987). *Public and private high schools: The impact of communities.* New York: Basic.

Coleman, J., Hoffer, T., and Kilgore, S. (1981). Questions and answers: Our response. *Harvard Educational Review* 51, 526–545.

———. (1982). *High school achievement.* New York: Basic.

Cook, T. D., and Campbell, D. T. (1979). *Quasi-experimentation: Design and analysis issues for field settings.* Boston: Houghton Mifflin.

Fraker, T., and Maynard, R. (1987). Evaluating comparison group designs with employment-related programs. *Journal of Human Resources* 22(2), 194–227.

Green, W. H. (1997). *Econometric analysis.* 3d ed. Upper Saddle River, N.J.: Prentice Hall.

Greene, J. P., Howell, W. G., and Peterson, P. E. (1998). Lessons from the Cleveland Scholarship Program. In B. C. Hassel and P. E. Peterson (eds.), *Learning from school choice.* Washington, D.C.: Brookings Institution, pp. 376–380.

Hoxby, C. M. (1996). Evidence in private school vouchers: Effects on schools and students. In H.F. Ladd (ed.), *Performance-based approaches to school reform.* Washington, D.C.: Brookings Institution.

Maddala, G. S. (1983). *Limited dependent and qualitative variables in econometrics.* Cambridge, U.K.: Cambridge University Press.

Metcalf, K. (1999). *Evaluation of the Cleveland Scholarship and Tutoring Grant Program, 1996–1999.* Bloomington: Indiana Center for Evaluation, Indiana University.

Murnane, R. J. (1981). Evidence, analysis, and unanswered questions. *Harvard Educational Review* 51(4), 483–489.

Peterson, P. E., Myers, D. E., and Howell, W. G. (1999). *An evaluation of the Horizon Scholarship Program in the Edgewood Independent School District, San Antonio, Texas: The first year.* Paper presented at the annual meeting of the American Public Policy and Management Association, Washington, D.C.

Peterson, P. E., Myers, D. E., Howell, W.G., and Mayer, D.P. (1999). The effects of school choice in New York City. In S. E. Mayer and P. E. Peterson (eds.), *Earning and learning: How schools matter.* Washington, D.C.: Brookings Institution and the Russell Sage Foundation.

Snedecor, G. W., and Cochran, W. (1989). *Statistical Methods.* Ames Iowa, : Iowa State University Press.

Witte, J. F. (1991). First year report: Milwaukee Parental Choice Program. Unpublished manuscript, University of Wisconsin, Department of Political Science, and Robert M. La Follette Institute of Public Affairs.

Witte, J. F., Bailey, A. B., and Thorn, C. A. (1992). Second year report: Milwaukee Parental Choice Program. Unpublished manuscript. Madison: University of Wisconsin, Department of Political Science, and Robert M. La Follette Institute of Public Affairs.

14

Designing Education Voucher Experiments: Recommendations for Researchers, Funders, and Users

FRED DOOLITTLE AND WENDY CONNORS

Education voucher proposals are increasingly a part of the policy debate and could play an important role in education reform. The topic of vouchers is important for those involved in the policy debate and for funders of programs, education administrators and teachers, parents, and students. The debate about vouchers raises important issues about public funding and provision of educational services, the role of the public and nongovernment sectors, the key educational outcomes for policy, and ways in which research findings can support an informed debate on controversial topics. Evaluators are sometimes called into the

The authors wish to thank Howard Bloom and Ramona Ortega of the Manpower Demonstration Research Corporation for their special help with this chapter and Robert Weber for his editorial assistance.

fray in the midst of these discussions to expand the empirical knowledge base underlying the policy debate.

This chapter offers guidelines for undertaking and designing experiments to test the implementation and impacts of education vouchers. Although the term "experiment" is often used broadly to mean a test of a proposed initiative, this chapter argues that in this context there are reasons to focus on a more precise definition: a multisite random assignment impact evaluation of vouchers linked to a study of the program's implementation. Random assignment (which can be thought of as akin to a lottery) is used to identify two similar groups for study: a program group that is offered access to educational vouchers, and a control group that is not. Both groups are followed over time, and any differences in key outcomes represent the impact of providing access to education vouchers.[1]

The offer of education vouchers is a program that lends itself to and calls out for a study through a random-assignment experiment. Vouchers are individualized treatments (the offer of a subsidy to a specific student versus something like a whole school reform) of great policy import and potentially considerable expense. They are currently being tested on a limited scale to assess their appropriateness for broader implementation. As such, there are many questions about how people will respond to the offer of vouchers and what effects the vouchers will have on the educational experiences of those who do and do not receive them. Further, there are serious problems with alternative methods that are sometimes used to study program impacts, as discussed later in this chapter.

Other fields of public policy have faced questions similar to those posed by education vouchers and, hence, have mounted a series of program evaluations of alternatives. Public finance economists have long argued that it is important to distinguish various aspects of public involvement in providing key services that serve redistributive goals; the crucial distinction often concerns public-sector *funding* of a service versus public-sector *production* of that service. For many services, there are alternatives beyond public production: contracting with nongovernment agencies, providing assistance to individuals or families to purchase the service in a market, or providing cash assistance to raise households' overall incomes and thus support higher levels of consumption of the service.[2]

The goal of this chapter is to provide a detailed framework for deciding on and designing experiments for education vouchers. It focuses on key questions that must be resolved in order to make an experiment worthwhile and to produce useful findings. Evaluations can bring frustration as well as enlightenment, as anyone involved in this work no doubt has experienced. One frustrating result is to produce findings that seem to matter little in the policy debate; the choice turns out to be driven by considerations other than the type of empirical information produced by research. A second source of frustration is an evaluation that produces uncertain findings: "It could be this, it could be that; we cannot tell you which." The framework offered in this chapter seeks to avoid both of these disappointing outcomes.

This chapter is organized around questions that designers of an experiment must face. The first set of questions concerns the policy environment and the nature of the proposed program. The second set focuses on specific research design issues such as the appropriate methodology, considerations in conducting follow-up with sample members over time, and ways to calculate and interpret findings. The chapter draws on past experience studying education vouchers to illustrate many of the points being made.

Key Policy-Related Questions

This section describes four important threshold questions that must be resolved to make a study of program impacts worthwhile. First, there must be a well-defined program model; vaguely specified programs do not lend themselves to impact studies. Only if there is a reasonably concrete description of the program can we know if we are testing the right thing. Second, this program must be different enough from other alternatives available in the community to warrant and permit a test of its impact. Third, there must be some level of agreement on the key goals (intended outcomes) of the program. Otherwise, it will be impossible to design a study that addresses the appropriate questions. Finally, studies of this type (which require a substantial resource commitment) should be done only if the type of empirically based findings they provide will be seen as useful in resolving policy questions of importance.

Can the Program Be Defined Precisely?

In deciding whether to conduct an impact study and in selecting the appropriate experimental design, it is critical to define the intended treatment—in this case, vouchers—for which impacts will be estimated. Understanding who is eligible and which selection criteria exist for the program is necessary in order to specify the appropriate random-assignment procedures.

Defining Key Program Elements.   The premise of vouchers rests on the idea that creating a market-based system for education will allow parents more flexibility in choosing schools for their children while prompting the public schools to become more efficient and consumer-driven.[3] Vouchers are often presented as a vehicle to provide disadvantaged families with greater choices and control, thereby easing general dissatisfaction with the public school system (particularly in inner cities).[4] In some cases it is argued that vouchers will drive institutional reform by diminishing bureaucratic control.[5] While considering the varying theories on vouchers, it is also important to recognize that there is no single voucher system; instead, there are many approaches that can use the voucher mechanism.[6]

Therefore, understanding specific program elements (such as the size, i.e., value, of the voucher or the length of time for which the subsidy is being offered) becomes critical in designing an experiment to measure program impact. The size of the voucher needs to be large enough to cover a substantial portion of tuition at a particular school as well as to warrant other adjustments, such as changing schools or related transportation issues. Moreover, the longer the voucher offer is open, the greater the likely sign-up rate; given the required adjustments and possible negative effects of mobility on students, parents would be less likely to use a voucher if it were available only for a short time.

To demonstrate the variability of approaches, it is useful to look at two existing voucher programs. In New York City, the School Choice Scholarships Foundation (SCSF) offers 1,300 scholarships for low-income families to apply to tuition at either religious or secular schools. The scholarships are worth up to $1,400 annually and can be used for at least three years.[7] The Milwaukee Parental Choice Program, in contrast, pays participating private schools the equivalent of the state aid that Milwaukee public schools receive per pupil ($4,894 per student in 1998–1999). In 1998–1999, an estimated 5,800 students participated. In addition, during a three-year period 15,000 students have been allowed to participate.[8]

The information available to parents and the accessibility of that information are important components of any voucher system. Because education is a complex service,[9] in order to enhance choice consumers need to rely on information about a school's attributes, such as the quality of its teachers and its ideology, academic program, and average class size. If information is not readily available, research demonstrates that the more educated, motivated, and English-speaking parents will be more inclined to seek out information on alternative options. To mitigate this possible inequity, information dissemination may include a technical assistance component to identify hard-to-reach families and inform them of their options.[10] Other supportive components, such as establishing networks to help parents and children adjust to a new setting or providing transportation to facilitate attendance, also affect how the voucher mechanism is structured. The SCSF, for example, has assisted families in finding private school placement, which may have led to higher sign-up rates than for families who were simply granted a voucher.[11]

Specifying the Eligibility Requirements and Selection Process.   In defining the voucher mechanism, it is also critical to determine who will be eligible for the program and how selections will normally be made. Does eligibility depend on educational achievement, on income, or on some combination of the two? Is the voucher more widely available to children currently enrolled in a public school? If the latter, then how long do children need to be previously enrolled in order to be eligible for the voucher? To illustrate, the SCSF program requires that children live in New York City to be eligible for a scholarship. In addition, they have to be enrolled in grades one through five, attend a public school at the time of application, and be eligible for the free school lunch program.[12]

All these considerations influence the selection process, which may take form as either a lottery or an application process or may be based on income and/or achievement. For example, the SCSF eligibility rules combine achievement and income characteristics by allocating 85 percent of the scholarships to children who attend low-performing schools and who are eligible for the free school lunch program. Thus, although a lottery is used to select families, students from low-achieving schools have a higher probability of winning a scholarship.[13]

Is the Program Truly Different from Other Options?

After the program elements and the characteristics of eligible participants have been identified, the question emerges about how distinctive the services available to the treatment group are from what is already available and would be available to the control, or comparison, group. If a voucher is small relative to the cost of education, it might not be worth it for families to adjust school choice because of the associated costs of the transaction. Yet families not selected for the voucher program (but who are otherwise eligible) may be inclined to seek out alternative sources for similar financial support. This shifting from public to private schools is illustrated by some families in Milwaukee who were not selected in the lotteries to participate in the program; instead, they received scholarships from a privately funded program (Partners for Advancing Values in Education) to attend primarily religious schools. Very likely the remaining portion of the group that was not selected for vouchers was systematically different from those selected in the lotteries, preventing a comparison of voucher lottery winners with those not selected who did not find alternative aid.[14]

A second consideration that could weaken the distinctiveness of the program under study lies in the question of available supply. Unless enough private and alternative public schools are authorized and willing to take students with vouchers, the offer has little real meaning for most lottery winners. In Milwaukee, for example, the number of participating schools and available slots therein were initially limited because schools were restricted from accepting vouchers from more than half their students. Furthermore, because only 1 percent of Milwaukee's public school students (expanded to 1.5 percent in 1994) were actually able to participate in the program, few new schools initially emerged to serve voucher students.[15] Choice may have been further constrained because many participating schools had relatively poor facilities,[16] low teacher salaries, and high teacher turnover.[17] It would appear that parental choice was hindered and, therefore, that the distinction may have been weakened between the educational options open to students with and without vouchers.

Which Intended Outcomes Should Be Tracked?

The intended outcomes of any policy affect significantly what one chooses to track in an evaluation. Key outcomes may be prioritized and identified differently by various groups (such as politicians, administrators, students, and parents). Even within groups, there may be divergence and, hence, potential confusion about which outcomes matter. Finally, the theory of change itself may argue that certain outcomes are intermediate and thus require assessment at various stages of the evaluation.

Existing studies on vouchers have looked at outcomes (such as student achievement, parental satisfaction, class size, truancy, student characteristics, attendance, and graduation rates) for both the control and the treatment groups. However, the key outcomes for those whose decisions the intervention is intended to affect—that is, the parents and the students—may differ from the key outcomes for policymakers and educators. Although student achievement, for example, is an objective and equitable measure for comparing data across schools or school systems, some research indicates that achievement may not be the outcome of primary interest to parents, who instead may give greater priority to the school's location, values, or religious instruction.[18] Alternatively, parents may report that they choose school quality (as indicated by preliminary results from a voucher study in Washington, D.C.), but they define "quality" in terms of parental involvement, curriculum, or class size.[19]

Divergence in terms of how parents and policymakers view key outcomes may also make it difficult to identify which outcomes to study. For example, policymakers may design a choice program that does not include the option of choosing religious schools because of questions about the constitutionality of using public dollars to fund them; but parents may be seeking a school that offers more value-laden instruction rather than rigorous academics. When determining which outcomes to study, the key is to understand the varying viewpoints of the parties involved.

Certain outcomes may require assessment at specific stages throughout the evaluation. A priori, one may theorize that students need a certain amount of time to adjust to a new setting before certain outcomes, such as achievement, are measured. D. Kerbow (1996) did find that student mobility can have a negative impact on achievement, at least for the first year of adjustment, but that students appear to recover during the following years. This study suggests that initial data about choice students' achievement should be examined carefully and that perhaps other outcomes would be helpful in understanding a program's impact. As Kerbow (1996) points out, however, the negative impacts of mobility can be mediated by a systematic entrance/exit strategy whereby participating schools share an individual student's background information and incorporate the student more smoothly into the new school.

Are Research Findings Relevant in the Policy Debate?

Social experiments can often answer critical questions about the impact of particular treatments. However, if decisions or hardened positions already exist regarding the adoption of a program, then research findings may not be considered useful. Some examples of the debate surrounding school vouchers suggest that the positions of the parties are strongly influenced by larger issues about the future of public schools and that the type of information that an impact study could supply would be only marginally useful.

An additional consideration in evaluating the potential utility of research findings stems from an argument regarding who should be served by the voucher program. To be politically relevant, a study must have the right sample. T. E. Moe (1995) argues that vouchers should be inversely correlated with income in order to promote social equity. However, M. Carnoy (1993) suggests that large subsidies for low-income families have not been supported historically by the American public. If the program to be evaluated targets low-income families only, then an impact study may inform only policies considering such a reform. If the sole politically viable option is providing equal vouchers for all children, then findings from the study of a narrowly targeted program would be incomplete and would not address some key political considerations.[20]

A final concern is the standard of evidence that will be used to assess program impacts. If a reform involves great costs (fiscal, administrative, political), then it is likely to be adopted only if it produces very large gains in the relevant outcomes. And if only very large gains would matter, it may not be necessary to use the most rigorous method to estimate impacts. However, if there is interest in having solid estimates of the magnitude of impacts and of how impacts on some outcomes or some subgroups compare with others, then a more reliable research method should be employed.

Key Research Methodology Questions

When a possible experiment meets the threshold of potential policy relevance, a series of issues arises related to the appropriate research design for the study. Among the broad issues to resolve are the scale of the program, the generalizability of findings to other settings, the proper methods for estimating program impacts, the feasibility of implementing research procedures without disrupting program operations, the appropriate follow-up strategy, and the proper scope of linked implementation and participation analysis.

Can the Program Be Large Enough in Scale to Allow for Evaluation of Impacts?

Very small programs may be able to produce many lessons about implementation issues, but they cannot support the type of impact analysis that is the subject of this chapter. In the context of education vouchers, three considerations are important. First, for an impact study to be successful, the sample of students and parents whose experiences are tracked must be large enough to produce findings of sufficient statistical precision to allow the researchers to discern whether a difference between those in the program group and those in the control group is large enough to be "real," that is, unlikely to have occurred by chance. Second, there is an interaction between the questions to be answered and the needed sample size. In this context, the issue revolves around the relative importance of understanding the impact of offering a voucher versus the impact of using the voucher. Third, to the extent that an important consideration is whether institutional adjustment processes could be triggered by vouchers, the sample must be large enough to stimulate such changes. Each of these considerations is discussed separately in the following sections.

Statistical Considerations About Estimating Impacts. Those conducting experiments often rely on the concept of "minimum detectable effects" to decide on the needed sample size for an impact study. The approach has the following goal: to identify the sample size needed to allow the researcher to detect *as statistically significant* estimates that are of a policy-relevant size. Deconstructed, this statement says that the approach focuses on a choice available to the designers of a program and study: How large should the study sample be? It recognizes that one major purpose of a study is to determine whether the program has any impact on the key outcomes of interest (in our case, student achievement could be a focus), or whether the program makes no real difference (i.e., the impacts are zero). Any impact estimate has a "confidence interval" around it, reflecting that any particular experiment may disclose chance differences between the program and control groups (sampling error) because of the specific individuals who are assigned to the two groups.[21] Estimated impacts that are close enough to zero to include zero within their confidence interval are not different from zero in a statistical sense. The analyst cannot be sure that impacts are large enough to make it unlikely that they arose by chance.

A frequent goal in designing an impact study is to have a sample that is big enough to detect program impacts that would "matter" in a policy sense as being statistically significant. The magnitude of policy-relevant impacts is always subjective, reflecting judgments about the importance of making any difference in addressing a problem, past experience with other approaches intended to address the same problem, and the program's financial and other costs.

Intuitively, the needed sample size is a function of:

1. *The size of the impact* to be detected. The smaller the impact (the difference in average outcomes between the program and control groups) that researchers want to be able to detect, the bigger the needed sample.
2. *The variation in the data* for which impacts will be estimated. The stronger the relationship between the program's treatment and a particular level of outcome, the smaller the sample needed.
3. *The degree of desired confidence* that results are correct. The more confident researchers want to be, the bigger the sample needed.

Using this framework and some assumptions about variance and the degree of confidence desired, it is possible to illustrate the size of program impacts that are detectable (as statistically significant) with different sample sizes.[22] Encouragingly, the sample size needed to detect relatively small impacts is well within the bounds of feasibility and similar to the sample sizes of several past and ongoing tests of vouchers. Table 14.1 shows the sample sizes needed to detect various levels of impacts, with the impact defined as the difference in average outcomes between the program and control groups expressed using the concept of effect size. "Effect size" is defined as the multiple of the sample standard deviation. An effect size of 1 would have an impact equal to the sample standard deviation for that outcome.

Although the judgment of how small a minimum detectable effect to seek is subjective, past experience in education reform evaluations can provide some

TABLE 14.1   Illustrative Minimum Detectable Effect Sizes for a Voucher Experiment

If the total sample size is:	Then the minimum detectable effect size is:
100	.35
500	.16
1,000	.11
1,500	.09
2,000	.08

NOTE: This table presents the total sample size, with program and control groups combined. The minimum detectable effect sizes are for a one-tailed test of statistical significance, at the .05 level of statistical significance and 80 percent power. The minimum detectable effect size for a two-tailed test would be approximately 12 percent larger.

context for the information in Table 14.1. A meta-analysis reviewing numerous evaluations of education reforms suggested that effect sizes of .02 or less be characterized as a "small effect," effect sizes of .05 be characterized as a "medium effect," and effect sizes of .08 be characterized as a "large effect."[23] Thus, the minimum detectable effect sizes shown in Table 14.1 imply that with relatively small samples (for example, 500 members) even small effect sizes can be detected. Based on this first consideration, the sample size requirements are well within the range of past tests of vouchers and do not pose any special barriers to this type of study.

The Possibility of Nonuse of the Voucher by Members of the Program Group.   The previous analysis focused on average impacts for the entire program group and assumed that the primary focus of the analysis was the impact of offering vouchers (the policy option available to funders).[24] To the extent that a substantial percentage of those in the program group do not use the voucher, then additional sample size concerns come into play. This is a real issue; in a recent report on the New York City voucher program about 75 percent actually used the voucher to purchase educational services.[25] The actual percentage of the program group (those offered the voucher) who use it will vary depending on the sample intake process, the size of the voucher and conditions on its use, the characteristics of the sample, and the available sources of educational services. But it is unlikely that every program group member will actually use the voucher.

In measuring the impact of the offer of a voucher, the minimum detectable effect size is a function only of the sample size and—when this approach is used— the explanatory power of the independent variables (covariates) used in the regression analysis to increase the precision of the impact estimate. However, the actual size of the impact generated per offer will itself depend directly on the proportion of people in the sample who actually use the voucher (assuming impacts come only or primarily through use of the voucher). Incomplete use of the voucher dilutes the treatment contrast between the program and control groups: The probability of attaining a given impact per voucher offer decreases as the usage rate decreases.[26] Therefore, if researchers anticipate that a substantial percentage of the program group will not use the voucher, their expectations for the likely *impact per voucher offer* would need to be adjusted downward. Consequently, a larger sample would be needed to be able to detect this anticipated smaller impact per voucher offer.

Triggering Broader Adjustments.   The literature on education choice and vouchers as well as on influences on student achievement highlights a variety of possible adjustments that a large-scale voucher program could stimulate. Implicit in the voucher model is the goal of triggering changes in the supply of educational services. As public schools face new competition, they could improve the educational services they offer. Alternatively, public school services might decline in quality with the withdrawal of students and funding. New private school alternatives could emerge to respond to the new demands for private alternatives, and existing private schools could change their offerings in response to a new clientele. To fully exploit the advantages of a market for education and choice about schools, informed choice is important, and new kinds of information about schools might emerge over time.

The research literature also suggests that other adjustments might emerge because of the importance of peer effects both in parental choice of education institutions and in the "production" of educational achievement within a school. If vouchers were broadly available and used, this would give a new group an effective demand for private alternatives. As these vouchers are used, there could be a change in the composition of the student body in many schools, both private and public. If (as the literature suggests) parental choice of schools is affected by who else is attending a school, then school choices by parents could become interdependent over time. One might imagine a situation in which parents and students make their school choice, arrive at the school to discover a different mix of students than they expected, and then make changes in their school choices over time. The extent to which this will happen, the degree to which choices will stabilize or school-switching will disrupt the educational experience of students, and the extent to which the process leads to homogeneous or heterogeneous groupings of students appear to be open questions at this point. Beyond presenting the potential for a complex choice process, the mix of students might also directly affect student outcomes. Some literature suggests that the mix of students in a school affects student achievement, with the clearest effects coming for students at the lower end of the achievement distribution.

Finally, vouchers could stimulate larger political effects on public support for education funding. Withdrawal of students from public schools and public support for private alternatives might lessen public support for education and might lead to greater support because of new service offerings.

If these factors do affect the operation of a voucher system in important ways, then an evaluation of a small-scale program might miss important effects. Further, there is no obvious way to identify whether using a small sample study would over- or underestimate program impacts. The many different factors might pull in different ways, and the nature of the misestimation then depends on the relative importance in the real world of the competing influences.

This possibility calls for one of several strategies: (1) small-scale tests of whether there is substantial sign-up for the voucher offer, changes in school choice, and impacts on individual student outcomes, which are followed by a large-scale study; or (2) studies with samples large enough to trigger adjustments; or (3) a so-called saturation study (where everyone who would be eligible in an area receives the offer) coupled with experiments.[27] For the third alternative, areas for voucher saturation could be selected randomly from matched pairs of sites to improve the design's ability to isolate the effects of vouchers versus other attributes of the local schools.[28] My personal sense is that the existing studies have resolved the threshold questions of sign-up, changes in school choice, and arguable student outcome impacts, so the future choices should focus on the second and third options.

Can the Test of Vouchers Provide Findings of Broader Applicability?

If informing education policy is a goal of the voucher experiment, its designers need to consider the context in which the program operates. When the participating schools are representative of other school systems, it is easier to generalize evaluation results to a broader population. Thus, a useful question to ask is whether the public schools in the program area are typical of other public school systems.

Given the variability of private schools, it is also important to understand the private alternatives that are available to choice students. For example, the Milwaukee Parental Choice Program was initially limited to independent secular schools. But because most private schools in Milwaukee were religious, the participating schools were not representative and, therefore, were unable to inform policy more broadly.[29] If court rulings uphold expansion of Milwaukee's voucher program to include religious schools, this may provide a greater opportunity to inform other cities considering such a reform.

Finally, other ongoing developments in a school system may be so far-reaching and disruptive of normal practice as to undermine the generalizability of findings. For example, the Cleveland voucher program began in September 1996—one year after a federal judge presiding over an existing desegregation order had placed the city's public schools under direct control of the state superintendent of public instruction. In addition, because of budget cutbacks in 1995, Cleveland's public schools system had eliminated full-day kindergarten in all nonmagnet public schools. Forty-two percent of the participants in the voucher program in 1996 were kindergarten students, suggesting that parents may have been seeking full-day kindergarten (as opposed to choosing an alternative situation), an option that was available only in private schools.[30]

Should and Can Random Assignment Be Used to Assess Program Impacts?

The Case for Random Assignment.   Substantial literature assessing the various ways to estimate the impact of social programs highlights the statistical, operational, and ethical pros and cons of different approaches.[31] My sense is that there is no single best method, and the appropriate choice depends on the nature of the intervention being evaluated, the questions to be answered, and the programmatic setting in which the research will be conducted.

As a starting point, some types of changes are not amenable to study through random assignment of individuals or families. These include changes in the nature of the organizational unit that provides the service (e.g., whole school reforms), or changes in policy and programs for which some—or even much—of the effect could result from changing the community's expectations about program services (e.g., comprehensive community initiatives or major overhauls of welfare that emphasize individual responsibilities). For programs providing services to individuals, it is most important to choose a statistically grounded impact estimation approach when the process of selection for eligibility is complex, involving voluntary individual actions to apply for the intervention and numerous decisions by schools about whom to accept.[32] This last situation has characterized most education voucher tests conducted so far.

Consequently, in the absence of a well-executed random-assignment design, it has been very difficult to identify an appropriate group of parents and students against which to compare the experiences of those offered the voucher. For example, almost by definition parents and students who do not apply for vouchers are not the same as successful voucher applicants, even if they appear "similar" on standard measures of socioeconomic status, demographic traits, and student achievement. Some more subtle but important differences—access to information about services; satisfaction with the student's existing level of achievement and educational progress; interest in the vouchers and alternative sources of education; the ability to follow through; and satisfaction with the existing school— somehow led them *not* to apply. And these factors could also influence such key outcomes as attendance, engagement in school, achievement, and promotion. Thus, several things that can affect outcomes (some important, hard-to-measure characteristics plus access to the program) differ between successful applicants and similar nonapplicants, making it difficult if not impossible to attribute any differences in outcomes over time to the intervention under study.[33]

The appropriateness of random assignment also rests on there being more people who would be interested in the service under study than could participate with available funds. This factor has also characterized several recent tests of education vouchers, and it will be discussed in greater detail later in this chapter. Given such a circumstance, some method of allocating scarce program slots has to be devised, and the use of a lottery is a natural choice. Thus, most recent tests of vouchers have included this central element of a random-assignment impact study. The natural application of random assignment and the need for it to address the problem of identifying an appropriate comparison group have led to fairly broad acceptance of random assignment as the best approach for impact studies of vouchers.

The Operational Feasibility of Random Assignment. Beyond the analytical appeal of random assignment in the context of vouchers, it must also be possible to implement the research design without unacceptably disrupting program operations. Four key procedures are discussed in the following sections: (1) developing a standard intake process whereby all those served—and everyone in the research sample—are identified; (2) collecting baseline background information on members of the sample (to describe the sample and identify important subgroups for analysis) and securing informed consent from sample members, if needed; (3) using a lottery at the appropriate point in the intake process to select program group members; and (4) monitoring that members of the program group do receive the offer of a voucher and that members of the control group do not. It appears that each of these procedures is feasible in a test of vouchers for volunteers and in an offer of vouchers to a sample of those who appear to be eligible under program guidelines.

A Standard Intake Process. During a program's initial stages of development, there may be some informality in the application and intake process. During the pilot stage, for example, the goal may be to get some people into the program quickly in order to identify and correct implementation problems. After an impact evaluation is planned, however, intake must be standardized enough so that research procedures can be put in place at all the possible "doors" into the program. If there is decentralized intake or multiple routes into the program, these must be specified concretely enough so that research procedures are consistently applied. In the case of a random-assignment impact study, everyone who ends up in the research sample must have gone through the lottery. Otherwise, the program and control groups will not be comparable, and the core comparison used to produce estimates of program impacts will be invalid.[34]

In the context of a voucher test in which people apply to receive the vouchers, intake can easily be standardized by requiring all applications (even if they are collected in a decentralized way) to be routed through a central point, where a final determination of eligibility is made, applications are reviewed for completeness, and choices are made from among the pool of applicants. In a test of a voucher offer to a sample of those who appear to meet possible eligibility rules; researchers can work with program staff to assemble a list of the eligible pool, a sample can be drawn, and members of this sample can be randomly assigned to the program and control groups. Then program staff can conduct outreach to those in the program group to inform them of their eligibility for the voucher offer.[35]

Collection of Baseline Information and Informed Consent. In cases where people have to apply for the program, as part of this process the staff typically collects background information. Researchers can work with staff to develop a common research and program application form, can rely on the existing program application information, or can supplement that with additional questions. When the test involves offering vouchers to a sample of the eligible population, then researchers either have to rely on whatever information can be gleaned from other existing records (a good strategy when the sample is drawn from those participating in some other program), or have to draw a research sample from the eligible population and contact them before random assignment to collect background information.[36]

The issue of informed consent is handled in many ways. In cases where people apply to receive a voucher, the application process can include information about the study, the lottery for selection, and future data collection. In cases where a sample is drawn from an eligible population and the study is a test of a new opportunity that would be used at the option of the recipient, informed consent is not always sought. If there are special consent requirements for access to data needed for the study follow-up, as may be the case in the test of a voucher, then informed consent is needed. It could be part of a baseline survey done before random assignment.[37]

Use of a Lottery to Allocate Slots. Random assignment of sample members to the program and control groups is appropriate only if it does not result in reducing the number of people who have access to the program. Typically, there is a set amount of money for program services, which implies a maximum program scale. If program services go unused, this can raise ethical issues and is very likely to produce resistance among program staff.

In the context of voucher programs for which individuals volunteer, past experience suggests there can be excess demand for vouchers, with applicants exceeding available vouchers. The extent of excess demand is a function of many things: public outreach and publicity about the voucher program; the level of dissatisfaction with existing schools; the appeal of alternative services; perceptions about whether voucher holders can access these alternative services; the size of the voucher relative to the cost of the alternative services; and conditions placed on the receipt and use of vouchers. Because some of these factors are within the control of designers of a voucher experiment, it appears to be feasible to have an excess demand for the vouchers.[38]

In the context of a test of vouchers for a sample of the eligible population, the concept of demand does not directly apply. However, tests of this type most likely will have program funding that provides far fewer vouchers than would be needed to serve the entire eligible population, thus again requiring some way to allocate access to vouchers.

Consistency of Treatment and Random Assignment Results. For random assignment to produce accurate estimates of impacts, the voucher has to be offered to the program group but cannot be offered to the control group. If this protocol is not followed—either through confusion during the process of informing people or because the program staff does not support the research approach—the resulting impact findings will be undermined, because the program group's experience will not represent the effect of making the voucher offer and the control group's experience will not represent the "world without a voucher." In the center of a program like education vouchers, the offer can be made through a standardized process that ensures voucher payments can be made only to members of the program group. Furthermore, it is important to develop a consistent and clear way to make this offer so that members of the program group will understand the opportunity being presented.

Are There Ways to Build Staff Support for the Study?

A random-assignment study is much easier to implement if the staff involved in program implementation support the goals of the study, understand the reasons for the research approach, and participate in developing detailed plans for the study. This approach produces a better, more realistic set of research procedures and greater staff buy-in to the research effort; it also reduces the cost of monitoring compliance with research protocols.

Past experience suggests that a first important step is listening to the staff's insights and misgivings about the research plan. In this way, many staff concerns can be addressed, and the participatory process creates a sense of ownership in the evaluation. Second, it is important to fashion an analysis plan that will provide findings of interest to the program staff. Many central questions of a study will be relevant to their interests, but it may be possible as well to include special studies of operational issues that are important to them. Third, throughout the project it is vital to recognize in presentations and reports the central role that staff plays in the research.

At What Point During Intake Should the
Random Assignment Lottery Be Inserted?

Both operational and analytical considerations are important influences on the proper point of inserting random assignment, and the research design often represents a balancing of differing perspectives. As discussed above, it is important to seek a point in the intake process where program operations will be disrupted as little as possible. A related operational consideration—relevant in studies of applicants for a voucher—is the burden on staff and potential sample members. The later in the intake process that the lottery is inserted, the greater the administrative burden on program staff. For steps leading up to the lottery, material must be processed for all interested applicants, including those who will eventually end up in the control group. Furthermore, as applicants progress through additional steps in pursuing their applications, staff may form emotional bonds with individuals, making it harder to accept the results of random assignment and perhaps increasing the disappointment of applicants who are assigned to the control group. These considerations call for an insertion point that is early in the intake process.

Other analytical considerations may call for a different decision about random assignment, depending on the key questions the study seeks to answer. If a central purpose of the evaluation is to understand the effect of making an offer of a voucher to those eligible under program guidelines, then random assignment should be done before any formal application process, as shown in Figure 14.1. Staff would be given a list of those randomly assigned to the program group and would contact them to present the voucher opportunity. Thus, operational and analytical considerations would coincide.

Other evaluation purposes would call for later points of random assignment, for example, if the purpose is to understand (1) the effect of access to a voucher on eligible persons who volunteer, or (2) the effect of using a voucher to attend a different school. In the first case, the lottery must come after an explanation of program services, expression of interest, and formal determination of eligibility, as shown in Figure 14.2. In the second case, researchers might also want to assess applicants' circumstances to learn more about whether they would be highly likely to use a voucher if they received one and whether they would be likely to find an alternate school that would accept them, as shown in Figure 14.3.

In the extreme, one might postpone random assignment until the probability of using a voucher is very high—possibly waiting until applicants are accepted in a school where the voucher can be used. In this case, the trade-off with opera-

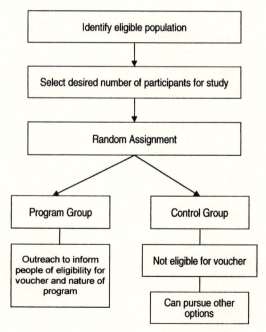

Figure 14.1 Effect of Offering a Voucher to a Representative Sample of Those Eligible

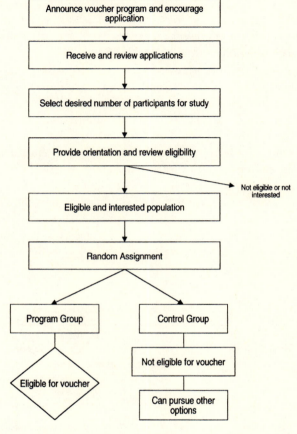

FIGURE 14.2   Effect of Offering a Voucher
to Volunteer Applicants

tional concerns is clear. Furthermore, analytical considerations may argue against very late random assignment. The later that random assignment occurs, the more likely the sample will consist exclusively of parents and students who are highly motivated to switch schools. This raises the probability that those who end up in the control group will continue their search for a way to switch schools, which will increase the percentage of the control group who end up switching schools through other means. Thus, even in this extreme case, there is a need to balance different considerations in selecting the point of random assignment.[39]

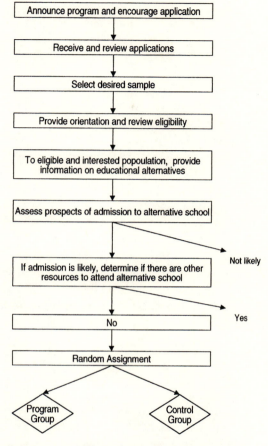

FIGURE 14.3   Effect of Using a Voucher to
Attend a Different School

Particular rules of the voucher program may call for special random-assignment research designs. For example, if the program under study limited eligibility for vouchers to those currently attending public schools, then others might have an incentive to transfer temporarily into the public school system in order to "pick up" the voucher and then return to a nonpublic school. Findings based on a study with a sample made up exclusively of people currently in the public schools could underestimate the participation rates and costs of a full-scale program. This can be avoided through changes in program rules.[40]

What Amount and Type of Baseline Data Should Be Collected?

A random-assignment experiment typically uses baseline information in the following ways:

- *To describe the research sample*, portraying the eligible population or the applicant pool, depending on the type of study. This can be an important part of an implementation study.
- *To identify key subgroups* for special analysis of program implementation, participation, and impacts. These could be groups of special interest to policymakers (for example, those defined on the basis of family income, race, or prior educational achievement) or whose responses to the program warrant special attention.
- *To increase the precision of impact estimates,* which will be based on program and control group comparisons.[41]
- *To determine whether there are response bias problems* in follow-up data and to attempt to correct those that do exist. As discussed later in this chapter, serious problems can arise if follow-up data are unavailable for a large percentage of the overall sample or if specific groups in the sample are underrepresented in the data.[42]

It is also important to note two things for which baseline data are *not* used in an experiment: (1) estimating preprogram trends in key outcomes for use in comparing impacts before and after the program; and (2) matching program group members to others to form a comparison group for impact estimation. These uses would require extensive data about historical trends and subtle descriptive information that are not a part of the impact estimations in an experiment.

Because of the limited purposes of baseline data in an experiment, the extent to which they are collected becomes a strategic choice in research design. In many cases, researchers have chosen to secure baseline data by relying on relatively short survey forms completed by sample members, or even by using administrative records. They instead shifted finite study resources to support a larger sample for the analysis, better follow-up data, and enhancements to the implementation research.

How Can Researchers Ensure That the
Program and Control Groups Get Different Treatment?

The issue of distinctive treatment must be addressed both at the time of random assignment—when the two research groups are formed—and during the subsequent period. When the results of random assignment are first known, program group members quickly should be given a clear explanation of their status and the nature of the vouchers they may access. If the offer of vouchers is a complex message, they may need to hear the information more than once to understand it, and they should be told where they can receive further explanations and follow-up help. It is a mistake to expect members of the program group to undergo several administrative steps before they receive enough information to understand the potential value of the voucher offer; to create the incentive to follow through, one must tell potential users early how they can access the vouchers. Similarly, control group members should receive clear explanations of what they cannot access (the vouchers under study) and what they can do (look for other resources in the community).

In the period following random assignment, it is important to continue monitoring the treatment difference. Are program group members actually receiving an explanation of the voucher offer that they understand, and is there a way for them to get answers to their questions? Are the logistics of following through to use vouchers simple enough so that the program group can accept the offer and use them? Are applicants who have already gone through the lottery (and been assigned to the control group) trying to reapply and get another chance? If so, is the program staff able to identify them (e.g., by consulting a roster of those already randomly assigned) and inform them that they have only one chance and will remain in the control group?

In experiments across many different topics, it is common for some members of the control group to find alternative sources of aid. But a major problem arises if many controls find alternative aid during a study whose goal is to understand the effect of attending private schools instead of public schools. If this happens, it could reflect a poor choice of site (because there are too many sources of similar aid) or poor timing of random assignment—it comes so late that it produces a control group made up of eager and attractive private school applicants who aggressively continue their search for ways to attend these schools.

Can Key Outcomes Be Tracked for Acceptable Costs?

Program impact estimates rest on a comparison of the behavior and experience of members of the program and control groups over time. For an experiment to succeed, researchers must be able to measure key outcomes for a large percentage of the sample over an appropriate follow-up period (discussed further below).

Identifying Proper Measures of Key Outcomes. Agreement about key outcomes is a threshold requirement for undertaking a study (as discussed above), but it is also important that there be ways to measure the key outcomes for acceptable costs in terms of both dollars and intrusion into the lives of sample members and school staff.

In the case of school vouchers, much attention has been focused on the program's effects on educational achievement. Often, this outcome can be tracked using existing student records, including test scores.[43] In most recent studies, these have been supplemented by surveys of parents to understand their reactions to their children's schools and educational progress. Given the relatively small samples in most recent studies, it has been possible to mount a survey despite the substantial costs per survey completion.

Some types of outcomes have proved difficult to track in this setting. For example, it is prohibitively expensive in staff time and intrusiveness to conduct classroom observations for each member of the sample. Instead, measures of the educational experience have typically been collected by surveying the impressions of parents and—for studies of high schools—students.[44]

Ensuring Uniform Measures and Means of Data Collection.   Because impact estimates from an experiment rest on comparisons of the program and control groups, it is vital that the plan to collect follow-up data be the same for both groups—that the same measures of outcomes be used for both groups and that these data be collected in the same way from the same sources. Otherwise, observed differences in key measures might be a function of differences in data-collection methods rather than indicating changes in behavior or experience resulting from access to the program.

One common issue related to data collection concerns documenting participation in programs like the one under study. In the context of a voucher study, depending on its focus, the data might measure people's access to sources of financial aid (the vouchers or some other assistance) or their attendance at private schools. It is very useful to use program records to describe the implementation of the vouchers and the extent to which members of the program group actually made use of the services offered. However, when the focus of the analysis shifts to estimating the difference in activities between the program and control groups, it is not proper to use the participation data from the program under study unless similar records are available for alternatives that the control group might have used.[45]

The timing of data collection and the point in time against which follow-up is measured must also be the same for both groups. To illustrate the first point, imagine that some key outcome is increasing over time for both the program and the control groups and that follow-up data are being collected by a survey. Also, assume that the survey is completed more quickly for members of the program group, per-

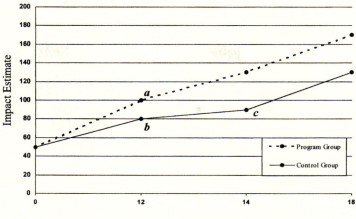

Month Since Random Assignment

Correct impact estimate = *a-b* = 20.
Incorrect impact estimate = *a-c* = 10.

FIGURE 14.4   Effect of Different Timing of Data Collection
SOURCE: Adapted from Larry L. Orr, *Social Experiments:*
Evaluating Public Programs with Experimental Methods
(Thousand Oaks, Calif.: Sage Publicatons, 1999), p. 177.

haps because they are easier to find. Figure 14.4 illustrates the situation. If the impact estimate rests on a report of status at the time of the survey, the difference in the timing of survey completion would produce an artificially small estimate of program impacts because the control group would experience the upward trend for a longer period. For example, in Figure 14.4 the true program impact with the same follow-up period would be 20 points (point *a* minus point *b*), whereas the estimate linked to the different timing of the surveys would be 10 points (point *a* minus point *c*). Although special efforts are needed to keep response rates and the timing of responses similar across the two research groups, for some outcomes it is possible to collect historical data (perhaps by month) so that comparisons can be made at comparable points in time.

It is also vital to start the "follow-up clock" at the same point for both the program group and the control group. Most often this issue arises because program proponents want to focus the analysis on the period when program group members have started to use the services.[46] In the context of a voucher plan, this might lead a researcher to compare the experiences of program group members *after* they accessed a voucher with the experiences of control group members who do not have access to the services. There are two problems with this approach. First, there is no obvious comparable point in time for the control group members. Second, if the analysis is limited to program group members who access the voucher, then this can distort the impact estimate, for these voucher users are almost certainly not a random sample of the full program group.

The way to resolve this dilemma in experimental impact studies is to make all follow-up observations relative to the point of random assignment, because that date has meaning for both groups and because that is the point at which the two similar groups were identified through a random process. By reporting impact estimates by periods relative to the date of random assignment (the first period after random assignment, the second period after, and so forth), the researcher's basic experimental impact comparison remains valid. Further, it is possible to focus analysis on different phases throughout the follow-up period: a phase when program group members are accessing the program, a phase when they are using program services, and a phase after they have received program services.

High Completion Rates for Follow-Up Data.   Even though random assignment produces comparable program and control groups, if the follow-up data-collection strategy does not generate information about a large percentage of both groups, then the basic experimental comparison can be undermined. (The research literature often labels this a "response bias" problem.) Randomly distributed nonresponse does not alter the expected values of the average outcomes for the program and control groups (so it does not bias impact estimates), but it does reduce the sample size and, thus, the statistical power to find impacts of a given magnitude. However, when nonresponse is greater among either research group or among members with certain characteristics (such as boys), then impacts may be biased somewhat unless corrected for nonresponse.[47]

The problem of low or different follow-up completion rates is often thought to be associated with surveys, but it can also occur when students' school records are used. For example, if records are available only for a certain school district, and/or it is hard to track individual students' records if their family status or residence changes, then researchers can fail to collect follow-up information for a substantial portion of the sample. A program group–versus–control group difference in follow-up rates can arise if the program stabilizes students' residences and household experiences or if contact information is collected from those administering the vouchers (who are in touch with members of the program group) but no comparable contact information is available for members of the control group.

How Long Should the Subsidy Offer and Follow-Up Period Be, and Which Outcomes Should Be Tracked at Various Stages?

Before deciding on the duration of the voucher offer and of follow-up research and the analytic focus at different stages of the project, it is useful to clarify the assumptions of program designers and operators about how vouchers lead to improvements in educational outcomes. Two underlying aspects of the program's theory of change can inform the design of an impact study. At one level, vouchers are intended to raise educational outcomes by helping students move from weaker schools to stronger schools, thereby improving the educational services they receive and supporting their efforts to learn. At another level, the theory of vouchers rests on the notion that enabling parents to select an educational-services supplier in a market will lead to improvements in educational outcomes both by helping students find the right supplier for them and by stimulating innovation and improvements among existing suppliers as well as entry of new suppliers.[48]

What findings could emerge from a short (perhaps one- or two-year) follow-up? This period of follow-up would reveal changes in school choice and would provide estimates of the effects on intermediate outcomes such as attendance in school, engagement in the learning process, time on task, and so on. It is also possible that impacts on student achievement could emerge this quickly.[49] But this short-term follow-up will probably not provide the full story, because it may take more time for the new school's educational approach to affect student outcomes; there may be a settling-in period as students and parents get used to the new school setting and become integrated into the educational process and as the school learns how best to teach its new students.

The market metaphor for vouchers suggests that the perspective of a much longer time is needed to reveal a full picture, and that short-term impacts should be interpreted as the effects of the first level of market adjustment. This conclusion rests on three considerations.

First, adjustments by parents, students, and schools are not costless, and the voucher offer has to be seen as lasting long enough to warrant responding to it. A very short-term test of a subsidy would prompt a more modest response (only the easiest things would be done) than an offer that is seen as stable enough to be incorporated into long-term planning. Many different experiments with subsidies have faced this issue (sometimes called "duration bias"), including tests of health insurance, housing assistance, income support, and earnings subsidies for low-income workers. Two approaches have been taken: offer the subsidy for a very long time,[50] or consciously vary the length of the subsidy for members of the sample and try to learn about likely long-term effects from the variation (or lack thereof) observed across different-length treatments.[51]

Second, creation of a market does not imply immediate improvements in customer satisfaction and outcomes; there is no guarantee that in a new market consumers and producers will make the proper choices the first time out. Markets have strength as a means of making resource choices because of the pressures they create for continued adjustment and improvement through individually expressed demand motivated by self-interest, competition on the supply side, and growing information about market conditions, the production process, and costs. In markets for frequently purchased products where new suppliers face few barriers to entry, adjustments can be rapid (luncheonettes come and go quickly), but choices about schools and the emergence of new educational options are often linked to an annual school-year cycle, implying a much slower adjustment process.[52]

Third, in the market adjustment process the choices of consumers and producers are interdependent. Parents' and students' reactions to a school are affected by who else attends it; the choice of a school also implies the choice of a peer group. This is important in several ways. Parents may be seeking a student body that reflects their values (diversity of race and class or lack thereof, common perspectives on religion or school discipline, etc.). Further, there is evidence that students' educational achievement is influenced by the peer group in the school. This peer-group effect on achievement may be more important for students who are performing at lower levels and be less important for those at the higher end.[53] At any rate, the adjustment process can be complex as parents adjust to the previous choices of other parents and schools adapt to a changing student body—a process that can continue for a considerable length of time.[54]

What Are the Key Questions for Implementation Research in a Voucher Experiment?

Impact findings alone—without an understanding of program implementation—are difficult to interpret and provide few lessons for future policy and administration. Therefore, experiments should include an analysis of the nature the sample, the treatment under study (and, to some extent, other services received by sample members), participation in services (those being studied and other related services), and program costs. Such an analysis can then build to an assessment of whether the program received a "fair test" and how to interpret any observed impacts.

The Characteristics of the Sample.   Describing the sample intake process and the nature of the resulting sample is one of the initial steps in most implementation research, and it should be part of voucher experiments as well. Baseline data can usually be used to outline the characteristics of those in the study; to make comparisons with other groups, such as the eligible population; to assess whether the program reached those it was designed to serve; and to identify any key subgroups within the sample that warrant special analysis. Further, it will be possible to analyze the level of interest in the program, the number of applicants, differences in application rates among subgroups (defined by such things as race and prior student achievement), and whether anything in the intake process may have affected the sample's composition.

Implementation of Program Services.   Next the focus is on describing what the treatment actually turned out to be. Research and evaluations are strewn with examples of implementation problems and major differences between a program's theory and practice. In the context of education vouchers, it is vital to learn how the offer of a voucher was delivered and what the members of the program group understood the offer to be. Although the concept of education vouchers seems simple in theory, many aspects of voucher use need to be explained to members of the program group: detailed eligibility rules, the amount and duration of the subsidy, lists of schools where vouchers can be used, and other conditions of participation. Probing to learn sample members' understanding of these topics and their reactions to the offer will contribute to an understanding of the program and its impacts.[55]

In a program intended to stimulate new school choices and changes in the available educational offerings, it is also important to look for the emergence of new schools or new approaches in existing schools in order to encourage parents and students to select those schools. Further, there is the possibility in the long run that the schools that voucher users leave will experience a decrease in services and/or degradation of the educational experience because of a change in the student body or declining funding of educational services outside the voucher program.

Participation in Services.   In a voucher experiment, the program group represents the experiences of those given access to vouchers; the control group repre-

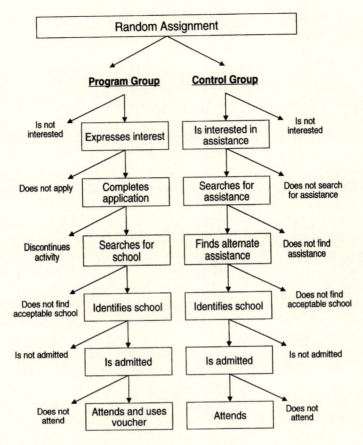

FIGURE 14.5   Eligible Population's Potential Responses in
Test of Vouchers

sents the experiences of those who are not eligible for vouchers but can search for
and access other community resources. It is likely to be true that some members
of the program group will not take advantage of the offer and that some members
of the control group will succeed in finding alternative ways to attend
schools where vouchers can be used. Thus, in interpreting observed differences in
key outcomes over time, it is vital to know what the members of the program and
control groups actually did.

Figures 14.5 and 14.6 illustrate the complexity of the responses that members
of the program and control groups might have to the options open to them.

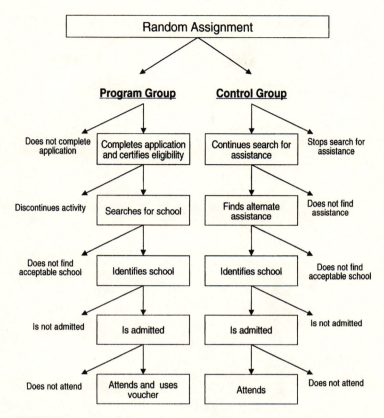

FIGURE 14.6   Volunteers' Potential Responses in Test of
Vouchers

These figures highlight the importance of studying program participation in order to answer questions like those below. Many of these questions can be addressed through a follow-up survey of parents, which would also focus on the key outcomes for the impact study. Some questions for the program group include:

- What proportion of the program group followed through the various steps needed to access and use the vouchers?
- Why did people pursue the offer or choose not to?
- At which schools did people use the vouchers, and what were the schools like?

- What did parents think of the schools, both in absolute terms and relative to prior schools?
- Over time, was there changing use of vouchers or shifts in schools chosen?
- What were people's overall reactions and plans for future school choices?
- For those not using vouchers, which schools did students attend and why, and what were their reactions to these schools?

Questions for the control group:

- Were people able to access other sources of financial assistance?
- Which schools did the students attend, and what were their reactions to these schools?

Information on participation in the program under study and similar programs will be the basis for describing the "treatment difference" between the program and control groups. To illustrate the importance of this, imagine that in a study focusing on the effects of offering vouchers one found that a small percentage of the program group actually accessed a voucher and that some in the control group found alternative aid. This would lead one to expect small impacts on educational outcomes but—should they occur—it would *not* lead to the conclusion that offering financial aid had little effect on student outcomes. Alternatively, if one found a large difference in treatment (many in the program group took up the voucher offer, and few in the control group found alternate assistance), then one would expect larger impacts if providing access to financial aid "worked" to improve student outcomes. Impacts of a small size would be evidence of the ineffectiveness of raising student outcomes by providing financial aid.

Program Costs.   Program operators often have information about the costs of services provided to the program group—for example, how many members used vouchers, of what amounts, and for how long. They also often have the information needed to estimate the administrative costs of running the program. Usually researchers rely on these data to calculate program costs, often excluding any costs arising because the program was part of a research project that involved special data collection. It is common to calculate costs after a start-up period, when the program is operating at a larger scale in somewhat of a steady state. Cost information is often presented in a standardized way as the *cost per program group member.*

In the context of an impact study, researchers typically also develop a cost estimate for similar or substitute services provided to the control group outside the program under study. This cost estimate can then be combined with the cost per program group member to estimate a *net cost of the program*, that is, the cost of the added services received by the program group. Because impact estimates represent the improvement in outcomes produced by the extra services that the program group receives, the net cost of services per program group member is the appropriate comparison in weighing program benefits and costs.

A Context for Impact Estimates: Did the Program Get a Fair Test? One way to summarize implementation findings in the context of an impact study is to discuss whether an experiment provided a "fair test" of a program. This involves a judgment as to whether the program was implemented well enough to represent what the experience would typically be when the program is operated. The normal problems of implementation (a busy staff and clients who make competing demands on their time, the difficulties of recruiting and retaining staff at given salary levels, normal management and communication problems, etc.) would not make a test unfair. But problems caused by the research (such as a design that seriously hampers program intake or participation, excessive burdens of data collection that diverts staff from operational responsibilities, etc.) could make a test unfair in this sense. In addition, extraordinary problems arising outside the scope of the study (a major natural disaster disrupting services and daily life, an agency closing, unforeseen unusual events that drive up costs, etc.) would lead one to conclude that an experiment was not a fair test.

One complicated issue arises when an experiment produces a small treatment difference between the program group and the control group. If this occurs because the program did not appeal to those who were offered access and so participation was low, this is an important finding in itself and does not invalidate impact findings. However, if the small treatment difference occurs because of unexpectedly high levels of control group services (e.g., another educational financial aid program opens), then the researchers cannot estimate the impacts of the program under study.[56]

What Impact Estimates Are Appropriate, and How Should They Be Interpreted?

The basic experimental impact estimates rest on comparisons between the experiences of all members of the program group and all members of the control group. Often, outcomes are measured either as averages (such as average test score) or as rates (i.e., some percentage of the group achieved some outcome) for each group. Findings are usually presented in simple ways, for example, by presenting direct comparisons of the outcome levels for the program and control groups and reporting the resulting difference as the impact, with an indication of whether the impact differs from zero by a statistically significant amount. When baseline information is available, researchers often estimate impacts by running a regression, with the outcome of interest as the dependent variable and with baseline characteristics and a treatment dummy variable as dependent variables. The coefficient of the treatment dummy in this regression is the impact estimate. This regression approach increases the statistical precision of the impact estimate but does not change the expected value of the impact estimate.

Within the full sample, impacts can be calculated for subgroups *defined at the basis of prerandom assignment characteristics.* Examples might include subgroups defined by gender, race, or previous educational achievement. Such comparisons are possible because individuals with any of these characteristics were assigned to the program group and the control group randomly. Subgroup impacts are calculated by applying the full-sample approach to specific subgroups (e.g., calculating impacts for boys in the sample and then calculating impacts for girls). Thus, impacts are estimated by comparing boys in the program group with boys in the control group, and by comparing girls in the program group with girls in the control group.[57]

Efforts to calculate impacts for subgroups defined on the basis of postrandom assignment experience carry the analysis beyond the realm of experimental research. An example of this type of subgroup is one whose members attended private school for more than one year or attended for one year and then returned to public school. Many techniques have been tried for this work, but such an analysis does face the basic problem of all nonexperimental research: finding a statistical technique that avoids selection bias. Because people who fall into a subgroup based on postrandom assignment behavior are not a random sample of the full program group, it is very hard to identify their control group counterparts—as would be needed to support a valid comparison.

Given Nonparticipation Among Program Group Members, Can Impacts Be Estimated per Participant?

If a substantial percentage of the program group does not participate in a voucher program, this is an important finding. Researchers should place this finding in the proper context (e.g., was the sample randomly drawn from the eligible population or from volunteers?) and should try to understand the reasons for nonparticipation. In some cases, there will be an independent interest in estimating the impacts of *using the voucher*, separate from the standard impacts of *offering the voucher* (the latter rests on a comparison of the entire program group and the entire control group).

As a starting point, it is not appropriate to compare those members of the program group who used vouchers with members of the control group. It is virtually certain that people in the program group who used vouchers are different in some important ways from those who did not. They may differ on things like knowledge of educational alternatives, ability to negotiate through agencies and schools, time available to seek educational alternatives, and dissatisfaction with their existing school. All these factors could also affect key outcomes. Thus, a comparison of voucher users and the control group could not isolate the effect of using vouchers, because other characteristics of the two groups also differ. Further, because control group members never have the option of participating, it is not possible to identify the control group counterparts of those in the program group who participated.[58]

Two techniques (which are equivalent under certain conditions) have been used to estimate impacts per user or participant. The more intuitive of the two approaches rests on the assumptions that in a voluntary program all the effects of the program occur through participation or use of the program, and that those who choose not to participate are unaffected by the program.[59] The overall impact on the program group is a weighted average of the impact on participants and the impact on nonparticipants, where the weights reflect the proportion of the program group in each category. If the assumptions mentioned are correct, then the impact on nonparticipants is zero, and the overall impact equals the impact on participants multiplied by the proportion of the program group that participates. The no-show adjustment is fundamentally different from a comparison of voucher users with the control group in that the no-show adjustment makes no assumption that users and nonusers are similar; it assumes only that all impacts come through use of a voucher.[60]

To illustrate the use of the adjustment, imagine that in an experiment three-fourths of the program group use the voucher and one-fourth does not. This is approximately the split in the ongoing New York City School Choice Scholarships Foundation study.[61] Thus, if the impacts per program group member were 100 points on an outcome, then the impact per voucher user would be 100 divided by .75, or 133.

This approach, often called the "no-show adjustment," does not affect the statistical significance of impact estimates. Estimates of impact per program group member that are not statistically significant do not become statistically significant when converted to a per-user basis.[62] Further, the adjustment does not "create" impacts where none previously existed: If there are no impacts per program group member, then there are no impacts per user.

In applying the no-show adjustment to a study of vouchers, it is important to consider outcomes individually and to assess the appropriateness of the key assumption of the adjustment. For some outcomes—such as changes in class size, teaching methods, the school facility, and the like—it seems safe to assume that observed impacts for the program group are driven by those members who use the vouchers to change schools. For an outcome like parental satisfaction with the existing school, however, it is possible that even those parents in the program group who do not use the voucher might be affected by having the voucher as an option. They may feel less "trapped" in the existing school but have decided to stay there after investigating other options; this might affect their level of satisfaction with the school. When there is a possibility that the voucher might have had some impacts on nonusers, the no-show adjustment would produce an impact estimate that should be seen as the "upper bound" estimate of the impact per user.

Conclusion

Experiments using random assignment to study education reforms are not common events. The nature of many education reforms may make random assignment the wrong analytic approach, or the local administrative and political setting may make random assignment infeasible. However, for pilot tests of education vouchers, a random-assignment experiment does seem to be a natural approach for evaluating program impacts. In fact, operational considerations have often led program staff to include the central element of random assignment—a lottery for entrance—in the normal applicant-selection process.

The choice of random assignment as the method for estimating program impacts is only the first step, and this chapter has offered a series of questions to help designers of research make the most of this experimental approach. Many questions arise in using random assignment to study vouchers—most of them questions that have surfaced and been addressed in other contexts. It is hoped that by identifying basic issues and proposing options to resolve them, this analysis will increase the chances that research on education vouchers will answer important policy and social questions.

Notes

1. This chapter will offer a specific definition of experiments to try to lessen some of the confusion in the literature evaluating education vouchers. Many different types of analy-

sis are being called experiments, but many do not rely on the basic comparisons at the heart of a random assignment study.

2. For a review of this issue and the role of evaluations, see Stephan D. Kennedy, "Direct Cash Low-Income Housing Assistance," in Howard S. Bloom, David S. Cordray, and Richard J. Light, eds., *Lessons from Selected Program and Policy Areas: New Directions in Program Evaluation* (San Francisco: Jossey-Bass, 1988).

3. Henry Levin, "The Theory of Choice Applied to Education," in William Clune and John Witte, eds., *Choice and Control in American Education, vol. 1: The Theory of Choice and Control in Education* (New York: Falmer Press, 1990).

4. John F. Witte, "School Choice and Student Performance," in Helen F. Ladd, *Holding Schools Accountable: Performance-Based Reform in Education* (Washington, D.C.: Brookings Institution Press, 1996).

5. John E. Chubb and Terry M. Moe, "Choice Is a Panacea," *Brookings Review* 8(3) (Summer 1990): 4–12.

6. Levin, "Theory of Choice."

7. Paul E. Peterson, David E. Myers, and William G. Howell, *An Evaluation of the New York City School Choice Scholarships Program: The First Year* (Cambridge: Program on Education Policy and Governance, Harvard University, 1998).

8. John F. Witte, "Achievement Effects of the Milwaukee Voucher Program" (Madison: University of Wisconsin, Department of Political Science and the Robert M. LaFollette Institute of Public Affairs, 1997). Alex Molnar, "Educational Vouchers: A Review of the Research" (Milwaukee: Center for Education Research, Analysis, and Innovation, University of Wisconsin–Milwaukee, 1999).

9. Richard F. Elmore, "Choice as an Instrument of Public Policy: Evidence from Education and Health Care," in Clune and Witte, *Choice and Control.*

10. Terry M. Moe, "Private Vouchers," in Terry M. Moe, ed., *Private Vouchers* (Stanford: Hoover Institution Press, 1995).

11. Peterson et al., *An Evaluation.*

12. Ibid.

13. Ibid.

14. Cecilia Elena Rouse, "Private School Vouchers and Student Achievement: An Evaluation of the Milwaukee Parental Choice Program," *Quarterly Journal of Economics* 113(2) (May 1998): 553–602.

15. Jay P. Greene, Paul E. Peterson, and Jiangtao Du, "Effectiveness of School Choice: The Milwaukee Experiment" (Cambridge: Program on Education Policy and Governance and Center for American Political Studies, Harvard University, 1997). Later amendments to the program expanded its scale.

16. Ibid. (on facilities); Witte, "Achievement Effects."

17. Elmore, "Choice as an Instrument."

18. Peterson et al., *An Evaluation.*

19. Depending on the patterns of impacts seen, a study of a broad program might produce findings that support narrower targeting.

20. For a discussion of the statistics behind social experiments, see Larry L. Orr, *Social Experiments: Evaluating Public Programs with Experimental Methods* (Thousand Oaks, Calif.: Sage Publications, 1999).

21. The calculations presented assume use of a random-assignment impact analysis de-

sign with an equal number of program and control group members, a confidence level of .05 for a one-tailed test, a statistical power of 80 percent, and an R^2 of .05 for a regression of prerandom assignment covariances and treatment status on the outcome for which impacts are being estimated.

22. Mark Lipsey, *Design Sensitivity: Statistical Power for Experimental Research* (Thousand Oaks, Calif: Sage Publications, 1990), pp. 54–55.

23. As discussed later in this paper, the core impact estimates are those estimated per voucher offer; they come directly from a comparison of the program and control groups.

24. Peterson et al., *An Evaluation.*

25. As the rate of nonuse increases, for a given impact per voucher user the observed impact per voucher offered declines.

26. The housing assistance field faced similar issues and developed a combined approach somewhat like that mentioned. See Kennedy, "Direct Cash." Some efforts have been made to model within a simulation framework the complexities of school choice under a voucher system. See Charles Manski, "Educational Choice (Vouchers) and Social Mobility," *Economics of Education Review* 11(4) (1992): 351–369, for an example. As Manski illustrates, the resolution of this complex topic depends on a variety of factors.

27. See Howard Bloom, Johannes Bos, and Suk-Won Lee, *Using Cluster Random Assignment to Measure Program Impacts: Statistical Implications for the Evaluation of Education Programs* (New York: Manpower Demonstration Research Corporation, 1999).

28. Rouse, "Private School Vouchers."

29. Dan Murphy, F. Howard Nelson, and Bella Rosenberg, "The Cleveland Voucher Program: Who Choses? Who Gets Chosen? Who Pays?" (Washington, D.C.: American Federation of Teachers, 1997).

30. For a nontechnical summary of various approaches, see Peter Rossi, Howard Freeman, and Mark Lipsey, *Evaluation: A Systematic Approach* (Thousand Oaks, Calif.: Sage Publications, 1999). For a somewhat more technical review, see Lawrence B. Mohr, *Impact Analysis for Program Evaluation* (Thousand Oaks, Calif.: Sage Publications, 1995).

31. In the literature on evaluations, this problem is discussed under the label "selection bias." If the process that people go through to be selected for the program is complex and involves subtle, difficult-to-model decisions by parents, students, and schools, then it is hard to identify other parents and students who would have been selected for the program if they had applied.

32. Some programs allocate slots on a first-come, first-served basis, and it is tempting to compare successful applicants with those denied entry or placed on a waiting list. Once again, however, there are likely to be differences between those early, successful applicants and others who applied.

33. In past studies, it has proved feasible to set aside some program slots for people who are not included in the research sample but who "need" to be served because of local political concerns or special needs for service. But the larger the number of "excluded" program slots, the more there can be concerns about the ability of the research sample to represent the experiences of the type of people who will be part of the ongoing program.

34. Depending on how eligibility is defined, there may not be any overall list of the eligible population. If eligibility is linked to income, there may be ways to use lists of students eligible for other income-tested programs, such as free or reduced-price school meals. It is also possible to conduct a community survey of residents of a target area where the voucher is to be tested to identify households that meet the eligibility rules.

35. In some studies, background information has been collected immediately after random assignment. This is possible only if contact with sample members can be made quickly (so their circumstances do not change) and if researchers do not need informed consent (which requires a personal contact and explanation before the subject enters the study).

36. In some studies, follow-up is done through surveys of sample members whose participation in the survey is requested but not required. In that case, advance informed consent may not be needed.

37. In the New York City School Choice Scholarships Foundation program, for example, 20,000 people submitted initial applications to receive 1,300 scholarships, and voucher experiments in Washington, D.C., and Dayton, Ohio, also had initial applications far exceeding available scholarships. See Peterson et al., *An Evaluation*. In the Washington, D.C., Scholarship Fund Pilot Program, more than 7,500 people submitted initial applications for approximately 1,000 scholarships. In Dayton's PACE program, about 3,800 people submitted initial applications for about 800 scholarships. See Paul E. Peterson et al., *Initial Findings from an Evaluation of School Choice Programs in Washington, D.C., and Dayton, Ohio* (Cambridge: Program on Education Policy and Governance, Harvard University, 1998). The experience in Milwaukee suggests that excess demand is not always the case. There, the scale of the program did not reach the permitted size in its early years. See John F. Witte, *First Year Report: Milwaukee's Parental Choice Program* (Madison: University of Wisconsin, Department of Political Science and the Robert M. LaFollette Institute of Public Affairs, 1991).

38. As phrased here, this could sound like a problem that is unique to random assignment and that might be avoided through nonexperimental techniques. But a similar problem exists with those methods. The more the statistical technique is successful in identifying a comparison group made up of people who have not expressed an interest in finding an alternate school before entering the sample (thus reducing the chance that they will subsequently make this switch), the more likely it is that the comparison group will be different in important ways from the program group.

39. Perhaps eligibility could be limited to those who have been in the public schools for a specified time period. Alternatively, researchers could put in place a more complex random-assignment design or could attempt to estimate any changes in the normal rate of transfers into the public schools while the voucher offer is in place. For an effort to address a similar issue in a financial subsidy program, see David Card, Phillip Robins, and Winston Lin, *How Important Are "Entry Effects" in Financial Incentive Programs for Welfare Recipients? Experimental Evidence from the Self-Sufficiency Project* (Ottawa: Social Research and Demonstration Corporation, 1997).

40. In a regression analysis, baseline characteristics are often used as independent variables along with a dummy variable for the program group, with the dependent variable being the outcome under study. If there are small differences in baseline characteristics between the program and control groups, this regression adjustment will increase the precision of the impact estimates.

41. In some experiments, baseline data are also used for nonexperimental comparisons beyond the basic comparisons of program and control groups. A relevant example would be seeking to identify the control group counterparts of program group members who actually use the vouchers. If this were possible, then one could estimate nonexperimentally the effect of actually using the voucher. Researchers have not had great success in devel-

oping reliable methods to do this, inasmuch as it presents the same problems of selection bias that prompt use of random assignment in the first place.

42. Some types of educational impact studies are plagued by differences in the tests used by different schools or by changes in a school's tests during the period of study. The experimental research design is actually an advantage in this regard, as long as all members of the sample in a site are affected by the test change. Because experimental impact estimates rely on a comparison of program group–versus–control group outcomes rather than on an analysis of trends in outcomes, test changes can be accommodated. Greater problems emerge if members of the program and control groups are measured using more than one test; at times researchers have been forced to administer special achievement tests or to use other data to convert test scores to a common metric.

43. Although classroom observations are often conducted as part of a study of program implementation, findings are not individualized and connected to specific sample members.

44. In some studies, researchers have tried to use participation data from the program under study to document participation in its services and then to use a follow-up survey to ask sample members about participation in all other programs. This approach is likely to have two problems: Sample members often have trouble determining the source of assistance they received (was it from the program under study or some alternative?), and respondents to surveys tend to underreport the extent to which they participated in services. Both problems could lead to misestimation of the service difference between the program group and the control group. See Orr, *Social Experiments,* pp. 176–180, for some examples of the problems that might arise and the pros and cons of various strategies. The following points in the text are also discussed by Orr (see, e.g., chapter 5 in his book).

45. When a study is examining a program that offers services of a set duration, the comparable analytic focus would be on the postprogram period, that is, after program group members have had time to complete the program and begin to see its effects.

46. For example, if a study had follow-up data for 80 percent of the program group but only 60 percent of the control group, it is likely that the two samples available for impact estimates would no longer be comparable. The control group follow-up sample excludes those who were hard to find, possibly because of changes in residential location, household composition, or school attended; these characteristics are also likely to lead to lower educational outcomes. Experience suggests that the best research strategy is to devote enough resources to follow-up data collection to avoid differential rates of nonresponse, because statistical methods may not be able to correct problems after the fact. Orr reaches the same conclusion in *Social Experiments,* pp. 215–218.

47. Various economists have argued for this position, most notably, Milton Friedman in *Capitalism and Freedom* (Chicago: University of Chicago Press, 1962). More recently, John E. Chubb and Terry M. Moe have raised a similar argument in *Politics, Markets, and America's Schools* (Washington, D.C.: Brookings Institution Press, 1990); and "Politics, Markets, and the Organization of Schools," *American Political Science Review* 82 (1988): 1065–1087. For a discussion of this view of vouchers, see also "Market Approaches to Education: Vouchers and School Choice," *Economics of Education Review* 11(4) (special issue, December 1992).

48. See, e.g., Peterson et al., *An Evaluation,* for first-year impacts from the New York City School Choice Scholarships Foundation program.

49. It can prove difficult to maintain the offer in place for a long time. In the Negative Tax Income experiments, one research group was offered twenty-year eligibility for the

income support program. But as support for the study declined, the researchers had to buy out this research group after only eight years of eligibility.

50. This design could be accomplished by randomly assigning members of the sample either to the control group (not receiving any subsidy) or to program groups that receive one of several subsidies of varying length.

51. Even very dissatisfied parents will weigh the likely educational disruption of a midyear shift against the hoped-for gains from a "better" school.

52. For a brief summary of the research on this topic and references to other studies, see Henry M. Levin, "Educational Vouchers: Effectiveness, Choice, and Costs," *Journal of Policy Analysis and Management* 17(3) (Summer 1998): 381–382.

53. For discussions of the complex school choice and adjustment process that may occur even within a simulation model, which involves simplifying assumptions, see Manski, "Educational Choice"; and Steven M. Glazerman, "Determinants and Consequences of Parental School Choice," Ph.D. dissertation (University of Chicago, 1997).

54. Many other studies of subsidies for low-income people have discovered that the details of program rules were hard to convey. This was an issue in the New Hope Demonstration, the Canadian Self-Sufficiency Project, and even the Negative Income Tax experiments.

55. One exception would arise if the supply of financial aid were expanded to see whether there was unmet demand and this expansion did not result in increased use.

56. The approach described would calculate impacts for subgroups that can differ on characteristics other than the one used to define the subgroup split. For example, boys in a sample might have different prior attendance patterns or achievement scores than girls. Some analysis also controls statistically for these differences and seeks to isolate whether the individual subgroup characteristic under analysis leads to a difference in impacts. See Bernard Ostle, *Statistics in Research* (Ames: Iowa State University Press, 1975), for the logic of this approach; and for an example of its use see George Cave et al., *JOBSTART: Final Report on a Program for School Dropouts* (New York: Manpower Demonstration Research Corporation, 1993).

57. Once again, efforts to use statistical techniques to avoid this selection bias face the same difficulties as any nonexperimental impact evaluation.

58. See Howard S. Bloom, "Accounting for No-Shows in Experimental Evaluation Designs," *Evaluation Review* 8 (1984): 225–246.

59. The second technique for estimating impacts per participant or user involves the instrumental variables approach. It is used in Peterson et al., *An Evaluation.* The no-show adjustment and instrumental variables produce the same result if research status (program versus control) is the only instrument used to estimate an equation predicting participation.

60. See Peterson et al., *An Evaluation.*

61. Basically, the standard error of the estimate is scaled up by the same factor as is the impact estimate. Because the t statistic of an impact estimate is a ratio of the impact estimate and its standard error, scaling up both the numerator and denominator leaves the ratio unchanged. See Bloom, "Accounting for No-Shows."

References

Bloom, H. S. (1984). Accounting for no-shows in experimental evaluation designs. *Evaluation Review* 8, 225–246.

Card, D., Robins, P., and Lin, W. (1997). *How important are "entry effects" in financial incentive programs for welfare recipients? Experimental evidence from the self-sufficiency project.* Ottawa: Social Research and Demonstration Corporation.

Carnoy, M. (1993). School improvement: Is privatization the answer? In J. Hannaway and M. Carnoy (eds.), *Decentralization and school improvement.* San Francisco: Jossey-Bass.

Cave, G., Bos, J., Doolittle, F., and Toussant, C. (1993). *JOBSTART: Final report on a program for school dropouts.* New York: Manpower Demonstration Research Corporation.

Chubb, J. E., and Moe, T. M. (1988). Politics, markets, and the organization of schools. *American Political Science Review* 82, 1065–1087.

_____. Choice is a panacea. *Brookings Review* 8(3), 4–12.

_____. (1990). *Politics, markets, and America's schools.* Washington, D.C.: Brookings Institution Press.

Elmore, R. F. (1990). Choice as an instrument of public policy: Evidence from education and health care. In W. Clune and J. Witte (eds.), *Choice and control in American education,* vol. 1. New York: Falmer.

Friedman, M. (1962). *Capitalism and freedom.* Chicago: University of Chicago Press.

Glazerman, S. M. (1998). *Determinants and consequences of parental school choice.* Ph.D. diss., University of Chicago.

Greene, J. P., Peterson, P. E., and Du, J. (1997). Effectiveness of school choice: The Milwaukee experiment. Cambridge: Harvard University, Kennedy School of Government, Program on Education Policy and Governance.

Kennedy, S. D. (1988). Direct cash low-income housing assistance. In H. S. Bloom, D. S. Cordray, and R. J. Light (eds.), *Lessons from selected program and policy areas: New directions in program evaluation.* San Francisco: Jossey-Bass.

Kerbow, D. (1996). *Patterns of urban student mobility and local school reform: A technical report.* Report No. 5. Baltimore: Center for Research on the Education of Students Placed at Risk (CRESPAR).

Levin, H. M. (1990). The theory of choice applied to education. In W. Clune and J. Witte (eds.), *Choice and control in American education,* vol. 1. New York: Falmer.

_____. (1998). Educational vouchers: Effectiveness, choice, and costs. *Journal of Policy Analysis and Management* 17, 381–382.

_____. (ed.). (1992). Market approaches to education: Vouchers and school choice. *Economics of Education Review* 11(4) (special issue).

Lipsey, M. (1990). *Design sensitivity: Statistical power for experimental research.* Thousand Oaks, Calif.: Sage Publications.

Manski, C. (1992). Educational choice (vouchers) and social mobility. *Economics of Education Review* 11(4), 351–369.

Moe, T. E. (1995). Private vouchers. In T. E. Moe (ed.), *Private vouchers.* Stanford: Hoover Institution Press.

Mohr, L. B. (1995). *Impact analysis for program evaluation.* Thousand Oaks, Calif.: Sage Publications.

Murphy, D. F., Nelson, H., and Rosenberg, B. (1997). The Cleveland voucher program: Who choses? Who gets chosen? Who pays? Washington, D.C.: American Federation of Teachers.

Orr, L. L. (1999). *Social experiments: Evaluating public programs with experimental methods.* Thousand Oaks, Calif.: Sage Publications.

Ostle, B. (1975). *Statistics in research*. Ames: Iowa State University Press.

Peterson, P. E., Greene, J. P., Howell, W .G., and McCready, M. (1998). *Initial findings from an evaluation of school choice programs in Washington, D.C., and Dayton, Ohio*. Cambridge: Harvard University, Kennedy School of Government, Program on Education Policy and Governance.

Peterson, P. E., Myers, D., and Howell, W. G. (1998). *An evaluation of the New York City School Choice Scholarships Program: The first year*. Cambridge: Harvard University, Kennedy School of Government, Program on Education Policy and Governance.

Rossi, P., Freeman, H., and Lipsey, M. (1999). *Evaluation: A systematic approach*. Thousand Oaks, Calif.: Sage Publications.

Rouse, C. (1998). Private school vouchers and student achievement: An evaluation of the Milwaukee Parental Choice Program. *Quarterly Journal of Economics* 113, 553–602.

Witte, J. F. (1991). *First year report: Milwaukee's Parental Choice Program*. Madison: University of Wisconsin, Robert M. LaFollette Institute of Public Affairs, Department of Political Science.

Witte, J. F. (1996). School choice and student performance. In H. F. Ladd (ed.), *Holding schools accountable*. Washington, D.C.: Brookings Institution Press.

Witte, J. F. (1997). Achievement effects of the Milwaukee Voucher Program. Madison: University of Wisconsin, Robert M. LaFollette Institute of Public Affairs, Department of Political Science.

About the Editor
and Contributors

Henry M. Levin is the William Heard Kilpatrick Professor of Economics and Education at Teachers College, Columbia University, and Director of the National Center for the Study of Privatization in Education. He is also the David Jacks Professor Emeritus of Higher Education and Economics at Stanford University, where he served from 1968 to 1999. He is a specialist in the economics of education and human resources and has published fourteen books and almost 300 articles on these and related subjects.

Martin Carnoy is Professor of Education and Economics at Stanford University, a faculty member since 1969. He writes on labor economics and educational issues in the United States and internationally and has a special interest in the relation between the economy and the educational system.

Christopher Connell is an author and consultant based in Falls Church, Virginia, who writes frequently about education and health policy. A former Associated Press education writer and assistant chief of the AP's Washington, D.C., bureau, Connell is the author of *A Survivor's Guide for Presidential Nominees*, published in November 2000.

Wendy Conners is Associate Director at Giving New England. Formerly a development analyst at the Manpower Demonstration Research Corporation, Conners currently oversees the research and development of a venture philanthropy project, applying venture capital strategies to support young nonprofits. Conners received a master's degree in program evaluation from Stanford University.

Fred Doolittle is a Vice President of the Manpower Demonstration Research Corporation and is Deputy Director of its Department of Education, Children, and Youth. Doolittle's current research interests include the implementation and effects of whole school reform at high schools and middle schools and new methods to estimate the impacts of school reform on student outcomes.

Pearl Rock Kane is an associate professor in the Department of Organization and Leadership at Teachers College, Columbia University, where she also directs the Klingenstein Center for Independent School Education. She has conducted charter school studies in New Jersey and New York.

Frank R. Kemerer is Regents Professor of Education Law and Director of the Center for the Study of Education Reform at the University of North Texas–Denton. He has written extensively on school choice and vouchers and is the author of a number of books on education law and public policy. He was co–principal investigator of a four-year study of public and private school choice in San Antonio.

Arthur Levine is President and Professor of Education at Teachers College, Columbia University. Prior to Teachers College, he served as Chair of the Higher Education program and Chair of the Institute for Educational Management at the Harvard Graduate School of Education. His research in the field of higher education, primarily of undergraduate students, has more recently included distance education.

Ellen Magenheim is Associate Professor of Economics at Swarthmore College and is Coordinator of Swarthmore's Concentration in Public Policy. She specializes in the economics of industrial organization, and her research on child care focuses on the market for child care and early childhood education. Magenheim's research on child care has been supported by the Rockefeller Foundation, the Smith Richardson Foundation, and Swarthmore College.

Patrick McEwan is Visiting Assistant Professor of Educational Policy Studies at the University of Illinois at Urbana-Champaign and previously Assistant Director for Research at the National Center for the Study of Privatization in Education. He is an economist whose recent research projects include the evaluation of a large-scale voucher plan in Chile. He is also coauthor, with Henry M. Levin, of the second edition of *Cost-Effectiveness Analysis: Concepts and Methods*.

Lee D. Mitgang is currently Communications Director of the Wallace–Reader's Digest Funds, following a nearly thirty-year career as an award-winning journalist, author, and foundation researcher. His latest book is *Big Bird and Beyond: The New Media and the Markle Foundation*.

David Myers is a senior fellow at Mathematica Policy Research. His areas of substantive interest focus on issues of access and equity in education. Myers's recent work has emphasized the impacts of school choice on students' academic performance and the performance of schools, and interventions targeted at preparing economically disadvantaged students for postsecondary education.

Gary Natriello is Professor of Sociology and Education at Teachers College and the editor of the *Teachers College Record*. His research interests include school organization, the social dimensions of evaluation processes, at-risk youth, and online learning.

Caroline Hodges Persell is Professor of Sociology at the Department of Sociology, New York University. Her areas of specialization include sociology of education, stratification, and education and technology. Her current research interests include educational privatization, the effects of the Internet on student learning, civil society and social tolerance, and social inequality and infant mortality.

Mark Schneider is Professor of Political Science at the State University of New York–Stony Brook, where he also serves as department chair. He is the author of several books and more than fifty articles on political science, sociology, and public policy; his newest book, *Choosing Schools: Consumer Choice and the Quality of American Schools* (written with Paul Teske and Melissa Marschall), was published in August 2000. Schneider is currently working on several projects concerning the flow of information about schools and how modern information technologies can aid parents in finding better schools.

Janelle T. Scott is Assistant Director for Program Development at the National Center for the Study of Privatization in Education, Teachers College. She is a doctoral candidate at UCLA's Graduate School of Education and Information Studies and a former elementary school teacher. She specializes in the politics of education, school governance, and race and education. She recently completed a study of educational management organizations and charter schools.

Geoffrey Walford is Professor of Education Policy and a Fellow of Green College at the University of Oxford. He is author of more than 100 academic articles, chapters, and books and is Joint Editor of the *British Journal of Educational Studies* and Editor of the annual volume *Studies in Educational Ethnography*. He is Director of a Spencer Foundation–funded project on faith-based schools (a comparative study of England and the Netherlands) that runs from 1998 to 2001.

Amy Stuart Wells is Professor of Educational Policy at UCLA's Graduate School of Education and Information Studies and Visiting Scholar at the Russell Sage Foundation. She is a sociologist of education whose research and writing has focused broadly on issues of race and education and more specifically on educational policies, such as school desegregation, school choice, charter schools, and tracking.

Index

WITHDRAWN